D0097618

A BRIEF HISTORY OF

THE
ANGLO-SAXONS

GEOFFREY HINDLEY

CARROLL & GRAF PUBLISHERS
New York

Carroll & Graf Publishers
An imprint of Avalon Publishing Group, Inc.
245 W. 17th Street
11th Floor
New York, NY 10011-5300
www.carrollandgraf.com

AVALON
publishing group incorporated

First published in the UK by Robinson,
an imprint of Constable & Robinson Ltd, 2006

First Carroll & Graf edition, 2006

ISBN-13: 978-0-78671-738-5
ISBN-10: 0-7867-1738-6

Printed and bound in the EU

GEOFFREY HINDLEY, educated at University College, Oxford is a lecturer and writer. He was three times an invited participant at the International Congress on Medieval Studies at Kalamazoo, and has regularly lectured in Europe and America on Medieval social history, European culture and the history of music. From 1994 to 2000 he taught English civilization at the University of Le Havre. He is also President of the Society for the History of Medieval Technology and Science of Oxford and London. His many books include *The Shaping of Europe, Saladin: A Biography, England in the Age of Caxton, The Book of Magna Carta* and *A Brief History of the Crusades*. He lives in Peterborough, England.

Praise for Geoffrey Hindley's *A Brief History of the Crusades*

'We are clearly entering a new phase of an old war. Hindley's book fills in the historical background to it and should be widely read.'

Paul Johnson, *Mail on Sunday*

'Hindley's accomplished book is informative, never descending into the sensational – but not avoiding the horrors either.'

Good Book Guide

'Hindley's book magnificently explores the motives of knights and peasants . . . and presents an heroic tapestry of Europe on the move.'

Oxford Times

Other titles in the series

A Brief History of 1917: Russia's Year of Revolution
Roy Bainton

A Brief History of the Birth of the Nazis
Nigel Jones

A Brief History of the Boxer Rebellion
Diana Preston

A Brief History of British Kings & Queens
Mike Ashley

A Brief History of British Sea Power
David Howarth

A Brief History of the Celts
Peter Berresford Ellis

A Brief History of the Cold War
John Hughes-Wilson

A Brief History of Christianity
Bamber Gascoigne

A Brief History of the Circumnavigators
Derek Wilson

A Brief History of the Crusades
Geoffrey Hindley

A Brief History of the Druids
Peter Berresford Ellis

A Brief History of the Dynasties of China
Bamber Gascoigne

A Brief History of Fighting Ships
David Davies

A Brief History of Globalization
Alex MacGillivray

A Brief History of the Great Moghuls
Bamber Gascoigne

A Brief History of the Hundred Years War
Desmond Seward

A Brief History of Infinity
Brian Clegg

A Brief History of Medicine
Paul Strathern

A Brief History of Mutiny
Richard Woodman

A Brief History of Napoleon in Russia
Alan Palmer

A Brief History of Painting
Roy Bolton

A Brief History of the Royal Flying Corps in World War I
Ralph Barker

A Brief History of Science
Thomas Crump

A Brief History of the Tudor Age
Jasper Ridley

A Brief History of the Vikings
Jonathan Clements

To Diana

CONTENTS

Acknowledgements   ix

A Note on Names and Measurements   xi

List of Illustrations   xiii

Maps   xv

Chronology   xxi

Selective Genealogy of
   the Royal House of Cerdic/Wessex/England   xxix

Introduction: An Idea of Early England   xxxi

1 Invaders and Settlers:
     Beginnings to the Early 600s   1

2 Southern Kingdoms, AD 600–800   31

3 Northumbria: The Star in the North   60

4 The Mercian Sphere   92

5 Apostles of Germany   120

6 Alcuin of York and the Continuing
     Anglo-Saxon Presence on the Continent   150

7 Viking Raiders, Danelaw, 'Kings' of York   176

8 The Wessex of Alfred the Great   205

9 Literature, Learning, Language and
     Law in Anglo-Saxon England   234

10 The Hegemony of Wessex:
        The English Kingdom and Church Reforms   262
11 Danish Invasions and Kings: Æthelred
        'Unraed', Cnut the Great and Others   291
12 Edward the Confessor, the Conquest and
        the Aftermath   321
Appendix 1: The Bayeux Tapestry   354
Appendix 2: The Death of Harold and
    His Afterlife?   361
Appendix 3: Royal Writing Office
    or Chancery?   364

Notes   365
Select Bibliography   379
Index   395

ACKNOWLEDGMENTS

Since the publication of the second edition of Peter Hunter Blair's *An Introduction to Anglo-Saxon England* in 1977 (reprinted in 2003 with a new introduction and updated bibliography), there has been a wide range of books, articles and journals on all aspects of Anglo-Saxon history and culture. This *Brief History* has drawn on this wealth of publications as well as the classic work of scholars such as Frank Stenton and Dorothy Whitelock to present a rounded and, to the best of my ability, up-to-date account of the history, language and literature of what was undoubtedly one of the most formative cultures in Britain and Europe. Of the many distinguished scholars to whose work I am particularly indebted, I would like to mention here: James Campbell, Simon Keynes, the late Patrick Wormald, Michael Lapidge, John Blair, Pauline Stafford, Rosamond McKiterrick, Timothy Reuter, David Rollason and David Hill. Many others are acknowledged in the notes and bibliography.

More personal thanks go to my editors at Constable and Robinson, Becky Hardie and Claudia Dyer; to the specialist reader; and to David Rose who copy-edited the entire text with great thoroughness; to Christopher Shaw for reading the page proofs and Helen Peters, to whom I am indebted for the index. For those errors that remain, I am of course to blame.

A number of the pictures used are thanks to the generous help of my friends Gordon Monaghan and Rex Winsbury, who made many special journeys in pursuit of photographs of crosses and eagles, statues and churches. For some of the artwork that enriches the plates, I am gratefully in the debt of Mr Monaghan, a celebrated draughtsman in the world of stained glass design, who works in partnership with his wife Yvonne.

Finally I would like to say thank you to the staff of Cambridge University Library; the staff of Peterborough Museum and Art Gallery; the Peterborough Central Library; and the staff at Yaxley Library, in Cambridgeshire, for their expertise and assistance.

A NOTE ON NAMES AND MEASUREMENTS

Spellings and place names

The territory we now call France covered, during the Anglo-Saxon period, various regions with different names, for example Gaul, Neustria, West Francia or Frankia. Like other writers in this field, I have done my best to tread a rational path through the minefield of usage. In the last case both spellings are found in recent literature. On the assumption that the usage derives from a Latin formation and that Latin at the time still used the letter 'C' for the consonantal 'K', and having no other letter, I have adopted the spelling 'Francia', though the word would no doubt have sounded like Frankia.

Personal Names

When it comes to the spelling of Anglo-Saxon and Scandinavian personal names and transliterations from Old English, Old Norse or Danish usage, one finds a rich diversity of modern variants. From Æthelred/Ethelred, Eiric/Erik, Sweyn/Swein, to Cnud/Cnut (even the somewhat old fashioned Canute) and so forth. Alfred/ Ælfred is the classic example. One of the recent biographies of the king refers to him throughout as 'Alfred' while the book jacket features a manuscript in Old English where the name is clearly shown as 'Ælfred'. It seems to me that 'Alfred' is the inevitable choice here. In other cases I have endeavoured to follow what one might call 'best practice' in the knowledge that common usage may change by the end of this decade. Within the last decade, two major books have been published on the leading dynasty of Wessex nobility: the title of one concerns the 'Godwins', the other, the Godwines. I have adopted 'Weland the Smith' in place of the 'Wayland' for the name of the figure of pagan legend. A note about Egbert or Ecgberht: it is now increasingly common to find the spelling Ecgberht, not only because it is more true to the original but also because in Anglo-Saxon 'ecg' sounds like 'edge' not 'egg'.

The Scandinavian raiders appear as 'Vikings' even though it is likely that 'viking' may have originated as a generic term for a young raider or pirate. Technically, the lower case spelling might seem preferable. In fact, I have followed the predominant convention and capitalized it.

Measurements

In the interests of my American readers I give dimensions in the common usage of the world's largest trading nation, namely the old English mile, yard, foot and inch, with the European metric equivalents given in brackets where useful.

LIST OF ILLUSTRATIONS

Gordon Monaghan took all photographs featured unless otherwise stated.

Frankish ship's figurehead
(*Held at the British Museum and drawn by Gordon Monaghan*)

The Castor hanging bowl
(*Courtesy of the Peterborough Museum and Art Gallery*)

A reconstruction of the princely burial chamber excavated at Prittlewell, Southend-on-Sea, Essex
(*Drawn by Faith Vardy, Museum of London Archaeology Service*)

Disc brooch from the burial site at Alwalton near Peterborough
(*Courtesy of the Peterborough Museum and Art Gallery*)

The golden belt buckle from the ship burial at Sutton Hoo
(*Courtesy of the British Museum*)

The portrait page of St Mark from the Lindisfarne Gospels
(*Courtesy of the Bridgeman Art Library*)

The Coppergate Helm
(*Held at the York Museum Trust and drawn by Gordon Monaghan*)

The Bewcastle Cross, Cumbria
(*Photograph by Rex Winsbury*)

Detail from the front panel of the Franks casket
(*Held at the British Museum and drawn by Gordon Monaghan*)

The annual Whitsuntide Dancing Procession of Echternach, Luxembourg
(*Photo: Ed Kohl © Luxembourg Tourist Office – London, used by kind permission*)

The Hedda stone, Peterborough Cathedral
(*Courtesy of the Dean and Chapter of Peterborough Cathedral*)

The gold mancus of Coenwulf of Mercia
(*Held at the British Museum and drawn by Gordon Monaghan*)

All Saints' Church, Brixworth

Alfred the Great of Wessex
(*Courtesy of Winchester City Council*)

Platz Bonifacius, Fulda, Land Hessen, Germany
(*Courtesy of Stadt Fulda*)

The lower half of the frontispiece to King Edgar's charter for the New Minster, Winchester
(*Held at the British Library and drawn by Gordon Monaghan*)

Detail from the 'Five Senses' on the Fuller Brooch
(*Held at the British Museum and drawn by Gordon Monaghan*)

All Saints' Church, Earls Barton, Northamptonshire

The 'flying angel' from the church of St Laurence, Bradford on Avon
(*Drawn by Gordon Monaghan*)

'Christ in Majesty' from the church of St John the Baptist, Barnack
(*Courtesy of the PCC*)

The 'death of King Harold II at Hastings' from the Bayeux Tapestry
(*Courtesy of the Bridgeman Art Library*)

Important archaeological and architectural sites in Anglo-Saxon England

Lindisfarne
Yeavering • • Bamburgh

Bewcastle •

Ruthwell •

Tyne
Hexham • • Jarrow
• Monkwearmouth

Tees

West Heslerton •
Ripon •
Cuerdale viking hoard • • York
Ribble
Humber
Barton upon Humber

Chester • • Sandbach Crosses
Dee
Trent
Repton • Brancaster •
• Barnack • Alwalton
Tamworth • • Norwich
Severn
Brixworth • *Ouse*
Earl's Barton •
Burgh Castle

Bradwell •

Hereford • • Gloucester
• Deerhurst
Wye
Thames
Bradford- London Sutton Hoo
Bath • on-Avon Kingston • Mucking • Prittlewell
Rochester •
Richborough
Glastonbury • Hinton Winchester • Canterbury
Athelney • St Mary Lullingstone
Hamwic (Roman villa)
Exeter • Dorchester • Porchester
Tamar Fishbourne

N

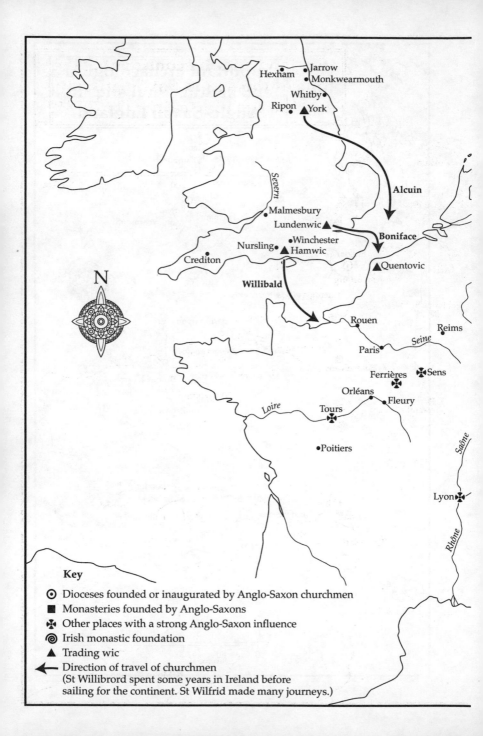

Hexham • Jarrow
• Monkwearmouth

• Whitby
Ripon • ▲York

Alcuin

Severn

• Malmesbury
Lundenwic ▲

Nursling ▲ • Winchester
Crediton • ▲ Hamwic

Boniface

▲ Quentovic

Willibald

Rouen •
Reims •

Seine

Paris •

Ferrières ✠ Sens

Orléans • • Fleury

Loire

Tours ✠

• Poitiers

Saône

Lyon ✠

Rhône

Key

⊙ Dioceses founded or inaugurated by Anglo-Saxon churchmen
■ Monasteries founded by Anglo-Saxons
✠ Other places with a strong Anglo-Saxon influence
◎ Irish monastic foundation
▲ Trading wic
← Direction of travel of churchmen
   (St Willibrord spent some years in Ireland before
   sailing for the continent. St Wilfrid made many journeys.)

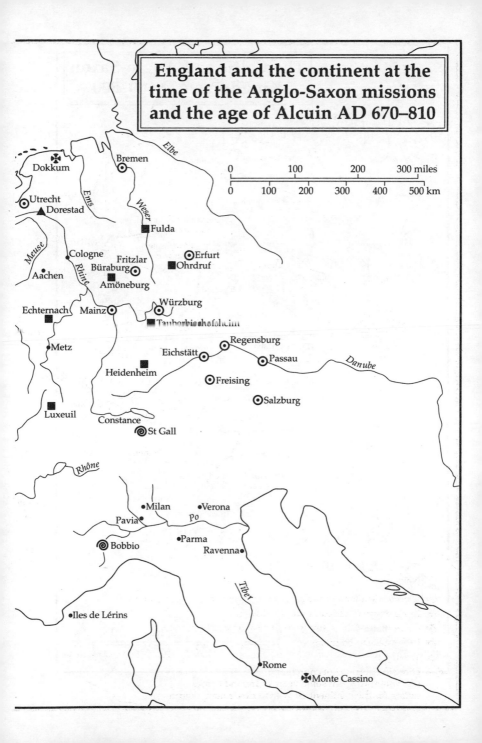

England and the continent at the time of the Anglo-Saxon missions and the age of Alcuin AD 670–810

Dokkum

Bremen

Elbe

0   100   200   300 miles
0 100 200 300 400 500 km

Utrecht

Ems

Dorestad

Weser

Meuse

Cologne

Rhine

Fritzlar

Fulda

Erfurt

Aachen

Büraburg

Ohrdruf

Amöneburg

Echternach

Mainz

Würzburg

Tauberbischofsheim

Metz

Eichstätt

Regensburg

Passau

Danube

Heidenheim

Freising

Salzburg

Luxeuil

Constance

St Gall

Rhône

Milan

Verona

Pavia

Po

Bobbio

Parma

Ravenna

Tiber

Iles de Lérins

Rome

Monte Cassino

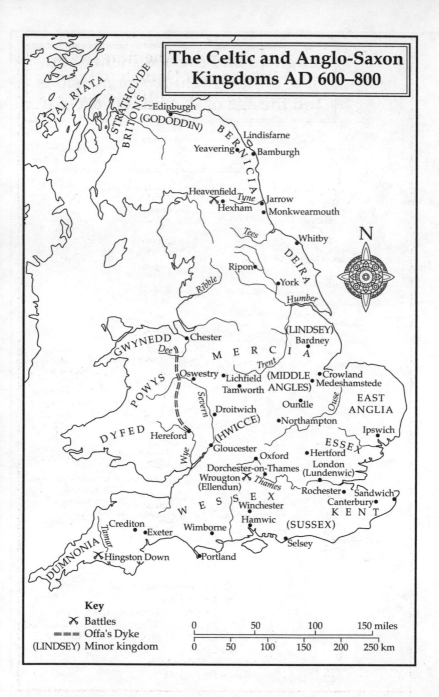

The Celtic and Anglo-Saxon Kingdoms AD 600–800

DAL RIATA

STRATHCLYDE BRITONS

Edinburgh
(GODODDIN)

BERNICIA

Lindisfarne
Yeavering • Bamburgh

Heavenfield ✕ *Tyne* • Jarrow
Hexham • Monkwearmouth

Tees

• Whitby

DEIRA

Ripon •

Ribble

York •

Humber

GWYNEDD • Chester

Dee

(LINDSEY)
Bardney

M E R C I A

Trent

POWYS
Oswestry • Lichfield (MIDDLE • Crowland
Tamworth ANGLES) Medeshamstede

Severn • Oundle EAST
ANGLIA

Droitwich

DYFED
Hereford (HWICCE) • Northampton • Ipswich

Gloucester Oxford ESSEX
Dorchester-on-Thames • Hertford
Wrougton ✕ *Thames* London
(Ellendun) (Lundenwic)

Rochester • Sandwich
Canterbury •

W E S S E X Winchester
KENT

Crediton • Hamwic (SUSSEX)
Exeter Wimborne

DUMNONIA *Tamar* Selsey

✕ Hingston Down • Portland

N

Key

✕ Battles
=== Offa's Dyke
(LINDSEY) Minor kingdom

0	50	100	150 miles
0	50 100	150 200	250 km

England at the time of the Viking and Danish invasions in the 9th and 10th centuries

STRATHCLYDE BRITONS

BERNICIA

Bamburgh

Carlisle
Tyne
Hexham
Community of St Cuthbert
Durham
Tees

Norse Viking presence
Gosforth

Isle of Man

Viking rulers (8?7–954)
Ripon
Ribble
York (Jorvik)
Humber

Vikings from Dublin

Anglesey
Chester
Dee

WELSH KINGDOMS

Torksey
Gainsborough
Lincoln
Derby
Trent
Nottingham
Repton
Leicester
Stamford
Elmham
Peterborough
Thetford
Ely
Hoxney
Cambridge
Ipswich
Ouse

Bridgnorth
Severn

WORCESTER
Hereford
Gloucester
Wye
MALMESBURY
OXFORD
WALLINGFORD
Maldon
Mersea Island
Chippenham
Thames
London
Bath
Edington
Ashdown
Kingston
SOUTHWARK
Sandwich
Sherborne
WATCHET
Athelney
WINCHESTER
SOUTHAMPTON (HAMWIC)
Canterbury
Appledore
Lewes
Hastings
EXETER
SHAFTESBURY
St Germans
Tamar
WAREHAM

N

Key

◇ The five boroughs
⚑ Bishop's See
△ Adapted by Danes as raiding base
⌇ Approximate boundary between Wessex- and Danish-controlled territories (880s–920s)
✗ Battle
LEWES Alfredian burh
=== Offa's Dyke

0   50   100 miles
0   50   100   150km

CHRONOLOGY

360s   Incursion of the Scotti (inhabitants of Ireland), the Picti (inhabitants of Scotland) and the Saxones from northwest Germany, or already resident as *foederati* (mercenaries in the service of the empire) into the province of Britain

410   The sack of Rome by Alaric the Visigoth
Honorius, the western Roman emperor, notifies the Romano–British *civitates* that thenceforward they must fend for themselves

429   Germanus, bishop of Auxerre, makes first visit to Britain in response to request by the British church

431   Palladius sent by Pope Celestine as first bishop 'to the believers in Ireland'

443   *Anglo-Saxon Chronicle* (*A-SC*) date for Britons' appeal to Aetius, the principal Roman commander in Gaul, for aid against the barbarian incursions

447   Second visit of Germanus; he dies in Ravenna the following year

449   *A-SC* date for arrival of Hengest and Horsa

470s   *A-SC* notes landing of Aelle on coast of Sussex

490s   *A-SC* notes landing of Cerdic and his son Cynric in the Solent

c. 500   British victory at Mount Badon under 'Ambrosius Aurelianus', location unknown. The battle checks the incursions of the heathen Angles and Saxons for 44 years, according to Gildas, who was born in the same year

c. 540   Gildas writes his *De excidio et conquestu Britanniae* ('Concerning the Overthrow and Conquest of Britain').

	It inveighs against the moral decadence of the British and attributes their defeats to this
563	Irish monk Columba comes to Britain and founds the monastic community at Iona
570	Presumed death of Gildas
590	Gregory I (the Great) becomes pope
591	Columbanus, monk at Bangor in Co. Down, goes '*in peregrinatio*' to the Frankish kingdom of Burgundy and soon thereafter founds the monastery at Luxueil
592–616	Northumbrian Kingdoms: the pagan Æthelfrith, king of Bernicia from 592, rules also in Deira from *c.* 604
597	Augustine and his party, sent by Pope Gregory I to preach Christianity to the English, arrive at the court of King Æthelberht of KENT and his Christian queen, Bertha of Paris; Æthelberht is baptized no later than 600
603	Northumbria: Æthelfrith defeats the king of Dál Riata at the battle of Degsastan and within twelve months succeeds, by right of his wife, to Deira, forcing her brother Edwin into exile (604)
613 or 615	Æthelfrith wins major battle against the Britons (possibly of Powys) at the Battle of Chester
c. 615	Possible date for the promulgation of the first code of laws in a European vernacular by Æthelberht of KENT
616	In Kent, the death of Æthelberht is followed by a brief pagan resurgence under his son Eadbald
	Rædwald, king of East Anglia, with his client Edwin of Deira defeats and kills Æthelfrith at the Battle of the River Idle. Edwin becomes king in Northumbria
c. 619	At about this time Edwin marries Æthelburh of Kent, who is accompanied north by Paulinus, later bishop of York
c. 625	Death of Rædwald of East Anglia; paganism strong in the kingdom
627	Edwin of Northumbria baptized at Easter with his baby daughter Eanflæd
630/31	East Anglia: Sigeberht, in exile in Burgundy under Rædwald, returns as king and installs Felix as bishop
633	Penda of Mercia and Cadwallon of Gwynedd defeat and kill Edwin of the Northumbrians at the Battle of Hatfield
634	Oswald of Northumbria defeats and kills Cadwallon at the Battle of Heavenfield, near Hexham

635   Cynegils of Wessex baptized by Birinus, bishop of
       Dorchester. Oswald founds Lindisfarne
642   Penda of Mercia defeats and kills Oswald of Northumbria
       at the Battle of Maserfelth. His brother Oswiu becomes
       king in Bernicia, and his cousin Oswine in Deira
651   Oswiu becomes king in Deira, though his rule is resisted
       there
653   Penda of Mercia's son Peada, sub-king of the Middle
       Angles, converts to Christianity. Cedd is sent to Bradwell
       on Sea in Essex; the following year Cedd becomes
       bishop of the East Saxons
655   Penda of Mercia and allied Britons force Oswiu of
       Bernicia to restore plunder at an encounter near Stirling
       on the River Forth. On 15 November Oswiu crushes
       the allies at the Battle of Winwaed and kills Penda
658   The Mercians drive out Northumbrian forces and make
       Wulfhere king
664   Synod of Whitby
       Oswiu of the Northumbrians aligns the church in his
       dominions with Rome in the calculation of Easter and
       matters of ritual
669   Theodore of Tarsus, consecrated in Rome as archbishop
       by Pope Vitalian, arrives at Canterbury. That year he
       installs Wilfrid as bishop of York and arranges the
       appointment of a bishop in Mercia
670   Oswiu of Northumbria dies peacefully
674   Benedict Biscop founds his monastery at
       Monkwearmouth
678   Wilfrid, expelled as bishop of Northumbria, leaves
       England to appeal to the pope; Theodore divides the
       huge diocese into three, Bernicia, Deira and Lindsey, all
       kingdoms or former kingdoms
679   Synod of Hatfield convened to affirm the allegiance of
       the church in England to orthodox Trinitarian
       Christianity and refute the monothelete heresy.
       Theodore presides with the style 'archbishop of the
       island of Britain and of Canterbury'
       At the Battle of the Trent, Æthelred of Mercia defeats
       Ecgfrith of the Northumbrians
681   Benedict Biscop founds the monastery at Jarrow, with
       Ceolfrith as its first abbot

685	Ecgfrith of Northumbria defeated and killed by the Picts at the Battle of Nechtansmere
686/8	Cædwalla of Wessex absorbs the Isle of Wight; he makes a pilgrimage to Rome, where he receives baptism from the pope. He dies there
688	Ine succeeds as king in Wessex; some time within the next ten years he promulgates his Laws
690	Death of Archbishop Theodore
	St Willibrord begins his mission to the Frisians from Utrecht
695	Laws of Wihtred, king of Kent
706	Wilfrid restored as bishop of Hexham
709	Death of Wilfrid
710s	Nechtan mac Derile, king of the Picts, applies to Monkwearmouth for help in adopting Roman Easter and in building a stone church
714	St Willibrord baptizes the future Frankish king, Pippin the Short
716	Abbot Ceolfrith leaves for Rome, bearing the Codex Amiatinus
719	Pope Gregory II at Rome mandates St Boniface to mission in Germany
725	Æthelbald of Mercia exerts *imperium* in Kent on death of King Wihtred
732	Battle of Poitiers: Charles Martel ends Arab advance north of the Pyrenees
735	Death of Bede
	Bishop Ecgberht becomes the first full archbishop of York
742	St Boniface convenes 'Germanic Church Council', dated AD, Bedan style
744	Foundation of abbey of Fulda
747	Third Council of Clofesho
751	Coronation of Pippin the Short as first non-Merovingian king of the Franks
	St Boniface present at the ceremony
754 or 755	5 June, St Boniface on mission to Frisians martyred at Dokkum (aged 78?)
757	Æthelbald of Mercia murdered, and his successor too. Offa accedes
776	Battle of Otford; Kent reasserts independence of Mercia for a time

787   Council of Chelsea confirms the elevation of Lichfield to
            an archbishopric
            Ecgfrith son of Offa anointed king of Mercia, perhaps on
            this occasion: co-ruler with his father
793   Vikings sack Lindisfarne
796   Death of Offa of Mercia; succeeded by his son Ecgfrith,
            who is murdered soon after. Revolt in Kent against
            Mercia led by Eadberht Præn
798   Coenwulf of Mercia deposes Eadberht Præn
800   Christmas Day, Charles the Great, king of the Franks,
            crowned emperor by Pope Leo III
825   Battle of Ellendun: Ecgberht of Wessex defeats
            Beornwulf of Mercia
820s   Historia Brittonum with its 'Arthurian' elements set down
            at Welsh court of Gwynedd. 'Nennius' one of the
            writers associated with it
854   Æthelwulf of Wessex and his son Alfred travel to Rome
865   The 'Great Army' of Danish Vikings campaigning in East
            Anglia
867   York falls to Viking force
            Æthelred of Wessex adopts Mercian 'lunette' penny type
            and thus in effect inaugurates a monetary union that
            anticipates the Anglo-Saxon kings' nationwide unitary
            coinage
869   Battle of Hoxne and death of King Edmund of the East
            Angles
870   Battle of Ashdown: victory for King Æthelred of Wessex
            and his brother Alfred over the Viking Danes
871   Alfred becomes king of Wessex
873–4   The 'Great Host' winters at Repton in Mercia and
            defeats King Burgred, who goes into exile at Rome,
            where he dies
875–6   Vikings under Halfdan settle lands in Northumbria
876   Danes divide Mercia with Ceolwulf
878–9   Following surprise Danish attack at Twelfth Night, Alfred
            is a fugitive in marshes of Athelney. He regroups.
            Following victory at Edington he stands sponsor at the
            baptism of their king, Guthrum
880   Danes settle in East Anglia
885   Submission to Alfred of all the English not subject to the
            Danes
886   Alfred 'inaugurates' burh at London

899	Alfred, king of the Anglo-Saxons, dies
903	King Edward (the Elder) crushes rebellion of Æthelwold
910	Battle of Tettenhall: Edward defeats Northumbrian Danes
918	Death of Æthelflæd, Lady of the Mercians. Mercia taken over by Edward, king of the Anglo-Saxons
924	Death of Edward, accession of Æthelstan
925	Coronation of Æthelstan at Kingston Æthelstan coinage with style 'REX TOTIUS BRITANNIAE' Grately Code issued about this time
934	Æthelstan makes pilgrimage to shrine of St Cuthbert at Chester-le-Street
937	Battle of Brunanburh: Æthelstan's victory over the Vikings of York and their northern allies
939	Death of Æthelstan and accession of Edmund
943	Baptism of Olaf, Viking king of Dublin and York, Edmund standing as his sponsor
946	Murder of Edmund at Pucklechurch, accession of Eadred
952–4	Eadred achieves submission of York Vikings Eric Bloodaxe killed at Battle of Stainmore
955	Death of Eadred, accession of Eadwig
957	Edgar king in Mercia and Northumbria
959	Death of Eadwig, Edgar king of all the English kingdom Dunstan, archbishop of Canterbury
961	Oswald becomes bishop of Worcester and, two years later, Æthelwold bishop of Winchester. The three principal figures of tenth-century church reform now in post.
973	Edgar's 'imperial' coronation at Bath
970s	Edgar's reign sees reforms of Anglo-Saxon coinage with royal mints established nationwide
c. 973	Council of Winchester approves the *Regularis Concordia* (i.e. an accord for the 'regular' clergy, the monks), governing the reformed Benedictine monasteries throughout England
975	Death of Edgar, accession of Edward the Martyr
978	Murder of Edward, accession of Æthelred II
981	Seven Danish ships sack Southampton: the first incursion since death of King Edgar
990	Sigeric, archbishop of Canterbury, travels to Rome for his pallium. A detailed account of his journey survives
991	Battle of Maldon: Ealdorman Byrthnoth killed resisting Norse raiders.

	Archbishop Sigeric advises paying tribute of 10,000 pounds, the first in Æthelred's reign
994	Swein Forkbeard and Olaf Tryggvason of Norway lay siege to London
995	Community of St Cuthbert move from Chester-le-Street to Durham
1002	Wulfstan becomes archbishop of York and bishop of Worcester. St Bryce's Day Massacre
1009	Arrival of army of Thorkell the Tall
1012	First levy of *heregeld*, tax levied nationwide (Europe's first such impost) to pay Danish mercenaries. Payment continued until 1051, revived under the Norman kings and last raised in 1162. Martyrdom of St Ælfeah
1013	Swein of Denmark invades; Æthelred and his family flee to Normandy
1014	Death of Swein
1015	Return of Æthelred; Cnut campaigns against Edmund Ironside
1016	Death of Æthelred; accessions of Cnut and Edmund, who dies 30 November
1017	Cnut marries Queen Emma
1020	Cnut's first letter to the English
1021	Thorkell the Tall exiled
1027	Cnut's journey to Rome
1035	Death of Cnut; Harold I proclaimed at Oxford
1040	Death of Harold I, accession of Harthacnut
1042	Accession of Edward the Confessor
1044	Robert of Jumièges appointed bishop of London
1051–2	Expulsion and return of the Godwine family
1053	Reputed visit to England by Duke William of Normandy
1055	Tostig Godwineson appointed earl of Northumbria
1063	Earls Harold and Tostig campaign successfully against the Welsh
1065	Rising in the north against Tostig
	Harold has King Edward appoint Morcar of Mercia earl of Northumbria
1066	January, King Edward dies; Harold crowned king in Westminster Abbey
	Harald of Norway invades England with Tostig but Harold defeats them at Stamford Bridge, 25 September; William invades, 28 September.

	William defeats the English army at Hastings, 14 October.
1068–9	Northern rebellions against William
1071	Rebel force on Isle of Ely surrenders to William; Hereward the Wake makes good his escape
1075	Death of Edith, queen of Edward the Confessor, at Winchester. King William has her body brought solemnly to Westminster to be interred beside that of her husband in the abbey
1085–6	The Domesday survey
1087	Death of William the Conqueror
1088	William II, facing rebellion led by Odo of Bayeux, 'summoned Englishmen and placed his troubles before them [and they] came to the Assistance of their lord the king . . .'
1092	Death of Wulfstan, bishop of Worcester – the last English bishop in post
	The last consecutive entry in the *Anglo-Saxon Chronicle*

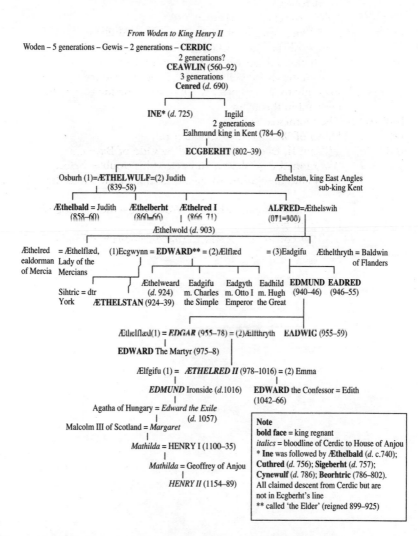

From Woden to King Henry II

Woden – 5 generations – Gewis – 2 generations – **CERDIC**
2 generations?
CEAWLIN (560–92)
3 generations
Cenred (*d.* 690)

INE* (*d.* 725) Ingild
2 generations
Ealhmund king in Kent (784–6)

ECGBERHT (802–39)

Osburh (1)=**ÆTHELWULF**=(2) Judith   Æthelstan, king East Angles
(839–58)   sub-king Kent

Æthelbald = Judith   **Æthelberht**   **Æthelred I**   **ALFRED**=Æthelswih
(858–60)   (860–66)   (866–71)   (871–900)
Æthelwold (*d.* 903)

Æthelred   = Æthelflæd,   (1)Ecgwynn = **EDWARD*** = (2)Ælflæd   = (3)Eadgifu   Æthelthryth = Baldwin
ealdorman   Lady of the   of Flanders
of Mercia   Mercians

Sihtric = dtr   Æthelweard   Eadgifu   Eadgyth   Eadhild   **EDMUND EADRED**
York   **ÆTHELSTAN** (924–39) (*d.* 924) m. Charles   m. Otto I m. Hugh   (940–46) (946–55)
                                the Simple   Emperor   the Great

Æthelflæd(1) = *EDGAR* (955–78) = (2)Ælfthryth   **EADWIG** (955–59)

EDWARD The Martyr (975–8)

Ælfgifu (1) = **ÆTHELRED II** (978–1016) = (2) Emma

EDMUND Ironside (*d.*1016)   **EDWARD** the Confessor = Edith
(1042–66)

Agatha of Hungary = *Edward the Exile*
(*d.* 1057)
Malcolm III of Scotland = *Margaret*

Mathilda = HENRY I (1100–35)

Mathilda = Geoffrey of Anjou

HENRY II (1154–89)

> **Note**
> **bold face** = king regnant
> *italics* = bloodline of Cerdic to House of Anjou
> * Ine was followed by **Æthelbald** (*d.* c.740);
> **Cuthred** (*d.* 756); **Sigeberht** (*d.* 757);
> **Cynewulf** (*d.* 786); **Beorhtric** (786–802).
> All claimed descent from Cerdic but are
> not in Ecgberht's line
> ** called 'the Elder' (reigned 899–925)

SELECTIVE GENEALOGY OF THE ROYAL HOUSE OF CERDIC/WESSEX/ENGLAND

INTRODUCTION
AN IDEA OF EARLY ENGLAND

'Late Anglo-Saxon England was a nation state.' So wrote a leading historian some ten years back. The words were controversial then and they are controversial now. Yet Professor Campbell was quite explicit as to his meaning. 'It was an entity with an effective central authority, uniformly organized institutions, a national language, a national church, defined frontiers . . . and, above all, a strong sense of national identity.'[1] It is, perhaps, hardly a view that squares with the received wisdom outside the world of Anglo-Saxon studies. But England was certainly a nation state at a very early era of European history.

In this book I claim no originality of research, but want to tell the story of the first centuries of the English in Britain and in Europe and show how the historical reality of an English identity grew out of traditions of loyalty and lordship from the epic heritage of a pagan past embodied in the poem of *Beowulf* in a common vernacular language, and how the notion of a warrior church produced an expatriate community that made pioneering contributions to the shaping of the European experience. In the process we should see how, while there was 'a nation of the English centuries before there was a kingdom of the English',[2] that kingdom, based on a shared vernacular language and literature, at the time of its overthrow in

1066 had achieved a substantially uniform system of government that, for good or ill, was in advance of any contemporary European polity of a comparable area.[3] It was the culmination of a gradual coming together of separate political entities. As a result, the story comprises overlapping narratives of rival kingships – Kentish, Northumbrian, Mercian and so forth – up to the mid-tenth century, so that the reader will sometimes find the chronology running ahead of itself. Above all, this main account is of necessity interrupted by chapters not set in England at all but on the Continent of Europe, where three generations of expatriate English men and women made formative contributions to the birth of a European identity.

In the early 700s Wynfrith 'of Crediton' in Devon, otherwise known as St Boniface, patron saint of Germany, where he worked for most of his life, was in the habit of referring to his home country as '*transmarina Saxonia*' ('Saxony overseas'). He described himself as of the race of the Angles. His younger contemporary, the Langobard churchman Paul the Deacon, noted the unusual garments that '*Angli Saxones* were accustomed to wear' and in the next century Prudentius, bishop of the French city of Troyes, writes of: 'The island of Britain, the greater part of which Angle Saxons inhabit' (*Brittaniam insulam, ea quam maxime parte, quam Angli Saxones incolunt*).[4] Wilhelm Levison, the great authority on the English presence on the Continent in the early Middle Ages, actually suggested that the term Anglo-Saxon may have originated on the Continent to distinguish them from the German or 'Old' Saxons. However, most scholars now tend to accept that the name of the 'Angles' had earlier origins.

We have here a cluster of terms – Germany, Saxony, Langobard, French – that are not what they seem. The geographical identity of the island of Britain is still, give or take a coastline indentation or two, what it was twelve hundred years ago, but 'France' was part of the region known as 'Francia', the land of the western Franks. Gaul was the Roman term for the province and the term 'Neustria' is sometimes used for territories in southern Francia. The Langobards were a Germanic people who had established a kingdom in northern Italy remembered in the word Lombardy. What today we might call 'Germany' then comprised parts of the wesern regions of the modern state, mostly the lands of the East Franks – Francken (Franconia), Hessen, Lothringen, Schwaben (Swabia) and Bayern (Bavaria). The pagan Germanic-speaking tribes of Saxony (those 'Old' Saxons) had yet to be brought into the Christian domains of the eastern Franks, though they too were Germans.

This leaves us with the Anglo-Saxons. They were at first a mixed collection of Germanic raiders who had crossed over to the island Britain and would eventually become subsumed under the name of 'English'. Some may have settled as early as the 370s, following a great incursion of Scotti (from Ireland), Picts (from Scotland) and Saxons described by the Roman writer Ammianus Marcellinus for the year 367. In much the same way, the Germanic tribes on the east bank of the lower Rhine, known collectively as 'the Franks', who began to disturb that part of the Roman imperial frontier in the third century, were made up of three main groups: the Salian, the Ripuarian and the Chatti or Hessian Franks. As for the original inhabitants of Britannia, whose descendants still maintain their identity in Wales, they considered the English quite simply as Germans and continued to call them that as late as the eighth century.[5]

About the year 400, apart from the officers and men of the Roman military, a small group of colonial officials and possibly a few Christian clerics, the overwhelming majority of the inhabitants of Britain south of Hadrian's Wall could have been divided into two broad ethnic groups. The larger of these could claim descent from the original Iron Age peoples who occupied the islands before the Roman invasion of AD 43 and who still, some four centuries later, constituted the bulk of the population. The smaller group, a native establishment and ruling class, was of mixed Romano-British ancestry, the result of intermarriage. Most of them called themselves 'Roman'. Many could have spoken or written Latin, the rest spoke one of the languages of the British territories that were formerly client kingdoms to Rome. ('Roman', of course, was a civic rather than ethnic designation. The legionaries came from such provinces as Dacia (modern Romania), Iberia and Gaul, a few perhaps from Latium in Italy, and many from Syria.

What Professor Geoffrey Elton in his book *The English* (1994) termed 'the marauding bands of barbarians from the regions around Friesland and the mouth of the Elbe' were also diverse in origin. Elton believed that their languages over time 'turned into dialects of one Anglo-Saxon or Old English' language. As he observed, in its various forms this earliest form of English 'preserved extraordinarily few words' borrowed from the languages of the British peoples whom the newcomers displaced.[6] These newcomers introduced the ancestor of what is, at the moment, the dominant language of the world. In the centuries before its temporary eclipse by French and Latin after the Norman Conquest, they had fashioned something unique in the Europe of its day: a linguistic culture which, though it made use of Latin, used the vernacular in all fields from social intercourse to government and from law to learning and literature.

It appears to have evolved as a new language. In the opinion of John Hines of Cardiff University, it was an amalgam of Germanic dialects spoken in the Continental homelands of the Saxons, Angles, Jutes, Frisians and the rest. There, a divergence had set in within the North Sea Germanic linguistic community. In Britain, apparently, these language varieties converged, particularly in the matter of pronunciation. In England dialects developed in this new language without any identifiable correspondence to the homeland origins of the dialect groups.

In the 490s, when, we are told, the Saxon invader Aelle had carved out a kingdom for himself in the region now called the county of Sussex and extended his influence over neighbouring territories, the bulk of the population of southern Britain still displayed the same ethnic mix as a century before. Now, however, the small Romano-British upper class was being displaced, or subjected. Latin, one can assume, had disappeared as a language of social intercourse as well as of administration – though the sixth-century British scholar Gildas wrote in Latin for readers among the elite, and remnants of the British Christian Church kept the language in ritual use and for letters. (In AD 461 we find mention of 'Mansuetus, bishop of the Britons' at the Council of Tours.) The majority of the native inhabitants no doubt for a time kept to their British dialects; but by the late 600s the dominant linguist community from Hadrian's Wall in the north to the Channel coast in the south, and from the River Severn in the west to the east coast, was that of the Germanic incomers, already evolving their own literary culture.

Scholars are generally agreed that by the ninth century the concept of an 'English people' (in Latin, '*gens anglorum*', Anglo-Saxon, '*Anglecynn*') was commonly used to denote all people of Germanic origin in Britain. The emerging English language itself, adopted by the native British inhabitants, helped the evolution of a shared sense of nationhood. At the beginning of this particular story stands the venerable figure of St Bede, whose great book *Historia ecclesiastica gentis Anglorum* has the words in its title and who was to be one of the most widely read Latin scholars in Continental Europe as well as in England.

The Venerable Bede: England's first historian

Bede died in 735 about the age of sixty-five, having completed his *Ecclesiastical History of the English People* just three years before. It was a respectable though not an excessive age for a monk of his time. The pattern of monastic life, if seriously observed, is conducive to health. True, it is demanding. The daily singing of the office on a 24/7 roster makes for broken nights but also for a regular bodily regime. The healthful benefits of singing, long ago praised by England's great Tudor composer William Byrd, had been known for centuries before that. (Bede and his fellows were instructed by John the Cantor – from Rome – in Roman, presumably 'Gregorian', chant. This John may also have kept an eye open for heresy in the cloister.)

Food might be sparse in a well-run house but dietetically sound. Alcohol taken in moderation has known medicinal properties and the herb garden presided over by the monk apothecary provided the foundation of sound health provision. Reading for mental exercise, prayer for spiritual exercise, and meditation and physical activity are the three components of a monk's waking hours. Against the frustration of sexual abstinence can be set the strong psychological motivation of a belief system where bodily chastity is considered a high virtue rather than a tiresome anti-social idiosyncrasy and where the dedicated service of God is held to be not only deeply beneficial to the individual soul but also a prime community service.

Of course, all this was part of an ideal monastic observance. Like the modern political class, medieval churchmen were often 'only human'. But their ideal, if only they could manage it, was to help their society transcend the weaknesses of human nature – not to pander to them. People saw a fully functioning monastery as a barracks for God's cohorts in battle against the principalities and powers of Evil, and missionary monks as the church's field army against the devils infesting Europe's forests of heathendom.

From boyhood Bede, placed by his parents at the recently founded monastery of Jarrow on Tyneside, devoted his full strength of mind and purpose to the service of God and to the life of scholarship, where, being a creative genius, he achieved success in heaping measure, often working through the cramping cold of a Northumbrian winter in his unheated monastic cell. In his last year we know he dictated his books to a scribe. As a younger man he would have worked up the actual copy himself.

Besides the prepared parchment or vellum, and the horn well charged with ink (produced from a compound of lampblack and gum), a writer's tool kit comprised: a variety of pens made from birds' feathers (stiff pens, for example, were preferred for certain styles of script); a razor; and two types of knife – the penknife for cutting and trimming the pen, another for scraping the parchment or erasing mistakes. (It was the pleasure of Wulfstan II (c. 1008–95), the last Anglo-Saxon bishop of Worcester, who always carried such an implement about his person, to use it to trim any excessively luxuriant or well-perfumed locks of 'decadent' young courtiers respectfully bowing their heads to him. The young scoundrels lost the Battle of Hastings, nevertheless.) In addition the diligent penman required a whetstone block for sharpening the cutting edges; a stylus and wax tablets for making notes or inscribing exemplars to be copied by apprentice penmen; and parchment scraps. A veteran like Bede could expect to have his pens cut and sharpened for him by a novice, one of his team.

Bede tells us that he got some material by word of mouth. Jarrow and its brother house, like any other large and busy monasteries, were open to travellers, often distinguished guests visiting from long distance. We know of a monk who, preparing the biography of the English nun Lioba, would pump her friends 'being careful to make notes of anything he heard . . . jotting them down on odd pieces of parchment.'[7] One can imagine Bede perhaps at the refectory table of the guest house at Jarrow making the occasional jotting as he listened to the news of a visiting nobleman or distinguished traveller from abroad, perhaps like Lioba's biographer using a kind of shorthand. But we can be sure that his notes were more carefully archived. Lioba's biographer seems to have been a muddler and died before he could get his jottings in order; they were written up by a fellow monk.

It was probably from some traveller from afar that Bede came to learn of the havoc wrought by the Muslim armies from North Africa upon the Christian kingdoms of the Iberian peninsula. For English news he depended on a wide circle of correspondents in Mercia and Canterbury and other centres, possibly as far afield as Egypt. Bishop Daniel of Winchester wrote to him with news of events in the church of the kingdom of Wessex, in Sussex and the Isle of Wight. A correspondent at Rome even copied documents in the papal libraries for him.

For the early sections of the *History* he drew on a wide range of books that demonstrated the riches of his monastery's library. His account of the life and death of St Alban, the great martyr of the British Church, is taken from a Continental manuscript, the *Passio Albanis*. Chapter 2 of the *History*, dedicated to Julius Caesar, 'the first Roman to reach Britain', comes almost verbatim from *Historiarum adversus paganos Libri VII* (Seven Books of Histories against the Pagans) by the Spanish priest Paulus Orosius.

A (probably younger) contemporary of St Augustine of Hippo, Orosius had lived through historic times. In 410 the barbarian Alaric the Visigoth sacked Rome. The impact on the Christian Roman empire was immense. In 391 Emperor Theodosius had banned pagan sacrifices and the visiting of the old Roman temples; now, barely twenty years later, the 'eternal' walls were breached by a pagan army. To old-fashioned Romans it must have seemed a just vengeance by the old gods, to Christians, a punishment for their sins. The catastrophe prompted St Augustine of Hippo to write his monumental work *De civitate dei contra paganos* (Concerning the City of God against the Pagans). It set the fall of Rome in the eternal context of God's purpose and confronted the challenge of pagan religions and pre-Christian classical philosophy. Its ideas would reverberate throughout the Middle Ages and beyond. It was Augustine who suggested that Orosius produce a work to complement it.[8]

The result was a history of the world with the central argument that, even during times of pagan barbarity, humanity was guided by divine providence. Little wonder if it too became a textbook for scholars in Europe's new barbarian, but post-pagan, regimes. Little wonder also that it survives in more than 200 manuscripts, among them a number by Anglo-Saxon copyists. Like Bede's history itself, it was translated into Old English during the reign of King Alfred the Great of Wessex.

As to Bede himself, it is so unexpected to find a sophisticated methodology in a historian of the eighth century that it is easy to forget that he very definitely had an agenda. Writing in 1995, N. J. Higham observed that Bede wrote, as

> a committed exponent of Roman Christianity . . . at a time when that branch of the Faith was battling for the hearts and minds of the Anglo-Saxons and their distant cousins in Germany against paganism and other branches of Christianity.

Bede may have had the Continental Saxons in mind as part of his audience, but it seems that St Boniface, 'the Apostle of Germany', had no knowledge of the *History* more than a decade after its completion, though he did write to England asking for other works by the great scholar of Jarrow to be sent to him.

Nevertheless, in the English context Bede downplayed, when he did not distort, the doings of great pagan kings. We shall see that Æthelfrith of Bernicia, terror of the Christian British, is treated quite leniently. But Bede himself was almost certainly of Bernician descent and, in any case, the king was the founding father of the glories of Christian Northumbria as Bede saw them. In so far as he prepared the way for the triumph of the 'true faith', Æthelfrith was to be seen as an unwitting agent of the providential purposes of God. In much the same way there are still Marxist historians prepared to overlook the murderous tyranny of Stalin as an agent of historical progress.

Before he set pen to parchment Bede faced a quite basic problem: how was he to date the events he described. He was writing in Northumbria but his 'history of the English people' described events in many other kingdoms of Britain, events before the coming of the Saxons, events in Europe and even beyond. His source documents used differing dating systems; in Britain itself the various kings tended to date events by their own regnal years. Other systems involved some combination of the months of the Roman calendar, the regnal year of the pope, or the emperor, plus the year of the indiction. For example, when Pope Gregory II drew up a letter commissioning the Anglo-Saxon monk Boniface to preach on the Continent, it was dated by the papal chancery as follows: 'Given on the Ides of May, in the third year of our most august Lord, Leo, by God crowned emperor, in the third year of his consulship, in the second indiction.'[9] It was a cumbersome and paradoxical formula, in that the pope, who claimed the headship of Christ's church, honoured his lord the (Byzantine) emperor, Leo, but had nothing to say about his Lord Jesus.

There was just one simple and universal system available to a Christian historian; it was based on calculations about the birth and crucifixion of Jesus Christ made by the sixth-century church lawyer Dionysius Exiguus (i.e. Denis the Little) to help determine the date of Easter, the commemoration of that crucifixion. Bede decided to give all his dates as from 'the year of Our Lord' – (anno domini, now AD for short) or 'the year of the Incarnation'.

It was to prove an epoch-making decision in the literal sense of the term. According to Bede that papal letter was given on '15 May AD 719'. The system was becoming generally adopted in western Europe within a century of his death, thanks to the wide diffusion of his writings and to the English missions on the Continent. When Boniface himself came to promulgate the decrees of the Synod of the German Church of 742, the Concilium Germanicum, he dated them in Latin, 'anno ab incarnatione Christi septingentesimo XLII' ('the

year from the birth of Christ 700th 42').[10] The fact that today's international dating system, the Common Era, is the Christian era calculated from the supposed date of Christ's birth, is largely due to
Bede. No historian could boast a more lasting memorial to his work.

From Beowulf to bureaucracy

Pioneer of the modern world's dating convention, a historian in the
sense that we understand the word as one who endeavours to weigh
evidence on its merits of probability, a good son of the church, Bede
was also a member of the establishment of his own day and surely
familiar with bardic traditions and epics of the warriors' mead hall.
Scholars still debate the date of the manuscript of *Beowulf*, but most
seem to agree that some form of the epic itself had long been part
of the oral tradition. The ideals of loyalty to king or lord, courage
in the face of monstrous danger, the warrior worthy of the gifts of
the arm-ring giving lord were assumptions that formed a social
fabric. It was a fabric where over all and behind all looms the
undefinable presence of '*wyrd*'. It is associated with the ideas of fate
(Latin *fortuna*), the destiny that shapes and informs human affairs, a
space–time warp to which in the ancient Greek world even the gods
were ultimately subject. In the pre-Christian world of northern
Europe it was the continuum in which the 'Norns', the three Fates
of Norse legend, cradle and determine human affairs. The word,
but not the presence, survives in modern nursery English as 'weird'.
As late as Shakespeare it still held something of its dread: not for
nothing did he dub the three witches in *Macbeth* the 'Weird Sisters.'

Be that as it may, for both cleric and lay this Anglo-Saxon world
of rival kings and conflicting ecclesiastical jurisdictions, where
Canterbury and York would first try conclusions and where Christ
the King of Heaven triumphed over the heathen gods and their
attendant 'devils', 'lordship' was the core value. As John Blair notes
in *The Church in Anglo-Saxon Society* (2005), the monk's obligation

of obedience to his abbot chimed with the secular value of imperative loyalty to lord or kin. This loyalty to the lord could even override obligations to the king. A man who remained at home, rather than accompany a lord condemned by the king to exile, could expect disrespect from his peers. In 675 King Ecgfrith of Northumbria ordered Bishop Wilfrid of Ripon into exile, but the cathedral's clergy refused to follow him to 'realms across the sea'. When news reached St Aldhelm, bishop of Sherborne in Wessex, he wrote a contemptuous letter. If even laymen, ignorant of the divine knowledge, despise men who abandon a good lord when he falls on hard times and is exiled, what was one to say of clerics who protested love of their bishop when he fostered them in the good times but let him go into exile alone?

But a puzzling paradox will emerge in the course of this book: this world of *Beowulf*, heroism and legend also produced a state structure of closely organized authority. So that in that area east of Wales and south of the rivers Tees and Ribble (the area surveyed by the Domesday Book commissioners) England's pre-Conquest kings exercised a system of government more substantially uniform and extensive than any other European ruler. 'There is no question of there having been anything comparable to the English state in France.'[11]

And yet, equally, we can say that England did have a political society that had many points in common with Continental 'feudalism'. In England, as in Europe, men knew 'a form of lordship in which a tenant could owe "rent" in many forms', and had 'obligations to provide all sorts of service, including military service.' With the Norman Conquest, the elimination of the Old English social elite and its replacement by a new, alien landowning class resulted 'in a tightening of the bonds of lordship to a degree which was even more foreign to France (including Normandy) than it was to England.'[12] In other words, the essential elements of 'the feudal system' were present in England prior to 1066, and the Battle of Hastings merely intensified them.

But there was the English dimension – the courts of the shire and its subdivisions, all part of a system of royal justice that was in a significant sense popular, attended by and presided over by men residing in the locality. A principal key to the long success of the English state, it has been said, was 'the development of [local] loyalties to local units which had been created for the purposes of the central authority'.[13]

Living as we do in times when the encroachment of the state upon the liberty of the individual is increasing, and that state is becoming at the same time ever more remote and less accountable, it may seem somewhat perverse to laud the efficiency of the Anglo-Saxons' government apparatus. But at that time the idea of local loyalties in counterbalance to the central authority provided a useful buttress against autocracy. And there could be practical advantages. On his long forced march north to confront and defeat Harald Hardrada of Norway at the Battle of Stamford Bridge in September 1066, King Harold II of England, writes Emma Mason, was 'joined on the way by contingents from the regions through which they passed, which in itself indicates both the efficiency of his courier and also the national respect for Harold's authority'.[14] It is an example of a centralized state able to work for the benefit of its people. But that state would seem to have been ahead of its time; M.K. Lawson has commented on 'the slow decline under William [the Conqueror] and his successors of the powerful system of government developed by the late Anglo-Saxon state'.[15]

In the 400s the former Roman province of Britannia, that is the southern half of the island of Britain, was a zone of authority in disintegration; a century later the hazy idea of an *Imperium* (Bede's term), wielded by a 'high king' or 'bretwalda' (the term used in the Anglo-Saxon Chonicle to translate Bede's '*Imperium*') had emerged. Such an idea was known also in Ireland but no Irish 'high king' (and there might be more than one at any one time) ever achieved full recognition, so that even after Brian Boru's victory over the

Norsemen at Clontarf in 1014 successive high kings continued to rule only 'with opposition': that is, contested by minor 'under kings'.

In England, by contrast, the notion of a single 'over king', present from the very early days of the Anglo-Saxon settlement, evolved into reality. In 1065, the last full year of the Old English State, rebel leaders in Northumbria, discontented with the earl appointed by the southern-based court of Edward the Confessor, did not set up their own candidate but asked the king to appoint as their new earl a man with close links in the south. In years gone by Northumbria had had its own king but now its great men were content to accept as lord an appointee chosen by the king of all *Engla lond*, as the country had become known.

At the time of its conquest by William of Normandy, Anglo-Saxon England, including the increasingly integrated eastern regions known as the Danelaw, was subject to a fairly uniform administration that was unmatched in France, Spain or Italy; it was a government that wielded more effective central power than even the mighty German emperor, Henry IV. Overrun and plundered by its Norman conquerors though it was, this English state provided them with the wealth for a building programme of churches and castles unmatched in scale in any other comparable area, and the means to consolidate their power and build the foundations of dominance in the islands of Britain and beyond. I hope to suggest how it all started.

I

INVADERS AND SETTLERS
BEGINNINGS TO THE EARLY 600s

Anglo Saxons who knew their history believed that their ancestors had come to Britain from parts of northern Europe after the Romans had left the island, and that the leaders of these invading war bands and kinships had defeated British inhabitants and displaced them. Sagas and legends declaimed to the sound of harp or lyre at banquets and aristocratic assemblies recounted the deeds of kings and warriors from a heroic past and *Beowulf*, Europe's oldest pagan epic poem in any Germanic language, told a story set in southern Scandinavia of ancestral heroes and kings of the Geats (of whom Beowulf becomes king), the Danes and the Swedes.

The poem as we have it is in a manuscript, also known as the Nowell codex, dated according to scholarly opinion somewhere between the 990s and 1050s; the poem itself may have originated between the years 600 and 900, but apparently 'there is no current critical consensus'.[1] The work, by an anonymous Christian poet, presumably derives its materials from a pre-Christian oral tradition. It has been attributed to a Northumbrian king, the court of East Anglia in the early seventh century and the West Saxon court in the ninth century – some of the legends, characters and literary motifs are known to have been familiar in Wessex,[2] especially around the monastery at Malmesbury, in the time of King Alfred.

There are signs of links between East Anglian ruling families and Scandinavia at the extensive seventh-century site surrounding the famous ship burial of Sutton Hoo. Bede, however, named three peoples – Angles, Saxons and Jutes – and Frisians also contributed to the ethnic mix. (In his *Gothic Wars*, *c.* 550, the Byzantine historian Procopius wrote that Britain was inhabited by Britons, Angles and Frisians.) In general, Bede distinguished between the Saxons who settled the southern parts of Britain, principally Essex, Sussex and Wessex; the Angles who settled East Anglia, Mercia and comprised 'all the Northumbrian race'; and finally the Jutes who settled Kent and the Isle of Wight. Archaeologists have found that around the year 500 Anglian, Saxon and Kentish women's styles of dress were quite distinctive.[3] Yet Bede sometimes seems to use 'Saxons', 'Angles or Saxons' and then 'Saxons' again interchangeably

The details of how and when the migrations occurred are obscure. However, whereas about 400 Britain was a place of diverse non-Germanic populations, some two hundred years later, south of the Firth of Forth and east of the line of the River Severn, new Germanic kingdoms were emerging and at least one of the Kentish kings used Old English to record laws. This chapter deals with how the newcomers are thought to have arrived and their impact on the native inhabitants of Britain. But we start with the place itself and the British world they encountered.

The place

The term 'Pretanic Islands', the oldest version of the name 'Britain', is to be found in the work of the Greek historian Polybius, writing in the second century BC and recording the notes made by Pytheas, another Greek writer, navigator, geographer and astronomer, who explored the island about a century or so earlier but whose works are lost. 'The form' we are told 'implies for the name of the inhabitants, "Pritani" or "Priteni".' The form 'Prydain' for the island as a whole long continued in Welsh, as for example in the title of the early tenth-century Welsh heroic poem *Armes Prydein* (The Prophesy of Britain).

Following the Roman conquest under the Emperor Claudius in AD 43, the people of the province the Romans dubbed 'Britannia' came to call themselves Brittones. However, in the second century AD Ptolemy, the most famous Greek geographer of the ancient world, enumerated some thirty-three groups or tribes, those in the region we now call England and Wales included Iceni (Norfolk), Cantiaci (Kent), Dumnonii (Devon), Silures (Gwent and Powys) and so forth. From the late third century, it seems the island was under sporadic attack from Germanic sea raiders commonly grouped under the general designation of 'Saxons', with ports of origin along the Frisian, German and Danish coastline. A series of imposing Roman structures from Brancaster on the Wash to Richborough in Kent and Portchester in Hampshire would seem to be the remains of a defence system to protect what one source called the 'Saxon Shore'.

From the 360s the country was subject to sporadic raids from the Picti and the Scotti as well as Saxon sea rovers. A group of these, we noted, may have settled as early as the 360s, others perhaps a little later, possibly as mercenaries or *foederati* in traditional Roman manner. Excavations between 1965 and 1978 at Mucking, Essex, on the north bank of the Thames estuary revealed scores of sunken huts (German: *Grubenhäuser*) and two cemeteries, in occupation from the early 400s to the early 700s. The pioneer settlement may have been of such Germanic *foederati* brought over to defend the estuary.

The empire in Europe was under general attack and in 410 Alaric the Visigoth actually occupied Rome; Britain's military garrison was soon called back to Rome leaving the defence of the embattled province to the local Romano-British population and its civic leaders, the *civitates*. The Western Emperor Honorius sent word that thenceforward they would have to fend for themselves. (Recent

theory argues that the late fourth-century empire was still a going
concern and the end when it came was not so much a decline, the
conventional view, as a collapse).[4]

Nevertheless, the imperial administration in the West, harassed
by barbarian incursions and the rising costs of defence, had been
hampered by declining tax revenues. Prosperous local patricians had
been increasingly reluctant to fund the financial burdens of their
civic duties and obligations and had withdrawn to their estates.
Great country houses, 'villas', mushroomed. Supported by the
produce and rents of tenant farmers, and served by a full range of
resident craftsmen, blacksmiths and so forth, villa estates became
self-sufficient economic units. In France such estates often provided
the growing point for future towns. This is also the source of the
French word *ville*, meaning town. The main villa building of a
Christian proprietor might become a church – such evolution could
of course have taken place in Britain. Certainly, in Britain archaeology has unearthed or identified by aerial photography scores of
villas, from the great coastal estate at Fishbourne in Sussex to
Hinton St Mary in Dorset (with its Christian chi-rho symbol, the
Greek letters that begin the name *Christus*, set in a mosaic floor) and
northwards to Cheshire and Yorkshire. Since it is probable that they,
like their Gallic counterparts, had not been paying their full imperial taxes for decades, Britain's prosperous gentry could hardly
object if the empire withdrew its soldiery. Perhaps, it has been suggested, they were glad to see the back of them. If so, they would
soon have cause to think again.

Bede's Britannia

In the year 429 Germanus, bishop of Auxerre, together with Lupus,
bishop of Troyes, embarked at an unnamed port on the northern
coast of Gaul on a rescue mission. Ahead, across the Oceanus
Britannicus, lay the troubled land of Britannia – under threat not

only from barbarians but also, which was much more serious from the bishops' viewpoint, from false teachings of the Christian Faith. Britain's churchmen, alarmed by the threat of a heresy known as Pelagianism, had sent an appeal for help to the Continent and at a synod of the bishops of Gaul 'the unanimous choice fell upon Germanus and Lupus . . . [who were] appointed to go to the Britons and confirm their belief in God's grace' (Bede I. 17).

From the British point of view the situation was not only dangerous, it was embarrassing. Heresy was not unknown in the Roman province. There is evidence to suggest that Gnosticism, based on the idea that knowledge of god came not only through the scriptures but through hidden 'knowledge' (Greek, 'gnosis') known only to initiates, had found adherents in Roman Britain. Gnostics believed, among other things, that the soul after death was purified by an ascent through seven heavens[5] (the 'seventh heaven', opening to the state of bliss) and in general had forced Christians to formalize their doctrines to defend the authority of the New Testament and define their teachings on paradise and heaven (see chapter 9). But Pelagianism seemed to have originated in Britain itself.

The British monk and theologian Pelagius had arrived in Rome in his mid-twenties about the year 380. His austere and ascetic lifestyle, a dramatic contrast to the easy-going morals of fashionable socialites and clergy in the capital, soon made him a cult guru among the trendy – both priests and lay people. He opposed the doctrine of divine grace, freely available to all, as proposed by his great contemporary St Augustine of Hippo. If people could be saved to eternal life whether with or without merit, but simply through the freely given forgiving grace of God, then, he argued, the whole moral code was sabotaged. Pelagius also opposed the orthodox teaching of original sin, that people are innately wicked, and argued for the essential goodness of human nature and its capacity, indeed obligation, to win salvation by free will. Such a theory seemed to subvert the charismatic power of Jesus Christ as the intermediary between humanity and the creator, God. Archaeology indicates that Christianity was favoured among Britain's social elite from an early date. The church plate of the Walton Newton silver suite of early third century (among Europe's oldest), found near Peterborough, the site of Roman Durobrivae, carries the chi-rho symbol of orthodox belief. But new heresy threatened.

Help was on its way. But, we are told by Bede, the demons raged against Germanus and determined to halt his mission. Halfway across the Channel a storm erupted that shredded the sails and sent the sailors to their prayers. Like Jesus on the Sea of Galilee, Germanus was sleeping peacefully through the commotion until the others woke him up. Sprinkling holy water and making an invocation to the Trinity he addressed a prayer 'to the true God' and returned to his bedroll. The storm, of course, abated and the wind veered to give them a fair onward voyage.

On landing, they were met by cheering crowds of British Christians and soon convened a debate with the heretical clerics. These were routed in the argument; Germanus and Lupus convinced any waverers among the crowd with their miracles and then journeyed to the tomb of Britain's proto-martyr St Alban to thank him for his assistance. Germanus ordered the tomb to be opened and deposited in it relics of the Apostles that he had brought with him. The marvels witnessed that day swelled the local Christian community with new converts.

While all this was going on, Bede tells us, 'the Saxons and Picts joined forces to make war on the Britons.' (Were these Saxons some of the *foederati* already settled in Britain, rather than sea raiders?) A British Christian army, mustered to resist, called on the bishops visiting from Gaul for support. As Easter approached, they prepared for battle with Germanus at their head. He had the main force drawn up on the plain over which the enemy would advance, and stationed a large ambush in a valley out of sight on their flank. At an agreed signal the British troops, those waiting in ambush as well as the main body, burst out in shouts of 'Alleluia' as the enemy began the advance. Thinking themselves surrounded, the enemy panicked and fled the field. But despite this 'Alleluia Victory' Britain remained under increasing barbarian threat. At some time in the 440s, according to the British scholar Gildas, writing about a century later, some leading Britons sent a desperate appeal for help to Aetius, the chief commander of Roman forces on the Continent. None was forthcoming.

Gildas, who seems to have been writing about the year 550, was another important source for Bede's early chapters. His history *De excidio et conquestu Britanniae* (Of the Ruin [or overthrow] and Conquest of Britain) is about the incursion of barbaric Germanic tribes into the cultured Christian Britain he remembered. The first boatloads arrived by the invitation of a proud British tyrant ('*superbus tyrannus*') to serve as barbarians invading from the north of Britain. They were given lands in the eastern part of the island. More followed, but then the newcomers turned against their employers and ravaged the country. A British counter-attack under a leader called Ambrosianus Aurellianus had great success and, after further warfare, the Britons won a crushing victory over the Saxons at a place called Mons Badonicus or Mount Badon (of which neither location nor date are known, though *c.* 500 seems likely).

According to Bede, the parents of Ambrosianus had been of royal blood, though perhaps his source had garbled a tradition that the great man was in fact of Roman patrician family. His name has been associated with the victor at Mount Badon. One theory has proposed that Ambrosianus, if a Roman then presumably also a Christian commander, had used Roman military methods including the use of cavalry to create a (possibly mercenary) force engaged by various British kings in various parts of the country. This may have given rise to the legend of Arthur and his knights. The theory certainly fits the image of a charismatic Christian leader of a mounted force recorded in many parts of Britain from Tintagel in Cornwall to the north of England.

There is no written record of a King Arthur and his exploits before the early ninth-century manuscripts known as the *Historia Britonnum* associated with the name of Nennius. Local oral traditions flourished in Wales and Cornwall but the fount of the Arthurian legends is the fertile imagination of the Welsh writer Geoffrey of Monmouth, writing in Latin in the mid-twelfth century. His *History of the Kings of Britain* presented a compelling account of this ancient Christian hero, whom the Norman kings of England liked to see as their predecessor and whose deeds fired the imagination of all Europe.

A period of peace followed Mount Badon and this seems to have been the time when Gildas was writing. He deplores the ways of the corrupt priesthood and aristocracy of his day, who threw the triumph away and must surely suffer divine retribution for their moral turpitude. Little is known about Gildas, apart from his name and the fact that he was fluent in Latin and passed his life between Wales and Brittany, where he was honoured as a saint. He is said to have been the founder of the monastery there known as St Gildas de Rhuys (where Peter Abelard was abbot for a time in the early twelfth century).

Christianity survived in the west of Britain (and possibly as a minority cult in the main Anglo-Saxon territories), so that when St Augustine of Canterbury led Rome's first official mission to the country in the 590s he was able to put out feelers to native bishops. In the year 603, 'making the use of the help of King Æthelberht, he summoned the bishops . . . of the nearest British province to a conference.'[6] The meeting was held under an ancient oak, presumably a sacred site since the time of the Druids but soon known as 'Augustine's Oak'. It was inconclusive and the British asked for time to consult with their community. At the second encounter, Augustine opened the proceedings by urging the British to join him and the Roman church in brotherly relations. But arrogant body language seemed to belie the friendly words, as Rome's envoy had not risen from his ceremonial chair to greet the local deputation on their arrival. They refused to recognize him as archbishop.

Two words in Bede's account catch the eye: 'summoned' and 'nearest'. Then as now, Rome had no doubt as to her superiority in the universal church; she did not issue invitations. That can, perhaps, be taken as read. But the idea of a 'nearest' province of the British is revealing. Clearly there were others and hence a British Christian presence fringing the Anglo-Saxon world. Archaeological evidence bears this out. The hanging-bowls with cruciform mountings of clear Christian symbolism, such as the fish motifs flanking a pierced cross found at Faversham in Kent and other such pieces found in Anglo-Saxon graves, are mostly of British manufacture.[7] Bede estimated the great monastery at Dangor-is-Coed, Denbighshire, had some two thousand monks.

'There are in Britain today', he writes, 'five languages and four nations: English, British, Scots and Picts; each of these have their own language but all are united in their study of God's scriptures by that fifth language, Latin.' Thanks to archaeology we know today that each also had their own dress fastenings, so that a warrior's jewellery like the British ring brooch or the Anglian square-headed brooch may, it has been suggested, have proclaimed his identity.[8] Bede tells us that the only original inhabitants of the island were the Britons – who gave the place its name – and who, he thought came over Armorica i.e. Brittany. In fact, the name almost certainly derives from British emigrants who crossed the Channel in the fifth and sixth centuries, fleeing Irish raiders operating along the coasts of Wales, Cornwall and North Devon.

According to Bede, the Pictish inhabitants of northern Britain were descended from a party of sailors from a remote land he calls 'Scythia', who, blown off course, made landfall off the northern coast of Ireland. They begged the Scots then living there for a grant of land so that they could settle, but were told to move on and recommended to try the island not far to the east. The Picts did so.

Bede claims that Pictish royalty descended in the female line because, so went the tradition, the Irish Scots had provided the all-male pioneers with womenfolk on condition that, in the event of a disputed succession, the new king should be chosen from the female royal line. Sometime in the fifth century, at about the time the Saxons were crossing over from the Continent, a chieftain of the Irish Scoti in what is now County Antrim established an enclave across the North Channel in Argyll. In the course of time, and after war, betrayal and intermarriage, some time between the 830s and 850s the rival houses of Picts and Scots merged so that the Scottish kingdom of Dál Riata (Dalriada) and the Pictish realm began to come together under Kenneth MacAlpin (Kenneth I), who died in about 858 and was buried on the island of Iona.

Like modern Britons, Bede and his contemporaries recognized ethnic diversity as part of their countries' characters and also had doubts about the geographical origins of the invaders and their ruling families. Modern archaeology also questions the extent of the population displacement caused by the invaders in the south as well as the north. In its most extreme form it seems to question whether there was any significant Germanic invasion at all.

The Anglo-Saxons themselves had no doubt. Centuries later, celebrating the great English victory over Vikings, Scots and British at Brunanburh in 937, the *Anglo-Saxon Chronicle* hailed it as the greatest victory since the 'Angles and Saxons arrived . . . invading Britain across the seas from the east'. Following Bede, it also gives the year 449 for the landing of the first boatloads of settlers as distinct from raiders. A library of books has been written on the dating of the *adventus Saxonum* ('the arrival of the Saxons'). In one of his letters Alcuin of York, who had read his Bede, described the Viking sack on the Holy Island of Lindisfarne in 793 as happening 'nearly three hundred and fifty years' since 'our fathers [came] to this fair land'[9] and historian Paul Battles is convinced that the time of their arrival was 'essential to a

Migration Myth and so was central to the Anglo-Saxon definitions of themselves as a people'.

English origins and traditions

Given the various opposing views as to the Anglo-Saxon settle-ment – if indeed the word 'settlement' is not too strong – it seems that the one view that no one contests is that they came by sea! But here agreement ends. Were the ships powered by oars, by sails, by paddles or by a combination of these means? In his *Dark Age Naval Power* (1999), which reassesses Frankish as well as Anglo-Saxon naval activity, John Haywood points out that, like the Vikings after them, Saxon pirates raided from Orkney to Spain and, like them, they struck from the sea without warning. He believes that all the probabilities point to the use of a sail on long-range ventures, though paddles could have been used up river reaches. He cites the Gallo-Roman historian Sidonius Apollinaris, writing in the 470s, who says specifically that the Saxons raiding the Gallic coast used sailing ships. A simple rigged sail could have made up to 100 miles (160 km) possible in a twelve-hour day with a following wind on a calm sea, three times the distance possible for a team of rowers, who would in any case have had to rest up from time to time in similar conditions.

Haywood considers that the archaeology points to two phases of settlement, at first in the early 400s between the Humber and the Thames, with a notable cluster in the Upper Thames Valley, and then in far greater numbers in Kent and along the south coast from the 450s to the early 500s. He finds conclusive evidence that at this time there was a massive population movement out of the area between the River Weser and the Jutland peninsula. There is no doubt in his mind that in its early stages the Anglo-Saxon settlement represented a mass folk migration, not an aristocratic or political takeover. Given a sailing time of three to four days and skilled crews, several return voyages could have been made in a season. The early kingdoms certainly exploited naval power: the Northumbrian kings, for example, held the Isle of Man for a time and took Anglesey.

In fact, the attitudes of historians to the coming of the Anglo-Saxons and the formation of their settlements and kingdoms have ranged from dismissing the newcomers' leaders as 'flotsam' on the tide of history to describing them as judges who superimposed leadership in war on peaceful functions, and from deriding their followers as a riff-raff of settlers to rating them at fairly large tribal units 'whose commanders knew what they were doing'.[10]

According to the ninth-century version in the West Saxon Chronicle, in the south the first three, in supposed order of arrival, were Hengest of Kent (about 450), Aelle for Sussex (470s) and Cerdic for Wessex (about 500). Historians consider most of the detail of these early years as a matter of creative tradition. For example, archaeologists in Sussex unearthed Germanic cemeteries of early – rather than late – fifth-century date and at an inland location, which may suggest territory there had been ceded to incomers by the indigenous Romano-British population well before the 'first' arrivals. But the stories were accepted by later generations of educated Anglo-Saxons as reliable accounts of their origins and are in any case of considerable interest in their own right.

In the talk of kings and kingdoms that follows it is worth remembering that scholars often use the term 'extensive lordships' to describe the structures for exploiting the people and resources of post-Roman Britain. In such a system, powerful self-established elite groups, perhaps warlords and their entourages, exacted services and renders of food and other materials in kind from the population under their sway, rather than by the actual ownership of land. Given the logistics of transport, for centuries the king and his retinue of servants, clients and advisers moved to consume the 'renders' at points of assembly for the produce, perhaps a fortified royal residence or 'vill', which over the years might acquire some of the functions of a regional market town, perhaps the residence of a great man at the heart of his estate. About the development of these estates and their organization virtually nothing is known.[11] Sometimes a religious estate, or minster, might entertain the court: in 765, for example, Offa issued a charter in the presence of the abbot of Medeshamstede (later called Peterborough). One hopes the place got off more lightly than when, in the reign of King Edward II (1307–27), an eight-week stay by the king's favourite Piers Gaveston cost the then abbey of Peterborough more than a year's revenue.[12]

South of the River Humber

It is possible that Kent, where we start the survey, may have developed an exception to this pattern of itinerant courts and had a capital city. Apart from London, Canterbury is the only place in Britain known to Bede as a 'metropolis'. About 600 the Christian queen of Kent had had her private chapel just outside the place for the best part of twenty years. This suggests that her court, at least, was fairly sedentary. The name of the kingdom and its capital derive from the tribe of the Cantiaci who inhabited the area in Roman times. Archaeology has revealed traces of Germanic settlers in Canterbury in the late 300s but the main settlement is supposed to have occurred in the 450s, under the leadership of the warlord brothers Hengest and Horsa. Bede, who, it has been suggested, was probably using a Kentish source, says they were Jutes, a people whose origins have been much discussed but who are now generally assumed to have come from Jutland in Denmark.

Bede and the *Chronicle* tell us that they arrived with three boat-loads of followers, to serve as mercenaries at the invitation of a King Vortigern to help him against the Picts. It seems it was Bede who gave this 'king' a name, though he may have invented it from a word meaning 'chief lord' as a loose translation for the term *'superbus tyrannus'* used by Gildas.[13] Where, in Britain, did this 'Vortigern' have his palace? Was it in the northwest, as one might expect if his enemies were indeed the Picts, or in the south? Did he really reward Hengest with what is now the county of Kent? Or did the mercenary leader fall out with his employer, call in reinforcements and carve out a kingdom by conquest? Certainly, the king lists for Kent, drawn up probably as late as the 800s, give Hengest as the first king (later dated as reigning from 455 to 488). But the royal dynasty, the Oiscingas, is called after neither him nor his father, Whitgils the Jute, but after Oisc or Aesc, son of Hengest. The written record does not give Hengest the title of 'king' before his arrival in Britain – though Sir Frank Stenton thought it 'best' to regard him as a chief of 'very noble descent' who brought his retinue from over the sea to Britain. Intriguingly, however, he shares his name with a hero mentioned in *Beowulf* – Hengest of the Eotan tribe (translated as 'the Jutes' by Seamus Heaney).

This famous story of English origins, as told in Bede's Latin, was translated with particular fidelity in the ninth-century Old English version of Bede's history, suggesting to one historian of the migrations that it may have acquired 'canonical status'.[14] It certainly has its fair share of mythic associations. The fact that Hengest and Horsa were brothers recalls the twin brothers that feature in other Germanic origin myths: Ybor and Agio for the Lombards; Ambri and Assi for the Vandals. Romulus and Remus, twin founders of ancient Rome, feature on early English coinage, for example that of East Anglia in the eighth century. Also from East Anglia comes a scene of a pair of dancing warriors on one of the ornamental panel types of the Sutton Hoo helmet.[15] Then there is the association of the names with the words for horse – 'stallion' (*hengest*) and 'horse' or 'mare' (*horsa*) – and the suggestive fact that the horse played an important part in the cults and belief systems of the Germanic invaders of England. (The Roman twin gods Castor and Pollux, the 'Gemini' of the zodiac, were often portrayed as young horsemen.)

Set against such mythologizing theories are convincing historical details. In the version as told in Bede's source, the *Historia Brittonum*, the war leader Hengest springs his attack in the hall of Vortigern with the cry '*Eure nimath seaxas*' ('draw your [hidden] knives').[16] (The Latin source drops into the language of the invaders for a more 'faithful' rendering of the traitor's cry. And it is the more telling for those who knew that the Saxons supposedly were named for their characteristic short knife, the *seaxa* – and who did not know that Hengest and his men were supposed to be Jutes.) Then there is the fact that the historical King Æthelberht (*d.* 616), who brought Christianity to Kent, was unquestionably the son of Eormenric, who in turn was Hengest's grandson or great grandson. The balance seems to tip in favour of Hengest also being a historical figure and a distinguished ancestor.

That the Jutes of Kent had fairly extensive Continental European contacts is suggested by the fact that 'Eormenric' is the Anglo-Saxon variant of Ermanarich, the fourth-century Ostrogothic ruler of a vast territory in the Ukraine and a figure of Germanic lore and legend. It has even been suggested that Kent had a substantial percentage of Franks in its population and was subject to a Merovingian paramount power. But the Merovingians were Christian, whereas Kentish paganism seems to have flourished well into the reign of Æthelberht. Place name evidence indicates cult centres of Woden in the Canterbury region and the king remained faithful to paganism for at least twenty years after his marriage to a Merovingian Christian princess (chapter 3).

Next we come to Sussex, where paganism lasted fifty years longer. Today divided from Kent only by the county line, then it was separated from it and the Thames Valley basin by the no man's land of the Weald (Anglo-Saxon, 'forest'). In this isolated territory, perhaps in the 470s, a certain Aelle, accompanied by his three sons and three boatloads of followers, landed 'at the place called Cymen's Shore' (probably Selsey Bill) and forced a landing against a British defending force, which they drove back. Following the *Chronicle* account we learn that the intruders maintained themselves for more than a decade, facing down a British counter-attack in 485, before in 491 overrunning 'Andredesceaster', the Roman fort of Anderida, near Pevensey, and slaughtering all the inhabitants.

By the year 500 then, the family of Aelle seem to have established a viable territorial presence – call it a kingdom. Bede considered it so important that he described Aelle as the first English king to hold 'imperium' (i.e. 'rule') over all the kingdoms south of the River Humber. If this sequence of annals bears any relationship to actual historical events it opens another field of speculation. How big was a force of three boatloads? Did it comprise exclusively fighting men and did families follow on? Why did the British not make a second counter-attack? What was the population in Anderida doing all this while? Perhaps it was less pivotal an event than Bede would have us believe. Professor Susan Reynolds wrote

> A kingdom was never thought of merely as the territory which happened to be ruled by a king. It comprised and corresponded to a 'people' [*gens, natio, populus*] which was assumed to be a natural inherited community of tradition, custom, law and descent.[17]

Finally there is the case of Wessex. Here there seem to be at least two foundation myths. Bede has its kings begin as rulers of a people established in the Upper Thames Valley region under the legendary founder 'Gewis' (the Old English translation of Bede, done at the court of King Alfred, always calls 'the Gewisse' the 'West Saxons'). An eponymous Gewis does feature in the sixth generation from Woden in the West Saxon genealogy drawn up much later. The *Anglo-Saxon Chronicle* opens the story of Wessex with a landing of five boatloads that sailed up the Solent one day in the year 495 under two princes, Cerdic and his son Cynric, and landed in the face of armed British opposition at a place called Cerdic's Shore; where this was we do not know.

Over the next forty years, other episodes in this mythic account of early Hampshire and the region speak of the arrival of 'Port' and his two sons at Portsmouth, 'where they slew a young Briton, a very noble man' (it is hard not to think of the comment by the Greek historian Procopius that 'the noblest sacrifices' in Thule (the remote north) is the sacrifice to Ares the war god of the first captive in a war).[18] The defeat by Cerdic and Cynric of a 'Welsh' (i.e. British) king is followed by their kinsmen Stuf and Whitgar with three more ships who also won an opposed landing battle against Britons at Cerdic's Shore. The *Chronicle* marks the beginning of the 'rule of the West Saxon royal house' in the year 519, when Cerdic and Cynric won another victory over the Britons at 'Cerdic's Ford'. Some ten years later they took the Isle of Wight and in 534 Cerdic died, to be succeeded, we are told, by Cynric.

The terse annals, though written centuries after the events they purport to record, can be revealing. At his first appearance Cerdic is not only given no ethnic origin, he is not even given a Saxon name, but rather a Germanic version of the British-sounding 'Caraticos'. Arriving with a son of fighting age he dies forty years later, clearly a venerable patriarch. He acquires royal status years after his arrival in Britain. His kingdom is established through years of victorious struggle against the 'Welsh' and, with the Isle of Wight, which he takes with his son or grandson Cynric about 530, he makes a successful conquest 'across the sea'.

After Cerdic's death the story of steady conquest continues with Cynric (*d.* 560) and his son Ceawlin (*d.* 592), who win important battles against the British in the 550s. At this point the writer of the *Chronicle* gives us the royal ancestry, listing Cerdic as the great grandson of Gewis. Ceawlin, listed as the second bretwalda, defeated Æthelberht of Kent in the 560s and won a great victory over the British in the 570s – three of their kings were killed and

three towns, Bath, Cirencester and Gloucester, taken. Extending
from the Solent northwards to the River Thames and west to the
estuary of the River Severn, Ceawlin's kingdom now divided the
British of Wales and the Welsh marches from the British of Devon.
Moving northwards from Kent and Wessex, we come to Essex,
with the complex of Roman London, East Anglia, the Thames
valley and the Midlands. Written records for Essex are virtually
non-existent before the reign of Sæberht (*d.* 616/17), Æthelberht
of Kent's nephew. His father, Sledd, was acknowledged as the family
ancestor by all subsequent kings, but a genealogy drawn up about
800 traces the legendary descent not from Woden, claimed by most
Anglo-Saxon royal houses, but from the Old Saxon tribal deity
Seaxnet. It seems that the Essex kings were also unusual in their frequent practice of joint, usually dual, kingship – two brothers or king
and son, for example. There is also a hint that paganism was strong
in the kingdom at the time of King Sæberht's conversion to
Christianity. Mellitus, the first bishop of London, consecrated at the
start of the reign of King Sæberht in 604, was to have a rocky ride
in the next few years as the region reverted to paganism.

As in Essex, so in East Anglia written records, such as they are,
begin after the year 600 in the reign of King Rædwald, grandson of
Wuffa, founder of the Wuffinga dynasty, which claimed Caesar
among its ancestors. One historian called this period 'the lost centuries'; traditionally it is part of 'the dark ages' – dark because they
lack the illumination of records.

But if these are virtually non-existent, archaeology has told a tantalizing and now astonishing story. Early in 2004 excavations were
under way by the Museum of London Archaeology Service (at the
invitation of the Borough of Southend-on-Sea) that were to reveal
a find still being assessed as this book goes to press. The site was for
proposed roadworks to ease traffic congestion near the suburb-
village of Prittlewell. Since the 1860s the construction of roads and
railways to open up the London commuter belt have led to ad hoc

excavations producing grave goods – swords, spears, shields, jewellery – which suggest that five acres were in use from around AD
500 to 700 as the cemetery of the elite of a warrior society. The
new find at Prittlewell, as reported in the journal *British Archaeology*
(May 2004), dates from the same pagan/Christian transition period
in eastern England as Sutton Hoo. Two small gold crosses suggest a
Christian involvement and links with the southern German region
where they are common. Like Sutton Hoo Mound 1, its only rival
in the archaeological record so far, it is a breathtaking glimpse into
the warrior society in those 'lost centuries'.

The body of the great man had been laid in a wooden box or
casket in a wood-lined 'burial chamber of the highest status'. The
timber panelling had long since perished, but wood fibres were still
attached to a great copper bowl, which had originally hung against
it from an iron hook. The body was surrounded by ritualistic and
luxury objects. Hrothgar had rewarded Beowulf with a standard of
gold, a fitting emblem of honour for the hero who had slain Grendel
the monster; the lord of Prittlewell had an iron standard buried with
him. In addition were his weapons (sword, spear, shield), a solid gold
belt buckle, drinking horns and a folding camp-stool. As at Sutton
Hoo there is a lyre (see chapter 9 below). The excavators found dice
and fifty-seven gaming pieces, a Byzantine drinking flagon and a
Coptic bowl, evidence of the international trade of the time.

From East Anglia and Essex we move into the English Midlands,
home-to-be of the central kingdom of Mercia (the theme of
chapter 4). At its largest extent Mercia stretched from East Anglia
westward to Wales, from the Thames northward to the Humber. In
other words it was the heartland of Anglo-Saxon England.

North of the Humber

Finally, in this sketch survey of Anglo-Saxon origins during the
invasion/settlement period, we come to the lands north of the

River Humber, which was apparently considered the great divide of their territory by the Anglo-Saxons themselves. Someone, Bede most likely, coined the name 'Northumbria' for the kingdom that dominated the country here, between Humber and Forth, in his day. In fact the term subsumed two distinct kingdoms, each with its own royal house and each with a name that proclaimed British antecedents. The larger, to the north, bordering with the Picts and Strathclyde Britons, was 'Bernicia' with its main centre at Bamburgh; the smaller, with its northern frontier on the River Tees and its chief centre at York, was 'Deira'.

We do not know when the first Germanic settlers in the region arrived nor where they landed. Bede's account could be interpreted as linking their story with the first settlers in Kent. The author of the *Historia Brittonum*, his principal source here, was probably a Welsh/British scholar, like Gildas, though working later. He composed his account of history from the Creation to the 680s about the year 829 at the court of Gwynedd, although it survives only in a number of manuscripts from the tenth to the thirteenth centuries, among them one by a certain 'Nennius'. The *Historia* also includes extracts from a Kentish Chronicle, lists a number of Anglo-Saxon genealogies and seems to have known Bede's *History*.

Simplifying the Bede/*Historia* account, we learn that the Britons of those days, including their king Vortigern (whether he ruled in the north or south of the island), called in Saxons against the 'northern nations', which suggests we are dealing with the settlement of the north and not the south country. Three shiploads of 'Angles or Saxons' arrived. They win their first engagement against an enemy attacking 'from the north' but then sent messengers back to their homelands describing the fertile nature of the land and the lazy ways of the natives. More shiploads followed. All the newcomers soon turned on their employers and one group, making a truce with the Picts, went on the rampage – pillaging the land, slaughtering priests before their own altars and ravaging city and countryside before returning to their base. If the group allied with the Picts were the people led by Hengest and Horsa, it would mean that the Picts themselves, with their home base in modern-day Scotland, had penetrated Roman Britain as far south as the Thames. Of course, this is not impossible. But it seems to make better sense if the unnamed invaders who allied with the Picts were, instead of the Kent-based Hengest and his followers, the first Germanic settlers in the region of 'Northumbria' – leaders unknown.

Three models have been proposed to suggest how the transformation from British to English came about for, in the words of David Rollason, 'it is hard to avoid the conclusion that the population [of "Northumbria"] came to regard itself as predominantly English and was principally English speaking.'[19] First, the Roman or Romano-British regime, having called in the barbarian mercenaries against the incursive Picts, decided on a peaceful handover. In other words there was a simple change of elites. York, the Roman Eboracum founded about AD 71, had been a major military and administrative centre, the capital so to speak of the province of *Britannia inferior* ('Lower Britain'). It was here, in the year 306, that Constantine the Great, the first Christian emperor, was raised on the shields of the legionaries before beginning his march on Rome. It was here too that towards the end of the Roman period the *dux Britanniae*, head of the British military defences, had his headquarters. Here, if anywhere, an orderly handover of power to barbarian federate troops could have been made. But such an idea is speculative in the extreme. There is some archaeological evidence for Germanic settlements in Deira before the year 500 and the *Historia Brittonum* (written, remember, in the 830s), hints at a shadowy Anglian ruler of Deira in the 450s – and that is all.

The second hypothesis is that British kings, operating either from Iron Age hill forts or previous Roman power centres, having displaced the imperial administration in the early fifth century, conceded power to the invading Germanic elite after only a brief

resistance. David Rollason finds that the proposal for such a handover from a 'sub-Roman' authority is difficult to sustain. Dating of
archaeological finds, such as barbarian burial sites scattered along the
routes of Roman roads is problematical, since it can depend on key-
ins to written records that are themselves open to dispute. If such
finds can be shown to be early, then we may be looking at the graves
of federate troops posted to defend the road by their Roman or sub-
Roman employers; if they are later, then it is probably a case of
invaders who literally fell by the wayside as their companions raided
by forced marches into the interior. In other contexts he seems to
suggest that archaeology can be inconclusive:

> . . . a very small quantity of pottery of 'Anglian' date found on a site
> could as easily have been dropped accidentally on a ruined site as have
> been actively used in a building which continued in full use.[20]

Excavations at York Minster unearthed foundations of the impressive
headquarters building of the Roman military administration of
Eboracum. The great cross-hall or basilica would certainly have provided a fine palace for British kings of Deira, but there is no proof,
archaeological or otherwise, that it did.

Both these models for British to Anglo-Saxon transition
postulate a large majority British population in the subsequent
'Northumbrian' state, its native culture and language anglicized by
the incomers. The third model proposes an Anglian Northumbria
as the outcome of conquest combined with ethnic cleansing, either
by massacre or expulsion, its culture owing little to either native
British or imperial Roman antecedents.

An argument for cleansing by mass slaughter would be supported
by some evidence in the archaeological record of mass graves; alter-
natively the natives were subjugated to slave status en masse, and
slaves there certainly were in Anglo-Saxon, as in Romano-British,
society; thirdly the Britons may have headed westward in ragged
refugee columns before the advancing alien armed bands. But

maybe they just stayed put, accepted their new Germanic masters, and simply assimilated to their ways and adopted their language. John Blair reckons that by the early 700s most of the inhabitants of Britain from the Pennines to the south-west of the country had acquired what he terms an 'English' political and linguistic identity adopted from the ethnic minority of intruders.[21] As to the north: 'throughout Northumbria the dominance of English place names is extremely striking.'[22]

Place name evidence is always subject to caveats. Maybe the local invading lord gave a British village an English name and forced the locals to adopt it. Maybe the local peasantry not only adopted the invader's language in their dealings with him, but jettisoned their own for the sake of fashion (as has been suggested). In any case, it seems we can conclude with Professor Rollason that Bede was essentially right to consider that by his time that part of the Roman empire south of Hadrian's Wall and native areas to the north of it, both inhabited by the British, had been welded into a kingdom which was regarded by the English as inhabited by the 'people of Northumbrians', one of the other lands in which lived 'the people of the English'.[23]

The first king named for Bernicia is Ida, reigning in the sixth century (d. ?559) and followed by a confusion of names. For Deira the first name we have is King Ælle (d. 590s). If we can believe the punning anecdote by which Bede was to explain Pope Gregory's decision to launch the Roman mission to England, it seems that Ælle of Deira ruled a kingdom of Angles and lost at least one battle. One day in the 570s (that is, before he became pope), Gregory, so goes the story, was walking through the Roman slave market when he caught sight of two blond-haired youths for sale. (Christian Europe was no different from any other contemporary culture in accepting slavery, though dealing in Christians was forbidden.) On being told that they were 'Angles', from a kingdom called 'Deira' ruled by a king called Ælle, he quipped in Latin a pun that William

Shakespeare might have envied, with the observation that they should be called 'not "Angles" but "Angels"' ('*non Angli sed Angeli*'), that they should be delivered from the wrath (Latin, '*de ira*') [to come] and that 'Alleluiah' should be sung in their land when they were converted. The unfortunate boys may have been picked up by Frisian merchants at a clearance sale, following some battle between Deirans and Bernicians. The internecine warring came to an end under the Bernician king Æthelfrith, who emerges about 592 as the first known 'ruler of Northumbria'. He was a pagan king in the heroic mould, with a pedigree going back beyond Woden to Geat, a name mentioned in *Beowulf*.

Beowulf the hero – Beowulf the king

The poem of *Beowulf* opens in 'Heorot', the splendid mead hall of King Hrothgar, a Danish king. For twelve years the monster Grendel has terrorized the place, raiding at night and killing warriors as its food. A stranger arrives, a prince of the court of King Hygelac of the Geats of southern Sweden, his name Beowulf. He offers to rid Heorot of its terror. That night Grendel breaks down the door of the mead hall but Beowulf fights it to the death, ripping off its arm and driving it out into the darkness. The next day the hall carouses in triumph, but that night Grendel's mother takes vengeance, killing one of Hrothgar's men. Beowulf slays her and then, feted by Hrothgar and showered with gifts, returns to the land of the Geats. There King Hygelac, too, awards him the finest gem-studded sword from the Geat treasury and 7,000 hides of land, a hall and a throne. Shortly after, Hygelac dies and Beowulf reigns for 50 years. When his realm is ravaged by a fire-belching dragon, Beowulf rises to the challenge though all his men, save young Wiglaf, desert him. The dragon is slain but the hero is mortally wounded and the poem ends with his funerary rites and a threnody, a dirge of death.

Set in legendary pagan times, the poem is nevertheless shot
through with Christian sentiment and imagery. For all the killing, no
feud is set off. The poet uses more than twenty synonyms for the
word 'king' or 'lord', among them *frea*, which is thought to be connected with the name of the god Frea or Frey, in turn associated with
the Swedish royal dynasty at Uppsala; but *frea* is also used in other
poems in the sense of 'lord of mankind' and directly for the Christian
Lord. Pagan and Christian mesh at the most basic levels. The *Beowulf*
poet sets the scene of the heroes drinking in the royal mead hall; in
the 1960s archaeologists excavating at the site of King Edwin of
Northumbria's royal seat of Yeavering in Northumbria revealed a
great hall of dimensions and plan to match the poet's description –
but it also showed a close match to the great Northumbrian churches
of the period.[24] The house of the king and the house of God were
of like dignity. The merging of the concepts of kingship and godhead
found in Christianity helped in promoting the new Faith among the
heathen tribal folk once the king had decided to adopt it: as William
Chaney claims, 'the most fundamental concept in Germanic kingship is the indissolubility of its religious and political functions.'[25]

However charismatic his semi-divine aura might be, to his followers the early Germanic king in his capacity as warlord was the
fount not so much of honour as of wealth. Since the days of
Beowulf, generosity as 'ring giver' was the foundation of royal prestige. The ambitious young chief had to secure companions to stand
by him and men to serve him when war comes. The warrior strove
to win renown and honourable reputation summed up in the words
dom and *lof*, words with no exact equivalent in modern English
though perhaps most nearly equated to the French *la gloire*. When
the hero slew Grendel, King Hrothgar rewarded him with a gold
standard, a richly embroidered banner, a fine helmet and a sword of
state, an emblem of honour but precious in its own right.

Pagan imagery seems to thread through the verse of the saga in
a tapestry to counterpoint the Christianizing elements. Bede speaks

of the banners borne before the Northumbrian kings; from *Beowulf* we know such banners, with boar emblems, have their antecedents in the pagan world. The hero wears a boar helmet, and grave goods from Sutton Hoo and Benty Grange include helmets adorned with boar crests that protect not merely by deflecting the enemy's sword or axe, but also by divine potencies, the boar having sacred associations.[25] The stag or hart commemorated in *Beowulf* at Heorot (Hart Hall) is echoed by the royal stag-shaped standard at Sutton Hoo. It seems that the monster's of Beowulf's world lingered on in the mind of Christian Anglo-Saxon England – and beyond. At Queen's College, Oxford, they celebrate the famous *Boar's Head Carol* at Christmas time; at Abbot's Bromley in Staffordshire the annual horn dance seems a link with the ancient cult of the royal stag and, of course, in the Middle Earth of *The Lord of the Rings*, J.R.R. Tolkien (re)created Smaug the very dragon on his treasure hoard. But then Tolkien was a professional in this world and his articles on *Beowulf* were rustling the groves of academe long before the Nazgûl hissed along the banks of the Brandywine.

Kings and 'bretwaldas'

In the ninth–tenth centuries the *Anglo-Saxon Chronicle* added the name of King Ecgberht of Wessex to Bede's list of the rulers with *imperium*, giving him the English title '*bretwalda*', which perhaps equates to '*brytenwealda*' (literally 'broad ruler'), an ancient Germanic term for the Latin *imperator* ('emperor'). But was it an honorific title or, as is the view of Eric John in his *Reassessing Anglo-Saxon England*, 'an office that clearly mattered' and which, in his view, came to involve the taking of tribute and to entail, for a Christian *bretwalda*, 'important ecclesiastical power'.

Either way, it seems hard to see how the 'supreme rule' in Britain could belong to the first name on Bede's list, Aelle, king of Sussex, the pocket coastal monarchy well south of the Thames, flanked to the east by Kent, to the west by the burgeoning realm of the West Saxons, and hemmed in to the north by the Weald. We do not know whether the later kings of Sussex claimed him as ancestor. Even so, it is possible that Bede considered him the senior ruler of the Saxons in Britain at that time. Within the territory of 'Sussex' itself there seem to have been a few autonomous kinglet states – for example that of the Haestingas in the hinterland of Hastings, while to Aelle's west the territory that would become all-powerful Wessex had yet to evolve.

The fact that Bede calls him 'King' Aelle does not necessarily mean that he was a king before he came to England. Kingship proves a slippery concept if we try to define it among the Continental Saxons. According to the eighth century *Life of St Lebuin,* 'in olden times' the Saxons had no king but village 'rulers' and 'noblemen', who held an annual meeting in the 'centre of Saxony' where they confirmed the laws, gave judgement on outstanding cases and by common consent drew up agreed rules of action both in peace and for the coming year.[26]

The first-century AD Roman historian Tacitus reported that the Germanic peoples in his day took or chose their kings (*reges*) for their noble ancestry and their war leaders (*duces*) for their courage and skill in war. But one assumes that a successful war leader would have little opposition if he claimed the kingship; was the word 'king' connected with the word 'kin' and did it refer to the head of a kin group rather like a clan chief? And what did 'choosing' a king involve? Not so much 'election' in the sense of selecting between rival candidates but 'acclamation' rather: the public approval as leader by the followers, kin or war band of some nobleman or warrior who had won his ascendancy by a successful campaign or consistent display of leadership – or by force. Some form of public ceremony would have confirmed the elevation of the individual to his new status. Possibly the elevation was literal – a leader being raised on a shield and then paraded through the assembly of the people to shouts of acclaim. But it is also possible that it consisted of a the placing of a piece of ceremonial headgear, crown or helmet, on the head. As kings converted to Christianity, ritual was developed and Christian religious elements became central.

Pagan kings too had enjoyed spiritual legitimacy. 'The primal leader of the tribal religion was the ruler. The king . . . stood between his tribe and its gods. . . .'[27] He was, in the German term *heilerfüllt*, 'filled with salvation'. Generations before Clovis, king of the Franks, converted to Christianity, his dynasty, the 'long haired' Merovingians, enjoyed a pagan charisma that endured long after they had lost all power in the state. When Bede described King Oswald of Northumbria (killed in battle only thirty years before the historian's birth) as 'the most holy king', the phrase would have resonated with overtones of the ancient heathen sacral kingship for some of his older listeners. That Oswald himself, a Christian of only twenty years standing, harked back to the old thought ways, seems to be revealed by his last words, dedicating his soldiers to the divine protection, which entered into the folk memory. ' "God have mercy on their souls," said Oswald as he fell, is now a proverb,' Bede tells us. Now, proverbs embodied folk wisdom: the same words that one man might interpret as a Christian soul commending the souls of his fellows to their common lord, would, for a traditionalist, recall the king as the

> sacral figure which held the tribal world together and related it to the cosmic forces in which that world [and its gods] was enmeshed . . . [and] . . . that 'saved' his folk as much as did the gods themselves.[28]

Whatever form his inauguration took the ruler would later be expected to show that he could trace his ancestry to a hero or god; preferably the pagan figure of Woden.

In the ninth century, the *Anglo-Saxon Chronicle* speaks of 'Woden from whose stock sprang the royal houses of many provinces' and a Northumbrian addition confirms 'from this Woden sprang all our royal family as well as that of the peoples dwelling south of the Humber.' At about this time, too, king lists, supposedly drawn up by the royal scops (the equivalent of the poet chroniclers that formerly recorded the oral traditions of the African kingdoms) purport to demonstrate the descent of historical figures from this mysterious personage. In the case of the kingdom of Lindsey (approximately modern Lincolnshire), which in Bede's time was a province of Mercia, the king list is one of the few pieces of evidence of its one-time independent existence. At some later date a Christian gloss on an already fanciful lineage added an ancestor called 'Scaef', supposedly descended from Adam.

As always with oral traditions, the ear of faith is needed if one is to detect the 'truth', but it seems probable that the warrior aristocracies of eastern England may have believed this figure to be the father of Scyld, or Shield Scaefson, 'the great ring giver', whose ship burial forms the opening episode of *Beowulf*. The poet tells us that his warrior band, following the orders he had given them in life, bore the body out to the princely craft riding at its buoy in the harbour and there laid him out, by the mast, amidships. Then they piled his treasures around him, stepped a gold standard above him and launched him out on the waves alone in the sadly freighted vessel. 'No man might tell who salvaged that cargo . . .' The Sutton Hoo ship burial might have been a dry run for the scene – miraculously, over thirteen centuries were to elapse before it was recovered and in all that time it would seem 'no man had salvaged the cargo'.

After ten years research on Saxon ships, Edwin and Joyce Gifford concluded that the original, 90-foot (27-metre) long Mound 1 ship, powered by sail and 38 oars/sweeps, could have had 'a remarkable . . . sailing performance'.[29] A half-scale model indicated the ability to reach and run in winds of Force 4 on the Beaufort Scale and of speeds of up to 10 knots sailing, or 6 knots rowing. A journey time of three days from Suffolk to the Jutland peninsula would have been quite feasible, apparently. The shallow 2-foot (60 cm) draft would have ensured sailing manoeuvrability in shallow coastal waters and the ability to 'beach-land' in conditions of high surf. A full-scale craft would have been well adapted to the waters of the east coast of England, the southern North Sea and the coasts of north-west Europe. Such craft as these could have brought the ancestors of the Anglo-Saxons on the great raid of migration across the 'gannet's bath'.

2

SOUTHERN KINGDOMS AD 600–800

It has been a convention to describe the political map of England south of the Antonine Wall and east of the Welsh Marches, between the seventh and ninth centuries, as the 'Kingdoms of the Heptarchy' (Greek *hepta*, 'seven', and *archy*, 'rule'). But historians did not always agree as to which were 'the Seven' or just when the 'Age' might be said to have begun and when it ended. Some even contested the use of the word 'kingdom' at all. In the view of Geoffrey Elton, these 'kings' where little better than 'princelings' – the Anglo-Saxons themselves distinguished between kings (*regi*) and sub-kings (*reguli*), and which term should be applied to any given individual could depend on who was writing the story. South of the Humber, the people of what is now Lincolnshire surely considered their rulers as 'kings of Lindsey' and their territory a kingdom; Bede on the other hand considered it a 'province' (of Northumbria), co-extensive with a bishopric of the same name.

During those centuries we find many kingdoms, sub-kingdoms and tribal territories and regions south of the Humber. It may be helpful to list the most prominent: Lindsey as mentioned; East Anglia; Essex, which in addition to the modern county of that name also included parts of Hertfordshire and most of Middlesex and Surrey; Kent, comprising virtually the modern county (though early east and west Kent may have been independent, and the later kingdom encroached on the kingdom of Essex); the midland kingdom of Mercia; Wessex; the kingdoms of the Magonsæte and of the Hwicce that lay along the western frontier of the Saxons with the British/Welsh; Middle Anglia, a congeries of once independent tribal peoples; and finally the kingdom of Sussex. Westward lay the British/Welsh kingdoms such as Powys and Gwynedd and to the southwest the British kingdom of Dumnonia, roughly equivalent to the modern counties of Devon and Cornwall. North of the Humber lay the Northumbrian kingdoms Bernicia and Deira and in the northwest the British kingdom of Strathclyde. North again we come to Scotland, at that time divided between the Scoti of Dál Riata and the kingdoms of the Picts, or Pictland.

The pagan regions of northern Britain first received the Christian message from the Irish Scoti, and they had been sent a missionary from Rome by 431. In that year Pope Celestine sent 'a certain Palladius to the Scots believing in Christ to be their bishop' (Bede I.13). But it was the mission by St Patrick, a Romano-British nobleman's son seized by pagan Irish raiders and taken as a slave to Ireland, that really began the island's conversion and particularly the lands of the far west, 'in the lands controlled by the Connachta'.[1]

In 563 the Irish saint Columba founded a monastery on the island of Iona off the west coast of Scotland, in the territory of Dál Riata. (The story of how this Irish influence reached the Anglian kingdoms of Northumbria is given in chapter 3.) In 597 Roman Catholic Christianity arrived in the south, with the mission of St Augustine sent by Pope Gregory I to King Æthelberht of Kent and his Christian wife of long standing, Bertha of Paris. For any mission to succeed it would need support in the Frankish territories north of the Alps through which it would have to pass. At this time they were divided between the kingdom of Austrasia (roughly western parts of what is now Germany) and, to the west of that, a number of kingdoms, chief among them Neustria. Rome wrote to various rulers to solicit safe passage for the planned mission.

These rival rulers were all descendants of Clovis of the Merovingian dynasty, the pagan chieftain of a confederacy of barbarian tribes known as the Franks (see chapter 5). Clovis had defeated the last Roman prefect of Gaul in the 480s (about the same time that Aelle of the South Saxons was carving out his kingdom). When he converted to orthodox catholic Christianity, as taught by Rome and Constantinople, it was a turning point in the history of the papacy. At that time the bishops of Rome, the popes, felt in danger of being marginalized in the west by Europe's dominant barbarian rulers, Theodoric the Ostrogoth in Rome and the Visigothic kings in Spain who held to Arian Christianity, which taught that Christ was not God's equal and was heretical in Rome's view. Thus the conversion of Clovis, the rising barbarian star, to their version of orthodox Christianity was an important gain. The marriage of the Roman Catholic Merovingian Princess Bertha, eighty or so years later, into a heathen ruling house across the Channel, opened the way to a further extension of the pope's influence north of the Alps.

Princess Bertha's father, the Merovingian King Charibert I of Paris, had died, but a condition of the marriage had been that she should be able to continue to practise her religion – her entourage included her priest, bishop Liuthard – and a dilapidated Roman church dedicated to St Martin had been restored (probably in late sixth-century Merovingian style) for her use.[2] Kent lay within the sphere of influence of the Merovingian rulers of northern Francia. The cultural ties were evidently close. Mercantile and political contact between Kent and Francia and the presence of Franks at Æthelberht's court had familiarized some Franks with the language of the English and some of the Kentish court with Frankish.[3] Augustine and his Italian companions were worried about linguistic difficulties. Pope Gregory had arranged for Frankish priests to accompany them to act as interpreters. The queen's chapel meant that Latin, too, had a toehold. It also seems reasonable to suppose that these Latin clerics helped pioneer the adaptation of the Latin alphabet to the writing of Old English (see below and chapter 9).

The *Anglo-Saxon Chronicle*'s entry for 597 tells us that Pope Gregory I 'sent Augustine to Britain . . . who preached God's word to the English nation'. The future founding archbishop of Canterbury landed on the Isle of Thanet (now part of mainland Kent, but then separated from it by a wide channel) with some forty men, monks and presumably support personnel early in 597.

Augustine was prior of a Roman monastery that Pope Gregory had himself founded and many of his companions were from the same house. They were hardly willing recruits. Setting out in early 596, they stopped for some weeks in southern Gaul while Augustine returned to Rome hoping to persuade Gregory to recall the mission. He refused, but gave him letters of authorization and introduction to the secular and church authorities along the route. Rome's authority was by no means absolute in Europe, even in church matters, at that time. For one thing, as Augustine discovered, churches in Gaul observed a 'Gallican' rite different from that of Rome.

We do not know for sure why Gregory, pope since 590, decided to launch the mission. Jesus Christ had of course charged all true disciples to spread his message to all the world. But why to the English? Why now? In terms of church politics a new province owing exclusive allegiance to Rome and following the Roman rite would obviously be an advantage to the papacy. Possibly the famous episode in the Roman slave market triggered Gregory's decision. But the fact that the pagan English had overrun most of the Roman Empire's once Christian province of Britain was probably the underlying cause. Eric John has controversially argued that following the death, a few years earlier, of the powerful West Saxon king Ceawlin, who according to Bede was the second to wield the *imperium*, Æthelberht was already being accorded that status. To continue with John's analysis, because this status represented real seniority among the English kings, Rome may have considered the time was now opportune to activate its long-standing presence at the court of Canterbury.[4]

At all events, King Æthelberht formally received the Roman party a few days after their arrival, in an open-air ceremony. Maybe this was because he feared the newcomers could use sorcery against him in an enclosed space, as Bede believed; maybe because Anglo-Saxon pagan sanctuaries were generally in the open air; most probably because it was elementary PR to hold his first encounter with these important strangers in full view of as many of his council and people as possible. Before the end of 597 the king was converted and baptized.

Gregory, who termed Æthelberht 'king of the English' (rex Anglorum) now addressed a solemn communication to him and Queen Bertha, in which he reminded them of the example of the first Christian emperor, Constantine. The ceremony was to be understood as his solemn enrolment into the family of Catholic kings, of which the present emperor (that is the east Roman, Byzantine ruler at Constantinople), the most 'serene prince', as Gregory called him, was the father.[5] To be admitted as a member of this imperial family was probably the chief attraction of the new religion for Æthelberht. By this time, it has been said, it was 'the aspiration of Germanic leaders all over . . . Europe . . . to emphasize their right to rule by looking like the Byzantines in their use of gold garnet jewellery.'[6]

But we do not really know why the king took the new faith. Loyalty to his divine ancestors' religion had served Æthelberht pretty well. He seems to have won recognition as overking without the aid of the new god. The kingdom of the East Saxons, ruled by his nephew Sæberht (d. 616/17), was a client state and further afield Rædwald, king of the East Angles, treated him with respect. Place name evidence indicates Woden cult centres close to Canterbury where Queen Bertha had her chapel. The pagan cult did survive the king's conversion and in fact his son reverted to it after his death. So why the switch? Possibly the simplest answer is the right one. Had the king, perhaps, experienced a genuine spiritual epiphany?

The mission proceeded apace. A second team from Rome, under the leadership of Augustine's deputy Laurentius, arrived in England in 601; it brought the letters from Gregory and, for Augustine, the pallium of office as archbishop. He was duly consecrated and established himself – at Canterbury. Pope Gregory surely expected him to choose 'Londinium', a chief city of Roman Britain, as his metropolitan see. As surely, Augustine, the 'man in the field', must have found it impossible to present such an idea to the king of Kent. It has been argued that in fact, from the start, Christianity and Christian missions were tools of policy used and supported by kings as a means of extending their influence.[7] The suggestion that the senior sanctuary of the new religion of the English be set up, not in his dominions, the dominions of the senior king, but in the territory of his neighbour and nephew, Sæberht, king of Essex, would not, one feels, have amused Æthelberht. Sæberht followed his uncle's lead, being converted in 604, when London received Augustine's helper Mellitus as bishop. Justus, another of the Roman mission, was already installed as bishop in the Romano-British walled city at Rochester. With three centres established in less than a decade and influence established north of the Thames, Pope Gregory's plans seemed to be advancing well. In a letter to the pope, Augustine had been able to boast of no fewer than 10,000 converts in one baptism campaign.

On a visit to the court of Kent, Rædwald of the East Angles next became a Christian. It was a celebrity coup for the fledgling Roman Christian settlement in England. As the grave goods unearthed at the Sutton Hoo ship burial demonstrate, the warrior aristocracy of the East Angles and their lord represented a realm of immense wealth. But the conversion may have been no more than a gesture of political deference to his overlord. Returning to his people,

Rædwald permitted the practice of the pagan cult to continue, even sanctioning pagan and Christian altars in the same temple. Nevertheless Bede would list him as one of the holders of the *imperium*. The truth is Rædwald was to play a decisive role in the history of Christianity in Bede's world when he killed Æthelfrith of Bernicia at the Battle of the River Idle in 616 and so opened the way for Edwin, who would become Northumbria's first Christian king. The victory on the Idle left Rædwald the most powerful ruler in the England of his day, yet he receives scant treatment in Bede's history, written a century later. In fact he presented Bede, historian of God's providential purpose, with various problems. Praiseworthy as the patron of Edwin and as an early convert to Christianity himself, the East Anglian king proved ambivalent towards that religion and, worse still, evidently reverted to paganism. Yet a later kinswoman of his, the saintly Æthelfryth, founder of the abbey at Ely, was for a time the queen of Ecgfrith of Bernicia.

The transition from pagan to Christian made for complicated allegiances and was never smooth. There would be a momentary lapse back to the old ways even in Kent. Canterbury's first archbishop was dead by the year 610. Thanks to him, Kent was to be the home of the metropolitan see of the church in England. He was succeeded by Laurentius.

Kent: the first English government in action

Kent was unusual in many ways. Alone among the intruder kingdoms, it took its name from the local pre-invasion population, the Cantwara. Local customs here would prove especially tenacious: the longest lasting, 'gavelkind', an almost specifically Kentish form of land-tenure, was not abolished until 1926.[8] In Kent, local community divisions were different. Elsewhere there were 'hundreds' and, later, 'wapentakes'; Kent was divided into 'lathes' apparently centred on royal manors or vills. The principal seat of the king of Kent was in a city, Canterbury (Cantwaraburh); it was in close secular contact with the Continent – archaeology has unearthed a profusion of Frankish luxury articles in Kentish graves of the sixth century; and now Æthelberht was to break entirely new ground for an English ruler: the promulgation of a written law code. It still survives.

He enacted these 'judgements' we are told: (a) for his people, (b) following the example of the Romans, (c) with the counsel of his wise men and (d) had them written in the English language. They were still being observed, Bede wrote, in the early 700s. This all seems straightforward enough, but almost every item on Bede's list presents problems. It is unlikely that 'the Romans' referred to are the lawgivers of ancient imperial Rome herself. Perhaps the allusion is to the great code produced a generation earlier at Constantinople by the Emperor Justinian. It seems more likely, however, that Bede has in mind the Germanic successors to Rome in the West. The Byzantines looked down on them as semi-barbarians; Bede, a compatriot so to speak, would see in these opulent Germanic courts, with their garish trappings of would-be Latin gravitas, fit heirs to the Caesars, or at least to the Roman state in Gaul.

For us, the most startling element of Æthelberht's innovation appears if we reverse the order of Bede's priorities. Though they follow the pattern of the Alaman and Bavarian customary codes on the Continent, it was, so far as we know, the first time a European vernacular was used for a legal code – by a matter of centuries. The other Germanic codes, like the Visigothic, Lombard or Burgundian, were in Latin.

Talking of Æthelberht's code, the editors of one edition of Bede's *Ecclesiastical History* comment 'These Kentish laws in their original form seem to be the earliest documents written down in the English language.'[9] If they are right, it is reasonable to assume that the research and development needed to create a written vehicle for English was initiated by King Æthelberht, and for this purpose. The

Italian church scholars now at his court presumably led the project, but they themselves had no need of it in their own work – after all, the language of the Church and of their service books, being in Latin, already used the Latin alphabet. Why did Æthelberht issue his code? Personal prestige was presumably part of the point. Following the example of other European barbarian kings, he had decided, wrote H.M. Wallace Hadrill, 'to have his people's customs written down and attributed to himself'.[10] But, since the Continental laws were in Latin, if these Kentish laws were actually the traditional customs of the people, the use of English rather than Latin surely made it harder for the king and his council to claim authorship. Unsatisfactory as it may be to attribute honourable intentions to any executive or legislature, however ancient, one must consider it a possibility that the king of Kent and his council may have been aiming, in however limited a way, at 'open government'.

The code started with provisions dealing with the theft of ecclesiastical property, because, Bede tells us, the king 'wished to give protection to those whose persons and teachings he had received'. This is followed by compensation to be made for damage to the king's property or for injury caused in the king's presence, for instance where he is drinking; then come compensations owing to the higher and lesser ranks of free society: commoner and noble, in the legal jingle from Alfred's laws 'ge ceorl ge eorl', 'both husbandman and noble'. Payments due in compensation for injury are itemized, from limbs to teeth. A large number of clauses deal with the law relating to women and remarriage. Although issued in a council including clerics and recorded in a script and orthography that they may have invented, Æthelberht's code, apart from the compensation clauses at the top, 'is best seen as the law of the Cantwara'.[11] For the killing of a freeman payment is made to the king as 'lord ring', 'obviously an ancient term, belonging to a time when payment was made in rings'.[12]

A century later Kent's lawmakers seem to be contemplating a far heavier role for religion, attempting to enforce infant baptism and Sunday observance. Clause 6 of the code of King Wihtred (d. 725) prescribes the penalty due for a priest so drunk that he cannot perform his duties at baptism. One wonders whether such priests were accommodating their practice to popular religion like those Alcuin protested against: 'conventicles that leave the church and seek out hillsides where they worship not with prayers but with drinking bouts'.[13] Or was it just a case of wetting the baby's head in advance? In more general terms, Patrick Wormald, the great authority on Anglo-Saxon law, proposed that with Wihtred the law code is no longer just a record of custom but 'is becoming an arena for the making of new law'. Wihtred had come to the throne after a period of anarchy set off by raiding campaigns by Cædwalla of Wessex; Ine of Wessex (688–726) is the earliest non-Kentish legislator. Kentish clauses on the punishment of thieves follow similar wording in the two codes and both speak of laws 'abounding in godly purpose'.

Structure of society – king, thegns, ealdormen, ceorls, slaves

At this time, warfare was more or less endemic and slave trading was an inevitable by-product; after all, according to Bede, Gregory the Great's Christian mission to England was conceived in a Roman slave market. About the year 640 an English girl named Balthildis was bought in by the household of Erchinoald, chief minister of the Frankish king, Clovis II. Since the church forbade traffic in Christians, and supposing that the Christian king Clovis observed such niceties, she must have been a pagan and therefore, quite possibly, from Sussex – the conversion of the kingdom was still forty years in the future. Sussex girl or not, Balthildis was, one assumes, beautiful and certainly a woman of spirit and ambition since Clovis married her. When he died a few years later, Queen Balthildis became regent for their son Chlotar III and, incidentally, a campaigner against the slave trade. She was a generous benefactor of the monastic movement and in particular the convent of Chelles, near Paris, which she richly endowed and where she may have retired when ousted from the regency in 665. It became a favourite nunnery with English novices of noble birth.

Such a career was, of course, sensational. Few slaves became queens! And many people, even modest husbandmen, might own slaves. War was not the only route to slavery. It might be imposed as a sentence for a criminal offence: Clause 7 of the Laws of Ine of Wessex provides that if a man's wife and family connive at his thieving they may all be sent into slavery. In times of famine people might render themselves voluntarily into servitude. But slaves could gain their freedom. And in the laws of Alfred they even had some privileges; they were allowed holidays on four days of the year so that they might sell, if they wished, any gifts they had received as charity. The ceremony of manumission marked the transition by the giving of weapons. Freedom brought obligations as well as privileges; the freeman had the right to take his oath, he was 'law-worthy'; he might also be called upon to give his oath as an oath helper to support his lord at law. He also had the right to defend himself and his own, as well as the duty to defend his lord when called upon to do so. But if a kinsman or his lord were killed a freeman had not only the legal right, but also the moral obligation, to exact a life in revenge or settle for the blood money, the 'wergild', awarded by the law. However, even the ties of kinship and the pursuit of a blood feud took second place to the obligations of lordship.

Slavery was the big divide and *wergild* (literally 'man price') was the big test as to which side of it one stood. On either side there were degrees of social standing but one thing does seem to have been absolute: to whom was a person's wergild paid in case of injury or death? If you or your kin received the payment you were free.

If the money was paid to your lord or master you were a slave (*theow*). The list of charges found in the laws of Ine for the king's British subjects (*wealhs*) has, at the bottom of the heap, the landless man valued at no more than 50 shillings. He was taken to be the equivalent of a slave. Above him the scale rises to a landowner with a value of 600 shillings, the highest British rating. The equivalent figure for his English subjects would be twice that.

The West Saxons were pushing back the frontiers of British Dumnonia, which meant enlarging the British population within their frontiers and subject to their authority. In modern terms, discrimination against these new subjects by wergild values may seem unacceptable; however, insofar as a man without a wergild had no standing at all in law, the Welsh/British population was now in principle within the system.

Wergild was basic to that system in all the Anglo-Saxon kingdoms. Not only was it the blood money due to a victim or his or her family in case of injury or death, it was also the measure of compensation payable by him/her in the case of serious breaches of the law and the value of the oath required to clear him/her of the accusation. In short it was his/her value at law; if charged with some major offence, one had the right to vindicate oneself by finding 'oath helpers' of sufficient standing to swear to one's innocence.

Above the unfree we find a broad swath of social ranks in the loose category of the 'ordinary free man' or ceorl. Historians disagree over the exact extent of the freedoms he enjoyed, the degree of his economic and judicial obligations to his lord and his actual economic standing. His standing seems to have varied according to time and place. In early eighth-century Wessex, the ceorl who accepted a cottage from his lord was no longer free to leave his land holding and might find himself facing a heavy fine if he tried to flee. On the other hand, under Alfred a ceorl with a wergild of 200 shillings seems more like a prosperous yeoman farmer. He attended the local meeting of freemen as of right; fought when called for in the royal army and might well be better off than the young landless nobleman, feasting and sleeping at the king's expense in the king's hall. Such a man might be a royal companion or *gesith*, to use the old-fashioned term, but was still awaiting the essential land grant that would enable him to set up his own family establishment.

Canterbury and the organization of the church in England

As Christianity gradually extended across England, the ecclesiastical power centres, the bishoprics, came to exert ever more influence. By 604 there were three bishops in England. Augustine at Canterbury, the archbishop; Justus at Rochester (also in Kent); and Mellitus at London, in the kingdom of the East Saxons, whose cathedral of St Paul's was already being built under the protection of Æthelberht of Kent. But the archbishop was so uneasy about the future that he consecrated his own successor, Laurentius. This was strictly against church law, but it was a good decision. When Æthelbehrt died in 616 and his son Eadbald followed the pagan practice of marrying his father's widow, some thought it meant the end of the Roman mission. Both Justus and Mellitus retreated back to Gaul. Laurentius stood his ground and persuaded Eadbald to convert; his two timorous colleagues returned to their duties in England. The archbishop died in 619 but less than a decade later the king agreed the marriage of his sister to the pagan King Edwin of Deira. Rome had reason to be grateful to Laurentius, for with this marriage its presence was to be established north of the Humber (see chapter 3). For five years Canterbury was in the hands of Mellitus, of whom the best Bede could say was that he was sound of mind; after him the ageing Justus headed the province, dying in 627. With the twenty-year archiepiscopate of Honorius (*c.* 630–53), who had come over with the second wave of the

Roman mission, the Christian presence in England was consolidated, though not always at the initiative of Canterbury.

In the 630s a monk named Birinus, of whom almost nothing is known, although he may have been of Italian origin, converted the equally shadowy King Cynegils of Wessex. King Oswald of Northumbria, the sixth in Bede's list to wield the *imperium*, stood as his sponsor at his baptism and presided over his donation of the old Roman fort of Dorchester-upon-Thames to Birinus as his see. (The Wessex see was later moved to Winchester.) In the other major zone of paganism in the south, the kingdom of the East Angles, Archbishop Honorius played a major role in the establishment of Christianity.

Around the year 630 there was a stand-off between the old and new religions. Rædwald's successor adopted Christianity on the persuasion of Edwin of Deira, but he was murdered by his subjects. His brother Sigeberht, who had been baptized while an exile on the Continent, now returned. He was evidently intent on restoring Christianity, but without promoting what one might anachronistically call the 'religious colonialism' of the Northumbrian ruler. In fact, he had probably found his man during his exile. Bede tells us that 'Bishop Felix', a man born in Burgundy and apparently already consecrated there, 'came to Archbishop Honorius and expressed his desire' for missionary work. It is hard to avoid the conclusion that he and King Sigeberht had already discussed the project. At any rate, Honorius gave him the job and Sigeberht gave him a place, called Dommoc, for the seat of his diocese. This was probably the then coastal town of Dunwich.

Employing scholars and teachers whom he recruited at Canterbury, Felix built up a cathedral school on the Continental model, with the help of the king. But there is a mystery about Sigeberht. His devotion to his new religion seems obvious – he abdicated the throne in favour of a kinsman to enter a monastery – but among the people at large, it seems equally obvious, he retained something of the aura of a pagan war leader. A few years into his retirement the kingdom came under attack from Penda, the great pagan king of Mercia. Courtiers begged Sigeberht to take command of the battle and, when he refused, dragged him from the monastery to the front line. Even then he refused to fight and, carrying only a staff (*virga*) in his hand, died on the battlefield if not in battle.[14] Such is the legend and it will find echoes over two centuries later in the legends of King St Edmund. When Peada, son of Penda and his father's sub-king in the east Midlands, married a Christian princess and converted to her religion as part of the deal, the days of paganism seemed numbered.

Honorius died in 653. The Roman church's position in southern England seemed at last well established. In addition, Honorius had consecrated the first native Anglo-Saxon bishop and was succeeded by the first native Anglo-Saxon on the throne of Canterbury, Deusdedit, a West Saxon. In 664, the year of his death, developments of immense importance for the whole church establishment in England were unfolding at the Synod of Whitby, in the kingdom of Deira (see chapter 3). Here we round off the story of seventh-century Canterbury with an improbable appointment and its astonishing consequences.

Theodore of Canterbury: a Greek in charge of the English Church 668–690

Like Pope John Paul II, Theodore of Tarsus was about sixty when appointed to his high office and, also like the late pope, he lived well into his eighties. He was born about 602 in south-eastern Turkey and was appointed to Canterbury almost by chance, dying in office in 690. By bringing the English churches under a single authority, he laid the groundwork for the church in England (for centuries the country's premier organ of state as well as of religion). He shared a third characteristic with John Paul: Theodore was a considerable scholar. The cathedral school he founded at Canterbury became a major factor in the development of Anglo-Saxon learning, including in its curriculum studies in law and astronomy as well as the composition of Latin metrical verse. In one department, that of hagiography, it was indebted to its founder's Greek background. A basic text for English hagiographers (saints' biographers) was the *Life of St Antony* (*d.* 356) by the Greek writer Athanasius, a young contemporary of his subject, in a Latin translation of the 380s that Theodore introduced into the school at Canterbury. Among the many books modelled on this was the first life of the northern saint Cuthbert.

Theodore himself had long studied in the libraries and at the university of the imperial city Constantinople, where, in addition to biblical studies, he would have attended lectures on philosophy, medicine and astronomy. Then in 648 we find him working at Rome with others to refute the doctrine of 'monotheletism', that Christ had only one (divine) will, proposed by Emperor Heraclius years before and a fiercely contentious issue between empire and papacy.

That same year the eighteen-year-old Emperor Constans II had forbidden debate on the topic with an imperial *typos*, or edict. He was surely influenced by the advance of Islam. Five years before, in the second year of his reign, the teenage emperor and defender of the Faith had seen the Muslim armies conquer Christian Egypt and threaten Constantinople, capital of the Christian world. Islam's unswerving monotheism was a direct challenge to the Christian idea of a Three-in-One deity – it would seem even more of a challenge to the concept of a Trinity not united by a single Divine Will. Islam was triumphing.

The bishop of Rome, the pope, condemned the doctrine on theological grounds. In 649, twelve months after the imperial ban on the debate, Pope Martin I presided over the Lateran Council that repudiated the monothelete doctrine. Emperor Constans ordered

Martin's deposition and exile. Theodore of Tarsus had been party to the Lateran deliberations; some twenty years later that fact would shape a decisive moment in his career. Vitalian, the pope at that time, had been ratified in his position by Constans, following his election in 657, only on condition that he swore not to raise the issue of monotheletism. But the pope's theological objections remained. Then, with tension between pope and emperor still high, Wigheard, the Anglo-Saxon archbishop of Canterbury elect and Deusdedit's successor, arrived in the Holy City to receive his pallium (the scarf-like vestment of office worn by senior members of the church hierarchy), but died of plague. Theodore was, by chance, also in the city at this time.

Rather than send to England for another candidate to be elected, Vitalian decided to seize the moment and promote his friend and champion of orthodoxy. In March 668 Theodore, having had his hair tonsured in the Roman manner, was consecrated and left for England in the company of the Anglo-Saxon nobleman Biscop Baducing, a frequent visitor to Rome and patron of the church in Northumbria (see chapter 3). For the pope, the moment was opportune. With Theodore at Canterbury, Christendom's newest province was secure in the faith and Rome's influence strengthened. That year Emperor Constans died.

Installed at Canterbury in 669, Theodore launched a programme of change and centralization in the English church. A number of bishoprics were vacant; these he filled. He convened the first nationwide synod of the English churches at Hertford in 672 or 673. This provided for regular synods in the future at a place called Clofesho. We do not now know where this was: the case has been put for, among others, Brixworth in Northamptonshire, where there is still what is arguably the finest seventh-century church north of the Alps, and Hitchin, in modern Hertfordshire. Both exhibit the topographical feature indicated by the name, 'a cleft or cloven hill spur of land'.

The second general synod of the English church, convened by Archbishop Theodore for 17 September 679 at Hatfield, was a great occasion on the international stage. It was a decade since the death of Emperor Constans but the monothelete controversy was still unresolved. No one was better qualified than Theodore to bring matters to a head. Hatfield was convened specifically to endorse the decrees against the heresy. The ceremony was designed to impress. Following the practice of the early Church councils, the proceedings were presided over, so to speak, by a great illuminated Gospel book 'enthroned' on a special book stand and displayed to the synod as the assembly affirmed the decrees of five previous oecumenical councils. The following year the Sixth Oecumenical Council of the universal church adopted those *acta* against monotheletism so solemnly promulgated at Hatfield with full papal approval.

Theodore created new dioceses in the English church, which meant reduction in powers for bishops and brought him into conflict with the brilliant and powerful bishop of Northumbria, Wilfrid of York, whom he deposed and who promptly appealed to Rome. He won his case, retained his see at York and was reconciled with Theodore. Nevertheless Bishop Wilfrild's see was reduced in size and the first archbishop of York was not consecrated for another sixty years.

Wessex and her first Christian kings

It is obvious that the sequence pagan England–Augustine of Canterbury–Christian England is hardly an approximation to the reality of seventh-century history, even to the events as we know them. But it is easy to forget how unsteady the early decades were. In Kent Queen Bertha had been celebrating mass for the best part of a generation in her chapel at court before her husband followed suit; and when he died their son relapsed to paganism for a time. A similar relapse befell Essex on the death of its king Sæberht, at about the same time. To judge from the grave furniture at Sutton Hoo, Rædwald of East Anglia was planning to keep his options open at his death in the 620s and the Christian cause was to suffer a serious setback in the Northumbrian kingdoms within its first ten years.

But this was the world of the warrior code and of ring-giving lords: for the fighting men on all sides, Christian or pagan, British or Saxon, the struggle was as important as the outcome. The year that Oswald of Northumbria stood sponsor at his baptism, Cynegils of Wessex led a victorious campaign into the recently Christian kingdom of Essex (according to Bede, the East Saxons had relapsed into paganism and this was their punishment).

When Cynegils died in 643, Wessex once again found itself under pagan rule as his son Cenwalh flirted briefly in alliance with Penda of Mercia, taking the pagan king's sister as his queen and then, for reasons best known to himself, separating from the queen; her furious brother drove him from his throne. Cenwalh found exile with the East Angles where he reconverted to Christianity. When he recovered Wessex in 648 he founded the minster of St Peter's, Winchester, and, with the installation of the Frankish churchman Agilbert, seemed to have secured the new faith in Wessex.

Cenwalh (d. 672) continued to ply the royal trade of war leader. Success in the 650s against the Christian British/Welsh near Bradford on Avon and the annexation of areas of what is now Wiltshire and Somerset, was followed (661) by humiliation at the hands of Mercia as its new, now Christian, king drove a triumphant campaign south to occupy the Isle of Wight. The West Saxon dynast seemed in eclipse. His widow Seaxburgha, the only queen regnant of the Anglo-Saxon period, held the centre until her own death in the early 670s. In the next decade the throne was seized by a pagan warrior claiming descent from the royal house, despite his apparently Celtic name of Cædwalla. In three ruthless years (685-8) he conquered the kingdoms of Kent, where he installed his brother Mull, later burnt alive in a general uprising, and Sussex, recently converted by the exiled bishop Wilfrid of York. He, it seems directed Cædwalla to Christianity; he certainly received large estates in the Isle of Wight, which the king also conquered. Cædwalla's origins are obscure, his military success indisputable. It guaranteed him the spoils of war and the kind of fame as lord and ring-giver that in turn guaranteed followers. (We shall meet another such, St Guthlac of Croyland, in chapter 4.) Like Guthlac, Cædwalla adopted the life of faith. He had lived as a pagan warlord but his return to the new religion confirmed it in Wessex beyond further question. In 688 he abdicated the throne he had seized and went, a pilgrim, to Rome; one of the first of the many English kings to do this. There he accepted baptism and, ten days later, died.

Weapons – the honoured tools of war

Thanks to the archaeologist, the early medieval king-warlord and his war band of companions or *gesiths* stand before us as men of extreme wealth and extravagant display; ostentatious on the battlefield and in the pomp of death. The largest pieces of equipment, helmet and shield, are at the same time the most majestic emblems. (Though even here makers might attempt to cut corners. King Æthelstan's Grately code (*c.* 930) warned shield-makers not to use sheepskin, in place of true leather.) Made of wood and covered with tan-toughened leather, the heavy round shield, up to three feet (91 cm) in diameter, mounted with a central boss to deflect blows or be used as a bludgeon at need, could be a weapon of offence as well as defence. It was also a platform for display. Relief ornaments, in copper with applied silver-sheet embellishments, are exquisitely worked in animal forms – birds of prey, for example, or reptilian bodies – reminiscent in shape of the creatures that inhabit the scrolls and tendrils of the monks' illuminated manuscripts, and mounted seemingly at random for maximum decorative effect, but almost certainly in arrangements that conveyed symbolic meanings to the initiated.

For the fighting man himself the sword was surely the most valued tool of his trade in practical, but also in almost mystical, terms. The *Beowulf* poet writes of a sword treasured from the days of the giants, the envy of warriors, that only the hero himself could wield. As in the *samurai* culture of Japan, such high-status swords might pass through many hands, possibly as a gift from lord to *gesith*, possibly from father to son, certainly at the highest social level. They might be embellished, sometimes by successive owners, with gold fittings or other rich ornaments.

The sword-smith was highly rated in this warrior world: a craftsman of the highest calibre and respected social status. In the law code of Æthelberht of Kent the killing of the king's smith commands special compensation. As in many African traditions, the ironworker as such was held to be under divine patronage and, like the Roman god Vulcan, the legendary Weland the Smith of the Anglo-Saxons was lame. But whereas Vulcan was born so, Weland, it was believed, had been crippled deliberately by a king to prevent his escape from the royal smithy.

In the early centuries, the finest swords were produced by 'pattern welding'. The process, as depicted by Kevin Leahy,[15] begins by twisting strips of iron of the required length and then hammering them into flat ribbons. Four such 'ribbons' are next fire-welded onto an iron core and hammered out so that the twist marks, flattened into oblique lines, may create a chevron or 'herringbone' pattern. A strip of steel is next welded to either side of the core unit to provide the cutting edges. These are now ground and the whole polished to bring out the chevron effect – the blade's badge of fighting quality and inherent value. By the mid-ninth century, though, furnace improvements and refinements of the smith's technique made possible the production of quality blades without the need for pattern welding.

Weapons of all kinds, such as spears, light throwing axes or short single-edged dagger-swords (*seaxes*), which according to one tradition gave the Saxons their name, and, less frequently, swords, are excavated as grave goods and it seems reasonable to assume that the bones with which they are found are those of a warrior whose social status and fighting specialisms can be deduced from their presence. But, by an extensive analysis of some 1,660 male burials in Anglo-Saxon cemeteries, concentrating on sword-bearers, Heinrich Härke of Reading University concluded that this does not necessarily follow. For example, some 'weapon burials' were those of children aged as young as twelve months, and some of men too severely disabled ever to have seen action. Then there were skeletons presenting combat wounds but not accompanied by weapons of any kind.

Such facts and others have long persuaded scholars that weapon burials had a largely symbolic meaning. But Dr Härke has proposed a further hypothesis. Analysis shows that those adult males buried with weapons tended to be up to two inches taller than those without – more or less the height difference revealed, by other studies, as that between the Anglo-Saxon and Romano-British populations. Härke has argued that the [taller] immigrant Germanic [community] 'used weapons in the burial rite . . . perhaps . . . to demonstrate that they were ruling [the land] by force; a material culture version of the conquest myth'.[16] But it could be that these opulent inhumations, which would have had to be highly public events to make such an aggressive demonstration, were, rather, exclusive family memorials to kinship solidarity. The ceremony attending the baby boy buried with the family sword 'that any warrior would envy and only a hero could wield in battle' would, surely, have been one of howling private grief, not of ethnic triumphalism.

Eighth-century Wessex: the first West Saxon law code and the first shires

It was the view of Bishop Stubbs, the great nineteenth-century scholar of medieval studies in England, that when the House of Commons appears it is largely as an assembly of representatives of other, older assemblies. (He was writing at a time when the House of Commons was of some consequence.) He traced this in part back to the shire courts of Anglo-Saxon England. Nearly all were in place by the year 1000 and some, as Professor Campbell has pointed out, were much older: 'At least three were former kingdoms. Such a shire as Hampshire is much older, as a unit of government and authority, than is France.'[17]

The eighth century opened promisingly for the kingdom of Wessex. The name was coming into general use for the territory stretching from the lands of the Gewisse people, around the upper Thames, southwards to the coastal lordship established by the semi-legendary Cerdic two centuries earlier. It is not clear how or by whom the two regions were united, but the ruling dynasty held to the title of the Cerdingas. With King Ine (688–726) the historic heartland kingdom of the later Anglo-Saxon period secured its own core territories. The men of Kent were forced to pay compensation for the killing of Mull; Surrey was effectively a frontier province (bordering on Essex); while Sussex, it seems, was generally a bidd-able ally helping Ine in a campaign against the British king Geraint of Dumnonia.

The reign of Ine remains important for his law code, the first by a Wessex king, which survives as an attachment to the code of Alfred and holds the first references to the shire court presided over by a royal agent or *scirman* ('shireman'). It seems that the core West Saxon shires of Hampshire, Wiltshire, Dorset and Somerset, though based on existing administrative subdivisions, may have been estab-lished under this king. By a wide margin the Western world's oldest organs of local government still functioning, the West Saxon shires were already, in the classic English manner, of different type. The first two take their names from royal residences (*vills*) at [South] Hampton and Wilton. Dorset and Somerset, on the other hand, were named for the local folk, the settlers (*sæte*), in the vicinity of the forts of Dorchester and Somerton. Ine's laws are concerned that a malefactor might escape his lord's control by getting into a neighbouring shire. Apparently 'crossing the county line' has been an option for fugitives from justice for well over a millennium.

The shire with its subdivisions, such as the hundreds, was headed by a royal appointee originally in Wessex known as an 'ealdorman', though the term in general came to denote an official of higher status; by the year 1000 most of England had been divided under successive rulers into shires, each with its royal official known as the *scir gerefa* (the 'reeve'), an administrative officer of the shire (certain Canadian municipalities still have an official known as 'reeve'). The modern English sheriff has limited, often ceremonial functions. In the US his equivalent, inherited from the colonial period, remains an important local law enforcement officer. Familiar to all aficionados of the Western film, at the time of the western frontier the sheriff was empowered to recruit a 'posse' of the county's citizenry to help him at need. Like the man, the term derives from medieval England, from the (post-Conquest) Latin *posse comitatus*, the 'force of the county'. In some US states the posse may still be deployed as a citizen police force, to patrol shopping malls, for instance.

It is also under Ine that the term 'ealdorman' first appears in West Saxon documents, the first West Saxon coins were minted and the king first began to interest himself in commerce. In fact, it appears that King Ine, whose laws on the regulation and protection of foreign merchants encouraged the commercial development of Wessex, probably stimulated the kingdom's economy by the carefully planned development of the port of Hamwic, adjacent to the royal vill of Hampton. Population was resettled from the surrounding countryside; gravel and other building materials were shipped on site at the king's expense; and a new port was ready to join the international Channel–North Sea network of centres, given the generic name of 'emporium' (plural 'emporia') by historians of the period.

In the 710s Boniface of Crediton, then a monk at Nursling, en route for his mission to Germany, twice went by road to Lundenwic (London) to make the sea crossing from there. As a Wessex man he may have considered himself to be still on home territory. In the early 700s the law code of King Ine mentions the East Saxon Eorcenwold, bishop of London, as 'our bishop', which suggests that the West Saxon king considered he had a controlling interest in the place. Twenty years before that, a reference in the Kentish law code refers to the 'king's hall' and the king's *wic gerefa* ('wic reeve') – presumably the hall within the Roman city area and the reeve based in the wic (or trading area) to watch over the king's interests in the emporium's trade. Given its place on the Thames and at the convergence of many frontiers, and its status as an international emporium, we can assume that all adjacent authorities wanted their fingers in the honeypot and that London's merchant magnates knew how to restrict access.

Boniface had already made his mark when King Ine and his church councillors chose him to head a deputation to Canterbury. Churchmen had been among the advisers, both lay and clerical, the king had consulted when drawing up his legal code, which, among other things, legislated to enforce both infant baptism and the payment of tithes, levies due to the church. During his reign the kingdom, up to that time a single church province, was divided between two new bishoprics, Winchester and Sherborne, where the devout and scholarly Aldhelm, apparently of the royal kin, was installed. In Alfred's day it was believed that Ine built the first monastery in the vicinity of the numinous site of Glastonbury

Tor and he certainly was a patron to the abbey of Malmesbury where Aldhelm, who had long been a student at Theodore's Canterbury school, was abbot from the 680s. On the western edge of Anglo-Saxon settlement and conquest, the abbey had a sizeable number of Britons among its dependent population. As Della Hooke explains in *The Landscape of Anglo-Saxon England* (p. 40)

> Although large numbers of Anglo-Saxon immigrants followed the initial raids . . . [or wars, we might say, such as that of Ine and his Sussex ally against Dumnonia] and settled across England . . . the bulk of the population, especially in the west, must surely have remained Romano-British stock.

The original name of the minster of Malmesbury was Maildubhi Urbs the 'city' of Maildubh, in Old English Maeldubh's burh, and tradition holds that it originated around the hermitage of an Irish monk of that name. Irish monks may also have had a presence at Glastonbury. Certainly non-Roman Christianity was strong in the region. About 700 we find Aldhelm, writing to King Geraint of Dumnonia, spelling out the Roman way of calculating the date for Easter and urging that his British clergy adopt it. The approach to the West Country 'Celtic' Christians seems to have had some success. Bede claimed that the British already within the West Saxon borders were convinced of the Roman way. Apparently, however, the British across the Severn, the Welsh, refused to eat with 'the Roman party' and imposed a penance of forty days on priests who had anything at all to do with the Romans.

One of the pillars of Anglo-Saxon spirituality in Wessex was to be the new foundation at Wimborne, inaugurated with King Ine's sister Cuthburg as its first abbess. Married for a time to King Aldfrith of Northumbria (685–705) and later a nun at Barking in Essex, she lived a career typical of the kind of networking that was possible for women between the kingdoms of the Heptarchy.

Dynastic rivalry was also part of the royal scene and, though Ine fended off his rivals, such family feuding would return sporadically to disrupt later reigns. Like his predecessor, Ine abdicated to make the pilgrimage to Rome, where he would die. Men said it was he who founded the Schola Saxonum, the English quarter near St Peter's. In a reign of some forty years he had maintained the prestige and standing of Wessex and opened up the field of royal government beyond the activities of warlord and conqueror.

The *Chronicle* tell us that Ine was followed peacefully by a kinsman who ruled from 726 to 740. A family member named Cuthred, in turn, succeeded him. There is evidently drama behind the brief entries for these decades. We learn that in 733 Æthelbald, king of Mercia, captured the West Saxon royal vill of Somerton and that in this year the sun looked like 'a black shield'. Seven years later, Cuthred took the war to Æthelbald. Three years after this the two men were allies against the Welsh. For a time Cuthred was endangered by domestic rivals and no doubt he faced other threats not recorded in the *Chronicle's* terse chronology. In fact, between the seventh and the ninth centuries, the rule in Wessex rarely seems to have passed from father to son; perhaps the succession should be rather understood as an almost institutionalized pattern of challenge and counter-challenge among families of the establishment who laid claim to descent from Cerdic. In the year 752 Cuthred went against Æthelbald once more and this time 'put him to flight'. Four years later, Cuthred died.

There followed twelve months of conspiracy and murder among the ruling establishment, in which the new King Sigeberht was driven from his throne by his successor Cynewulf. Forced to flee, an outlaw, into the forest of the Weald, he was assassinated by a herdsman – on Cynewulf's orders, it was supposed. The next thirty years belong to Cynewulf who, we are told by the *Chronicle*, could trace his paternal ancestry in direct line back to Cerdic, and who fought many 'great battles' against the Britons. For all that, one of the longer, and it would seem more successful, reigns in English history receives little attention from the *Chronicle* bar the mention that it ended with the king's murder by Cyneheard, the brother of Sigeberht, whose own death Cynewulf too had contrived some thirty years previously. Cyneheard too was killed and the succession was secured by Beohrtric, another direct descendant of Cerdic. He may well have owed his throne to Offa of Mercia (see chapter 4); he married his daughter. Beohrtric was opposed by Ecgberht, connected with the West Saxon and Kentish royal lines, and grandfather 'to be' of Alfred the Great. Although Wessex won a momentary independence, Ecgberht was driven from 'the land of the English' i.e. England by Beohrtric who was assisted by Offa, and Ecghberht was forced to live at the court of Charles the Great, king of the Franks, for several years.

No doubt the overbearing Mercian looked upon Wessex as at best a client kingdom, at worst a subject province. According to King Alfred, who recounted the tradition to his biographer, Asser, many years later, Eadburh's malevolent period as royal consort explained why the wife of a West Saxon king was never consecrated queen. A true daughter of her father, she ruled the court circle by tyranny and intrigue, but had to flee the country when a plot misfired and she almost poisoned her husband. Whether any of this was true (was she following instructions?) or whether we are dealing here with a simple case of misogynistic gossip, the kings of Wessex did not, after her time, honour their wives with the title of queen and held their ceremonial 'crown wearings' in solitary state. It was a change from earlier times. In the seventh century the West Saxons had been briefly ruled by a queen regnant and as late as the 740s a king's wife was witnessing charters as '*regina*' ('queen').

Beohrtric's reign (786–802) witnessed an event of terrible omen for the English. 'In these days', records the *Chronicle*, 'came the first three ships of Northmen' – it seems they may have been from the region around Hardanger Fjord in western Norway. One report has them landing at Portland. The king's *gerefa* rode out to meet them because he did not know what they were, although, presumably they were not traders, since otherwise they would have been heading for Hamwic. Maybe they had steered a wrong course. It was the reeve's duty to have newcomers report themselves to the king's town. They killed him.[18]

It was a portent of things to come. Ecgberht, the next king of Wessex (802–39), who was king of Kent, Surrey, Sussex and Essex from 825, and was awarded the title of 'bretwalda' by the *Anglo-Saxon Chronicle* as eighth in line of the wielders of the *imperium* named by Bede, would spend the last years of his reign combating recurring incursions of such 'northmen' or 'Vikings'

3

NORTHUMBRIA: THE STAR
IN THE NORTH

I have argued in chapter 1, with David Rollason, that by the time
of Bede it was 'right to regard Northumbria . . . as essentially
English'.[1] This chapter argues that the Northumbrians of the
seventh and eighth centuries were, considering their numbers and
the size of their territories, among the most important, in terms of
their cultural contribution to contemporary Europe and influence
on the future, of any of the tribal successors to imperial Rome at
that time. Their kings founded the possibility of success; their
scholars and artists gave birth to it; and a succession of missionaries
of determination, faith and courage, and often of administrative
genius, established a presence in Europe that would prove formative
in the history of the Continental church.

The European setting and Northumbrian actors

In the late seventh century and the early eighth, Northumbria, that
is the united kingdoms of Deira and Bernicia, was England's dominant power. Warfare was a condition of the age throughout Europe.
In Spain a century of conflicts between various Visigothic rulers prepared the ground for the catastrophic reign of King Rodrigo (*d.* 711),

when Moorish mercenaries from North Africa were called in. Within months others followed and by mid-decade virtually the entire Iberian Peninsula was in the hands of Islam. Not until the reign of Abd ar Rahmann II, Emir of Cordova (822–52), did the full glories of Moorish Spanish culture begin to unfold. In Italy the Lombards, a Germanic people given to internecine war, produced a great ruler and lawgiver in King Liudprand (712–44), with his court at Pavia. But the pope at Rome, fearful that he might become the Lombards' puppet, called on the protection of Charles the Great, King of the Franks, and in 774 Charles added the iron crown of Lombardy to his other trophies.

The Frankish kingdom, which comprised most of western Europe north of the Alps, had been founded by Clovis, barbarian turned Catholic (not Arian) Christian in the early 500s. From 600 up to the early 700s it fractured in the wars of his successors, the Merovingian kings, and their chief ministers, 'mayors of the palace'. Then in 714 the Northumbrian-born St Willibrord, bishop of Utrecht, baptized Pippin, son of the 'mayor' Charles Martel. When he grew to manhood, this Pippin the Short, with the full approval of the pope, displaced the last Merovingian ruler. In the year 751 he became king of the Franks, in a ceremony of consecration conducted, we are told by the *Frankish Royal Annals*, by another English cleric, St Boniface, archbishop of Mainz and today patron saint of Germany. Towards the end of the century, his son, Charles the Great (in German Karl der Grosse, in French Charlemagne), presided over the 'Carolingian renaissance', the first great cultural flowering in Europe since the fall of Rome in the West, with the Northumbrian Alcuin of York his principal director of studies.

Leading roles in Northumbria's golden age (an overworked term in the view of some modern historians of Mercia!) go first to the five kings: Æthelfrith the pagan and his Christian successors Edwin, Oswald, Oswiu and his son Ecgfrith. Next, to the churchmen and women, mostly of noble stock: Abbess Hild (Hilda) of Whitby, who

presided over the Synod held there in 664 with momentous conse-
quences for Europe; Cuthbert, charismatic monk-bishop and
hermit; Benedict Biscop, monastic founder, patron of learning and
library builder and frequent visitor to Rome; Wilfrid of Ripon and
York, a prince bishop on the European stage and Archbishop
Ecgberht, a king's brother who, along with his successor Archbishop
Ælbert, created northern Europe's principal seat of learning, where
Alcuin would dazzle the continent. Greatest of all was Bede.

Soon after their deaths Cuthbert and Wilfrid were subjects of
notable biographies. Cuthbert's, completed some time between 698
and 705, almost certainly prompted the *Vita Wilfridi* written by
Stephen, a monk at Ripon, shortly after Wilfrid's death at Oundle in
709 or 710. There ensued what has been called 'a virtual "pamphlet"
war'. Bede himself was very much on the side of the modest Cuthbert
as opposed to the fiery Wilfrid, who it has been said 'came into
conflict with almost every prominent secular and ecclesiastical figure
of the age'. He founded many monastic communities and every year,
at the liturgical commemoration of his death, readings from the biography, delivered no doubt in a dramatic manner, would have revived
memories of that towering physical presence and sonorous voice.

Formation of a kingdom

The name 'Northumbria' may actually be Bede's coinage, but the
state originated in the two constituent kingdoms of Bernicia to the
north and Deira to the south. In 600 Deira was ruled by King Ælle
and Bernicia by King Æthelfrith, who was married to Ælle's daughter Acha. Her brother Edwin, their father's heir in Deira, was
robbed of the succession when Ælle died in 604 and the Bernician
king drove the young man into exile – a century later the Deirans
would still regard this as the act of a tyrant. Edwin found asylum at
the court of Rædwald of the East Angles and survived at least one
assassination attempt ordered by his brother-in-law.

Æthelfrith won decisive victories over his Christian neighbours, the Scots Irish of Dál Riata to the northwest and the British of the kingdom of Rheged, to the west.[2] Such border kingdoms were almost a symbiotic necessity for an expansionist English king. Either they paid tribute or he could distribute their land and wealth among his warrior thegns as befitted a ring-giving lord in the Beowulf tradition. Bede, perhaps here a better Northumbrian than Christian, admired Æthelfrith the pagan warrior lord. Reporting his victory at Degsastan (Degsa's Stone) over the Scots in 603, the monk compares the heathen war leader to King Saul of ancient Israel. Like Saul, Æthelfrith exterminated or enslaved the defeated population to open the conquered territory to settlement. Bede duly notes that, unlike Saul, Æthelfrith 'was ignorant of the true religion'.

Describing the destruction of the Britons of Strathclyde at the Battle of Chester in 614, Bede's triumphalism is open. The British had a detachment of monks praying for victory in the sight of the enemy. Æthelfrith attacked these first, 'fighting against us even if unarmed', slaughtering some twelve hundred before dealing with the rest of the 'accursed army', as Bede puts it. And why does he say 'accursed'? First, because their British ancestors had made no attempt to teach the faith to the invading pagan English; secondly, the British church refused to submit to Rome. With kinsfolk among the aristocratic tradition Bede himself was not so far 'divorced from the warrior mentality of Beowulf'.[3] His description of Æthelfrith as a man 'most desirous of glory' (*gloriae cupidissimus*) recalls the word *domgeorn* (literally, 'glory-eager') used in Anglo-Saxon literature of heroic warriors and Bede may have known a now lost epic praising the hero-king.

Æthelfrith's reign ended at the Battle of the River Idle in 616, when he was defeated and killed by Rædwald of East Anglia, who had taken up the cause of Edwin the exile. Now it was the turn of the dead king's sons (Edwin's nephews) Oswald and Oswiu, aged twelve and four, to seek asylum, apparently in Dál Riata.

In exile for seventeen years, they acquired fluent Irish and were baptized Christians, probably at the island monastery of Iona. Edwin, holding at first to the old pagan religion, extended Northumbrian power over the shadowy British kingdom of Elmet (in modern west Yorkshire). He imposed tribute over the islands of Anglesey and Man and, for a time, over Mercia. The campaigns of Æthelfrith and now Edwin were prising apart the British rulers of Wales to the south from those of Strathclyde in Cumbria to the north.

Edwin, the most powerful figure of his day and rated the fifth wielder of the *imperium* by Bede, moved among his manors and estates in quasi-imperial pomp. Banners were borne before him when he rode to war with his thegns (*ministris*) and also in time of peace as he travelled his territories, consuming the food rents owed by his subject lords. Behind this lay an administrative structure of cities (*civitates*), estates (*villas*) and provinces (*provincias*, possibly sub-kingdoms), Whenever the entourage made a progress from a great royal hall, it was preceded by a standard bearer or 'a type of standard Romans call a *tufa*, English call a *thuf*'. To such accounts we can add remarkable archaeological finds made in the later twentieth century near the village of Yeavering in Northumberland.

It is an extensive site, originally of pagan cult significance, stretching over about a quarter of a mile (*c.* 400m) with prehistoric remains at either end, a stone circle and a Bronze Age barrow, both modified in the later sixth century. Post holes and other traces indicate that in the early seventh century a number of monumental timber halls were built and also a unique structure best described as a segment of an amphitheatre. In the opinion of Professor Blair the complex was the royal vill of King Edwin and the site of the massive baptismal campaign following his conversion to Christianity (see below). Whether one of the timber halls ever served as the royal mead hall is unclear. That it was an Anglian royal vill raised in a place of traditional religious veneration seems certain.[4]

In 625 King Edwin married the Christian Princess Æthelburh (Ethelburga), sister of the king of Kent. She was to be allowed to practise her Roman Catholic faith at his court, under her priest Bishop Paulinus – consecrated before leaving Kent by Archbishop Justus of Canterbury (like him a founder member of St Augustine's mission) – and his assistant James the Deacon. Edwin was to convert at some future date. The following Easter he narrowly escaped an assassination attempt. The attacker, sent by the king of Wessex and posing as a courier, suddenly drew a concealed sword on being admitted to the royal presence and thrust at the king, who was only saved by a loyal thegn hurling himself forward to take the blow. The same evening, we are told, the queen gave birth to a baby girl. Edwin vowed to be baptized if the Christian God gave him victory over Wessex and meanwhile allowed his daughter Eanflæd to be baptized 'the first of the Northumbrian race'. The king, we are told, went into Wessex 'with levies', where he slew 'five kings'. He prepared to follow his daughter to the font.

Why Edwin should have opened himself to the new religion from the south is not clear. He was the most powerful king in the north, poised to achieve the *Imperium* throughout the Anglo–Saxon world. But it was an age when Europe's kings were aping the style of 'Roman' rulers, of which the religion based in Rome was an important part; perhaps Edwin decided to adopt it for reasons of modernity and prestige. His 'southern' marriage was an important political alliance. And it is always worth bearing in mind that there may have been an element of genuine religious sentiment involved. He anticipated objections from his pagan courtiers, but, if we accept Bede's account, the decisive council meeting went smoothly. First, the pagan high priest, Coifi, readily agreed the proposed overthrow of the kingdom's traditional religion – and might he be permitted to lead the desecration of the temples with the cast of a spear into the sanctuary? After all, he observed, he had been the most assiduous servant of the pagan pantheon, yet many other men had received more of the king's bounty than he. Surely if the gods had any real powers he would have been more favoured.

A more thoughtful courtier compared a man's life on earth to the flight of a sparrow that blunders into the king's banqueting hall with the fire blazing on a blustery winter's evening. After a few moments in the warmth and light, it flies out again into the storm. In the same way we pass a few moments in the glow of life from birth to death. But we know nothing of what went before or of what will come after. A religion that can give us information on such matters is surely worth a try. The council agreed and Coifi, riding the king's stallion, headed for the old temples, spear in hand. The stallion is important, not only because as high priest Coifi was officially permitted to ride only a mare, but also because the horse as such played an important part in the Anglo-Saxons' pagan religious beliefs.

Edwin was baptized, at York on 12 April 627, in a wooden chapel dedicated to St Peter built specially for the purpose. Apparently Roman 'Eboracum' had no Christian church building from the Roman period to match the ruined chapel of St Martin's at Canterbury. Urged by Paulinus, Edwin ordered the building of a basilica of stone, which enclosed the king's baptismal chapel.

Mass baptisms followed in what sounds more like a military campaign than the dove-like ministrations of the Holy Spirit. Bede tells us that Paulinus, a tall stooping figure with an aquiline nose set in his gaunt face, and his assistant James the Deacon spent thirty-six days instructing, presumably through an interpreter, and baptizing in the River Glen near the royal palace of *Ad-gefrin* (no doubt from Brittonic, 'hill of the goats'), that is Yeavering. Bede accounts for the success by the 'great desire . . . for baptism among the . . . Northumbrian people',[5] but presumably the known wishes of the king had something to do with it. Perhaps, also, a number of these many converts were 'closet' British Christians relieved to 'come out', even if the official Roman version of the Faith was not exactly theirs. Paulinus was established as bishop at York with James the Deacon at his side, and they began to preach in the subject kingdom of Lindsey. When, in November 627, Justus of Canterbury died, Paulinus consecrated his successor as archbishop, with papal approval. On 10 October 633 catastrophe struck. King Edwin was killed at the Battle of Hatfield Chase by the combined forces of Penda, the pagan ruler of Mercia, and Cadwallon, the British/Welsh Christian, king of Gwynedd. For twelve months the British king revenged the rapine, slaughter and rape his people had suffered at the hands of Æthelfrith, the pagan, years before. No doubt the aim was 'to wipe the entire English nation from the land of Britain'.[6] Retribution would follow. Later in the century the monastery of Ripon received endowments of holy places abandoned by British clergy 'fleeing the hostile swords' of the English.

Bishop Paulinus fled Deira, by ship, with Queen Æthelburh and her children for her brother's court in Kent. Deacon James held out at York, and in fact was to live to a ripe old age. Expert in church music, he taught 'after the manner of Rome'. Liturgical music was an important vehicle for spreading the Roman way. But in that dreadful year of 633, as Deira and Bernicia fell apart and their short-lived kings, Osric and Eanfrith, reverted to paganism before being killed by Cadwallon, it must have seemed that the Christian flame in Northumbria was extinguished. Events at the other end of the world would threaten Christendom itself. The death of Muhammad in Medina just four months before Hatfield had opened the way to the *tsunami* of Islamic conquest that was to wash away the East Roman Christian empire in North Africa, Egypt and Syria.

Heavenfield and renewal under the Irish influence

Oswald, Edwin's nephew, returned from exile in 634 and demolished Cadwallon and his army at the battle of Heavenfield near Hexham the following year. He claimed to have won with divine aid, in the sign of the wooden cross that he had raised before the battle with the aid of his soldiers. Oswald was now lord of the two northern kingdoms.

With the flight of Bishop Paulinus, Roman Christianity in Northumbria was in disarray. A Christian baptized into the Irish tradition, Oswald sent to Iona for a monk bishop who would re-found the Northumbrian church there. They sent Aidan and in 635 the king gave him the tidal island of Lindisfarne as the seat of his bishopric. Thus was inaugurated the monastery on Holy Island, destined to be the numinous heart of Northumbrian golden age culture. For the next thirty years the Irish clergy, with growing ranks of Northumbrian acolytes, were to prove an essential ingredient in the mix of Northumbria's golden age.

The first Irish mission to Britain had been that of St Columba or Colm Cille (c. 520–97), who was probably of royal kin and descended from Niall of the Nine Hostages of Meath. He was ordained at an early age and was associated for a time with Kells, then a royal residence, before founding monasteries in Ireland at Derry and Durrow. Then, in his mid-forties, he crossed the North Channel on a personal pilgrimage, possibly of penance, and together with twelve companions established a monastery on the island of Iona. The Book of Durrow is one of the inspirational manuscripts associated with what is sometimes called the Hiberno-Saxon tradition of illuminators, of which the two masterpieces are the Book of Kells and the Lindisfarne Gospels. Sometime in the 660s the Anglian churchman Ecgberht crossed over to Ireland and established himself at Rath Melsigi (probably Melfont in County Louth). This monastery attracted Englishmen such as Wilfrid and Willibrord, interested in the ways of the Irish missionaries or *peregrini*, as they are commonly termed in a technical sense (see below). Probably the most famous of these was St Columbanus, who had founded such monasteries as Luxeuil in the Vosges mountains and, most famously, Bobbio, near Piacenza in Italy.

Aidan's monastery on Lindisfarne recruited English boys for training as missionaries among their still largely pagan compatriots. Aidan himself, though he did travel his diocese on foot, had little English and he seems to have been most effective in his mission at court, where the king, a fluent Irish speaker, interpreted for his ealdormen and thegns. But top down conversion was the Anglo-Saxon royal way, as well as the Roman way. Being a king, Oswald wanted results, though systematic missionary campaigning in partnership with the authorities was not the Irish style, in fact was 'unique as far as the Irish are concerned'.[7] Aidan was followed by Irish monks, some ordained as priests, who could baptize as well as preach. They and their Anglo-Saxon disciples were basically responsible not just for the conversion of Northumbria but also for continuing the work begun by Paulinus south of the Humber.

In general Irish monks undertook pilgrimage for spiritual self-improvement rather than as a missionary vocation. The Latin term *peregrinus* (pilgrim) is often used in a technical sense for these Irish religious travellers, who combined pilgrimage with missionary activity. One might preach to the locals; he might move on; a group of *peregrini* might found a monastery, less to work among the surrounding community than as a retreat. Island monasteries like Iona were favoured. When St Wilfrid arrived in pagan Sussex, years later, a small Irish monastery had been established in the woodland wastes by the coast at Bosham for some years, with no discernible effect on the locality. Wilfrid converted the entire kingdom in short order.

Oswald of Northumbria: royal saint or pagan icon

In a reign of eight years Oswald so dominated affairs throughout Britain south of Pictland that, in Bede's view, he achieved the *imperium*. He annexed the kingdom of Lindsey, where Mercia also had an interest, and married the daughter of Cynegils of Wessex on the condition that her father convert to Christianity. Oswald stood godfather and, as we have seen, is named as joint donor when Cynegils confers Dorchester-upon-Thames on Birinus, first bishop of Wessex, as the seat of his diocese: a practical exercise of the kind of authority implicit in the word *imperium*.

It seems that Oswald's influence reached even into Kent. Bede tells us that Edwin's widow sent her children across the Channel to the court of the Merovingian King Dagobert for fear of Oswald. He also claims that the kings of Dál Riata and Pictland recognized Oswald's supremacy, while another contemporary flatteringly refers to him as 'ordained by god, *imperator* of the whole of Britain' [*totius Britanniae imperator a deo ordinatus*].[8] But, despite Oswald's victory at Heavenfield, Penda was still a threat and on 5 August 642 the pagan king of Mercia defeated and killed his Christian Northumbrian rival at the battle of Maserfelth. The location of Maserfelth is still disputed, favoured candidates being Oswestry (i.e. 'Oswald's tree') in Shropshire and a site in Lindsey.

Writing a century after the king-saint's death, Bede retails many miracles attributed to Oswald, both to his relics and even to the blood-soaked ground where he fell. Behind all these anecdotes seems to loom the backdrop of a pagan king cult. After the battle, his dead body was taken up and ritually dismembered under the gaze of the pagan King Penda. The head and the four limbs were then hung from the branches of a tree: 'In this hanging of parts of the king's body we can almost detect a ritual offering to Woden the god of war and himself known as the Hanging God.'[9] For two centuries the head was venerated at Lindisfarne; later, Willibrord's foundation at Utrecht claimed to hold it in a reliquary and there are numerous other marvels as the cult spread in Europe.

Besides the dismemberment of the body, some of the Oswald stories display other pagan elements. A horse fell into convulsions and was cured after rolling on the very patch of ground where the king fell. That a horse should benefit from the saint's miraculous powers seems odd, until we remember the important role of horses in Anglo-Saxon pagan beliefs. Horses were believed to conduct the souls of their masters to paradise after death.[10] A burial excavation at Lakenheath, Suffolk, in 1998 revealed the skeleton of a warrior of the early Anglo-Saxon period, sword in hand, with the skeleton of his horse, legs flexed, lying at his side.[11]

The most famous of all Oswald relics was the right forearm and hand (important in the pagan cult of the praying sacral king), which apparently remained fleshy and firm long after death. At one Easter banquet, Bede tells us, the king had been distributing food to a crowd of beggars. When supplies ran out, he called his smith to break up the silver platter into coin-size pieces for distribution. Bishop Aidan made a blessing. 'May this arm never perish.' Four centuries later, transported south from its shrine at Bamburgh, the right arm was still working its magic in Peterborough Abbey. The cult was to become widespread on the Continent. In one version a raven is mysteriously involved and the pagan Germanic associations are echoed in other ways.

From the battle of Maserfelth to the Synod of Whitby

From the start, dynastic and religious policy were enmeshed: the church hoping to exploit court influence to win converts and acquire endowments; kings supporting the missions as a way of projecting their influence. In 643 Oswiu recovered the severed head and arms of his dead brother, intending to create a royal cult. He founded a new church to St Peter on the rock at Bamburgh, the ancestral home of the Bernician dynasty, to accommodate the arms, which were enshrined there in a silver reliquary before the 730s. The head was assigned to Lindisfarne. One feels that the popular allure of this royal cult owed a good deal to its association with pre-Christian beliefs and customs and that the church's version aimed to sanitize it.

The imperishable forearm (testified as incorrupt by Alcuin in the late eighth century) remained at Bamburgh until the 1050s.

Politically, the death of Oswald split the two kingdoms once again. While his brother Oswiu succeeded in Bernicia, Deira broke away under their cousin Oswine, whose father, Osric, had been the ruler who had led the kingdom back to paganism during the dark days after Maserfelth. Despite this ancestry, Bede considered Oswine the perfect Christian king, while the Deirans themselves long resisted the rule of Oswiu. He, however, was determined to achieve a united kingdom.

Setting aside an earlier British/Irish wife, Oswiu now embarked on a marriage that made dynastic sense but had religious complications. He sent south to the court of Kent where his cousin, the Roman Catholic Eanflæd of Deira, was still living in exile. The two were well within the degrees of kinship considered incestuous by church law, but Rome made no objections, although the pope would surely have been informed about the marriage of this Christian princess. Oswiu saw the marriage as the way to affirm his dynastic rights in Deira; Rome may well have hoped for more far-reaching consequences. Either way, the Deirans were not impressed. Oswiu prepared to invade. What followed involved breaches of both the Christian and pagan codes that governed the world of the Anglo-Saxon noble. Oswine disbanded his army in the face of the enemy, itself shameful, and then went into hiding with one of his honoured companions, a *gesith* for whom loyalty to one's lord was supposed to be an absolute obligation. In fact this man betrayed Oswine to his enemy, King Oswiu, who had him killed. Still the Deiran nobles refused to accept Oswiu as king and chose a remote cousin of Oswine's to lead them.

Oswiu married one of his daughters to Penda's son Peada, who converted to Christianity, and a son to Penda's daughter Cyneburh. He also persuaded Sigeberht, king of the East Saxons, to be baptized. Penda's response to what we might call Oswiu's 'religious diplomatic offensive' came on 15 November 655. At the head of a massive army, and with the East Angles and the men of Deira at his side, he confronted the heavily outnumbered Bernician king at the River Winwaed, possibly near Leeds, and was himself destroyed. The Northumbrians' success in battle was, no doubt, an important element in their wealth. War booty was a prime source of income for a warrior society. As it advanced, the northern kingdom absorbed British kingdoms on the Pennines, such as Elmet, while their British enemies further west could exploit the gold mines of North Wales. Nor should one forget that Eboracum (later York) was one of the richest of Roman centres. The conquest of Pictish territories to the north (at one point the Bernician kingdom embraced what is now Edinburgh 'Din Eidyn' or 'Edwin's burh', according to rival theories) no doubt yielded profits.

Most theories relating to post-Romano-British society and the transition to the Anglo-Saxon kingdoms rely on speculation. The archaeological evidence for continuity can be ambiguous and limited even at such extensive and complex settlements as West Heslerton in North Yorkshire. But a peaceful transition from late Romano-British occupation to Anglian overlordship in the southern regions of Northumbria would have yielded dividends in terms of agrarian organization and prosperity.

Northumbria was secure and, in a gesture of triumph that would have been understood by every warrior, King Oswiu annexed to himself land in North Mercia reputedly 7,000 hides in area – exactly the extent of the lands that Hygelac, king of the Geats, awarded to Beowulf when he slew Grendel. He also founded twelve monasteries, among them Gilling, the site of Oswine's murder, and Whitby (then called Streanæshalch). Deira was obliged to accept his son, Alchfrith, as its sub-king. But even now Northumbria's southern kingdom still followed an independent line, above all in religion.

In addition to the short-lived dynastic alliance with Peada (to whom he gave the kingdom of Southern Mercia, but who died soon after that), Oswiu dispatched Irish and English clergy into Middle Anglia and beyond, and persuaded Sigeberht, king of the East Saxons, to accept both baptism and Cedd, of Lindisfarne, as bishop. Cedd built a church dedicated to St Peter at Bradwell-on-Sea, Essex, which is the oldest Anglo-Saxon building still more or less intact. Built on the site of a Roman fort about 653, using the original brick, it was in later generations used as a farm building. At the time it was an outpost of Northumbrian Irish Christianity, deep in the sphere of influence of the archbishops of Canterbury. Cedd also built a church at Tilbury, a further encroachment by the Ionian–Bernician bishop well beyond the boundaries of Northumbria but a fitting extension of influence for an appointee of Oswiu, holder of the *imperium* in Britain.

But now, under Alchfrith, Deira was going the Roman way. He ejected the Irish monks at the monastery of Ripon and in their place established his mother Queen Eanflæd's dynamic favourite, Wilfrid. There were numerous points of difference between the Roman and parts of the Irish church: points of doctrine and biblical teaching; the style of the monks' tonsure; and the date for the celebration of Easter. There were at least four systems for its calculation, one of which was used in the Roman church and by Canterbury, and another used in parts of Ireland and at Iona and Lindisfarne, and hence in Northumbria. The Northumbrian court was blessed with two factions: the king's, what one might call the Iona/Lindisfarne party, and the Canterbury Queen's party. At the very least it was inconvenient for the court to be celebrating this major religious event on days that might vary by as much as four weeks – and was led up to by forty days of fasting. But Oswiu and Eanflæd had accommodated the inconvenience for the best part of twenty years. Why was it that in 664 the king decided to settle the allegiance of the Northumbrian church? It is hard not to see Wilfrid as the prime mover.

Kings and noble clerics

It is now time to look at three of the most influential men in seventh-century Northumbrian society and politics, all born around the year 630 and entering their teenage years when King Oswiu came to the throne in 642, and all churchmen of aristocratic family: Cuthbert (d. 687); Benedict Biscop (originally Biscop Baducing, i.e. descendant of Baduc, d. 689); and Wilfrid (d. 709). Their careers, in different ways, illustrate the court church network in action; it could be close – Eanbald II, archbishop of York, apparently travelled his diocese accompanied by a sizeable guard of armed retainers, having given protection to enemies of the king.

There were recognized ranks of aristocratic status. A king's companion, an established man of property or count (comes in Latin, gesith in Old English), came above a minister or knight (miles in Latin, thegn in Old English), but probably began his career as one. Then there were men of 'ceorlisc' standing, what we might call the minor gentry (like Alcuin's family, in all probability), who as modest landholders were free but expected to defer to others of higher social status. Bede tells us that Benedict Biscop, churchman and artistic patron, was aged about twenty-five and a 'minister' of King Oswiu when the king gave him possession of land due to his rank. Virtually the same career pattern of royal land gifts raising a young warrior to the rank of companion is to be found in Beowulf. And the imagery of Christian warfare is always in the background. One of Biscop's young relatives, Eostorwine, was a household warrior of King Ecgfrith (reigned 670–85) until aged twenty-four, when he laid down his arms and 'girded himself for spiritual warfare' as a monk.

Documentary sources, though scant, reveal a body of mid-seventh-century nobles both extremely wealthy and extremely powerful (others were landless and vagrant). Nor were the accoutrements of nobility necessarily discarded in holy orders. In one of his letters St Boniface deplores flamboyant styles in clothes by high churchmen and berates some who still bear arms after taking orders. And yet quality arms were as much part of the noble's lifestyle as the monk' tonsure was part of his. A father was expected to kit out his son's debut at court, if only for the family honour. To appear at court poorly equipped would be a shameful thing.

Young noblemen tended to resent being bossed about by other young noblemen, however holy. Ceolfrith, Bede's abbot at Monkwearmouth Jarrow, was forced to resign and withdraw from the abbey because of jealousies and violent criticism from some of the noble brethren on account of his strict discipline. According to Boniface there were English churchmen who dressed in garments embellished with 'dragons' (oriental silks?). On the other hand, life in the church could offer challenge and openings to intelligent and ambitious minds.

Cuthbert, the first of our nobleman clerics, was being recognized as the unofficial patron saint of the Northumbrians within a generation of his death in 687; in 1987 he was focus of a notable 1,300th anniversary celebration. He entered the monastery of Melrose on the River Tweed aged about fourteen; the fact that he made his arrival mounted on horseback, carrying a spear and attended by a servant backs the assumption that his family were members of the nobility. Tradition speaks of him guarding his lord's sheep, but in a society where, witness Old English law codes, sheep rustling was rife (as, according to press reports, it is again today on England's northern fells) this could as well have been the armed service of a retainer as the duty of a peasant shepherd. (The shepherds carved on the mysterious Franks Casket (see page 86) carry spears.) In fact, Cuthbert may first have considered the military way – an anonymous 'Life' speaks of the boy having served with an army 'in the face of the enemy'. In the early 650s, before Winwaed, with the pagan forces of Mercia constantly probing the defences of Bernicia and with 'noblemen from many a kingdom flocking to serve the bountiful Oswine of Deira', a warrior's career would have been a natural choice for a young Christian aristocrat. After Winwaed, service in the *militia dei*, the 'army of god', would have made more sense. Cuthbert had easy relations with the royal family: he rose to be first prior and then bishop at the royal foundation of Lindisfarne; the gold and garnet pectoral cross, preserved as his in the treasury at Durham Cathedral, is a nobleman's jewel. And yet St Cuthbert was, and is, honoured for his humble piety. Raised against his will to be bishop of Lindisfarne in 685, he ended his days as a hermit on the island of Inner Farne, the death of this 'child of God', Bede's favourite name for him, 'being signalled to his community on Lindisfarne by the waving of torches from the cliff top'.[12]

Cuthbert is one of that select band of medieval personalities in England, like Julian of Norwich or Henry V, who still enjoy recognition status. Of greater importance in the story of Northumbria's European Golden Age, Benedict Biscop (i.e. the bishop) was originally a prominent young courtier in the hall of King Oswiu. (In later life he would appoint a deputy for his religious duties precisely because he was so often called away to consult with kings.) In 652/3, when they were both about thirty, he left England for Rome in company with Wilfrid, another young noble. This was the first of numerous visits. In 666, returning from his second trip, Biscop stopped off at the monastery on the Iles Lérins, across the bay from Cannes, thus anticipating Lord Brougham's preferred Riviera retreat – though, in contradistinction to his lordship, taking the tonsure as a monk. Only six years earlier the monks had adopted the monastic Rule of St Benedict; Baducing adopted Benedict as his new name in religion.

Benedict returned to Rome and there (as we saw in chapter 2) encountered Theodore of Tarsus, the newly appointed seventh archbishop of Canterbury. They journeyed together and Benedict was able to introduce Theodore at the court of King Ecgberht of Kent. For a time he served as abbot of the monastery of Canterbury until Theodore's assistant, Adrian, arrived. After yet another Rome visit Biscop returned for a time to Northumbria.

For twenty years he had been tracking the north–south route across the shifting frontiers of warring semi-barbarian Christian kingdoms, all the time buying books, assembling treasures and making useful contacts. It was now time to begin a project that was to feed back into Europe's culture for generations to come. In the year 673, on a tract of land given to him by King Ecgfrith, he began the building of the monastery of St Peter at Monkwearmouth, with the help of stonemasons recruited in Gaul/Francia, and apparently following a Continental layout. In 678 he was in Rome again, this time with Ceolfrith, who would succeed him as abbot at Monkwearmouth, and returned with a cantor in church music. Back in Bernicia, he began building the monastery at Jarrow, some seven miles north of Wearmouth on the River Tyne. As at St Peter's, archaeology has revealed that the main stone buildings were decorated with coloured paintings, sculptures and coloured window glass and plaster.

Wilfrid, appellant to Rome

St Wilfrid of Ripon and York, the third of our networking clerics, is remembered (thanks to one of the finest biographies from the Middle Ages, written by his disciple Eddius) as the most brilliant and substantial figure in England in the seventh century and, so far as the records go, in Europe. As the son of a gentleman, the boy was expected to attend to the needs of the house guests, 'whether they were kings' companions or their slaves', in the family home. But undefined trouble with a hostile stepmother led him to leave, about the year 648, aged fourteen. He evidently left without his father's blessing since, his biographer tells us, he himself found the funds to 'clothe, arm and mount both himself and his servants'.

Wilfrid would not win his sainthood through the Christian virtue of humility. Court politics was tied in to church politics. King Oswiu followed the tradition of Iona, with Lindisfarne the kingdom's senior episcopal see. Queen Eanflæd, baptized as a child at York by Bishop Paulinus and then exiled in Kent, adhered to the Roman tradition. Wilfrid became her protégé. About the year 652, after a brief time at Lindisfarne, he left Northumbria for Kent and the court at Canterbury, where the queen still had friends. From there, aged just twenty, a young aristocrat of substantial private means, he set out for his first sight of Rome in company with Biscop Baducing, some five years his senior and a very rich man. James Campbell has gone so far as to surmise that 'had Biscop wished to provide his father with a really lavish, old fashioned burial – ship, . . . splendid personal adornments – the likelihood is that they would hardly have dented his resources.'[13] One pictures him and Wilfrid as a couple of eighteenth-century milords on the Grand Tour, rather than as pious eight-century pilgrims.

In Rome Wilfrid set himself to master the Roman method of the *computus*, the calculation for the date of Easter. On his return journey he strengthened his Continental allegiances, with a three-year stay at Lyon, where he also became a monk. Back in England in the early 660s, he was made abbot of Ripon. About 663 the Frankish churchman Agilbert, who for some years had been a bishop in Wessex, ordained Wilfrid priest at Ripon. Agilbert's name, equivalent to Æthelberht, has led to the suggestion that he may have had ties with the royal house of Kent. The following year, 664, he led one of the factions at the historic Synod of Whitby (then called Streanæshalch) convened by King Oswiu at the abbey under the aegis of its abbess, Hild, to settle the Easter controversy.

Related to the royal house, she had been baptized by Bishop Paulinus at York in 627, aged thirteen, together with King Edwin. She was well into her thirties when she decided to become a nun, possibly with the idea of joining her sister at Chelles, near Paris (see chapter 2). In fact, she was installed by Aidan as abbess of the convent of Hartlepool, and then by King Oswiu at his new foundation at

Whitby. It was a 'double' foundation, that is for both men and women, with no fewer than five bishops among its alumni during Hild's abbacy. Archaeology has revealed evidence of its Continental contacts. King Edwin's relics were buried here, as were Hild's, though later translated to Glastonbury.

The Synod of Whitby and after

The problem posed by the computation of Easter comes from the fact that the crucifixion of Jesus Christ, the anchor date for many major festivals in the Christian year, is related to the Jewish Passover, which in turn is related to the Jewish lunar year. And since the lunar calendar is moveable relative to the solar calendar, and since Christians celebrate Easter according to the lunar date, elaborate calculations are required to determine the date. The following of Rome on the matter of Easter, just as following Rome in the use of Jerome's Latin Vulgate bible and the Gregorian chant of the musical rite, was a marker of Rome's authority in western Christendom. So the decision at Whitby would not only be important to the Northumbrian court but also, through Northumbrian missionaries in the German territories and the Frankish church, in Europe. (The date of Christmas is no problem because it is fixed relative to the pagan Winter Solstice festival of the solar year.)

Oswiu favoured Iona over Rome, but one feels his real interest was a unified observance rather than the triumph of a doctrine. The line-up of the opposing parties was: for Iona, Abbess Hild and the bishops Colman of Lindisfarne and Cedd of the East Saxons; for Rome, Queen Eanflæd, Bishop Agilbert the Frank and Wilfrid, who acted as Oswiu's English interpreter and spokesman. As the technical debate ploughed on, Wilfrid observed that his side was advocating the system ordained by the pope in Rome, the successor of St Peter, holder of the keys of heaven. Colman had to admit this was so. At this point the king smilingly intervened to rule that since St Peter must surely know the answer, the Northumbrian church would follow the Roman way. (Bede reports the debate but in fact, after his death, Rome later came to adopt the *computus* proposed by Bede himself.) Later that year Oswiu nominated Wilfrid bishop of York. He crossed the Channel to be consecrated at Compiègne, where, with ceremonial pomp exceeding anything to be seen in England, he was borne into the oratory, by nine bishops seated upon a golden throne. But, then, everything to do with Wilfrid would appear to have been more than life-size. For St Peter's, Ripon, he commissioned a copy of the Gospels in lettering of purest gold done on purpled parchment and bound in a gold case studded with costly gems. According to his biographer, Wilfrid's church at Hexham, with its columns and side aisles, grand proportions, winding passages and spiral staircases, was unequalled by any structure north of the Alps; it was, need one add, designed by Wilfrid himself. Both here and at Ripon he built crypts as if to imitate that feature in the Church of the Holy Sepulchre in Jerusalem.

Because of Wilfrid 's two-year absence on the Continent, the king made Chad bishop in his place. Canterbury intervened to depose Chad and restore Wilfrid, but when, in 677, Theodore went on to divide the diocese of York its bishop made his way to Rome to appeal to the pope. (On his way, this being Saint Wilfrid, he took time off to make the first conversion of the Frisians, having with him relics of St Oswald; see chapter 5). It was the first such appeal to the papal see and was a welcome boost to its authority at a time when it was in protracted controversy with the emperors at Constantinople over which was the ultimate authority in the universal church. Rome accepted the division of the York diocese but ordered the restoration of Wilfrid and authorized him to appoint the new bishops. But Rome also provided that the numerous monasteries ('the kingdom of monasteries') owing allegiance to Wilfrid be exempt from visitation by other bishops and be subject direct to Rome – a further accretion of papal influence.

Two kings and a bishop

In May 670, six years after Whitby, Oswiu died. He was followed by his son Ecgfrith, who checked the resurgent power of Mercia with a victory over its king, Wulfhere. But Bishop Wilfrid at York remained the dominant figure on the northern scene. Thanks to his persuasion the king's wife, a virgin for twelve years of marriage, took vows as a nun. But King Ecgfrith rejected the papal settlement regarding York and, with the concurrence of Theodore of Canterbury, in 678 Wilfrid was forced into exile. No doubt there was political calculation behind the king's decision: from Stamford (in modern Lincolnshire) to Perth in Scotland Wilfrid had spiritual rule of a 'kingdom of churches' of his own foundation to match the king's secular realm.

Naturally Wilfrid took his case to Rome again and meanwhile stayed for a time in Sussex, where, as we have seen, he converted the kingdom and founded the see of Selsey. Next he was given a bishopric by the king of Wessex, who also endowed him with extensive lands on the Isle of Wight.

Ecgfrith continued Northumbria's expansionist war-making with raids into Ireland and Pictland, where on 20 May 685 he was killed at the battle of Nechtansmere. He was succeeded by his half-brother Aldfrith, called 'the Learned' (d. 705). An exile during the previous reign, he had found refuge among the Irish and had acquired a mastery of the language. Theodore, the ageing archbishop of Canterbury, brokered an agreement between Wilfrid and the king and for a time peace reigned. But, with his once great diocese divided and his influence reduced, Wilfrid took himself to Mercia, where he lived for a decade under the protection of King Æthelred and fostered the mission to Frisia. Where once he had ruled as a 'clerical emperor' in England, now he was principally confined to the foreign mission field of Frisia. In 703, however, the new archbishop of Canterbury decreed Wilfrid suspended from episcopal powers. Again Wilfrid went to Rome; again he won a partly favourable judgement. He and the archbishop were reconciled in 705. In the same year King Aldfrith died and was succeeded by Osred. For St Boniface, writing years later, his reign (706–16) marked the onset of Northumbrian decline. As to Wilfrid he lived three years into the new reign and died aged seventy-five, at Oundle in the territory of the Middle Angles, part of the kingdom of Mercia where he had been very active in the later part of his life. He left a will in the aristocratic mode, designating his successor as abbot at Ripon and bequeathing his extensive wealth between his following, the poor and two important churches in Rome. A great prince of the church had died; at Ripon he was immediately acclaimed a saint. His feast day is 12 October.

The waning of the kingdom

King Osred must have had some redeeming qualities since Wilfrid had adopted him as his spiritual son. For Boniface his principal offence seems to have been his abuse of the network of wealthy minsters that had sprung up within the 'rhythms of elite secular life'. Often built in the precincts of Roman fortress or 'city' complexes, always richly endowed, usually centres of artistic output as well as meditation, they could be the private bailiwicks of noble or royal families, often with the 'aspects of a special kind of nobleman's club'. Remembering the duties of monastic hospitality, the convention of the itinerant court, and the fact that minsters comprised female as well as male establishments, one can appreciate that when Boniface referred to King Osred on a fornicating rampage through the kingdom's nunneries he was almost certainly not speaking metaphorically.[14]

Political rivalry and in-fighting made Northumbrian society increasingly lawless and the rewards for successful violence and oath breaking ever more tempting. Towards the end of his *History* Bede recounts the tale of a pious local man called Dryhthelm, who warned his family of the dangers of hell awaiting those who fell for such temptations – revealed to him in what, today, we would call an 'out of body experience'. He had died and a man in a shining garment had guided him through the realms of the afterlife (rather as Virgil would lead Dante through Hell). They pass through three zones of sinners in various degrees of discomfort awaiting paradise until the final glimpse through a dazzling haze of the perfect in thought, word and deed, who have entered paradise immediately after their death.

In some ways the passage anticipates the evolving concept of Purgatory, to which this Anglo-Saxon perception seems to have contributed. But the notion of an 'interim paradise' has been called 'a necessary, influential and ideologically charged concept . . . within Anglo-Saxon England'.[15] Such an idea of an afterlife abode with various levels would seem also to chime with the Norse Asgard, the home of the gods, where are to be found twelve 'mansions'. The chief of these was Valhalla, the hall of Odin and the destiny of warriors slain in earthly battle. Anonymous Old English religious poems tell of heaven ('*heofon*') as a treasure-filled hall (echoes of the booty-filled mead hall of the heathen warrior world), of its entrance through a huge door 'bound with precious treasure and wrapped with wonderful fastenings' and of warriors thronging in 'the heavenly kingdom where the Trinity rules the glorious mansions'.[16] As in the Franks Casket, discussed below, the heroic tradition has parallels with Christian imagery (see page 86).

In fact, eighth-century Northumbria, which saw Bede's dedication of his *History* to King Ceolwulf, the European prestige of the cathedral school at York and its library, and the glory days of Hexham, was often on the edge of political anarchy. Sixteen kings in a hundred years: murders, depositions, abdications, usurpations, nobles contesting with the royal kin. Ceolwulf was briefly deposed in a nine-year reign before abdicating to retire into a monastery.

For some twenty-odd years King Eadberht (735–58) reigned in relative stability represented by more or less regular coinage issues. For Alcuin (born about 740), given as a child into the care of Archbishop Ecgberht, brother to the king, these were happy years for the kingdom, 'ruled over in harmony by the one wearing upon his shoulders the pallium sent by the pope, the other wearing on his head his ancestors' ancient crown'. Eadberht abdicated to become a monk at the urgings of the patrician Æthelwold Moll. Murdered by palace servants after the briefest of reigns, Eadberht's son was in fact succeeded by Æthelwold Moll. His six-year reign (759–65) brought a degree of stability to the proceedings. Of high noble standing, though not of royal blood, his claim may have been no worse, if no better, than that of Eadberht. As to him, David Rollason thinks it 'notable' that he accepted only after his brother had achieved the influential position of archbishop and states flatly 'That the Northumbrian church was also involved in the dynastic disputes is beyond doubt.'[17] There are indications that Alcuin himself had kinship links with the patrician king.

Moll's son Æthelred was driven from the throne after having ordered the killing of three courtiers in 779. His successor, Ælfwold, was murdered following a conspiracy by the 'patrician' Osred II (788–90), who was himself forcibly tonsured and exiled on the Isle of Man. Osred was deserted by his 'soldiers' while attempting a comeback in 792 and murdered by order of Æthelred, who had regained power. Then came another 'patrician', Osbald, king for a reign of twenty-seven days in 796. Alcuin knew about all this and in a letter speaks of the 'blood of kings, princes and people shed through you and your family'. The turmoil continued. In 806 King Eardwulf was driven from the kingdom; he found sanctuary, according to a Frankish source, with Emperor Charles the Great who ordered his restoration. Whatever the role of great churchmen in dynastic disputes they seem to have brought the kingdom another problem, through evolving the concept of chartered *bocland* to secure landed endowments in perpetuity. Unscrupulous laymen realized that by founding a family monastery they could convert land into an hereditable possession by such a book or charter. The number of private monastic foundations rose and the stock of loan land available to the king in his capacity as gift-giver, and so his ability to recruit warriors to his service, went down. The defence of the kingdom suffered.

The ninth century would see the continuing decline of Northumbria. The sack of Lindisfarne in 793, which seems such a marker to us, was probably less significant for the Northumbrians than the rise of Ecgberht of Wessex, who was claimed to have ravaged the northern kingdom and forced tribute. In 867 the Great Heathen army took York and the kingdoms of the Northumbrians were a thing of the past. But the glories of their golden age live on.

Carvings and calligraphy

When he came to the throne King Aldfrith was a man in his early fifties. Educated at Iona, he was fluent in Irish and in Bede's opinion of 'great learning' (*doctissimus*). He was reputed to have offered Benedict Biscop land equivalent to eight peasant farms for a Mediterranean manuscript on cosmography: a man of culture.

The mysterious carved box known as the Franks Casket (after the benefactor who bought and donated it to the British Museum) has teased people ever since its discovery in the early 1800s in a private house in the French village of Auzon, Haute Loire. It is Anglo-Saxon work of unknown provenance and is presumed to have been taken to the continent in the eighth or ninth century. It would have found an admiring audience of educated nobles and learned clerics at Aldfrith's court. Oblong in shape, it comprises two side panels, two end panels and a lid, carved from whalebone ivory (a whale – *the* whale? – features among the carvings).

Three pairs of scenes are depicted, each of which seems to oppose a pagan episode with a theme of Christian thought. It seems the

designer must have had access to variant biblical readings and com-
mentaries, variants that were to be found in books in Northumbrian
libraries.[18] The themes of kingship and empire, recurrent in the
pages of Bede and *Beowulf*; of exile, a common experience of royals
and nobles; of salvation and the afterlife, all seem present in the
casket's riddling interplay of words and images. The scene depicting
the legendary Weland the Smith of pagan mythology is typical of
the kind of cross-cultural fusion of Christian and English aristocratic
culture that led one commentator to suggest that a churchman might
have commissioned the piece. (One scholar has even proposed that
Beowulf itself, a work using aristocratic secular stories in an essentially
Christian context, may have been produced in a monastery or community of clergy.)

   T. D. Kendrick, in his classic work on Anglo-Saxon art, considered that, in the sixty years between the arrival of Theodore as
Archbishop of Canterbury and the death of Bede in 735, learning
and the arts 'in the remote [Church] province of England . . .
achieved a position that without exaggeration may be described as
supreme in western civilization'.[19] Today, majestic carved stone
crosses from southern Scotland and northern England tell some of
the story.

   When he was about three the future Northumbrian saint,
Willibald, whom as a baby his parents had adored as a 'loveable little
creature', was suddenly attacked by a contraction of his limbs.
The illness made it almost impossible for him to breathe. Fearful that
he was going to die, they offered their little boy up at the foot of
the 'Holy Cross of our Lord and Saviour' – one of the crosses, 'held
in great reverence', that it was the custom of 'nobles and good men
of the Saxon race' to erect in a prominent spot on their estates so
that their neighbours or travellers could make their daily prayers.[20]
Probably it was one of the many, more modest, wooden crosses, put
up on their lands by prosperous gentry. Even so, the stone Bewcastle
Cross has an Old English inscription in runic characters, now much

defaced, that seems to commemorate some aristocratic patron. At all events Willibald recovered and went on to a missionary career in Germany, where the cathedral at Eichstätt in Bavaria is named after him (and which is about twenty miles from the birthplace of the opera composer Christoph Willibald Gluck).

The carvings on the cross at Ruthwell, Mediterranean in style, were no doubt brightly painted but their iconography is deeply sophisticated. They may have served a liturgical purpose or had a propaganda function to promote the Roman Catholic orthodoxy; certainly they are closely related to theological Roman developments in the late seventh century. An example is the panels depicting the 'Lamb of God' ('*Agnus Dei*'), imagery expressing the chant of that name introduced into the service of the mass at that time. At Ruthwell passages from the Old English poem *The Dream of the Rood*, in which the Cross ('Rood') tells the story of the Crucifixion and laments its own fearsome implication in the killing of God's son, is inscribed in runic letters on the edges of the cross. It also speaks of Jesus accepting the Cross by an act of his human will and so combats the heresy of monotheletism. Abstruse and irrelevant to our generation, it was, we have seen, highly topical in the 680s. This controversy between the Eastern and Western churches, the emperors and the popes had reverberated across Roman Christian Europe as far as Theodore's Canterbury and up to the frontiers with the Irish/British tradition (see chapter 2).

Ruthwell also has a scene of the Annunciation to the Virgin Mary, which was coming into the Roman liturgy from the East at this time. Was such a monument on the boundary between Northumbrian and the British kingdoms to the west erected as a triumphalist statement of Roman Christianity: an aping of the obelisks and triumphal columns of ancient Rome, consciously 'appropriated [by Northumbria] . . . to its own imperial project'? On the other hand, Ruthwell also has important Irish non-Roman elements. It is part of a Bernician group of crosses, at Bewcastle, Ruthwell,

Rothebury and Hoddom, that have certain similarities of detail – treatment of the vine scroll decoration, for example – which suggest a common centre of production and a common vocabulary. Painted in bright colours and possibly further embellished with glass and metal decorations, these monuments in the landscape would have been 'highly visible' and, to modern eyes, garish intrusions on the countryside.[21] To contemporaries they and their inscriptions would have been religious statements to complement the superb manuscripts created in the monastic scriptoria.

The art of calligraphy has been honoured in many cultures. In imperial China, a sample of the emperor's own hand was treated with almost religious reverence; among the most valued treasures of Istanbul's Topkapı Museum is a remarkable series of Korans in the exquisite calligraphies of the sultans; in the Jewish tradition, the scrolls of the Holy Torah have been inscribed by calligraphers of artistic genius. In the mid-twentieth century the 'white writing' canvases of the Wisconsin-born US Baha'i artist Mark Tobey introduced a calligraphic-based style into easel painting.

In Western Christendom from at least the fourth century the books of the Latin Bible, and above all the Gospels and the New Testament, were lovingly transcribed in monastery scriptoria on parchment or vellum in manuscript hands of immense beauty, clarity and, often, opulence of ornament. None outshine and few equal the work of the Northumbrian school of the seventh and eighth centuries with its crowning jewel the Lindisfarne Gospels, '. . . one of the world's great books – a breathtaking artwork and symbol of faith'.[22] Clearly modelled on an Italian model, indeed one scholar has called it 'a complete sixth-century Italian Gospel Book in disguise',[23] it is as clearly in execution and invention a northern masterpiece.

Remarkably for an artwork of its time, thanks to a note written into the manuscript some two centuries later (see chapter 9), we know the name of the individual who created it – Eadfrith, bishop of Lindisfarne (d. 721). Working between 715 and 720 this artist–calligrapher of genius wrote the entire text and created the staggeringly inventive and intricate ornamental capitals and 'carpet' pages that embellish the book. The rich binding adorned with precious metals and gemstones was plundered centuries ago. Detail after detail proclaims the cosmopolitan inspiration of the work. Every ornamental framework element is occupied by a sinuous interlacing ribbon–like line, which in turn is inhabited by fantasy 'birds' and 'dogs' and 'serpents' seemingly biting their own tails, reminiscent of the 'animal inhabited' art of the Irish monks who were the founding brothers of Lindisfarne. A boldly drawn and coloured full–length 'portrait' of the Apostle, following early (Roman) Christian models, and an elaborate illuminated initial letter occupying a single page introduce each gospel. In the so-called 'carpet pages' (Bede tells us that prayer mats were sometimes used in Northumbria, as in the Byzantine church) the disciplined riot of ornament can be dizzying and seem, dare one say it, obsessive. A sixteen-page sequence running through the text comprises canon tables, based on the work of a Byzantine scholar, that list passages where the Four Apostles agree with or differ from one another. The first carpet page is 'intentionally old fashioned' in colouring and design, evoking the art style of Coptic Egypt, the home of the monastic desert fathers like St Jerome, whose Latin 'Vulgate' translation of the Greek of the original Gospels provides the text of the work. The saints' titles use the Greek word '*Agios*' for 'holy', not the Latin '*Sanctus*'. Even the technology is intriguing – Eadfrith may be the first to have used a lead pencil (after all, the world's highest quality graphite would be mined near Kendal in Cumbria), while he was able to 'recreate a . . . Mediterranean palette from local materials'.

At its best, Northumbrian scholarship was fully in the classical tradition. Bede handled Cicero's rhetorical stylistic devices with mastery,[24] while the superb manuscript known as the Codex Amiatinus, the oldest extant complete Latin Bible of some 1,030 leaves, for long part of the collection of the Biblioteca Medicea

Laurenziana in Florence, was a masterpiece of biblical scholarship learning and penmanship. A Vulgate Latin text of the Bible copied from a text brought back by Benedict Biscop, and with additional commentary, it shows the maturity of a tradition able to develop and not just reproduce the culture and learning it fed on. It was produced at Monkwearmouth Jarrow to the commission of Abbot Ceolfrith and was intended by him for presentation at St Peter's, on a long-planned pre-retirement visit to Rome. When forced to resign by his fractious juniors, he was well prepared, having already commissioned not only the codex, but also two bibles, one for each of the monasteries. In fact he died on his way to Rome, at Langres in Burgundy in 716, so never presented the codex. It may have reached Rome nevertheless; for centuries it was held in the monastery of San Salvatore on Monte Amiata in southern Tuscany. At some point its dedication page was altered so that it now appeared to be the gift of: 'I, Peter of the Lombards (Petrus Langobardorum) . . .' Careful examination revealed that parts of Ceolfrith's dedicatory text has been erased and overwritten . . . for reasons no doubt best known to Peter of the Lombards!

Like the age of Italian Renaissance humanism, which was founded largely on ancient classical culture archived in Europe's monastic libraries, Northumbria's Golden Age had derived much of its impulse from elsewhere – in this case traditions of Christian culture originating in the Byzantine east, Continental Europe and from other parts of the British Isles. But like the humanists, Northumbria's scholars illuminated the Europe of their day and in institutions like the libraries at York, Hexham or Monkwearmouth-Jarrow boasted beacons of learning that would only be extinguished by the pagan depredations of the Viking raiders of the ninth century.

4

THE MERCIAN SPHERE

If only because of Offa's Dyke, the earthwork, immense in
European terms, that will surely lie along the marches between
England and Wales as long as the land lasts, King Offa is among
the most familiar names from the Anglo-Saxon period. (The
Danevirke, the early ninth-century rampart protecting southern
Denmark from the East Franks, is just ten and a half miles (17 kilo-
metres) long, running west from Hedeby, the settlement outside
modern Schleswig.) Offa held such sway in the policies of the
church, that most powerful international institution of the day, that
for a few years England had a third archbishopric. Thus at the
Council of Chelsea in the year 789 the king, 'with all his chief men
[*principes*]' was among the distinguished guests at the episcopal
assembly presided over by the archbishops of Canterbury and
Lichfield. Offa was also the only European ruler of his day to be
treated on equal terms by Charles the Great, king of the Franks. In
a famous letter he sent to Offa in the year 796, Charles recognized
'his dearest brother' to be 'a most strong protector of your earthly
country', as well as a defender of the 'holy faith'.

Offa may be said to have completed a process of Mercian
consolidation begun by King Æthelbald (716–57). Writing in 732,
Bede observed that all the peoples and church provinces south
of the Humber were 'subject' ('*subiecti*') to Æthelbald of Mercia.

Though he does not name him as holding the *imperium*, 'subject to' seems intended to convey the idea of an accepted, ordered authority. Bede's assessment may have been based on men like Nothelm, bishop of London, apparently close in the councils of the Mercian king. Nothelm also had good contacts at Rome and, with papal permission, had copied letters in the archive there which he 'brought' to Bede as source material for the *History*. He was to become archbishop of Canterbury, perhaps through Æthelbald's influence.

The beginnings of the English midlands

'Mercia' (the name from the Old English '*mierce*', 'boundary' [like the Slav 'Ukraine'], means 'the Marches' or 'Borderland'), that large area of fluctuating boundaries in central England between the Thames and the Humber, seems to have had its origins about the year 600 with a loose confederacy of Anglian tribes each under its own leader, who acknowledged as 'king' a single ruler drawn from one of their number, usually from the heartlands on the upper River Trent. Presumably the 'boundary' in question was the ever-moving westward frontier between the invading Angles and the native British – the 'Wild West', so to speak, as seen from East Anglia, the 'Wild East' as seen by the Romano-British Christian population.

Mercia grew around the historic centres of Tamworth, Repton and Lichfield where St Chad established the Mercian bishopric in 669. (A recently discovered panel of a sarcophagus made for his relics and displayed in the cathedral from February 2006, depicts the archangel, Gabriel. This rare example of early Anglo-Saxon sculpture has traces of its original paint work.)

Around this core we glimpse satellite peoples in tribal centres, under their own rulers or perhaps subjected by colonizing Mercian nobles, in names such as Wreocensætan ('settlers' round the Wrekin), Magonsætan (settlers west of the River Severn) and the

Pecsætan of the Peak District in Derbyshire. In the area around Leicester and Peterborough (at that time called Medeshamstede), tribal groups (some, it has been suggested, little kingdoms) known collectively as the Middle Angles for a time constituted a kingdom and diocese. Its first bishop, Seaxwulf (*d. c.* 690) was closely involved in the foundation of the abbey at Medeshamstede. The kingdom of the Hwicce, occupying parts of modern Gloucestershire, Herefordshire and Worcestershire around the see of Worcester, was the most important constituent of greater Mercia. It may have been a fully functional British kingdom, with an existing British ecclesiastical centre, simply taken over by a small Anglian warrior elite expanding from a family base in Winchcombe, near Tewkesbury, in Gloucestershire and briefly centre of its own shire, rather than a territory occupied by a scattered settler population. Early tradition held that the great King Offa grew up among the Hwicce; it was probably during his reign that Winchcombe began to be developed as a royal minster-like complex of churches within a defensive enclosure. The place also seems to have held a document archive.[1]

Although it was transcribed in the early eleventh century, a document known to historians as the 'Tribal Hidage' seems to offer insights into the early Mercian world. It is a list of some thirty-four kingdoms and tribal 'mini' kingdoms in 'Southumbria', each assessed by area according to its number of 'hides' (territorial units supporting a family farm). Peter Featherstone concluded that Mercia was at the forefront of the compiler's mind, the opening entry being for 'first Mercia', that is the traditional heartlands, assessed at 30,000 hides, and proposed that the Tribal Hidage figures probably carried a symbolic significance. For example, the people of the Hwicce are accorded a territory of 7,000 hides, surely reminiscent of the '7,000 hides, hall and throne' that Hygelac, king of the Geats, gave to Beowulf.[2]

Penda the great pagan: father of a kingdom

If it was the business of a king of the 'heroic' age to be a munificent
'arm-ring giver', to do honour to his lineage and so win followers
to his banner, for none was success in the bloody business of war
more important than for the leaders of the Mercians, 'the men of
the boundaries', the 'marcher lords' of an ever-moving frontier. The
seventh-century Mercian military establishment was well suited to
the extortion of plunder and tribute, but ill adapted to sustained
long-term conquest.

They enter history with Penda who challenged the supremacy of
Northumbria in a series of wars (see chapter 3). From a British perspective he appeared as the man who separated the central kingdom
from the northern kings of Northumbria. The reach of Penda's
power was demonstrated by his widespread campaigns from
Cirencester (628) in the south against Wessex to wars against East
Anglia, which ended in the deaths of the kings Sigeberht and, in
654, Anna. In the 640s he drove Cenwalh of the West Saxons from
his throne. Despite the disaster of Winwaed in 655, it was he, writes
Nicholas Brooks, 'who made the Mierce into a great kingdom'. He
argues if events and his own paganism had not combined against
him, Penda 'might have been known to us in English poetry, as a
great war leader, like some early El Cid.'[3]

From the mid-seventh century to the turn of the ninth, the
Mercians extended their sway to virtually all the lands between the
Thames and Humber. Many a minor kingdom and principality was
absorbed or lost status in the process. For example, in the 770s sub-
kings of the Hwicce were replaced by ealdormen. The impression,
then, is of patchwork ethnicity and tribally partitioned populations,
each under its own leader – a kind of Anglo-Saxon federated super-
power. Furthermore, enough fragmentary archival references
survive, together with cultural artefacts, to show that during the
eighth century and the early ninth this 'kingdom of the Mercians'

developed a considerable cultural heritage, before inundation by Danish invaders. The Mercian bishop Plegmund would become archbishop of Canterbury, and was a prominent member of the team that helped King Alfred of Wessex to achieve his great Anglo-Saxon recovery programme.

Mercian kingship might have had obscure origins but it would acquire for itself a serviceable genealogy. The actual succession depended largely on the ability of one or another claimant to secure sufficient support. The contestants were great men, ealdormen, 'princes' or 'dukes' who could canvas support 'from among their own number upon a king's death'. From one reign to the next the same names of this establishment of the great are found witnessing to royal charters. How they achieved that status in the first place is not so clear. It is possible that it reached back to the earliest days and that 'these *principes* or *duces* were themselves the hereditary or chosen leaders of different peoples within the extended Mercian world.'[4]

The beginning of Christian Mercia

We have seen Oswiu of Northumbria annex northern Mercia after his victory over Penda in 655, but he assigned a sub-kingdom of 5,000 hides in southern Mercia to the dead king's Christian eldest son Peada. He survived little more than a year before being murdered. Brief though it was, his reign saw the initiation of the abbey of Medeshamstede, one of the first foundations of Christian Mercia.

Northumbrian supremacy in Mercia lasted barely three years. In 657/8 a putsch by a group of ealdormen re-established the kingdom's independence under Peada's brother Wulfhere (*d.* 674). Acting on the advice of his sisters Cyneburh and Cyneswith, his brother the future king Æthelred (674–704) and of Archbishop Deusdedit of Canterbury, to name but a few, he confirmed the foundation of the minster at Medeshamstede. The *Chronicle's* entry on these events has fly-on-the-wall accuracy about the loving exchanges between Bishop-Abbot Seaxwulf and the king, who approved not only all the things the abbot wanted but all the things the king knew that he wanted. All present wrote 'with the finger', that is traced the crosses on the parchment with their finger. How much if any of this happened we cannot possibly know for sure: such 'creative accounts' and dubious charters were to be expected in the archive of any well-managed church establishment; papal bulls confirming the events and affirming that the abbot owed allegiance to the pope alone are also recorded. The Peterborough scribe, purporting to write a national narrative, gives the national synod of the church convened at Hertford in 672/3 just one line. But the figure of Seaxwulf reminds us of the 'veritable monastic empire' that he traditionally is said to have founded and Abbot Hedda first ruled, with 'colonies' from Breedon on the Hill in Leicestershire to Bermondsey, now in London's Docklands.

King Wulfhere invaded the Isle of Wight through Wessex in 661, disposed of lands in Lindsey, sold the see of London to a Frankish-born bishop, and subjected the king of Essex and the minor ruler of Surrey to his rule. Probably his presentation of Wight to the king of the South Saxons was as important in that king's final acceptance of Christianity as the preaching of St Wilfrid. Wielding power and influence on this scale throughout the island would seem to make Wulfhere a candidate to be numbered among Bede's list of rulers who wielded the *imperium*, the 'bretwaldas' of the *Anglo-Saxon Chronicle*. Then, in 674, he overstretched himself when, 'insatiable of spirit', he 'roused all the southern peoples' against King Ecgfrith of Northumbria and led them to defeat. He lost the province of Lindsey in the process and his life soon after.

It was only a temporary setback for Mercia. Within five years his brother Æthelred (ruled Mercia 674–716) had raided into Kent and, in 679, fought Ecgfrith of Northumbria to a standstill at a battle 'near the River Trent'. Mercia recovered Lindsey. Among the dead was Ecgfrith's brother, Ælfwine, 'much beloved in both kingdoms', Bede tells us. A prolonged feud was to be expected; instead, in a notable settlement negotiated by Archbishop Theodore of Canterbury, Ecgfrith agreed to accept the wergild payable for the death of a royal kinsman. The resulting peace stretched well into the next century, for in 704 King Æthelred abdicated to become a monk and subsequently abbot of Bardney, where he ruled until his death, presiding over the burgeoning cult of the Northumbrian saint-king Oswald. His wife, Oswald's niece, had brought the bulk of the relics there some years before.

Æthelred was followed on the throne by a nephew, Coenred, who also followed him into religion, abdicating in 709; he died on pilgrimage to Rome. The reign of his successor Ceolred (709–16) was troubled by the lurking presence of Æthelbald, an exiled distant kinsman who claimed descent from a brother of King Penda.

Æthelbald of Mercia – Lord of the Southern English 716–57

Æthelbald found sanctuary on the desolate island of Crowland in the Fens, where Guthlac, by this time a noted holy man, had made his retreat. This St Guthlac had won renown in a former life as a warband leader on Mercia's western frontier. A *Life of St Guthlac* was commissioned soon after his death by a king of East Anglia and two Old English poems, 'Guthlac A' and 'Guthlac B' also tell his story. Conditions on his island were ideal for the solitary soldier of Christ in battle against the demons of temptation, but hardly for a king-to-be. Guthlac dressed in skins and, by way of nourishment, indulged himself daily with a small piece of barley bread and a beaker of muddy fen water. On the other hand, the place was pretty secure; few, other than the saint and favoured pilgrims seeking the blessing of the holy man (and presumably the baker), knew the way through the treacherous, boggy terrain. The hermit saint prophesied that Æthelbald would become king, and the pretender vowed to build an abbey on the hermit's island should that happen. He may have honoured his promise – eighth-century timber piling, adequate as the foundations of a wattle and daub structure, have been unearthed.[5] Centuries later the Croyland/Crowland *Chronicle* would claim he had made extensive land grants. What little we know about Æthelbald indicates that an act of piety would have been out of character. The fact that he reigned for just over forty years in a violent age squares better with his reputation as a cruel and oppressive ruler. On the other hand, keeping faith with the deity might have seemed simple commonsense.

About the year 732, Bede noted, Æthelbald was the overlord of the East Saxons, East Angles, the West Saxons, the 'people who dwell to the west of the River Severn', the kingdoms of the Hwicce, and Lindsey, the Isle of Wight and the South Saxons. (Where King Aelle had first wielded the obscure powers of bretwalda, the once royal house now barely exercised the authority of a district governor.) A Mercian royal charter of 736 describes Æthelbald as 'king' of all the 'provinces' known as the Sutangli; and in a charter of this same year he features as '*Rex Britanniae*',[6] presumably a Latin equivalent for 'bretwalda'.

In the 720s the abdication of King Ine of Wessex to go on pilgrimage to Rome and the death of Wihtred of Kent had removed two powerful rivals on his southern frontier. The kings of the East Saxons (Essex) had to surrender control of London to Æthelbald and in 748 a Mercian royal council was held there. But his under-kings could exercise local authority. The Hwicce acknowledged him as 'king of the Southern English' ('*rex Sutanglorum*') and marched under his banners against the Welsh. But in 767 and 770 we find grants of land being made by their under-king.

Æthelbald's exercise of secular power outside Mercia was real enough. For a time in the 730s he occupied the West Saxon royal vill at Somerton; he made grants of Wessex land to the cathedral church at Canterbury; he enlisted the West Saxons, too, against the

Welsh; at the other end of England he ravaged Northumbria and made opportunistic alliances with the king of the Picts. His agents collected tolls from the shipping in London's emporium *Lundenwic*, and he disposed of lands in the territories of the Middle Saxons (Middlesex), formerly the preserve of the kings of Essex.

This was the man that St Boniface chose to lecture on sexual mores. He credits him with generous charitable donations and as a friend to widows and the poor; and he praises him as an upholder of law and order who kept 'a firm peace in [the] kingdom'. But against this Boniface sets reports he had heard 'about your excellency's private life', which not only breached the laws of God but damaged the king's standing 'among the people'. If Boniface is to be believed, Æthelbald was unmarried and so, presumably, had yet to father a legitimate heir (in fact he was to be succeeded by a cousin). He was also a notorious lecher and adulterer, violating not only other men's wives but also 'the brides of Christ . . . Creator of heaven and earth!' One supposes that many were jubilant when news broke in 757 that Æthelbald had met death at the hand of a bodyguard at Seckington, near the royal palace of Tamworth – probably under instructions from one or other party of the royal kin. After of the brief reign of Beornred, Offa, a kinsman of Æthelbald and quite possibly the chief plotter in his overthrow, emerges as the new monarch of the Mercians. With him we reach the most powerful of England's many kings before the reign of King Alfred of Wessex. Mercia had already overtaken Northumbria as England's dominant power.

The world of Offa, King of the Mercians: 757 – July 796

'The Age of Offa was perhaps the end of England's heroic age.' So wrote Patrick Wormald.[7] The king himself claimed descent from Offa of Angeln, one of the kings named in the *Beowulf* epic; Offa's

Dyke may well have been in part inspired by 'the boundary between
his own people and their neighbours' said to have been raised by this
heroic Scandinavian namesake; and the title *rex totius Anglorum
patriae* ('king of the whole fatherland of the English'), awarded to
him in a later copy of one of his charters, at least proclaims how big
he appeared to a later generation.

Asser, the Welsh biographer of King Alfred, describes Offa as
building an earthwork 'from sea to sea'. In fact, the structure we have
today stretches more than 64 miles (103 km) northwards from the
River Wye, near Hereford, to the vicinity of Mold in Clwyd. The
northern end of the great Dyke is backed up by the 49-mile (62 km)
Wat's Dyke, which overlaps it and continues on to the estuary of the
River Dee – one of Asser's 'seas'. We do not know when it was built.
Numerous excavations from 1931 onwards have failed to find any
signs of extensions to Offa's defence work, or garrison forts or
revetments or palisading. But at 30 feet (nearly 10 m) wide it was
undoubtedly a formidable obstacle. Following thirty seasons of excavation and research, David Hill and Margaret Worthington, in their
book of 2003 on the Dyke, argue that it runs along the line of the
border between Mercia and the Welsh kingdom of Powys and that
it may have been raised in the context of nine years of warfare
between Offa and his western neighbour. It is guarded on the Welsh
side by a wide ditch.

The building of a defensive dyke, however impressive, hardly
seems work for heroes. Even so, it has been suggested that the text
of *Beowulf* may first have been set down from the oral tradition in
Mercia, possibly during the reign of Offa or in the immediately succeeding period. Wormald pointed out that the hero's name itself is
very similar to that of Beornwulf, one later king of Mercia, and that
of Wiglaf, his last loyal supporter, to that of another. The poem's
'take' on Offa of Angeln, celebrated in Old Norse and Danish
sources (though hardly mentioned in Anglo-Saxon ones), calling
him 'the best king . . . on the face of the earth . . . honoured far

and wide for his generous ways, his fighting spirit and his far-seeing defence of his homeland', is certainly suggestive. Offa's actual grandfather may have hailed from the land of the Hwicce.

With Beornred disposed of, the way lay open for a king of ruthless ambition. For eighty years, between the accession of Æthelbald (716) and the death of Offa (796), Mercia dominated English history. With the exception of those few months in 757, just two men occupied the throne throughout that time, a record of dynastic tenure not to be outdone until the reigns of Henry III and Edward I (1216–1307), and quite remarkable for the bloodthirsty eighth century. His great predecessor had died without an heir, but Offa was determined to ensure the succession in his own family. He was also bent on supremacy over his neighbours – of achieving what Bede had called the *imperium*. It seems he owned a copy of Bede's *History*.

It was to be a new type of hegemony. Æthelbald had allowed a certain autonomy to subject regions. When Offa came to power three brothers apparently shared the rule of the Hwicce; some twenty years later these 'sub-kinglets' are heard of no more and the territory has been absorbed into greater Mercia. The kings of Sussex now administered the territory in Offa's name as his 'ealdormen'. In Kent, the first of England's Christian kingdoms and in regular contact with the continent, the process took a little longer. The *Anglo-Saxon Chronicle* records the battle of Otford between Kent and the Mercians in 776 but does not mention the outcome.

In 785 Offa makes a land grant in Kent in his own name, without reference to any Kentish 'king' or even 'ealdorman'. Other sources mention the shadowy figure of Ealhmund, who had been elected king in Kent by the native nobility. Unrest continued to trouble Offa in his Kentish province and then, in 786, Ealhmund's son Ecgberht, who also claimed descent from the royal family of Wessex, attempted to 'take the throne [there]', but was ordered into exile 'to the land of the Franks' by Offa and King Beorhtric of

Wessex (786–802). He stayed there for three years at the court of Charles the Great – did he perhaps meet Alcuin, the great Northumbrian scholar, at the Carolingian court (see chapter 6)? Wessex was independent; it was also a client state to Mercia, and Ecgberht did well to survive. Maybe the judicial execution of so prominent an æthling would have been too provocative. But things were not well in the Mercian supremacy. Offa's death witnessed a full-scale revolt in Kent. The pretender, by name Eadberht Præn, was reportedly an ordained priest, although he may also have been a Kentish æthling and so throneworthy. He held the throne for two years before being deposed and taken bound to Mercia, where he was blinded (the standard penalty for usurpers at imperial Constantinople) and his hands cut off – the penalty for theft.

There is circumstantial evidence to suggest that he had in fact been in exile on the Continent. The famous letter from Charles the Great to Offa, dealing with trade and other matters, also refers to 'the priest Odberht' who, along with a company of other exiles, had 'sought . . . our protection, being in fear of death'. It is apparent from the context that Offa wants him back in England and one wonders whether Odberht and Eadberht are one and the same person. Charles refers to letters from Offa that 'have informed us, that [these exiles] had bound themselves by a (religious) vow' but 'Odberht', claiming to be a pilgrim, wishes to continue his pilgrimage. Charles has decided to send him and his companions on to Rome where the pope and Archbishop Æthelheard, 'your archbishop', would judge their case. The Frankish king thinks it safer that the pope decide the status of the exiles, that is whether they are indeed 'religious', since 'the opinion of some people is different'. Is the allusion to a forced tonsuring of a throne claimant to debar him from candidacy? Charles makes no promise to return 'Odberht' to Mercia once he is back from Rome since his wish for pilgrimage must be taken seriously.

Connection with the royal kin, even if remote, was important for a successful claim on the crown. Offa could show descent in the fifth

generation of a collateral branch from the Mercian founding ancestor; in Wessex Ecgberht was the first of his branch of the royal house
of Cerdic to ascend the throne – his father was a Kentish king, presumably of Kentish stock. After his death a West Saxon genealogist
grafted him into the Cerdic family to produce what the historian
Richard Abels has called 'a useable past'.[8] Genealogy was very much
in vogue in the late eighth century and an important compilation
of family trees that survives from the 810s probably originated in
the Northumbrian court in the 760s. A Northumbrian provenance
is not surprising. In the hundred years up to 810 that kingdom had
had fifteen kings, of whom just three had died in office: of the
others five had been deposed, two exiled, two murdered and three
'killed'.

It is quite possible that the Mercian kings had been responsible
for some of these fatalities; their ascendancy was not a matter of
chance either within or outside their frontiers. In 794, according to
the *Anglo-Saxon Chronicle*, Offa ordered the beheading of King
Æthelberht of East Anglia, without reason given. Shortly after the
great king's death, writing to a Mercian ealdorman, Alcuin stated as
common knowledge 'how much blood [Offa] shed to secure the
kingdom on his son'. In the year 787 he had that son, Ecgfrith,
'consecrated'.

There are no details as to the nature of the ceremony, but it is
assumed that the word 'consecration' carried its traditional Christian
meaning of an anointing with holy oil and chrism (oil and balsam
mixed) administered by priest or bishop. 'King making' in early
Germanic society was more a matter of presenting the winner of a
ceremony of election, generally completed by raising the new king
on a shield. We do not know whether early Anglo-Saxon kings
were ever made in this way; Alcuin's reference to King Eadberht
at York 'wearing the crown of his ancestors upon his head' (see
chapter 3) indicates that Northumbrians at least thought that
crowning as such had a long tradition. Among Germanic kings on

the Continent the crown or diadem was presumably adopted from the ceremonial of the Eastern Roman or Byzantine empire, but from York itself comes that mysterious piece of headgear known as the Coppergate Helm with its religious Latin inscriptions – surely fitting furniture for the 'churching' of a Christian warrior king.

A few years before Ecgfrith's elevation, the pope had anointed two sons of Charles the Great. For the last ten years of the reign, Ecgfrith presumably held the rank of co-ruler, though given his father's imperious nature it probably had little practical significance. However, in 796, the year of his months-long reign, Ecgfrith issued a charter at the Mercian court assembly held at the 'famous' vill or 'minster' of Bath. The remains of the Roman city were almost certainly the subject of a short Old English poem *Ruin*, which reflects on the past glories of the work of giants and the marvels of the hot springs. It seems likely that the Mercian monarchy was looking to ape the new palace complex that Charles the Great was building near the hot springs of Aachen.[9] But the new king died in December 796. Alcuin believed he fell victim to 'the vengeance for the blood shed by his father'. Three years later Ecgfrith's successors began the development of Offa's royal vill at Tamworth as something approaching a 'capital' of the kingdom, also no doubt inspired by the complex at Aachen.

The Mercian Church

Ecgfrith was probably consecrated at the synod or ecclesiastical council of 786/7, attended by papal legates and presided over by King Offa. The council's decrees were promulgated both in Latin and the vernacular (in Southumbria presumably in Offa's name, and in Northumbria at a similar council held there), and were reported back to the pope by the legates. They dealt with the proper conduct of and the sacrosanctity of the office of king, the desirability of powerful men rendering justice, and various ecclesiastical provisions (apparently approved of by Alcuin of York, who was in England at this time). It was the latest in a series of councils of the church in England south of the Humber that had begun with Archbishop Theodore's synod at Hertford back in 672 (when the delegates had agreed to a yearly convention thereafter at the place called Clofesho). The series had contributed to the growth in the power and unity of the English church as a whole.

At Hertford, Theodore styled himself 'bishop of the church of Canterbury'; in September 679 at the assembly at Hatfield he was now designated 'by the grace of God archbishop of the island of Britain and of the city of Canterbury'.[10] The council at Clofesho in 747, presided over by Archbishop Cuthbert of Canterbury, another cleric of noble kin, who had received the pallium in person from Pope Gregory III in Rome, required that every priest learn and explain to the people in their own tongue the Creed, the Lord's Prayer and the offices of mass and baptism. More significant was that Cuthbert sent to Boniface a report of the council's proceedings by his deacon Cynebert, probably a direct response to the criticisms by St Boniface of both king and archbishop – a remarkable testimony to the saint's prestige and authority.[11]

During the later part of Offa's reign, and particularly the reign of Archbishop Jænberht (765–92) at Canterbury, there was recurrent friction between king and church over the question of the elevation of Lichfield to the status of a metropolitan see, and over the Canterbury mint, for the archbishop struck his own coins with his name on one side and that of the king on the other. Archbishop Jænberht died in August 792. In a Council at Clofesho before the close of that same year King Offa made an important grant of privileges to the churches of Kent. Had Jænberht perhaps persuaded Offa to ease his policy towards the Kentish church as a gesture of appeasement?

Although much of the agenda was presumably worked out in advance this, the first Clofesho council in forty-five years, was necessarily presided over by the new archbishop of Canterbury, Æthelheard (792–805), who was evidently a Mercian by birth and, according to Charles the Great of the Franks, 'Offa's archbishop'. In fact his blatant pro-Mercian sympathies made it advisable for him to withdraw from his see during the unrest under Eadberht (796–8).

In the last year but one of the eighth century Æthelheard assisted his king at an assembly unique on two counts in the history of the English church. First, the 799 Council of the Southumbrian bishops was held, in the presence of King Coenwulf, on a royal estate – the great Mercian centre of Tamworth in Staffordshire. Secondly, it was presided over by two of three English archbishops Æthelheard of Canterbury and Hygeberht of Lichfield. Hygeberht's moment of glory was brief enough. Four years later, at the last important Council of Clofesho in October 803, and armed with two papal privileges, Æthelheard delivered a double blow to King Coenwulf (796–821) and the Mercian monarchy. First, he asserted the independence of all churches from secular authorities and, secondly, he reaffirmed the dignities of Canterbury and declared the abolition of the archbishopric of Lichfield.

From the 740s through to the 820s England's middle kingdom was witness to what has been termed a fairly frequent 'ecclesiastical road show' at Clofesho, its chief venue, but also at Tamworth, Chelsea and other sites. These were remarkable gatherings – in the view of Sir Frank Stenton amounting to 'a new type of deliberative assembly' – attended by the great kings of Mercia, their under-kings and provincial governors, ealdormen and household officials, their chief men or *principes*, and swarms of servants and hangers-on, as well as the archbishop(s), bishops, abbots and lesser clergy. No church or single building could accommodate such a throng and we must visualize, rather, grazing land with acre upon acre of pavilions, huts and temporary shelters, probably grouped around a great church such as Brixworth, with villagers and peasants trudging in with supplies and food-renders from the neighbouring estates. The scene belongs to a world where the church was a power in the councils of government, a focus of wealth and employment, and for many a spiritual stronghold against the forces of evil.

The international dimension

In 787 Offa had succeeded in having Lichfield raised to the status of an archbishopric, despite the inevitable and fierce opposition of Canterbury. Only the pope could authorize the change and here Offa may have been helped by his generally friendly relations with Charles the Great. The pope, Hadrian I (772–95), was very much Charles's man and he had reason to be. With Rome under threat from the Lombard kingdom he had appealed to Charles, who duly invaded northern Italy and assumed the title 'king of the Lombards'. Then he made over large tracts of Byzantine imperial territory, Venetia and the duchies of Spoleto and Benevento, supposedly once the patrimony of St Peter, to the popes: 'Whatever had remained of the Lombard kingdom ceased to exist in 794.'[12]

In response Hadrian ceased to date papal documents by the year of the emperor at Constantinople but instead, in gratitude, by the regnal year of Charles, king of the Franks. Coins in the papal territories no longer carried the emperor's effigy but the pope's. A mosaic floor laid in the Lateran depicted St Peter handing a standard of battle to Charles and a pallium to Hadrian. But Rome was a place of endemic factional politics and, in a letter to Charles, Hadrian referred to rumours he had heard that Offa, 'king of the people of the Angles', had suggested that the Frankish king 'ought to evict us from the Holy See . . . and . . . establish another rector there from among your own people'.

Such a rumour, implausible as it might be, could only help Offa. It might be true; it might be wise to placate the Englishman. The existence of permanently manned *scholae*, or hostels of young

Anglo-Saxons, Franks, Frisians and so forth, right next door to St
Peter's, ready to come to arms to support the pope in case of Saracen
attack, might assume another significance in time of peace. Perhaps
their presence could be influential on papal policy.[13]

In the scant surviving records of the dealings between Charles
and Offa we can see guarded, sometimes prickly but generally ami-
cable relations. Charles was willing to discuss the marriage of a son
of his to one of Offa's daughters, but bridled at the suggestion that
an English prince should take one of his daughters to wife. There
are dealings about asylum seekers. A certain lord named Hringstan,
who had found refuge at the Frankish court claiming he had fled
Mercia in fear of his life, has died and Charles is no longer willing
to maintain his followers at the palace. He urges his 'dearest brother'
that their lord would have been the king's faithful liegeman 'had he
been allowed to stay in his own land' and by implication urges him
to treat them kindly. We don't know what happened to these failed
asylum seekers on their return.

Trade is a central concern. As today, merchants might attempt to
evade customs duties and a favourite ruse was the pretended pilgrimage. Charles complains about people who have fraudulently
joined up with pilgrims (evidently from Mercia) whose goal is
profit, not religion: if they are really traders they must pay tolls. As
to merchants (negotiators), there may be faults on both sides.
Mercian merchants may not have been always treated properly in
Francia and in future must have justice; but Frankish merchants in
Mercia must have the same. In the same letter he responds to an
earlier request by Offa, presumably on behalf of a merchant peti-
tioner, to look into the matter of certain 'black stones' (possibly
Rhineland lava stones used in the manufacture of grinding
querns)[14] to be imported into England and ask in turn that the
woollen cloaks be subjected to more rigorous checks as to style as
well as quality.

The material resources of monarchy

The proceeds of trading activity were one source of royal revenue, though not necessarily the most profitable: we shall turn to them in a moment. A chief resource was the king's power to enforce others to work on his projects. For example, royal initiatives in fortress building, once thought to date from the reign of Alfred in Wessex, were part of royal policy in the Mercian sphere in the eighth century. King Æthelbald in a general grant of privileges to the Mercian churches at the synod of Gumley in 749 reserves the 'necessary defence of fortresses against enemies'.

Frequent warfare, lavish church endowments, costs of embassies to Rome, building campaigns, of which much survives in the archaeological record, and the trappings of luxury that accompanied the royal and aristocratic lifestyle of the Anglo-Saxon kingdoms, all proclaim wealth and revenues. Unfortunately, evidence of where they were sourced and how they were steered into the royal treasuries is scanty. The great abbey church of All Saints at Brixworth in Northamptonshire, today the second church in the diocese of Peterborough and possibly a daughter house of the cathedral's predecessor Medeshamstede abbey, is a monument not only to the splendours achievable in the architecture of Anglo-Saxon England but also to the management skills as well as the material resources available to the builder.

The main body of the church as we see it today, probably of the eighth century and one of the largest structures of its period north of the Alps, is smaller than originally designed. It comprises a massive west tower embellished with stone ribbonwork or lessenes typical of Anglo Saxon architectural ornament (a stair-turret blocking the original west door and spire are later), and nave, choir and apse some 130 feet (40 m) long and 40 feet (12 m) wide at its west end. The interior, with its great round-headed arches of reclaimed Roman brickwork and clerestory windows above,

presents a monumental effect but would have been yet more impressive during its early centuries, when it was flanked with a series of
chambers (*porticus*), subsequently demolished. Although the monks
may have been subordinate to Peterborough, the actual stone for the
building was not taken from Peterborough's quarry of Barnack,
even though it offered easy transportation up the River Nene. In
fact, extensive study in the 1980s of the materials used revealed that
'this whole church (and not just the brick arches) was constructed
from reclaimed fabric derived from a number of Roman buildings.'[15] Much could have come from the ruined Roman city of
Leicester, about 30 miles (50 km) away and some from still further
afield. Was this because quarrying skills had been lost thanks to the
Anglo-Saxon invasions? Or was it that the sub-king of the Middle
Angles, in whose territory Leicester and Brixworth lay, commissioned the building on condition it were built from recycled material in his possession? Either way the labour costs and transport
arrangements would have been considerable and complicated,
calling for a highly competent master of works. Were ruined
Roman structures, as has been suggested, the principal (perhaps the
only) source of building stone until late on in the Saxon period?
Certainly, the classical legacy was commonly plundered on the
Continent – witness, most obviously, the Colosseum.

Minsters and emporia

In 650, John Blair tells us in *The Church in Anglo-Saxon Society*
(2005), England had no 'central places' that 'can sensibly be
called . . . towns', and still by 750 no cities in any sense we would
recognize today. But, he argues, there were two new types of
settlement offering centres for trading activities, 'coastal and estuar-
ine emporia and . . . complex monastic sites', generally known as
'minsters'. These enjoyed a considerable boom between the 670s
and 740s. The way in which such minsters could contribute to

economic development and provide growth points for market towns has points of similarity to the later evolution of the fortified 'burh'. The words were certainly not rigidly applied. There are eighth-century charters that call the church of St Paul's in London '*Paulesbiri*'. By the end of that century minsters, which had burgeoned as urban-style centres of high religious culture, looked likely to become ever more secularized.

In the case of Mercia what looks like a notable remnant of a minster complex is to be found at the parish church of St Mary, Deerhurst, beside the River Severn near Tewkesbury, the historic territory of the Hwicce people. The original church seems to have been raised on a Roman site but it developed over the centuries into a sophisticated structure adapted to elaborate liturgical programmes. A blocked doorway at first-floor level by the tower arch suggests the former presence of a gallery, which may have served for ceremonial appearances of dignitaries, perhaps even royalty. Carved animal-head corbels, once colourfully painted, flank the arch. The church has been much modified over the centuries since the Conquest, but surrounding it can be traced foundations of monastic buildings and possibly the minster wall ('*vallum monasterii*') of a once thriving complex. It was the building of such a wall at the minster of St Peter at Medeshamstede that led to its becoming known as Burh St Peter, Peters burh, hence Peterborough.

In the 1050s Deerhurst minster was generously endowed by Earl Odda. Near St Mary's can still be seen his private stone-built chapel, now an extension to a timber-framed Tudor farmhouse. Its classic, stolid Saxon chancel arch testifies to its founder's wealth and, by inference, the prosperity of the minister under his patronage. The chapel was consecrated in 1056 by Bishop Ealdred of Worcester who, as Archbishop of York, would officiate at the coronation of William the Conqueror.

London – city and emporium

From the seventh century onwards London was a powerful attraction to rulers whose heartlands lay at a distance – Essex, Kent, Wessex and, of course, Mercia. The emporium achieved a key position on an axis of influence and circulation that extended from the midlands down the Thames valley to the estuary and the highly commercial districts in eastern Kent and overseas. Minsters like Eynsham, on the upper Thames, could have loaded Cotswold wool on flat-bottomed barges to float down the meandering navigation. Trade certainly flourished in the great age of the minsters from the 680s to the 740s, as is confirmed by the profuse dissemination of the low value silver coins known as 'sceattas'.[16]

Recent archaeological finds offer tantalizing glimpses of the Mercian kingdom before the triumph of Ecgberht of Wessex at the battle of Ellendun in 825. In 2001 a gold coin of King Coenwulf (796–821) called a *mancus*, weighing just over 4.33 grams and in superb condition, was found near the River Ivel in Bedfordshire. It shows the king's head in profile facing to his left, his thick hair bound with what appear to be two braids fixed with a broach or hair clip, and bears the inscription COENVVLF REX M. He seems to be wearing an ornate shirt under a patterned cloak, which flows open from the neck. The design is clearly influenced by Roman coins, the lettering handsome and confident. This is the only gold coin known in Coenwulf's name. On the other hand, unlike the probably ceremonial piece known from Offa's reign, an Arabic gold dinar overstamped with the words OFFA REX, it is from an English mint. A Latin inscription on the reverse tells us that Coenwulf's coin was struck in the 'wic' or Saxon trading centre of London. This may have been in imitation of Carolingian practice: the reverse of a coin of Charles the Great bears the legend VICO DORESTATIS – i.e. Dorestad *wic*. on the Rhine delta. Equivalent to 30 days' wages for a skilled artesan, this beautiful piece of Mercian currency (the

British Museum accquired it for £357,832 in February 2006), reveals the close affinities between Mercia and Kent, where at this time Coenwulf's brother Cuthred was king. The royal portraits on the two currencies are similar in style and the London mint probably used a die supplied by a Canterbury engraver (possibly about 807).[17] With the Wessex victory at Ellendun and the expulsion of Cuthred's successor Baldred, the Kentish kingdom came to an end and the Canterbury mint had a new master.

Where did the gold come from? In the world of the *Beowulf* poet, gold treasure was part of the largesse expected of kings in the heroic warrior tradition and the grave goods excavated at Sutton Hoo and elsewhere show that expectations were realized. Since the gold mines of Ireland and Wales were beyond the control of the Anglo-Saxon kings, we must assume that they raised their gold in tribute from their Celtic neighbours or in trading loot and (pagan) slaves on the continental market. From the mid-seventh century on, Christian Europe's gold resource was depleted as Islamic conquest rolled across the Byzantine imperial territories of North Africa and Syria. Silver coinage came to the fore, and here the advance of Anglo-Saxon conquest brought silver-rich lead ores in eastern Somerset under West Saxon control, just as advances in Mercia had won control of the lead mines of the Derbyshire Peak. Here royal manors dominated the supply, so that during the 830s King Wiglaf's manor of Wirksworth supplied lead for church roofing to Canterbury. A principal source of revenue was the *salinae* or salt pits at Droitwich in Worcestershire. Here brine from the brine springs or wyches was boiled off in pits and boiling hearths of Roman origin in an industrial process under royal control. Tolls were also paid on the cartloads of timber and charcoal brought into the processing plant along the 'saltways' and the horse packs and cartloads of processed salt transported out for consumption at the manor centres. Increasingly researchers are seeing these manorial structures and trackway networks as communal/industrial patterns that reach back before the Anglo-Saxon period to Roman Britain, when a fort was built to protect the workings, and even Iron Age times. Their importance in Mercia is indicated by evidence that the royal vill at Droitwich served as a venue for the royal council.

Thanks to a scatter of charters between the 730s and 760s that grant exemptions of toll to various churches for their ships at the port of London or at Fordwich on the River Stour, we know that kings of Mercia and Kent were levying tolls on trade. The evidence may be 'woefully inadequate', but one presumes that tolls were levied at river ports such as Stamford on the Welland, in the east, and Hereford on the River Wye and Gloucester on the Severn in the west. The discovery in Hereford in 2004 of a lead *bulla* or seal of Pope Paschal I (817–24) casts a sidelight on the mechanics of Anglo-Saxon trade. Originally a disc, the little seal had been trimmed either side to produce an oblong-shaped weight (rounded top and bottom) of almost exactly one Carolingian ounce. Just as the English adopted the continental, Carolingian, system of coinage early, so it appears they were using continental weights and measures equally early.[18]

Lundenwic, to the west of Roman London in the area of modern Covent Garden, was one of a network of trading 'emporia' located around the North Sea and Channel coasts, such as Hamwic (Southampton) in Wessex, Gipeswic (Ipswich) in East Anglia, and, on the continent, the Frisian port of Dorestad (modern Wijk bij Duurstede) and Quentovic (towards the mouth of the Canche river). Large undefended settlements situated a little inland on navigable rivers, they were resorts not only for merchants but also for specialist craftsmen and proto-industrial producers. Like Lundenwic, perhaps a royal foundation, some were located on or near natural and political boundaries – in London's case the southern border of the kingdom of Essex and the River Thames. The sub-king of Surrey held sway on the opposite bank while Kent, Mercia and Wessex were within easy reach. Dorestad was just a three-day voyage away, travelling at 82 miles (130 km) a day.

Roman London may still have retained a degree of official status, with perhaps a Saxon royal hall, St Paul's and probably two other churches, along with the ruins of various Roman buildings, but at this time business and commerce lay outside the walls in the *wic*, remembered in the name Aldwych. At the height of its prosperity, in the 750s say, it may have covered as much as 60 hectares along the north bank of the river, roughly either side of the Strand as far as Trafalgar Square and the National Gallery and up to the site of the present Royal Opera House. Embankment timbers, excavated near Charing Cross station, give indications of the run of the water-front. Much of the trading was probably done here as if on a beach-side emporium. Rescue archaeology has recovered trade goods such as pottery and metalwork from Scandinavia, the Rhineland and Normandy; organic remains indicate that Londoners consumed, among other thing, quantities of oysters and eels. In the earlier period at least there was probably a slave market. Bede speaks of a Frisian purchase there in the 680s of a Northumbrian captive traded by Mercians. From the port, goods were distributed up the Thames and its feeder rivers, such as the Medway, but there was also a good deal of road communication with the hinterland. Excavations in the vicinity of the Royal Opera House revealed a network of narrow gravelled streets, including a road some three metres wide laid out in the seventh century and with drains either side. It was regularly resurfaced and continued in use for some two hundred years while the side streets running into it were also pretty well maintained. The gravel (and tons of it would have been needed) came from local pits – documents feature royal officials, for example a Kentish *wic gerefa* ('reeve'), regulating merchant activity. London's mints pro-duced some of the earliest English coins and the whole activity on the site was obviously of major importance in the evolution of the medieval English town and yet Robert Cowie, on whose article much of the foregoing is based, concludes, 'whether or not the Strand settlement was fully urban remains a moot subject.'[19]

Archaeology and documentary records indicate a number of major fires between the 760s and the end of the century. Timber, wattle and daub were the principal building materials. Later trade was hit by Viking attacks, the first recorded for the year 842, but military rivalries in the Frankish empire may also have weakened trading partners. What seem to be defensive ditches were dug at this time and numerous coin hoards unearthed at various sites, including the river bed, suggest what one might call wealth displacement in panic mode.

Control of London became a matter of mutual concern between West Saxons and Mercians linked by royal marriages and the sharing of a common monetary system. During the 860s and 870s the output of the London mint appears to have been greater than that of Canterbury, now under West Saxon control. In 874 the Danes drove Burgred of Mercia from his kingdom, replacing him with Ceolwulf II. For a moment Alfred struck coins at the London mint but three years later it was issuing coins in Ceolwulf's name and continued so to do until 879/80. It is true that when Guthrum retired from Wessex back into Mercia he shared out territory among his followers and 'gave some' to Ceolwulf. Yet this 'foolish king's thegn', so judged by the Wessex *Chronicle*, may have traced his ancestry to Ceowulf I (*d.* 823): he certainly exercised the powers of monarchy, granting land by charter and issuing coins in a monetary convention that had joined Wessex and Mercia since the 860s; their joint issues of cross-and-lozenge penny signalled a restoration of the silver content in both coinages.

Mercia in decline

In 825 Ecgberht, king of Wessex, defeated Beornwulf of Mercia at the battle of Ellendun (perhaps Wroughton in Wiltshire). The days of Mercian hegemony in the southeast and Mercia as a great power in the Anglo-Saxon universe were numbered. In the follow-up to the battle Ecgberht's son Æthelwulf drove Baldred, the last king of Kent and a Mercian client, from his kingdom; the Kentish satellites, the 'Surrey men', the South Saxons and the East Saxons turned back to Wessex. East Anglia followed and the year ended with the death of Beornwulf in battle against the East Angles. Two years later his short-lived successor was killed, together with Mercia's five leading ealdormen. Mercia's period of hegemony south of the Humber was over.

That the kingdom survived at all in more than name was thanks to the next king, Wiglaf, who, forced into submission by Wessex in 829, recovered independence within his borders the following year. He reigned for a further ten years and was succeeded by Beorhtwulf, who disappears from history with his defeat by the Danes. His successor Burgred seems to have attempted to maintain his kingdom's independence, but was expelled by the Danes and died a pilgrim in Rome in 874 or 875. After him came Ceolwulf II, the last man to bear the title king of Mercia, though despised by West Saxon opinion as a Danish 'yes man'. For half a century and more eastern Mercia fell within the Danelaw (see chapter 7).

From this point the story of Mercia becomes part of the history of the kingdom of the Anglo-Saxons (described more fully in chapters 8 and 9). As part of this development the shiring of Mercia began around the year 900.[20] Even so some of the old tribal/kingdom names long survived. The fact that we still speak of the Peak District is as much a matter of geography as tribal memory, but we find the 'Magonsætan' mentioned long after the Conquest in the twelfth-century *Chronicon* of John of Worcester. In 909 Æthelred, ealdorman of Mercia, and his wife Æthelflæd made a significant move to boost the swelling sense of Anglo-Saxon national identity when they arranged for the translation of the relics of St Oswald, held at Bardney since the days of Æthelred of Mercia, king and abbot, to their new minster of St Peter's at Gloucester. This was a comparatively small church but a notable building with its sumptuous adornments of sculpture and liturgical ornaments, and the translation added the Northumbrian king to the royal saints of Mercia. In the reign of Æthelstan his relics would become part of the halidom of the kingdom of England. As to the kingdom of Mercia itself, a sense of identity evidently did linger: as late as 1007 the Peterborough Chronicle refers to 'Eadric, ealdorman in the *kingdom* of the Mercians' [my emphasis] – more than a century after the death of the last man to bear the title of king.

5

APOSTLES OF GERMANY

When Boniface wrote his critical letter to Æthelbald of Mercia he was no stranger to the middle kingdom and its people; about one third of his surviving collected correspondence comprises letters to or from Mercians or related to Mercian affairs. The archive was probably assembled under the aegis of Boniface's helper St Lull, who would succeed him in the see of Mainz. Born about 710, Lull seems to have received his initiation into the religious life at the abbey of Malmesbury, with its 'catchment area', so to speak, across southwestern Mercia and northwestern Wessex. Lull met Boniface in Rome during the 730s and became one of his two chief assistant bishops (*chorepiscopi*) and a central figure in the English network in Germany. In the 770s a Northumbrian king naturally turned to him for help with a delegation to Charles the Great; a German bishop asked for his advice; he actively disseminated English learning on the Continent, such as the works of Aldhelm and Bede. Lull was the founder of the bishoprics of Hersfeld and Bleidenstadt. He was just one, if a distinguished example, of the numerous English churchmen active and influential in Europe during the eighth and early ninth centuries. How they came to be there and the role they played in the evolution of European culture is the theme of this chapter. They would have found the prevailing political conditions prevailing in the early 700s quite familiar.

The European background

Western Europe was a patchwork of rival power centres, Christian for the most part but with pagan outliers such as northern Frisia and, east of the Rhine, the remoter districts of Hessen, all struggling for control within their own fluid borders and for hegemony over their neighbours. North of the Alps the dominant power factor was the Merovingian dynasty, established in Gaul by Clovis about AD 500, around the time the Anglo-Saxons were settling in Britain. The dynasty derived its name from Merovech, the legendary hero of the Salian Franks who had settled, probably as *foederati*, within the Roman province in the marshlands of the Scheldt and Meuse river basin during the fourth century. He had been conceived, so went the story, by the coupling of his mother with a sea monster who surprised her while sea bathing. When, in 498, his descendant Clovis I converted to Catholicism, the descendants of this monstrous nativity acquired additional Christian charisma.

The conversion was a delayed thank-you note from Clovis to his Christian wife's god. Two years before, facing defeat by the Germanic Alemani tribe before the battle of Tolbiac, he had invoked the aid of Jesus and triumphed. The Merovingians' lands were divided between rival factions into an eastern branch in Austrasia, ancestor to the Holy Roman Empire, and later a western grouping called Neustria. The kings, however, were challenged by their own chief ministers ('mayors of the palace') as well as by powerful dukes, as in Bavaria and Thuringia. In the early 660s the Austrasian minister deposed his king, a child called Dagobert II, had him tonsured as a monk and sent him into exile in Ireland. Fifteen years of court politicking later, fortune pointed in Dagobert's direction. One of the factions looking for a puppet candidate contacted Northumbria's prince bishop Wilfrid for help. The great man complied. He had the Irish contacts and his years in Lyon had introduced him to Merovingian politics. In due course he invited young Dagobert over to Northumbria and then, having equipped him with a magnificent entourage, arranged for his return in style to the Austrasian throne in 676.

All this earned Wilfrid the enmity of the western Merovingian 'palace'. Two years later, embarking for another journey to Rome, Wilfrid decided to avoid the crossing to Quentovic and took the more easterly route to Frisia. So, fortuitously, he initiated what was to become a major episode in the history of Europe – the Anglo-Saxon mission campaign among the Germanic peoples. Held up in the arrangements for his onward journey to Rome, he put the delay to good use by talking Christianity to the local king. He received a friendly reception thanks, it seems, to the coincidence of a bumper fishing season with his arrival. Thousands were converted, we are told by his admiring biographer. Unfortunately the pioneering mission was short lived. The fishing grounds reverted to normal, the new religion lost credibility and then the crown passed to a fiercely pagan ruler named Radbod.

The Frisian mission was to be at length successfully re-established under St Willibrord today the patron saint of Utrecht, the Netherlands and Luxembourg. There had been a Christian presence in Roman times and a short-lived attempt at conversion in the early 600s but the Frisians, the dominant seafarers of their time in the North Sea, were comfortable with their pagan religion. Elsewhere, east of the Rhine, there had been Christian missions of greater or lesser effectiveness led by Irish monks or *peregrini* and some by German churchmen.

But this scattered Christian presence was not flourishing nor, from the papacy's point of view, duly subordinate to Rome. The new missionaries would encounter communities lapsing back into paganism and aristocratic prince bishops jealous of their independence and sovereignty within their ill-defined borders. They would find local clerics tolerating pagan practice within the context of supposedly Christian ritual, dubious marriage liaisons and numerous near heresies. Among these allegiances, beliefs and cult practices, the Anglo-Saxon intervention would prove decisive. St Boniface of Crediton, better known in Germany as St Boniface of Fulda, is regarded as the founder of the German Roman Catholic Church, respected by all German Christians. He and the cohorts of Anglo-Saxon churchmen and women – West Saxons, Mercians and above all Northumbrians – who flooded into Continental Europe can with reason be called pioneers.

In the context of Rome's dealings with the Anglo-Saxon world, the eighth century was payback time: Augustine's mission to Canterbury inaugurated a papal policy of expansion; Archbishop Theodore consolidated Rome's hold with his affirmation of Canterbury's position in a reorganized English church; and Wilfrid of York, by his appeals to Rome, was expanding the papal curia's jurisdiction in Western Christendom at large. Now some three generations of English monks, nuns and clergy were to make unquestioning allegiance to Rome the central assumption of the Western church, and so strengthen its position against the claims of the Byzantine emperors to suzerainty over the papal see. To quote Walter Ullmann a classic authority on the early papacy:

> In concrete terms strong ties especially between Anglo-Saxon England and the papacy came to be forged at exactly the same time as that at which the imperial [i.e. Byzantine] government had begun to terrorize the papacy.[1]

Willibrord of Northumbria: apostle of the Netherlands

For the best part of a century churchmen and monks from England criss-crossed the Channel or the North Sea. Many expected to spend most of their lives on the Continent, working among the pagan or recently converted pagan tribes bordering on the territories of the

Merovingian Frankish kingdoms. Back in England there was a good deal of interest in the missionaries' activities, particularly in the conversion of the German Saxons, the 'Old Saxons', whom the English considered their kinsfolk.

Wilfrid's first Frisian venture had failed but then, in 689, Pippin of Heristal, warlord and chief minister of the royal household of the Merovingian king Dagobert III, defeated Radbod and married his son Grimoald to Theodelinda, the daughter of the Frisian chief. Radbod reluctantly came to terms. This was the situation facing Willibrord, son of a devoutly Christian member of the Northumbrian minor nobility, when in 690 he landed with eleven companions, among them Suidbert, Hewald 'the Dark' and Hewald 'the Fair', on the coast of Frisia. He headed for an old Roman fort at Utrecht, some twenty miles away on the Krom branch of the Rhine mouth. The Romans had known the place as Trajectum ad Rhenum ('Ford across the Rhine'); in the 620s the Merovingian ruler of the day had conferred a chapel there on the Bishop of Cologne to be used as a missionary base. Nothing had come of that venture.

Now aged thirty-three, by the demographics of his day Willibrord was well into his prime. Sent by his father to Ripon, he had started his career under the influence of St Wilfrid and then, thanks to Wilfrid's contacts there, it seems, spent twelve years in Ireland at the monastery of Rath Melsigi under Ecgberht, who apparently had once dreamed of himself missionizing the Continent. (The fact that Willibrord sailed to Frisia directly from Ireland seems to have prompted the mistaken idea that he was Irish). From Wilfrid, Willibrord learned his unswerving allegiance to Rome; as a noble, he naturally gravitated to the royal court. He found an aristocracy beyond royal control; a king subject to his chief minister; a church establishment largely autonomous and indifferent to Rome; and a chief minister single-mindedly devoted to the advance of his own power and dynasty.

For Pippin, religion was a natural tool of policy with which to reaffirm Frankish authority over pagan neighbours, and this Englishman with his devotion to Rome was the natural lever in court politics against churchmen attached to the traditional dynasty and their group interests. Rome, where the popes still acknowledged the overlordship of the emperors at Constantinople, was secondary. Indeed, according to Wilhelm Levison, at this time 'the pope was of little importance to the Frankish church . . . [whereas] the English church was conscious of its Roman origin.'[2]

This suited Pippin well. By championing the Rome-orientated Anglo-Saxon missions he positioned himself in the eyes of the head of the church in the West as a staunch son of the church, in contrast to the dynastic loyalties of the Frankish church establishment and the ambivalent status of the royal house itself, whose traditional charisma rivalled, for many of their subjects, the spiritual aura of the Roman popes. Pippin and his house, ancestors to the Carolings, would prove stalwart advocates of the new Christian missions and of the papal patrons of those missions. As to the Frisians in the 690s, many, perhaps most, took the new religion resentfully. Baptism was to them less a sacrament to the Divine Being than 'a symbol of subjection to the Franks'. Radbod himself swore that he would rather spend eternity in the kingdom of Hades with his ancestors than in the Christian Heaven without them. For the moment, however, he bided his time.

With his mission established under Pippin's aegis, Willibrord travelled to Rome for the approval and blessing of Pope Sergius I. What was a natural move for a disciple of Wilfrid was 'a momentous decision' in a Merovingian context, but, as indicated, Pippin approved. The Englishman's visit strengthened his dynasty's dealings with Rome, which could only be good. Sixty years later the last king of the Merovingian house was to be replaced with papal approval as king of the Franks by his descendant Pippin III.

When Willibrord returned from Rome with holy relics for the new churches that were to be erected in their honour in the newly

converted territories, it was to find that his companions had elected
Suidbert as bishop. He was now in England being consecrated by
Wilfrid. It was less a case of politicking within a divided team, more
part of plans to extend the mission. The new bishop soon departed
for work in pagan Westphalia, Germany. Driven out by Saxon
raiders he retired to found a monastery under Pippin's patronage;
this was the origin of the settlement that became the town of
Kaiserswerth. The two Hewalds were martyred while attempting to
continue his work in Westphalia. Their shrine is still to be seen in
Cologne Cathedral.

Willibrord now made his headquarters at Antwerp,[3] under
Pippin's aegis, on the southern border of Frisia. Thanks no doubt
to the threatening Frankish presence across the border, by 695 Frisia
was ripe to become a new church province. Pippin sent Willibrord
on a second journey to Rome, this time for Pope Sergius to consecrate him as archbishop of the Frisians. He took with him gifts
from Pippin for the Holy Father and was duly consecrated in the
church of St Cecilia in Trastevere on 21 November. He returned to
Frisia and the following year received the fortress of Utrecht as his
bishop's palace at the hands of Pippin. An old church within the
walls of the former Roman fort became his cathedral. (In 1996 the
modern city celebrated its 1,300th anniversary with its patron St
Willibrord given due prominence.)

Pippin, theoretically the king's chief minister, was acting in every
way as a king himself, intervening at the highest level in the affairs of
the Frankish church and dealing through his and not the king's intermediary with the pope. If Willibrord was not just a pawn on the
chessboard of palace politics, he was certainly a very useful bishop!
The importance of his mission from Rome's point of view was surely
strengthened when Pope Sergius granted him the name in religion
'Clemens', after St Peter's successor as pope. He and his colleagues
pushed ahead with the extension of the Christian community in the
territories owing allegiance to King Radbod. Back in England,

friends of Wilfrid praised Willibrord, whom they saw as the continuator of his work. On a last journey to Rome about 703 Wilfrid,
accompanied by a young monk named Acca, spent time with
Willibrord. The two Northumbrian veterans reminisced over the old
days and the wonders worked by the relics of King St Oswald,[4] some
of which Wilibrord had with him. Years later Acca, now bishop of
Hexham, would tell Bede his memories of the meeting.

Willibrord had established a new base with a monastery at
Echternach, in modern Luxembourg, on land given to him by
Pippin about 700. He lies buried in the tenth-century crypt of the
church that bears his name and the town still celebrates his feast day
(7 November). This church also held relics of St Oswald and honoured Willibrord on the king's feast day. His pastoral care for the
community was not merely spiritual. On one visitation 'the saintly
man' found that the cellar was down to a single half-empty tun of
wine. He dipped his staff into the barrel with a blessing and went
on his way. That evening the cask was found brim full, to the delight
of the house steward. Willibrord swore him to silence. There is a
delightful seventeenth-century engraving showing the bishop-saint
with his wand of office, among the barrels of the wine cellar.

Willibrord extended his missionary activities to the Frisian
islands of Heligoland and Walcheren and even made some conver-
sions in Denmark. His standing in the Frankish kingdom was
evident when he was chosen to baptize the infant child of Charles
Martel, Pipin of Heristal's ambitious bastard son. The child, later
known as Pippin the Short, was the first king of the Carolingian
dynasty and father of Charles the Great. Pippin of Heristal died in
December 714. It was the signal for bitter internecine war between
his grandsons, their sponsors and Charles Martel, the illegitimate
son. In Frisia Radbod seized his chance. He ravaged the Christian
enclaves intruded into his territories by the Franks and drove
Willibrord from the country. The saint retired, for the time being,
to Echternach.

Four years later, in 719, the Merovingian political landscape was
transformed. A puppet still wore the crown, but old divisions were
to be merged into a single immense domain under the supreme
effective power of Charles Martel. On the northern frontier the
death of Radbod that same year opened the field to revived
Christian initiative. Although in his sixtieth year, Willibrord willingly returned. To help him he had a vigorous new assistant in
the person of Wynfrith of Crediton or Exeter, known to history as
St Boniface.

St Boniface of Crediton, patron of Germany: his early career

The newcomer was in his forties and the ageing Willibrord had
another twenty years of active life ahead of him. Given the general
assumption that medieval people had very short lifespans a word
about ages may be in order. The indomitable Wilfrid of York lived
to be seventy-six; Willibald, the English-born bishop of Eichstätt,
eighty-six. His brother Wynnebald, abbot of Heidenheim, died in
his sixties and their sister St Walburga, who succeeded him as head
of the abbey, was verging on seventy. The sweet-natured and much
beloved Lioba, abbess of Tauberbischofsheim, another alumna of
Wimborne, died aged about eighty. As to Boniface himself, when
he met his death in 754, aged about seventy-eight, it was not from
natural causes but as martyr of a pagan raiding party into his encampment at Dokkum during a final missionary campaign in northern
Frisia – his only shield a heavily bound Gospel book with which,
tradition holds, he tried to parry the sword blows of his attackers.

Wynfrith, said to have been born in Crediton, Devon, about 675,
was the son of a notable West Saxon family in the region of Exeter.
His biographer and kinsman St Willibald tells us that it was only
with reluctance that his father allowed the boy to attend the
monastery school of Exeter and then travel to the monastery of

Nursling in Hampshire. Here he was soon attracting students of his own by his academic reputation and the general admiration for his austere and virtuous life.

King Ine of Wessex and his advisers selected Wynfrith to head a delegation to the archbishop of Canterbury. Its success added the skills of a diplomat to his reputation. Inevitably, when the old abbot died the monks of Nursling begged him to take over the job. Instead, with two or three companions, he headed for the port of Lundenwic, bent on a Continental mission. A sea passage usually meant finding the skipper of a merchant ship willing to take passengers. Departure time could depend on how long it took the shipmaster to assemble his cargo. Having negotiated a fare, the monks waited for the shipmaster to set his sail for Dorestad, about twelve miles from Utrecht. It was the year 716 and Boniface found the Frisian opposition to the Franks in spate. He returned to England to reconsider his strategy.

The Continent was still the objective and Bishop Daniel of Winchester appointed another abbot at Nursling. The bishop offered advice on dealing with pagan rulers and their claims to descend from the gods. Don't argue, just listen to the genealogies with interest. And then point out that beings generated through the intercourse of male and female can hardly be eternal, so they must be not gods but men. And why, if against the odds they do have divine powers, do these gods of the north allow the Christian peoples to occupy the fertile southern regions of the world, rich in oil and wine, while they and their own worshippers are restricted to the cold regions? Above all the heathen are to be constantly reminded of the superiority of the Christian world. This must have been a difficult proposition to advance given the recent victories of Islam around the southern shores of the Mediterranean and its contemporary incursions into Europe; Boniface would later have to write to an abbess friend to delay her plans for a pilgrimage to Rome until the Saracen attacks on the Holy City had abated.

Once more Boniface left Nursling and set out along the road for
Lundenwic. It was the turning point of his life. He never lost touch
with England and would maintain a stream of correspondence with
friends and personalities in most of the English kingdoms, but he
never returned. Sailing from Lundenwic as before, though this time
on a 'small swift ship', Boniface and his party took a crossing to
Quentovic. Being a Wessex man he might have considered taking
ship at Hamwic, as St Willehad was to, and then up the Seine to
Rouen. But Quentovic was the principal Channel port and arrangements for the onward journey to Rome were probably easier. Even
so, lodging was a problem and the party had to pitch tents for shelter.

Warrior for Christ, ealdorman for Rome

King Alfred was to describe St Peter as having received the ealdor-
dom of Rome from God. The image well suits the role that
Wynfrith of Crediton would discharge for Rome in eighth-century
Germany, as the West Saxon ealdorman was the king's local deputy.
Wynfrith made his way to Rome and there, on 15 May 719, Pope
Gregory II 'commissioned him to preach to the unbelieving gen-
tiles'. It is the earliest such mandate to have been preserved.[5] It
specifies that any baptisms are to be conducted according to the
Roman rite and that Wynfrith, now named Boniface by the pope,
is to report back to Rome. There had been some papal contacts
with the peoples of northern Germany and bishops in the
Rhineland had been sending missionary expeditions eastwards.
While the English were not always first in the field, however, they
pioneered unquestioning authority to Rome. Boniface would later
boast of having made more than 100,000 converts.

It has been observed that:

What gave Boniface's work lasting success, compared with that of
some of the Irish monks who had preceded him, was his care for

organization and his realization that it was necessary to enlist the support of the state as well as the Church.[6]

He prepared the ground with a 'journey of inspection . . . to discover whether [the people] . . . were ready to receive the word of God.'[7] In Bavaria and Thuringia he consolidated and extended the existing Christian presence, whether in pockets centred upon baptismal churches established by lay lords or resulting from earlier sporadic Irish missionary work; there were some German initiatives, particularly to the west of Bavaria where Christianity already had some devotees among the aristocracy. His travels also took him into Lombardy where he was received by King Liutprand, though Boniface's biographer does not tell us whether he visited the monastery at Bobbio, near Pavia, founded by the Irish missionary St Columbanus a century before.

With the death of Radbod in 719 Boniface returned to Frisia where for three years he worked with Willibrord, re-establishing gospel teaching and destroying pagan temples and shrines and building churches. Now getting on in years, the 'Apostle of Frisia' wanted to make his dynamic compatriot a bishop and his second in command. Boniface pointed out that he had come to Germany under the aegis of the Apostolic See and had not formally sought Rome's permission to divert his energies to Frisia. Reluctantly, Willibrord let him return to the German mission field. At Amöneburg in Hesse, Boniface found the 'rulers', two brothers, 'practising . . . the sacrilegious worship of idols under the cloak of Christianity', though Willibald does not explain further. Boniface won enough converts to establish a chapel. He now commissioned 'an experienced and trustworthy messenger' to report his progress to Rome. By return he was commanded to come to the Holy City in person. Pope Gregory II questioned him on his creed and teaching, but it was immediately clear there was a 'communication problem', since it seems the Englishman could not easily understand the Italianized Latin that was evolving at the papal court. Saying, diplomatically, that he 'lacked the skill in the use of the tongue with which you are familiar' (a comment incomprehensible if it meant this renowned scholar could not understand Latin), Boniface asked permission to make a written confession of faith. This granted, he produced a piece 'expressed in polished, eloquent and learned phrases'. Gregory consecrated him bishop without a diocese on 30 November 722.

Like any liegeman he was required to take an oath, but where his fellow noblemen pledged loyalty to king or war leader, Boniface swore his allegiance in the first instance to St Peter 'and to his vicar on earth the pope'. From the outset his mission was pledged to Rome. Bishops of the sees adjacent to Rome (the so-called *suburbicarian* sees) made allegiance to the Byzantine emperor, that is the Byzantine emperor at Constantinople. Boniface pledged to uphold Catholic teaching and to report any bishop deviating from it to the Holy See. A few days later Boniface received letters of commendation from the Pope to the Thuringians, the Old Saxons and to 'Duke Charles', that is Charles Martel, mayor of the palace to the Merovingian Theodoric IV, informing him that the new bishop was charged with 'preaching the faith to the peoples of Germany who dwell on the eastern bank of the Rhine, some of whom are still steeped in the errors of paganism'.[8] Armed with a letter of protection from Charles, the new bishop returned to the land of the Hessians, where there was a superficial adherence to Christianity although many practised pagan rites and incantations to springs and trees.

Boniface led his war band of Christian warriors into the heart of enemy territory. The objective was an ancient and massive oak at a place called Geismar (probably the one near Fritzlar). The ancient tree, possibly with four trunks rising from the same bole, was sacred to Thor, the Germanic god of thunder and storm (known to the Anglo-Saxons as Thunor, and was the focus of a vigorous cult. Such tree cults were at the heart of north European paganism and lingered well into the Christian era. Instances are cited from sixteenth-century Prussia, while as late as the 1640s the priest of the little Normandy parish of Allouville-Bellefosse was battling with superstitious villagers over a great cleft oak tree at the heart of the community. Rather than risk the fury of the locals by chopping it down, the priest constructed a miniature wooden chapel-cell in the cleft, which is still on the tourist itinerary of the *département* of Seine Maritime.

St Boniface confronted problems similar to those facing that Normandy curé. In the Germanic pantheon, Thor was the special deity of warriors; the fact that the cloven trunk, no doubt the result of a lightning strike, continued in vigour suggested the indwelling presence of the god whose weapon was the thunderbolt, Thor's magic hammer. Undaunted by a largely hostile crowd, Boniface laid an axe to the main trunk. According to Willibald he had not completed the first notch on the fore side of the tree when it 'was smitten by a divine blast from heaven and crashed to the ground, shattering its crown of branches as it fell'. As if to confirm the miracle, the tree split into four parts, now found to be of equal length, without any further human intervention. Boniface ordered that the wood be used to build an oratory chapel, which he then dedicated to St Peter, patron of himself and of Rome.

Fulda, frontiersmen, English and German

Boniface now pressed on into Thuringia. He and his Christian pioneers, together with the scattered outposts of earlier missionary activity (perhaps from German sees) were harassed constantly. But little by little converts increased in number, ruined church buildings were reactivated as evangelizing centres and land cleared for a new monastery at Ohrdruf, near Gotha. Here the founding group 'grew their own crops and made their own clothes'. In due course the

monastery was put in the care of Wigbert, a Dorset man with a reputation for discipline who had come out to be abbot of Fritzlar, on
the Eder river, which together with the Fulda river was later an
important trade navigation.

News of the work attracted recruits from Britain, where 'readers,
writers and skilled men trained in other arts'[9] flocked to the villages
and forest settlements of Hessen, Thuringia and other German
lands. It has been argued that this exodus seriously depleted English
resources of educated men and women. Newly converted locals,
too, were inspired by the Englishman's example. When Boniface
decided on the foundation of the monastery at Fulda, where his
body still lies in its magnificent Baroque sarcophagus, he entrusted
the job to his Bavarian follower Sturmi (St Sturm).

Sturm's parents, noble Christian converts, entrusted the boy's
upbringing to Wigbert at Fritzlar. Ordained as priest, he retreated
with two friends to a wild, uninhabited spot to lead the life of a
hermit in huts they built themselves and roofed with tree bark.
Obviously self-sufficient, practical and determined, he was,
Boniface decided, just the man to find the site for his new venture.
It was the kind of prospecting expedition that would be a key factor
in the medieval clearance of Europe's forests. The final objective was
a self-sufficient community pursuing the contemplative life under a
disciplined monastic rule. The chosen site was a deserted spot in
well-watered, virgin terrain, capable of self-sustaining productive
exploitation. The outcome was an economic growth point and
centre for culture and learning.

After one false start, when several days rowing upstream along the
River Fulda produced no useful sighting, Sturm was told by
Boniface to try again. This time he set out alone, we are told, on a
single ass. By day he ambled through the trackless forest, checking
out the terrain, soil quality and above all possible drinking water
sources and access to the river. By night he cut saplings and brushwood to make a corral for the ass, using 'a tool which he carried in

his hand' – presumably some form of billhook . . . or an unclerical sword? We are told wild animals were a hazard. Then, on the bridge carrying the merchant road to Mainz over the River Fulda, he came upon a party of Slavs bathing in the river. They scared his beast and, 'as all heathen do', jeered at him. Fortunately, when they tried to do him harm, they were 'held back by divine power' – which rather tends to favour the sword theory.

Eventually, at a place called Eihloh, Sturm found a man with local knowledge who seems to have been invaluable in tracking down the 'blessed spot foreordained by God' – though Sturm, of course, attributed the discovery to the prayers of Boniface. Persuaded by Sturm's report, the latter took over and went to Carloman, the Frankish chief minister, to get his consent to the appropriation of the land.

The English role in Europe's Frankish Empire: I

Carloman was a member of the Carolingian dynasty that would soon dominate European affairs. It would come to owe a good deal to the Anglo-Saxon missions, as did the papacy. Boniface repeatedly sought papal decisions on the difficulties of canon law or to be informed on the rites of the Roman Church. As other churchmen followed his example, papal influence in the Frankish church inevitably increased. Above all, the English system of provincial church organization, originally approved by Pope Gregory the Great and brought to England by St Augustine, was now introduced into Frankish Europe as Boniface re-established councils as a relatively regular feature of Frankish church government.

By their own admission these [eastern] Franks had not held a council in eighty years and Carloman, Charles Martel's successor in the region, begged Boniface to convene a synod, promising to 'reform and re-establish ecclesiastical discipline' there. The so-called 'Germanic church council' of April 742, convened by Boniface under Carloman, proclaims by its very date the pervasive English influence. The chief minister did not at this time recognize any official Merovingian king and the proceedings of the council are dated by the Bedan AD method, the first official Frankish document to do so.[10] In this way the Anglo-Saxon missions pioneered the very era in German usage.

Growing papal success in Germany was counterbalanced by a deteriorating papal position in Italy itself. Once supervised by the Byzantine imperial governors at Ravenna, the popes were now in danger from the Lombard kings, with their capital at Pavia. It seemed they might become mere bishops of Rome, subjects not of the emperor but of a great Lombard monarchy. They looked for help from the Frankish kingdom across the Alps.

The title to power was still held by the Merovingians – later dubbed the *fainéants* (do-nothing) kings – at this point embodied by Childeric III, but action was the province of their Carolingian chief minister, now Pippin the Short. Even in its decadence the dynasty was held in awe among the people. With a charisma symbolized by the long uncut tresses of their hair, according to J. M. Wallace-Hadrill in *Early Germanic Kingship*, they retained privileged behaviour, notably open polygamy, from the pagan past. Straightforward assassination followed by a coup d'état might be possible for an ambitious member of the royal family; but the overthrow of that family itself was another matter. If the pope wanted help against the Lombards, he would have to offer help himself – to the ambitious ruler of the Franks.

Pippin aimed to oust King Childeric III; this required the authority, if not of God himself, then of as near as one could get on this earth. His family's cultivation of the successors of St Peter was about to pay off. Pippin sent a two-man embassy to Rome: Fulrad, abbot of Saint Denis near Paris and Burchard, bishop of Würzburg, an Anglo-Saxon and a Mercian by birth. They were to pose Pope Zacharias a question: 'Which of two should be king: the man who had the title but no power or the man who, in these difficult times, exercised the power but had not the title?' It was hardly a trick question and the pope, fortunately, knew the answer. He ordered that Pippin be made king, forthwith.

Yet the Merovingians were a hard act to follow and required special magic. In 750 the great minister's henchmen arranged for his election as king of the Franks at Soissons. Next, in early autumn 751 'King' Pippin, who had been baptized by Archbishop Willibrord, was, according to the *Royal Frankish Annals*, anointed by another Englishman, Boniface, by now archbishop of Mainz and 'Legate for Germany for the Catholic and Apostolic Church of Rome'. So it appears that the dynasty of Charlemagne or Charles the Great, King of the Franks, the dynasty that established the medieval, later Holy Roman, empire was raised to royal status in consecration by an Englishman.

English contributions in the field

Boniface had long depended on support from the Frankish authorities. In a letter to Bishop Daniel he explained that without their help the suppression of pagan rites and idol worship would be quite impossible; the protection of the clergy within the community could be hazardous; even discipline within the church itself could be difficult. All depended upon directives from the palace and the fear of sanctions if they were broken. But in this world of rival loyalties and sanctions Boniface had telling arguments on his own side when dealing with pagans: first his own allegiance to St Peter, founder of God's church on earth; second to that church itself, a monarchical hierarchy, and a fighting body, or church militant.

In a letter to Eadburga, abbess of Minster in the Isle of Thanet, he asks her to copy out for him in 'letters of gold' the Epistles of his lord, St Peter. There was a lot to commend the books to non-Christian lords and rulers. In the first place, Boniface's oath had been pledged on the earthly relics of their author, the first lord of the church militant – surely an important factor among men whose world was governed by oaths of allegiance. Secondly, the greatest of all the saints was no grey celibate but a married man who, like the many-partnered rulers the missionary was dealing with, had known all about the pleasures of sex. Thirdly, the books were 'compact', so to speak – just seven short chapters in total. But above all the glorious gilded lettering and luxurious quality of the illuminated manuscripts that Eadburga was to prepare for him would 'impress a reverence and love of Holy Scripture on the minds of the heathens to whom I preach'. He also writes that he is sending the costly materials for the work by separate messenger.

Of all the gifts he received from his own correspondents, Boniface particularly welcomed the books 'as lamps . . . [of the word of God] . . . to guide the feet of one working . . . in these gloomy lurking-places of the German people'. It is a telling glimpse of work in the great central forest of Dark Age Germany. Time and again we catch an echo of the workaday life of the mission field. The lack of a library to hand means that Boniface must check a basic date, like the year of Augustine's arrival in England, with Canterbury; he settles technicalities about the validity of baptisms performed in 'heathen tongues' and urges his co-workers to always instruct in the Catholic traditions of the see of Rome; he petitions the English clergy to pray regularly for the missionaries and to remember the pagan Saxons, '. . . people of the same blood and bone' and unable to honour the heavenly lord by death as members of his war band, so long as they are destined for hell.[11]

In Bavaria Boniface appointed three new bishops and with the support of Duke Odilo, who brought his nobles with him, divided the duchy into four dioceses and so laid out the basic ecclesiastical geography of the state for the next thousand years. Gregory rubber-stamped the arrangements and vested Boniface with 'apostolic authority' to attend a council shortly to be held on the banks of the

Danube as his representative. Outside Bavaria, as he reported to Gregory's successor Pope Zacharias (741–52), he had appointed three further bishoprics, Erfurt, Würzburg (then in Franconia) and Buraburg, near Fritzlar, the ancient meeting place of east Franks and Saxons. He begged the pope to give charter confirmation to the foundations 'so that there may be in Germany three Episcopal sees founded and established by St Peter's word and the apostolic see's command'.[12] The pope agreed this request.

Reform in the German church was certainly needed. Many a diocese had come into the hands of laymen who, although they claimed ordination, continued to behave like the members of a warrior aristocracy, riding into battle not only against heathens but also shedding the blood of Christians in their local feuding. In fact, since Europe's lay establishment pursued warfare as a way of life and since they often manned the upper reaches of the ecclesiastical hierarchy, the church could do little but compromise.

The principal means of establishing discipline in the religious life itself was the Rule of St Benedict of Nursia (proclaimed the patron saint of all Europe by Paul VI in 1964), founder of the monastery of Monte Cassino. The spread of the rule of St Benedict in Frankish monasteries owed much to English foundations such as the abbey of Fulda, which accepted it from the outset. So impressed was he by the Benedictine advance, promoted by the Anglo-Saxons, that Charles the Great was to ask the abbot of Monte Cassino for an authentic copy of the Rule. Many English monks spent years at the great monastery, among them Willibald the kinsman and biographer of Boniface, who had lived there for a decade before Boniface appointed him bishop of Eichstätt ('Oakstead'). But Willibald had led an action-packed life before retiring to the cloister and his biography, composed by a nun visiting his brother Wynnebald's abbey of Heidenheim, opens a window onto the great rival world of Islam barely a century old at that time.

Contacts with the world of Islam

Willibald had left England for Rome in his early twenties. After a
three-year stay in the great city he took ship from Naples for the
Holy Land with Wynnebald and another companion. Their desti-
nation, which had been within the territory of the Christian
Roman empire only eighty years before, was now under the
Muslim caliphate of Damascus, which was administered by gover-
norships and emirates. Christian–Muslim relationships were now
peaceful, if wary; trading vessels plied once more and some took
fare-paying passengers. Travel was feasible but some form of
identification or letters of introduction was advisable. The three
young monks reached Cyprus without trouble and found a passage
to the Syrian port of Tartus, formerly the Byzantine Christian city
of Antaradus. From here a day or two on the road took them to
Emesa, in the Orontes Valley. Birthplace of two Roman emperors
and then a seat of Christian bishoprics, since 636 it had been an
Arab city under the name of Hims (Homs), although still with a
sizeable Christian element and a number of churches. Without documents, Willibald and his party were immediately arrested as spies
because 'the pagan Saracens . . . [did not know] . . . to which nation
they belonged.' Luckily the local dignitary who first questioned
them had encountered other men from remote parts of the world
travelling in Palestine, 'eager to fulfil their [own] law', as he put it –
presumably equating Christian pilgrimage with the Muslim's obligation to the *hajj*. The party now applied to the governor for documents to cover their onward journey to Jerusalem. Instead, he put
them in prison awaiting further instructions from the 'king' of the
region, presumably the emir of Hims.

Their 'imprisonment' was not too arduous. Apparently impressed
by their loyalty to their religion, a generous local merchant fitted
them out in new clothes, sent them well-prepared meals from his
own kitchen and twice a week had them escorted to the local bath

house. On Sundays he took them himself to the local Christian church. (Christians and Jews were at that time allowed to continue the practice of their faiths on payment of a tax.) For a time, it seems, these 'young, handsome and beautifully dressed' Englishmen caused quite a stir in the town. Eventually they were cleared of suspicion and sent on their way. Arrested as spies they had emerged almost as friends at court. All this the biographer attributes to the benign workings of God, though we might think that Muslim generosity was part of the story. Willibald and company certainly returned with a wallet of travellers' tales: from the soured milk drink they shared with a company of shepherds (presumably a type of *kwass*) to a near-encounter with a mountain lion.[13] A century or so later the local inhabitants might well have been seen as dangerous. Upheavals in Islam brought in the less Christian-tolerant regimes; the local Christian community of Hims would be 'cleansed' and its churches demolished.

In fact, bands of Saracen raiders were harrying Europe soon after Willibald settled into his work in Germany. A letter of the 740s from Boniface bewails them as the punishment of God on a sinful people; more practically the saint warns an abbess friend planning to visit Rome that even here travel could be hazardous, given the prevailing incursions – the contemporary equivalent of an Islamist terrorist threat.

The tribulations of an old man

Such 'Saracen' attacks presented a physical danger but no threat to the Faith as such. Here the danger was the enduring resistance to the missions. The 'conversion' of the Saxon heartlands, for example, was to be achieved only after decades of warfare by the armies of Charles the Great that killed tens of thousands of Saxons. Meanwhile, Boniface had to contest against the corruption and debasement of his beloved religion's image by the conduct of the Christians themselves. His strictures against Æthelbald for his

immoral life owed much to the scandal they caused in pagan territories across the frontier where sexual fidelity was fiercely enforced:

> Thus, in Old Saxony . . . if a married woman commit adultery, they
> sometimes force her to kill herself by hanging; and when the body has
> been cremated they hang her seducer over the pyre . . .

The implied contrast with goings on among the Christian (Anglo)
Saxons under Æthelbald's dispensation is obvious.[14]

But then the lifestyle of the average, unreformed Frankish aristocrat bishop paid little heed to clerical niceties, either. Polygamy was
not unheard of among the episcopate – perhaps on the theory that
a bishop's ordination gave him something of the sacral mystery surrounding the king. Boniface reported deacons who slept nights with
four or five concubines in their bed, acknowledged bastard children,
and yet became bishops and celebrated mass. Part of the problem was
that the church permitted married men to enter the priesthood if,
admittedly, on what one might term a strictly one priest, one wife
basis. Neighbouring heathen tribes might understand such concessions to their own practices. What they could not stomach, Boniface
wrote, were pagan practices in Rome itself – January celebrations in
front of St Peter's, where crowds paraded the streets and gorged
themselves at food- and wine-laden tables and women, festooned in
ornaments, hawked pagan amulets and bracelets.[15]

Nor was Boniface much helped by the unsavoury reputation that
the clergy of his native island seem to have acquired on the
Continent. In his long letter to Archbishop Cuthbert of Canterbury
he complains about reports of drunken parish priests, and even
drunken bishops who encourage what sounds suspiciously like
binge drinking among their clergy. Even then the English had a
reputation for excessive drunkenness, which later in the same letter
Boniface laments as 'a vice that is peculiar to the heathen and to *our
race*, and that neither the Franks nor the Gauls, . . . Lombards, . . .
Romans, nor Greeks [indulge in]' [my emphasis].[16]

Apparently, although he never read Bede on the 'English', Boniface was perfectly aware of an ethnic identity that distinguished him from other peoples of Europe – including, it would seem, the heathen Saxons. It is also worth pausing to notice that he distinguishes between 'Gauls', the original Romano-Celtic population of what we today call 'France', and 'Franks', the federation of diverse barbarian tribes that overran them. As to drink, perhaps Boniface himself was not averse to the occasional episcopal tipple. In a letter to Archbishop Ecgberht of York he not only asks for copies of the book of homilies and the commentary on the Proverbs of Solomon by Bede, 'inspired priest and student of the scriptures' (not 'historian', we note), but sends by the bearer two small casks of wine to be consumed 'in a merry day with the brethren'.

But books were always the great solace and book requests are a standard feature; with advancing age he had a particular need for large print versions 'with the letters written out clearly and separately', which were to be had in England but 'unavailable in this country'. The more serious troubles of old age in exile, such as the withering of friendship, could challenge even his determination. Recalling his original name 'Boniface also called Wynfrith' asks a West Country acquaintance from his youth to pity '. . . an old man worn out by tribulations in this land of the Germans'.[17]

The role of women

This section focuses upon St Lioba, for whom St Boniface had an intense regard. She is just one of a number of Anglo-Saxon women saints, such as Abbess Hild of Whitby, Abbess Æthelburga of Barking in Essex and Abbess Æthelthryth (also known as Etheldreda or Audrey), daughter of King Anna of the East Angles. Twice married, Æthelthryth nevertheless maintained her virginity so that her second husband, Ecgfryth of Northumbria, who evidently expected more from a 'peace weaver', as dynastic wives were called, released her for the life of religion so that she might found a double monastery at Ely, where she presided until her death. She was succeeded by her sister St Sexburga, dowager queen of Kent.

The double monastery/nunnery was a fairly common institution in the Old English church and in most cases headed by a woman rather than a man. But then the Anglo-Saxons honoured many women as saints, a practice that ended with the Norman Conquest; in the view of the distinguished historian Doris Stenton, 'Anglo-Saxon women were more nearly the equal companions of their husbands and brothers' than in Norman England. In her *Women in Anglo-Saxon England*, Christine Fell cities cases of women apparently in business on their own account in the craft of embroidery. In the 810s the bishop of Worcester granted a certain Eanswith 200 acres (80 hectares) of land in return for the maintenance and enlargement of the cathedral's vestments, which means she must have employed a team of craft workers. From the reign of Edward the Confessor we hear of Ælfgyth, who was made a modest grant from the royal revenues for teaching a king's sheriff's daughter the craft of gold thread embroidery (*aufrisium*).

Laws regulating relations between the sexes could be harsh. Adulterers were liable to severe penalties, but whereas a man might be subject to forfeiture of land, under Cnut's laws a woman offender faced bodily mutilation. But from the very earliest period, Anglo-Saxon codes provide clear and sensible legislation for the rights of women. A rapist could expect a heavy fine but the laws also specified compensations payable for different degrees of sexual harassment short of rape, from seizing the breast to throwing a woman to the ground. The 'morning gift' a man paid to his wife on their marriage became her personal property to dispose of as she saw fit and it could be a substantial amount, whether in money or land. Æthelfryth, a certain ninth-century lady, sold land equivalent to five peasant land holdings. The code of Æthelred II of 1008 protected a widow from forced remarriage, ruling that she must remain single for twelve months, after which time she could remarry if she wished, but was free to choose her husband. Some chose to enter the life of religion: noblewomen and others might already be literate and, as for men, the church could offer prospects denied them in lay society. Not all could be abbesses, but many could exercise lesser responsibilities, while some apparently learnt to excel at the demanding skills of manuscript illumination.

Like Jerome, Boniface enjoyed the friendship of women. But whereas Jerome seems to have had a more or less permanent entourage of female admirers, Boniface kept a wide correspondence with various nuns and abbesses – many, like him, of noble kin, but also expert in the disciplines and the skills of the religious life. We have seen him writing to Abbess Eadburga, asking her to make a luxury copy of the Epistles of St Peter. It is not a question of her commissioning the work from a master illuminator but it is clear he is confident of her skills in this highly sophisticated and complex technique. A princess of the West Saxon dynasty, she uses the vocabulary of royal triumph on hearing of Boniface's initial success against the Frisian King Radbod, 'the enemy of the Catholic Church, [whom] God humbled at your feet'. When she says farewell 'in love unfeigned', one senses feelings deeper than mere friendship. His mission certainly owed a good deal to her generous support in books, church furniture and money.

Probably the woman who made the greatest impression on Boniface, as she seems to have done on all who met her, was Lioba (also Leoba). At his request she was sent out at the head of thirty nuns, all able to read and write and with some Latin, to act as a sort of missionary back-up team.

In his biography of her, Rudolf of Fulda, writing about 830, tells us that St Lioba was born about 699 in the island of Britain, which, he adds, 'is inhabited by the English nation'. Her aristocratic parents had almost given up hope of having children and Lioba's birth, foreseen by her mother's aged nurse in a dream, seemed divinely ordained. Devout Christians, they vowed the child to the service of God – and rewarded the aged nurse, evidently a household slave, with her freedom. The girl entered the Wessex convent of Wimborne under Abbess Tetta, sister of the king and well known to Boniface.

The community had just come through a troubled time. Tetta kept a strict house, even guarding her girls from contact with clerics – and that included bishops (drunken or not!). But her deputy, still more severe and quite unwilling to apologize, had infuriated the younger sisters, who were mostly young aristocrats used to deference. In due course the termagant died. Within days some of the younger nuns were jumping on the grave and cursing the body. Ominous portents subdued the more rebellious spirits and by the time of Lioba's arrival Abbess Tetta was presiding once more over a docile community.

It was a sympathetic atmosphere for the serious-minded young novice, at this time perhaps something of a prig (bishop-proof certainly). But she was to become a model of spiritual commitment and wisdom, truly worthy of sainthood. Boniface knew about her, as she was 'related to him on his mother's side', and wrote to Abbess Tetta asking her to release Lioba for service in the German mission. Continually building churches and monasteries throughout Hesse, Thuringia and Bavaria he wrote regularly to England to rally recruits, not just as missionaries in the field but to head his new monastic communities, which were to be homes of both prayer and scholarship, as well as anchors for the scattered rural congregations of believers. Tetta released her community's most celebrated member with a bad grace. Boniface made Lioba abbess at the convent of Tauberbischofsheim and general superintendent of nuns throughout Germany. By the end of her career there was hardly a convent in the region that did not have one of her pupils as abbess.

Lioba was described as beautiful (angelic) in appearance, abstemious (her personal drinking cup was known as 'Leoba's little one') and unfailingly good natured. A woman of private means, she was generous in her hospitality, hosting banquets for her guests even when she herself was fasting. In summertime she took an afternoon siesta, observing that lack of sleep dulled the mind, especially for study. But she expected a scripture reading all the same. Younger nuns competed for the privilege and the fun of trying to trick the holy abbess. Even when she seemed most soundly asleep she would correct any slip or omission and no one was ever able to catch her out.

Serious to a fault, apparently she never laughed out loud. Quite averse to the courtier's world, she was nevertheless much respected in court circles, above all by Queen Hildegard, wife of Charlemagne, who 'revered her with a chaste affection and loved her as her own soul'. There are hints that Lioba detected undertones in the queen's regard. In response to a pleading letter that they might meet one last time, Lioba complied 'for the sake of their long-standing friendship'. She received the usual effusive welcome, but cut short the visit. Their farewell embrace was more affectionate than usual, Rudolf tells us. The abbess kissed her royal friend on the mouth as well as upon the forehead and the eyes, saying

> farewell dearly beloved lady and sister . . . most precious half of my soul . . . we shall never more enjoy one another's presence on this earth. May Christ . . . grant that we meet again without shame on the day of judgement.

Shortly after, returned to her convent, Lioba fell into a terminal illness and was given the last rites from her English priest and confessor Torhthat.

The consequences of a pioneer age

Summing up what we know of the English missions in Germany during the eighth century reveals an episode of immense consequence in the history of the European continent. By its constant allegiance to Rome and the popes, the English mission assured the ascendancy of the Roman rite in the Western Church's liturgy until the Reformation of the early 1500s and, for good or ill, the survival of papal authority over Western churches. By its organization of the German church hierarchy the mission and its leaders prepared, under papal direction, a structure that proved central to the administration of the medieval, later Holy Roman, empire. So much for the future. At the time, contemporaries recognized its leaders as men of importance at the very summit of European affairs. According to tradition, the seventy-year-old Boniface anointed Pippin the Short, ancestor of the Carolingian dynasty, king of the Franks in 751. At the local level English clerics and monks were doers and role models admired and long remembered in the lands of the old Germany hegemony. Willibrord of Echternach, Willibald at Eichstätt and Boniface are only the most notable in the roll call of Anglo-Saxon names who were fundamental in the formation of early European history.

The reform spirit created by the Anglo-Saxons was alive in the Frankish church and the ecclesiastical policy of these Carolingians on the whole may be regarded as the continuation and the heritage of the work of St Boniface. Of crucial significance, according to Professor Rosamond McKitterick, were their methods of teaching, their conviction of the importance of papal authority, their emphasis on synodal authority and the energy they devoted to establishing a coherent diocesan structure.[18]

Professor McKitterick showed also that there is 'abundant manuscript evidence' of English men and women at work on the Continent in the form of the books they copied, both west and east of the Rhine. Even where, as at Jouarre, near Paris, the work is in Merovingian Frankish style there may be 'unmistakable insular traits' indicating connections with England. From the regions of Germany where Boniface and his colleagues were active, manuscripts in distinctively insular script styles indicate many more men and women from England than would be expected. McKiterrick found similar evidence of English scribes in Bavarian records,

Frankish ship's figurehead, dredged from the Scheldt, near Antwerp. It is possible that Britain's Anglo-Saxon invaders used similar figureheads.

The Castor hanging bowl: bronze, probably seventh century and possibly British work. Castor was the site of a Roman palace-villa and a seventh-century abbey.

A reconstruction of the princely burial chamber (early 600s), excavated at Prittlewell, Southend-on-Sea, Essex, 2003–4. Once timber lined and floored, it was sunk some 5 feet (1.5m) deep.

Disc brooch, *c*.600, from the burial site excavated at Alwalton near Peterborough.

The golden belt buckle from the Sutton Hoo ship burial, *c*.620. An outstanding example of a high-status ornament.

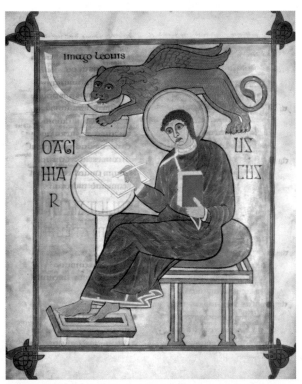

The portrait page of St Mark from the Lindisfarne Gospels, 715–20. *Agius* is a form of the Greek word *agios* meaning holy and the Lion is St. Mark's emblem.

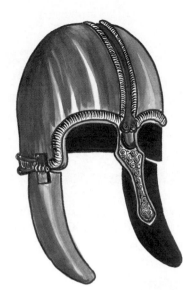

The Coppergate Helm
(*c.* early eighth century) before
its full restoration. The helmet
bears a Latin dedication to
'All Saints'.

The Bewcastle Cross,
Cumbria, 725–50.
It now stands some
14 feet, 6 inches (4.3m).
The carvings include
figures of Christ and
St John the Baptist.
Such monuments (see
page 88), originating in
Northumbria, are found
elsewhere, such as
Sandbach.

Detail from the front panel of the Franks casket, (now at the British
Museum) depicting the pagan legend of Weland the Smith (left) and
the Magi paying homage to the Christ Child (see pages 86–7).

The annual Whitsuntide Dancing Procession of Echternach,
Luxembourg, for centuries held to honour the Northumbrian
St Willibrord (d. 739) buried here in the church that bears his name.

The Hedda stone, Peterborough Cathedral, dates from probably the late 700s . The sarcophagus-like block with figures of Christ, his Mother and certain disciples, is some 5 feet long (1.5m).

The gold mancus of Coenwulf of Mercia (*d*. 821) was found by metal detector in 2003 and is now in the British Museum.

All Saints' Church, Brixworth. The church was completed by 800 and, at 150 feet (about 50m) in length, it is England's largest surviving pre-Viking church. Italian influences have been traced. Originally the arches gave onto side chapels.

Alfred the Great of Wessex, Winchester, sculpted by Sir William Hamo Thornycroft. The statue was erected in 1901 as the result of an international millenary commemoration of the great king.

Platz Bonifacius, Fulda, Land Hessen, Germany. The statue of Bonifacius (St Boniface of Wessex), 'the Apostle of Germany' (*b*. Wynfrith *c*.675) was erected in 1842 and was meticulously restored in 2002–3.

The lower half of the frontispiece to King Edgar's charter for the New Minster, Winchester (dated 966). The king, between the Virgin Mary and St Peter, presents the book-like charter to Christ in Glory, above. His dance-like posture recalls how King David 'danced before the Lord' (2 Samuel 6, 14).

Detail from the 'Five Senses' on the silver and niello Fuller Brooch, c.850. The disc is framed by 16 roundels with figured and floral motifs. The overall diameter is 4.5 inches (11.4cm).

All Saints' Church, Earls Barton, Northamptonshire, c.1000 (the battlements are post-Conquest). A nineteenth-century study of Anglo-Saxon architecture was based on similar stone 'strapwork' found on the tower of St. Peter's, Barton-upon-Humber.

The 'flying angel' from the church of St Laurence, Bradford on Avon. The little church (date unknown, though perhaps c.1000), its nave just 25 feet (7.6m) long, retains its sense of the numinous.

'Christ in Majesty' from the church of St John the Baptist, Barnack is about 3 feet, 4 inches (102cm) in height and dates from the 1060s.

The 'death of King Harold II at Hastings' from the Bayeux Tapestry. The Latin words 'hIC hAROLD REX INTERFECTUS EST' ('Here King Harold is killed') stretch over one figure who is perhaps pulling an arrow from his eye and another who has been felled by a horseman.

representing a continuous influx of Anglo-Saxon volunteers up to thirty years after the death of St Boniface.[19] Such a trend might help explain the low level of learning in England deplored by King Alfred in the next century. On the continent, the contribution of these Anglo-Saxon expatriates was undeniable.

Work by Professors McKitterick and Rollason in England and Joachim Ehlers in Germany, has revealed that Bede's *Ecclesiastical History* was widely influential on the continent from the late 700s. Presenting the English church as an extension of the primitive church and of the universal mission enjoined by Christ on his disciples, Bede belongs in the tradition of '*l'histoire universelle*', according to Georges Tugène. Continental copies, probably made at Aachen from manuscripts originating in Northumbria, such as the so-called 'Leningrad' Bede (completed about 746 and in St Petersburg since the early eighteenth century), arrived at monastic libraries from Würzburg to Tours and from St Hubert in the Ardennes to Trier. Recounting the conversion of a heathen people and the building of a Christian polity, Bede's work appealed to a Frankish elite pushing Christianization as a tool of imperial expansionism first among the Frisians, then the Saxons under Charles the Great, and under his successors (less effectively) among the Danes. When Europe's present *nomenclatura* wrote religion out of its failed 'constitution', it betrayed the convictions of Charlemagne himself, eponymous hero of its most vaunted prize.

At the time, the English example of diocesan organization was as important as Bede's historical schema. In the 760s, Abbot Gregory of Utrecht, a young Frankish nobleman, disciple of Boniface, took on an English auxiliary named Aluberht, who was duly consecrated bishop of the 'Old Saxons' at York; here a brilliant young scholar was making a Europe-wide reputation. His name was Alcuin.

6

ALCUIN OF YORK AND THE CONTINUING ANGLO-SAXON PRESENCE ON THE CONTINENT

The French historian and minister of education (1832–7) Guizot may have dubbed Alcuin of York 'Charlemagne's minister of education', but Alcuin himself looked upon his role, as did many aristocratic Anglo-Saxon churchmen, as that of a warrior in the service of Christ. Writing to Charles from his retirement at the abbey of Tours about 802, he begs not to be called once more to fight again and 'sweat under the weight of armour' having 'laid aside the soldier's belt'.[1] He was well aware of the honoured place the war belt with its costly buckle enjoyed in the rating of a warrior's equipment – the buckles at Sutton Hoo and Prittlewell tell the story.

Alcuin was born, it is now thought, about the year 740, into a well-connected kin group, perhaps of the minor nobility. He had also inherited 'by legitimate succession' the monastery of St Andrew built near the mouth of the Humber by Wilgils, father of St Willibrord, on little parcels of land given to him by kings and nobles. The career of Wilgils was not untypical of devout countrymen turning to the life of religion and attracting a small, sometimes 'distinguished' following so that their hermitage might evolve into a modest minster.

Alcuin's kinsmen included Willibrord, whose biography he wrote, and also Willehad, a cousin who would become the first bishop of Bremen. We have already noted that he almost certainly had relatives in Northumbrian court circles (see chapter 3). Another was Beornred, to whom he dedicated his two biographies of St Willibrord and whom he nicknamed Samuel. (The biblical Samuel, it will be remembered, had sponsored King David and 'David' was Charles the Great in Alcuin's system.) Beornred, who was abbot of Echternach from 775 and ten years later archbishop of Sens, was an important figure among the Anglo-Saxons in the Frankish administration of state as well as church: in 785–6 he shared with the abbot of St Vaast a two-man commission from King Charles to report on the condition of the church in Italy, which would also include the state of the papacy.

The aristocratic world of the court and the warrior is never far from Alcuin's correspondence. Writing to Archbishop Simeon of York in 801, who was at odds with King Eardwulf of Northumbria (the 'tyrant' as Alcuin dubs him), he urges him to resist and stand bravely like the standard-bearer in Christ's battle line, for if the standard-bearer leave the field what is the army to do? Later in the same letter Christ himself is compared as a war leader 'going before the ranks of his host . . . [who] first bore his cross to his Passion'.

Clerics shared the heroic and military culture of their class. Writing to another churchman, Alcuin seems to give us a glimpse round the screens of a cathedral monastic refectory where the readings, which should be from scripture or some improving book, may sometimes in fact have been from bardic lays or from *Beowulf* itself, with musical accompaniment. Specifically, Alcuin complains about the story of Ingeld or Hinield, a prince of the Heathobards, probably the one featured in the *Beowulf* epic, being declaimed to harp or lyre accompaniment. 'What has Ingeld to do with Christ?' he exclaims, 'Your house cannot have room for both.'[2] Since at least one modern scholar has surmised that *Beowulf* itself may actually have been composed in a clerical community, Alcuin's allusion becomes the more intriguing.[3]

Alcuin entered the cathedral school at York under Archbishop Ecgberht (*d.* 766), brother to the king. He made precocious progress, showing mastery of the Psalms of David and fluency in the works of Virgil well before the age of ten. They were happy days. His teachers seem to have been more indulgent than Alcuin himself would be with advancing age. We are told that Sigulf, a favourite pupil who followed him to the Continent and became an assistant teacher at Tours, would read Virgil with his own pupils but in secret because Alcuin would not approve.

The school at York was a stronghold of learning and its library 'a wondrous treasure' of many books under a single roof. In his long verse history of the church and saints of York, considered the first historical epic to survive in the literature of the medieval Latin west,[4] Alcuin recalled works in Hebrew and Greek, as well as the major Latin grammarians and classics such as Cicero and Virgil, but the library also held in its catalogue books by English scholars such as Bede and Aldhelm. In fact the library, built up by archbishops Ecgberht and Ælbert (*d.* 780) in the tradition of Benedict Biscop at Monkwearmouth-Jarrow, won repute throughout Europe for the range and depth of its learning. Alcuin, who in the 760s graduated to a teaching post in the school of York, was also becoming known on the Continent.

But he was deeply proud of the 'famed' city of his birth. His verse history tells of the high walls and towers of the Roman *castrum* Eboracum, which he believed had been built with the collaboration of the local tribes. The Britons of those days were not cowed and resentful, but worthy to stand as partners in an empire 'whose sceptre ruled the world'. By contrast their descendants had been cowardly and incompetent before the onslaught of a warrior race from distant Germany called 'Saxons', so called because they are 'hard as stone'. (No doubt Alcuin reckoned the derivation from the Latin word *saxum*, 'stone', more flattering than the one from the Germanic *seaxa*, the short stabbing knife, the Saxons' traditional weapon.) And there is a vivid landscape of the York, the emporium, he knew:

> a merchant town of land and sea . . . where sailors haste to heave their hausers out and ride at rest . . . a town . . . whose river flows through flowery meads to haven for its ships . . .[5]

The scholar never lost his loyalty to Northumbria, the country of his birth. Both as courtier and scholar he honoured the name of its warrior patron saint Oswald, describing him as a man powerful in virtue and the guardian of the fatherland (*'vir virtute potens, patriae tutator, amator'*).[6]

At about the time his reputation was taking off outside England, Alcuin made his first visit to Rome on the school of York's business travelling via the important abbey of Murbach in Alsace and the Lombard capital at Pavia. In 778–9 he was sent on a mission to the Frankish court and apparently made useful network connections with courtiers on his journey up the Rhine, though not meeting the king on this occasion. But the following year he was again in Rome to collect the pallium, or scarf of office, for York's archbishop Eanbald from the pope On his way back he had a momentous interview in the north Italian city of Parma with Charles the Great, king of the Franks, in March 781. As a result he was to become the leading member of the palace school, though perhaps not 'head' in a formal sense.

Ten years before he encountered Alcuin, Charles the Great had become sole ruler of the Frankish lands following the death of his brother Carloman. Called by Alcuin the father of Europe (an early instance of the use of that word in common parlance), he was a man of towering stature and ambition, bent not only on conquest and power but also on a cultural programme to revive learning we know as the Carolingian Renaissance (from Carolus, Latin for Charles). It was the view of the late Professor Elton that 'learned Englishmen like Alcuin . . . helped to civilize the court of Charlemagne.'[7] The

English were not alone, as Alcuin indicated in one of his letters, where he speaks of a new Athens in Francia (Athens having attracted men from all over ancient Greece) and perhaps rather flatteringly praises Charles as an example of Plato's philosopher king. A man of great intellect and wide familiarity with the studies of the men he recruited, Charles was also a ruthless evangelist determined to make the heathen, and above all the Saxons, 'submit to the mild and sweet yoke of Christ', whatever the cost in blood. War rumbled on round the more conventional missionary efforts of the churchmen. Back in the 740s these had already established an institution that would be vital to his great cultural initiative and that Charles himself was to enrich with valuable endowments – the monastery of Fulda, inspired by Boniface.

Fulda, foundation for the future

The building of Fulda had been a classic case of the application of practicalities to the achievement of great ideas. Having decided on the site, Boniface had gone to the man in authority, Carloman, the current mayor of the palace. A religious man who would later retire into a monastery, he willingly granted the site whole and entire, together with all the land that he may be 'supposed to possess' within a radius of three miles. The area in question is termed 'wilderness' and property boundaries are vague. In these last years of the Merovingian dynasty titles of authority are vague too: one source calls Carloman 'king of the Franks', another 'king of Austrasia'. Strictly speaking, he was not king at all.

A charter was drawn up and signed by the 'king' and an assembly of nobles of the region, who are told that the king 'requires' them to give any land they may hold in the area for the use of the monastery. Towards the end of March 'in the year of the Incarnation [i.e. AD] 744' (note the Bedan date)[8], Boniface visited the site. He was accompanied by a body of labourers and their supervisors who cleared the site of trees and undergrowth. A year later building work was well advanced and the archbishop came again, this time to give instruction in the Rule of St Benedict. It is apparent that the abbey already had a thriving water-powered craftwork production. Sturm had recruited workmen to divert a channel from the River Fulda under the abbey workshops, which 'conferred great profit upon the brethren . . . as is still obvious to those who use it . . . to this day'.[9] This strongly suggests that the abbey had installed a horizontal wheel water mill, no doubt similar to the type of machine, dated to about AD 700, of which traces were excavated at Ebbsfleet, Kent, in 2002 (as reported in *Current Archaeology*, no. 183).

While the king pursued his missionary work 'partly by conquest . . . partly even by bribes', Abbot Sturm focused on the cult centres, cutting down sacred groves and destroying temples. Not surprisingly the Saxons, clearly 'a depraved and perverse race', responded in kind. In 778 a particularly violent resurgence forced the community at Fulda to quit the monastery and carry the body of Boniface to temporary refuge at Hammelburg. Local forces in fact drove the Saxon threat back but Charles returned with a new army. Yet more campaigns against the Saxons under their famous 'duke' Widukind followed: in the mid-780s we find Abbot Beornred giving hospitality to his fellow Englishman Willehad, forced to abandon his missionary work because of the war. When Widukind finally submitted to the Frankish king and his religion of love in 785, Willehad 'resumed his work among the Saxons with obvious success'. He was consecrated bishop of Bremen on Charlemagne's orders.

The Sword in the Book – martyr and patron

The continuing influence of Alcuin's scholarship and teaching ran deep. More dramatic are the memories of Willibrord of Utrecht and

Boniface, the patron saint of Germany, who ended his life in martyrdom. In his seventies he had decided to return to the mission
field of Frisia. There on 5 June 754, as he and his party were reading
in their tents, they were set upon by a robber band and the saint
felled by a sword cut to the head – he died, we are told trying to
fend off the blow with the Gospel book in his hand.

Today it is tourists as much as pilgrims whose money bulks
the municipal income of Echternach on the celebration of
Willibrord's saint's day (7 November), but for Roman Catholics in
the Netherlands after its independence as the United Provinces, he
and his great assistant Boniface meant much more than a holiday. In
1583 the archbishopric of Utrecht was dissolved by the Protestant
States General and Roman Catholicism outlawed, following the
tyranny of the former ruler, Philip II of Spain. The religion went
underground. Its spiritual leader was a priest from Delft, Sasbout
Vosmeer, with his seat at Utrecht. According to the German historian Michael Imhof (2004), the cults of Willibrord and Boniface
enjoyed a resurgence and Vosmeer compared himself, surrounded
by heretics, to St Boniface surrounded by heathen. So, at the very
time when the English Protestant state, like the Dutch, was pro-
scribing Roman Catholicism, two Englishmen were venerated as
spiritual champions by an oppressed Catholic minority on the
Continent.

As to St Boniface himself, his cult in Germany flourished vigor-
ously at the time of the Counter-Reformation with paintings and
sculptures portraying him at his martyrdom or brandishing the
sword transfixing the Gospel book; this image became his emblem.
A fine statue of the saint (restored and refurbished in 2002–3) stands
in the main square of Fulda. For the purposes of this book, however,
it is a nice thought that this Anglo-Saxon gentleman from Wessex,
whose kin no doubt caroused to the lays of *Beowulf*, also found
himself, under the auspices of nineteenth-century greater German
nationalism, listed with Luther, Goethe, Beethoven, Mozart and

other German worthies as *Walhalla Genossen*, 'Companions of
Valhalla', the hall of the gods in Germanic legend.

Cultural campaign

The death of Boniface provoked controversy as to his body's final
resting place. His relic, full of numinous spiritual power, would be
a strong protector for the place where it lay: a generator of miraculous manifestations, and a powerful magnet for pilgrims and the
wealth they would bring. The chief contenders for the prize were
the saint's cathedral city of Mainz and its bishop, his friend and successor Lull, and Abbot Sturm at Fulda.

'A certain deacon' had a vision in which the dead saint had
insisted on burial at Fulda. The body was duly laid to rest there.
Abbot Sturm and his monks gave thanks to God. The following day
Bishop Lull, 'together with the throng of clerics and [towns] people'
who had come with him to protest, had to accept defeat and return
to Mainz. When Sturm was exiled to Jumièges in Normandy, people
said that Bishop Lull bribed King Pippin to place the monastery
under his jurisdiction. In the end Sturm was reinstated. The controversy had temporarily sapped the energies of the community at
Fulda, but it recovered and grew in numbers and wealth as noblemen competed in munificence of endowments. It was to become a
premier centre of learning under Abbot Rabanus (803–40), a pupil
of Alcuin.

In the opinion of one historian, the cultural contribution made
to scholarship and learning in Europe by both Boniface and Alcuin
may have been in part responsible for the decline of both in
England. 'Just as in Southumbrian learning one can trace a notable
decline once Boniface took a whole generation of the learned aristocracy off to the Continent to convert the Germans, so too
Alcuin's departure to serve as chief adviser to Charlemagne marks a
clear decline in Latin learning in the schools of Northumbria.[10]

Travellers and expatriates

Any study of the Anglo-Saxon intervention on the Continent, which for many of the men and women involved meant a permanent new home abroad, inevitably raises the question of why so many of them made the move. Travelling abroad for one's health, in other words flying for one's life into exile, was for a courtier a common hazard of existence. Eadburh, the daughter of King Offa of Mercia who married King Beorhtric of Wessex, ended her days in poverty in Pavia, we are told. In West Saxon tradition she emerges as a Lucrezia Borgia figure, manipulating court politics and disposing of rivals by poison. When the king himself fell victim to severe stomach pains, Eadburh supposedly escaped with as much of the royal treasure as she could conveniently carry and fled to the court of Charles the Great. Following a romantic episode with Charles himself and his son she once more took to the road in disgrace, heading south. Given its position on the approaches to the Alpine passes, Pavia was host to many such travellers.

But deeper motivations were at work for most of the Anglo-Saxon men and women who devoted themselves to the service of religion in the great age of the English missions. The anonymous Frankish biographer of St Lebuin (Leafwine) of Ripon, writing in the ninth century, describes England as a country 'productive of holy men [where] one finds laymen devoted to the service of God, virgins of exceptional virtue and monks of outstanding generosity'; then he goes on to explain that many had left their own country 'for the Lord's sake, either to expiate their sins, or benefit pagans and Christians by their teachings'.[11] In a religious age such motivations are to be expected; many also were fired by the call of Boniface to come over and help lead their cousins, 'the Old Saxons', into the way of heaven.

In addition to Christian altruism one is bound to suspect that for the English, then as now, simple curiosity about foreign parts was a powerful incentive. In the previous chapter we learnt something of an Anglo-Saxon view of the Middle East through the eyes of Willibald, bishop of Eichstätt, and he started life as a self-admitted travel enthusiast. Recalling his young experiences en route to the Holy Land one June day to an admiring circle in the monastery of Heidenheim, where he was presiding at the translation of his brother Wynnebald's remains, he explained that his plans for a pilgrimage had also been devised in part as 'a means of journeying to foreign countries that were unknown to him . . . and to find out all about them'. As he reminisced, Sister Huneberc (or Hygeburgor) of Heidenheim made notes so as to gather 'a kind of bouquet of the virtues [of this soldier of Christ] . . . and the scenes where the marvels of [Jesus Christ] were enacted'.[12]

Willibald persuaded his reluctant father 'to detach himself from the false prosperity of wealth' to go with him. They sailed on a west wind from Hamwic 'with a high sea running [and] the shouts of sailors and the creaking of oars', buffeted by the wind. The father died at Lucca, where he was venerated as a saint, and his son went on to Rome where he stayed for three years before getting the itch to travel again. In the Holy Land he saw the place in the River Jordan where Jesus Christ was baptized and the very cave where Christ was entombed, with its great square stone a replica of the one the angel rolled away. Leaving the Holy Land he coolly smuggled a calabash of expensive ointment or balsam resin through the Arab customs. Before presenting it for inspection he concealed a little cylinder of petroleum so that when the officers prised open the cover they would smell only the petrol fumes. He spent two years in Constantinople; he visited Sicily, and the volcano on the isle of Vulcano, where a Gothic king had been thrown into Hell for imprisoning a pope. Unfortunately Willibald could not look down into the crater because of the mounds of black 'tartar' drifting like black snow, as he told Huneberc. From Sicily he travelled to Monte Cassino and lived in the monastery there for ten years. Then, at last passing through the Trentino via Lake Garda and so through Bavaria, in 740/41 he arrived at Eichstätt, where he was ordained priest by Boniface and later consecrated as bishop. The travelogue of St Willibald as written down by Huneberc, who seems to have coined its title *Hodoeporicon*, is one of the most intriguing documents to have survived from the Middle Ages . . . and has already detained us far too long.

In her way, the authoress is also most interesting. A contemplative rather than a traveller, she seems a measure of the quality of woman to be found in the communities founded in the wake of the Bonifacian missions to Germany. Besides the *Life* of Willibald (*Vita S.Willibaldi*), of which the *Hodoeporicon* is part, she did a *Life* of his brother St Wynnebald (*d*. 761). Probably a Mercian or West Saxon, she, like St Boniface himself and many English writers, modelled her style on the ornate, mannered and neologistic Latin of Aldhelm of Malmesbury. Since Huneberc may well have entered Heidenheim during the abbacy of Walburga, Wynnebald's sister and successor, it is a pity that she did not write a biography of her.

A nun in the abbey at Wimborne, Walburga was sent to join Abbess Lioba, probably a kinswoman of hers, in Germany before taking up the position at Heidenheim that she inherited from her brother. Of the various monasteries founded by the Anglo-Saxons in Germany, Heidenheim is the only double house, for men and women. After her death in 780 this venerable abbess suffered the fate of having her memory embroiled with the pagan fertility goddess Waldborg, celebrated on 30 April, May Day Eve. Since the relics of Walburga were moved from Heidenheim to Eichstätt on May Day itself, the event came to be confused with the folklore excesses of the witches' Sabbaths supposedly held on the Brocken in the Harz Mountains on *Walpurgisnacht*.

English networking in action

The career of the Frisian Ludger, who died in 809 as bishop of Münster, is a marker for English networking in the Carolingian age.

Born about 744 near Utrecht, the pioneering see of the English mission, the young Ludger went to England where he studied under Alcuin at York until about the age of thirty. In 775 he was posted, presumably at Alcuin's suggestion, to Deventer in Friesland to reinvigorate the community that had been established there by another Anglo-Saxon, Lebuin of Ripon. Later in life he established the bishopric of Münster, with its 'minster'. Years later the memory of Alcuin's teaching at York was still remembered with respect in the cathedral school of his old pupil.

There were family contacts that give the lie to any idea that pre-Conquest England was cut off from the Continent. As we shall see, a German churchman, Egbert of Trier, was proud to trace his ancestry back to King Ecgberht of Wessex, as was Abbess Matilda of Essen. It was for her that Ealdorman Æthelweard (d. 998), a distant kinsman, wrote his Latin translation of the *Anglo-Saxon Chronicle*. He recalls anecdotes about the Anglo-Saxons' origins 'in the forests of Germany' to be found neither in Bede nor the *Chronicle* itself and wrote asking her for any information she might have about their family's doings in Germany. Right at the end of the period (1051) the marriage of Earl Tostig of Northumbria to Judith, half-sister of the Count of Flanders, had its own cultural resonance. When, after his death at Stamford Bridge, she married Welf I of Bavaria the dynastic union opened other avenues of influence linked to the cult of St Oswald in southern Germany.

Thus, it was Oswald of Northumbria, a man who never set foot outside the British Isles, whose cult left its mark at local level on the landscape and folklore of the continent from northern Italy to Scandinavia and Iceland, from the region around Metz (now in France) through Austria and Switzerland to parts of Eastern Europe. Its spread was, in part no doubt, thanks to the wide diffusion of Bede's *Ecclesiastical History*, but the admiring followers of the Northumbrians Wilfrid and Willibrord could be relied upon to sing the praises of the famous saint king of old Northumbria.

Bede's influence is to be traced in the biography of Oswald written about 1050 by the Flemish monk Drogo, though he also evidently had Continental sources to hand. In the next century the saint blossomed into a figure of romance as the eponymous hero of the *'Oswald' Spielmannsepike*, the kind of 'minstrel's epic' popular in aristocratic circles of the German empire. More than 3,500 lines long, and probably written at the imperial city of Ratisbon (modern Regensburg) during the reign of the crusader emperor Frederick I Barbarossa, the poem tells how Oswald falls in love with the daughter of a pagan king, Aron. The royal love quest involves the king's raven, magically able to speak; an expedition of warriors all fitted out with golden crosses at the king's expense; Oswald's marriage; and, need one add, King Aron's conversion to Christianity. In the tenth century the nun and playwright Hrotswitha of Gandersheim (*d.* 1000) wrote a book extolling the achievements of Emperor Otto I (*d.* 973) and claimed that his Anglo-Saxon wife Eadgyth, daughter of Edward the Elder, king of Wessex, also numbered Oswald among her ancestors. The genealogy is dubious but perhaps Hrotswitha took it for granted that any royal Englishwoman taken to wife by the German emperor must have the blood of England's most famous saint king in her veins. (This royal biographer also wrote a number of Latin plays, which she hoped would replace the works of the pagan Terence in monasteries. They probably did since, an advocate of chastity, Hrotswitha outlined in some detail the temptations attendant upon it.)

The place to stay

In the 790s Alcuin opened the pilgrim hostel of St Judoc's, near Quentovic, with funds provided by Charles the Great. This place, now St Josse sur Mer, near Etaples, had associations with English pilgrims since at least the days when St Boniface and his party had pitched their tents there back in the 720s. It soon became a natural rendezvous point for the English on business to the Continent. It would remain tied into a network of Anglo-Saxon/Frankish connections for generations. Alcuin was an important part of the explanation. Founder of the hostel, he was also made abbot of Ferrières by Charles the Great, where he was succeeded by one of his pupils from the York school, the Northumbrian monk Sigulf. Noted as a singer and an expert in the Roman style of plainchant,[13] he also developed Alcuin's traditions of learning at Ferrières. The house reached its peak as a centre of the late Carolingian Renaissance during the abbacy of Servatus Lupus (c. 850–62), like Alcuin also abbot of St Judoc's.

As a letter-writer Lupus prefigures aspects of Italian humanism; as a churchman he was very much involved in the correspondence networking patterns of the ecclesiastical confraternities (one might almost call them 'prayer gilds') introduced to the Continent from England. The house liber vitae, 'book of life', in which the names of departed brothers or of benefactors were inscribed so that they might be remembered in the monks' prayers, was basic. At first little more than single-fold 'diptyches', over the years these expanded into sizeable volumes as individual names were added. Sometimes an entire community would ask to be remembered in the prayers of a brother house, sometimes a neighbour, sometimes someone overseas. When he had finished his lives of St Cuthbert, Bede asked the monks of Lindisfarne to record his name in the 'album' of their house and hence of their confraternity.

Common in early English monasticism, the 'confraternity' was extended into a support network and bonding in the mission field. The letters of Boniface and Alcuin contain many examples of bishops, abbots and even kings included in their prayer families. There is also an excellent letter from Æthelberht II of Kent (725–62) to Boniface in which he mentions a saintly kinswoman of his and recalls how she told him Boniface had agreed to remember her in his prayers. He then asks if the saint would do the same service for him and draws attention to a couple of extremely valuable gifts he is sending with the bearer. Only in the last paragraph does he come to the point – a request for a quite specific and very clearly described type of falcon, which he is sure the churchman should be able to find without too much difficulty.

It was no doubt through his connections with the 'societies' between Ferrières and York that Abbot Lupus first got wind of the famous victory of Aclea won by Æthelwulf of Wessex over the Danes in the year 851. At the time the abbot was in desperate need of lead for the roof of his abbey's church of St Peter and was clearly well aware of the lead mines of Devon, by this time part of Wessex. He wrote to praise the king for God's grace in granting him the victory, praises him for his fabled generosity and offers him the chance of benefiting his soul by sending a sizeable supply of roofing material. He signed off not as abbot of Ferrières but of St Judoc's, knowing the English sentimental attachment to this saint. (In the early tenth century, when King Edward the Elder of Wessex had completed the building of his splendid New Minster at Winchester, the relics of the saint were translated there from across the Channel – as was recorded in the *liber vitae* of the Minster.) The links between England and the Continent forged in the era of the Anglo-Saxon missions would stretch across the centuries.

Distinguished guests expected and received distinguished treatment. On their journey to Rome in 855 the boy Prince Alfred of Wessex and the royal entourage of his father, King Æthelwulf, crossed the Channel to Quentovic where they were handsomely received at St Judoc's; from there they were escorted to the court of Charles the Bald at Soissons. After the mandatory exchange of diplomatic gifts, their host provisioned them for the onward journey and sent them under escort to the borders of his kingdom.[14] From there the way was through the lands of Charles's older brother, Emperor Lothar. The well-mounted column with its escort of household warriors passed unmolested along roads where bandits would pick off less well-protected travellers. It would have been well worth their attentions. Æthelwulf's treasure-house of gifts to St Peter included the sword of a warrior inlaid with gold and a crown of pure gold, four pounds in weight. Fortunately the successors to the Fisherman of Galilee have never had trouble in accommodating such largesse. The populace in general, cleric and lay, were treated to a distribution of gold and silver. Great men liked to make their mark at Rome and one imagines the West Saxon monarch succeeded.

Alcuin and his circle

From the year he joined the Frankish royal court, when he was about fifty, Alcuin passed much of the last twenty-two years of his life on the Continent. His advice was sought by both Frankish and Mercian churchmen. He was in England in 786, the year of church Councils in both Northumbria and Mercia, and again in Northumbria from 790 to 793.[15] Back with the Carolingian court, at Frankfurt, in the following year, he kept in touch with news from home. For example, a little later we find him writing of the affront offered to God by King Eardwulf ('the tyrant'), who is reported to have put away his wife and be living openly with his concubine. Considering that Charlemagne had repudiated a wife and kept six concubines, this seems a bit harsh on Eardwulf![16]

Alcuin's was not an original mind (he adopted 'Albinus', from a second-century AD Greek summarizer of Plato, as his nickname); in fact Latin grammar was his chief expertise. But this suited the times. Charles was less interested in thinkers who could open new directions in philosophy, than scholars who could help run his programme for the revival and consolidation of classical learning. A master of Latin literature and correct written Latin he was ideally qualified for a top position at the palace school, 'which soon became known as 'the School of Master Albinus'. Since Alcuin was also a noted authority on orthodox Roman theology and church liturgy he possessed key skills, given that Rome was keenly interested in Charles's plans in education and church organization – a continuation of the work of Alcuin's English predecessors.

Familiar with the conventions of courtly manners from childhood, Alcuin had quickly found himself at home in the palace school of the Frankish king. The king's consort, together with their sons Charles, aged ten at Alcuin's arrival, Pippin, five years old, and Louis, attended a class made up of sons of the nobility, sent by their fathers at the king's request, and sometimes the fathers themselves. Charles himself never learnt to read or write but he did attend class when he could – we know that he heard the lessons (that is, *lectiones* or 'readings') given by the Italian grammarian Peter of Pisa.

The Frankish court at this time, disdained as a semi-barbarian encampment by the opulent sophisticates at imperial Constantinople, was a remarkable experiment in terms of European cultural history. Charles, whose domains embraced much of the former Roman Empire in Europe, recruited an array of scholars, poets and theologians of diverse ethnic origins to a grand cultural project for the revival of Latin and ancient learning: as well as Alcuin, there were Italians, including Paulinus of Aquileia, the Spanish-born Theodulph, an ethnic Visigoth and the noted Lombard grammarian Paul the Deacon.

Following his conquest of the Lombard kingdom in northern Italy in 774, Charles had been troubled by a short-lived rebellion, in which Paul and his brother, noblemen from Friuli and members of the court at Pavia had been leading spirits. Subject at first to an elegant form of house arrest at Charles's court, Paul had eventually returned to Italy in the late 780s and settled into retirement at Monte Cassino where he devoted himself to his *Historia Langobardorum* ('History of the Lombards'), working on it up to his death in 799. The idea for the work could have been sparked by a conversation or in correspondence with Alcuin, or by a reading of

Bede's *History*, which was widely diffused on the Continent. Certainly his book 'accomplished for the Lombards what Bede's *Historia ecclesiastica* had done for the English, by giving literary expression to a sense of national identity'.[17]

The Carolingian court was a world of nicknames, puckishly distributed by Alcuin to royals and former pupils, all friends. Some seem obvious enough, like Candidus (Latin, 'white') for his English pupil and helper Hwita, who first came to the Continent around 793, or Columba (Latin, 'the dove') for the king's delightful young daughter Rotruda; others were not so immediately obvious, such as his own of 'Albinus' or 'Lucia' for Charles's sister Princess Gisela, abbess of Chelles. One would like to have known Fredegisus, one of his pupils who later joined the teaching staff and kept the Alcuin tradition alive in France, and was surely an impulsive individual: Alcuin always called him 'Nathaniel', the name of the disciple of whom Jesus once said, 'we have here a man without guile.' Angilbert, the young Frankish nobleman who passed through the palace school on his way to a distinguished career in the royal administration, was honoured as 'Homer' for his epic poem on the historic meeting between Charles and Pope Leo III. Arno, archbishop of Salzburg and 'my dearest and closest friend', was playfully dubbed the 'Overseer Eagle', a typical Alcuin pun, in fact a double pun. Like the Latin sourced 'super visor', the Greek word '*episkopos*' from which the Old English *biscop* or bishop ultimately derives, literally means 'over seer', in the sense of 'superintendent', while the archbishop's name was too close to the Old English *earn*, 'eagle' (modern English, erne) for his old friend to resist the wordplay. The image of the great lord of the air, high above the Salzach river plain, eyes peeled ready to swoop on any wrongdoer or malingerer in the cathedral's business, leaps off the page.

Playful and urbane, Alcuin's joshing of his colleagues can mislead us – they were not schoolboys but men of parts and in some cases of importance in the cultural evolution of Europe. These nicknames, though, are frequently cited between the 790s and the 810s in the documentary sources of the Carolingian Renaissance. Asking why it should have been Alcuin in particular who distributed these names, Mary Garrison suggested that it was his ambivalent position at court, as one of authority though not of the establishment, that gave him a reserved status, rather as in certain tribal societies artists and shamans, although not elders, are accorded the respect associated with witchcraft.[18] (It is surely intriguing in this context that in a 1990s French television dramatized series on the world of Charlemagne, Alcuin is featured in passing as a kind of Merlin figure encountered by Charlemagne in a woodland chapel.)

The 'Circle of Alcuin' radiated its influence through Europe to Fulda and, later, to the great Irish-born philosopher John Scotus Erigena at the court of Charles the Bald and to the school of Auxerre in the early 900s. An important text from the period dealing with philosophy and logic, and known to scholars as 'the Munich passages', was very probably the work of 'Candidus'; if true, it has been claimed this would make him the outstanding philosopher of his generation.[19]

Everyone around the court knew that the king was nicknamed 'David', after the great king of Israel, warrior and poet, reputed author of the Psalms. Charles's (dictated) letters reveal a sharp mind keen to debate serious issues and happy to correct textual faults in material sent to him. The year before Charles was to be crowned emperor by the pope, Alcuin wrote to 'the most religious . . . King David' and, among other things, thanks him 'for having the book which I sent on your instructions read in your hearing and its errors noted and sent back for correction'. Another letter, from the king's 'old soldier' – Alcuin was in his late sixties at the time – shows that the king's thirst for learning could, at times, be rather trying. 'A runner has just arrived with a sheet of questions urging this weak-witted old man to examine the heavens . . . to expound the erratic courses of the planets.' Protesting that the movement of the planets through the zodiac is not really his subject, he at first suggests Charles refer to the writings of Bede, 'the educator of our Land', or Pliny the Younger, before relenting and agreeing that if he can be sent a copy of Pliny he'll prepare some replies. We are left to guess as to what made the planetary movements of such pressing importance to Charles at this time, but it is entirely in keeping with what we know of that great man that he should send an express messenger to get the answer.

For more than twenty years York scholar and Frankish monarch were in regular contact, often by letter. More than 300 of Alcuin's letters survive (more than for any other Englishman of the Middle Ages, even Boniface). Since Alcuin often travelled with the peripatetic court and even once followed the king on campaign, their relations were generally close and, for the times, informal. But on those rare occasions when Alcuin felt he must question royal policy, he was careful to use the greatest formalities of address: 'To Charles, King of Germany, Gaul and Italy, the most excellent and devout lord', runs the opening of a strong critique on the question of tithes. This ten per cent charge, levied on agricultural produce and income for the good of the church and clergy, was resented even in well-established Christian communities. When Charles imposed it on newly conquered territories and recent converts, Alcuin feared that resentment could threaten rebellion and apostasy. He urged the king to forego the levy: it was better to lose the tithe than endanger the Faith.

News of the sack of Lindisfarne in June 793 prompted a long letter from Alcuin to Æthelred of Northumbria. He bemoans the desecration of St Cuthbert's church, the spattered blood of its priests and the plunder taken by the pagans. But he writes more in anger than in sorrow about what he calls the worst atrocity since the English arrived in Britain nearly three hundred and fifty years earlier (clearly he accepts Bede's date for the *adventus saxonum* of AD 449). In a Jeremiad that warns of worse to come if ways are not mended, he inveighs against 'fornication, adultery and incest . . . even among nuns', against 'greed, robbery and judicial violence', against luxurious dress and against the fashion for pagan hair style and beard trims. It appears that some clerics were so unprincipled as to hunt mammals with dogs! Soon after his elevation as archbishop of York, Eanbald, a pupil of Alcuin's, received a letter of exhortation that would have earned the moral approval of today's House of Commons. 'Let not your companions', he writes, 'gallop hallooing across the fields after foxes'; while elsewhere he deplores the frivolous novices at Jarrow who, he hears, prefer to dig out foxes' earths and go hare coursing rather than worship Christ.[20] Alcuin, who like Boniface had heard reports of drunkenness among English monks, urges sobriety. Elsewhere a telling aside reveals that, while regulations as to the correct vestments for the religious offices might be disregarded, people scrupulously observed due order 'of age and rank' at the refectory dinner table. It is another reminder that the ranks of English monastic life were well staffed with members of the upper social classes.

As to the actual conduct of the service in the chapel, he has much to say on music. First and foremost it should be sung according to the Roman rite. He, like his English predecessors in Europe, insisted on it. After his death, a cleric at the church of Metz remembered how as a boy Alcuin, 'the wisest teacher of our whole country', had taught his class the Roman (presumably Gregorian) chant. The boys would also have been told to sing in a disciplined manner, neither florid nor overloud, since Alcuin, like many another churchman, reckoned singers were all too ready to show off.

Teacher and scholar

Alcuin was one of the regular intimates participating in word games and verse exchanges at court, drafting correspondence for the king-emperor and taking a leading part in a public theological debate before Charles with a team of Spanish bishops. At this time, too, work began on assembling definitive written texts of the courses he had been teaching at the palace school for years, and much else beside.

He wrote guides to orthography, grammar and rhetoric as well as aspects of astronomy, was passionate about punctuation and prolific in writing analyses of biblical texts. He set new standards for accuracy in the copying of texts in the scriptorium It has even been suggested that his meticulous rules for the pronunciation of Latin (in his *Dialogus de Rhetorica*) may have influenced the direction of the emerging French language.[21] In the Romance-speaking areas of Europe, where Latin was evolving into the modern languages of French, Italian, Spanish and so forth, bad pronunciation, grammatical irregularities and slang idioms ('vulgarisms') were slipping into acceptability as 'Latin'. Alcuin's passion for rhetoric led him to one important and original development – the treatise addressed to the ruler linking rhetoric with the business of ruling. He was convinced that eloquence of speech was a tool by which the ruler could persuade men to do what was just and good. His treatise to Charles the Great on this theme was the first of many such works by scholars at courts of the Carolingian age.

Towards the end of his career Alcuin seems to have provoked jealousy among colleagues. In a letter to his community in York in 795 we find Alcuin protesting that he did not go to Francia 'for love of gold' but for the 'strengthening of catholic doctrine'. He did pretty well nevertheless. The revenues of no fewer than three religious houses (Ferrières, Maastricht and Troyes) were awarded to him, while the appointment as abbot of the immensely rich monastery of St Martin's at Tours meant a comfortable, if busy, life. In office there for just eight years and in the declining years of his life, he strengthened the place's reputation as a seat of learning, stocking the library with copies of 'rare learned books which I had in my own land' (that is, Northumbria). He writes to the emperor that everything he needs

can be supplied from York and asks Charles to pay the expense of
sending students north to 'bring back the flowers of Britannia to
Gaul . . . so that the garden of York may supply off-shoots of
paradise-bearing fruit', intended for what Alcuin called elsewhere
the smoky roofs of Tours.

During the seemingly placid career of a scholar, Alcuin had risen
to a position of eminence in the business of state and influence
over many of his fellow human beings: the head of religious houses,
adviser to a king-emperor, and director of programmes and cultural institutions such as the schools of those houses. Writing in
his *The Carolingian Empire* (Oxford, 1957), the German scholar
H. Fichtenau commented that 'Alcuin had crossed the English
Channel with a single companion. In the end he was lord of many
thousand human beings.'

In April 799 the new pope, Leo III, who had created Charles
'Patrician of the Romans', had been forced by opponents who
accused him of misdemeanours to flee the Holy City and seek
Charles's protection. In November 799 a commission appointed by
Charles restored the pope at Rome. In April 800 the king visited
Alcuin at Tours. We do not know what they discussed. Then in the
autumn he went to Rome in person to 'restore the state of the
church'. It seems that at this time Charles may have been planning
to assume the title of 'emperor' in the sense of 'a streamlined king
who ruled over several nations'.[22] On Christmas Day of that year,
800, however, at mass in St Peter's, as he rose from his knees, it was
to find Leo placing a crown upon his head and the crowd hailing
him as 'Emperor of the Romans'. One assumes that Alcuin, a good
churchman, approved the honour done to King 'David'; the recipient may have been less pleased.

Viking raids were to destroy much of the complex at Tours,
including Alcuin's tomb and epitaph, yet the cathedral school was
one of Europe's leading educational centres before the advent of
universities in the twelfth century. As Louise Cochrane observed in

her book *Adelard of Bath: The First English Scientist*, 'The develop-ment of the cathedral schools in Europe, stem[med] from that founded for Charlemagne by Alcuin of York at Tours and a later one by Fulbert at Chartres.'[23]

As he got older, Alcuin was subject to recurrent fits of illness, malaria has been suggested, and he may also have been troubled by a cataract. But he kept hard at work. In 800 he writes that the king, soon to be emperor, has charged him with a revision of the Old and New Testaments – in other words he was working on the text of St Jerome's Latin Bible known as the Vulgate, completed some 300 years earlier. Over the centuries the text had become corrupt thanks to copyists' errors and confusion over other old Latin versions. A major casualty had been punctuation, 'which greatly improves the style of a sentence' and, in Alcuin's opinion, was as much in need of restoration as was fine scholarship and fine learning.

The scriptorium at Tours was kept busy multiplying copies of the new Bible under Alcuin's supervision (it seems to have reached England by the 820s). They surely followed the injunctions of the 'General admonition' (*Admonitio generalis*) issued by Charles in 789 for the better ordering of church and society within his dominions. The imprint of Alcuin's concepts is to be found everywhere in the document, both in language and in content.[24] Typical is the instruc-tion that when a new Gospel or service book is to be copied, the work must be entrusted to a trained man not a boy. The copyists wrote in the elegant and highly legible 'Carolingian miniscule' let-tering, which would provide the model for some of the finest early printing types centuries later. Alcuin was responsible for the beau-tiful book design and reader-friendly page layout and ensured the distribution of the copies to monasteries and cathedral churches throughout the Frankish empire.

Among Alcuin's students were two young Germans, Einhard (770–840), the future biographer of Charles the Great, and Rabanus, a decade his junior. Aged nine, Einhard had entered the

school at Fulda, founded by Boniface; in 791 he graduated, so to
speak, to the palace school where Alcuin, its most prominent
teacher, numbered the king and his family as well as young courtiers
among his pupils. In later life Einhard recalled the great teacher as
'a man most learned in every field'.[25] Thus one of the most celebrated figures of the Carolingian Renaissance followed his entire
educational career in establishments either inspired by the ideals of
an English founder or conducted under the aegis of an English
teacher. It is generally supposed that when the Welsh bishop Asser
came to write his biography of King Alfred of Wessex he may have
taken the idea for writing a biography of his royal master
from Einhard's book on Charles the Great. This would hardly be
surprising, since both were in that wide circle of cultural exchange
initiated by the English missions to the Continent.

   Yet more important was Alcuin's influence on Rabanus (also
Hrabanus, c. 780–856), born at Mainz when Boniface's English successor, Lull, was still bishop. Nicknamed 'Maurus' by Alcuin, after
a disciple of St Benedict, he was trained at Fulda before being sent
by the abbot to spend a year or two at Tours under Alcuin. He was
then appointed director of the monastic school at Fulda. Under him
'the Tours of the North' became the leading centre of learning in
the German world. The English tradition is apparent. Like Alcuin's
beloved York, Fulda's library amassed a treasury of books. Like
Alcuin, Rabanus was a prolific if unoriginal author and his book on
grammar draws heavily on Priscian, Alcuin and Bede. In another
important way, the cultivation of the vernacular, Rabanus, remembered as *praeceptor Germaniae* ('Teacher of Germany'), may also have
been inspired by English precepts. By a decree of 748 Boniface had
insisted that priests should 'require from persons presenting themselves for baptism an affirmation of Faith and Renunciation of the
Devil in their mother-tongue'.[26] With the endorsement of Charles
the Great, the German church made use of the vernacular in parts
of the church liturgy.

The time that Rabanus was at Fulda (803–40) saw the creation of the long religious epic *Der Heliand* ('The Saviour'), written in Old Saxon by a poet possibly trained at Fulda. Since it is a retelling of the Gospel story, it is not a Germanic epic as such but it depicts the history of Jesus Christ in terms that would have been familiar to its target audience, the Old Saxons, and indeed to any Anglo-Saxon expatriates still to be found in the German religious world. This Jesus is a warrior king, a ring-giver (*bôggeðo*), and his disciples or '*theganos*' owe him the full allegiance until death due to a lord: in short, a Jesus from the world of Beowulf.

7

VIKING RAIDERS, DANELAW, 'KINGS' OF YORK

The sack of Lindisfarne in June 793, which caused Alcuin such anguish, had in modern terms been a catastrophe waiting to happen. The coastal site, so convenient for the raiders, had been chosen, like that of many another monastic community from Whitby in the east to Iona in the west, as a rugged retreat ideal for the contemplative life and remote from interruptions by the secular world. In the century that was to come the British Isles, like the rest of Europe, would become accustomed to incursions by alien and brutal raiders who targeted church properties as they would treasure hoards, and pillaged the countryside for supplies as well as for plunder. Richard Abels, a specialist in military history, estimates that a war band numbering in the upper hundreds would have consumed at least a ton of grain a day and its horses up to seven times as much in fodder.

These raiders terrorized the peasant population and displaced ruling dynasties; in the end they seemed likely to overturn the entire cultural project of Christian England. The tradition of fine script and manuscript production in Northumbria, such as the accomplished Roman display scripts (uncial and half uncial), for which Monkwearmouth-Jarrow was noted, appears to have been broken by the half-century of Viking disruption between 835 and 885.[1] Writing a century after the event, and one suspects with the wisdom of hindsight, the *Anglo-Saxon Chronicle* speaks of the year of Lindisfarne as one of dragons in the sky. The Vikings' dragon-prowed ships on the seaways would cause much more havoc.

This chapter aims to trace the history of devastation, warfare and resistance that saw the evolution of these raiders into settlers, like the Anglo-Saxons before them. The great work in which military planning, social restructuring and governmental initiative made possible the restoration of that culture during the reign of Alfred the Great of Wessex will be the principal theme of chapter 8. Here the king features as war leader against the raiders.

Many monks were killed at Lindisfarne and many treasures lost, but the relics of St Cuthbert and the great Gospel book survived, though we no longer have the original binding and cover. A 'book shrine' worthy of the sacred words it enclosed, it was adorned with ornamentation in gold, precious stones and silver gilding, the work of Billfrith the Anchorite. This, too, seems to have escaped the raiders of 793, judging by a note in the book in a mid-tenth century hand. Evidently the monastery's great treasure had been well guarded. Did it perhaps, have a full-time guardian? After all, the attack on that June day came, almost literally, out of a clear sky. If the great jewelled book had been seen by one of the plunderers, at the very least the encrusted cover would have been hacked off. Elsewhere, in later raids, the massive parchment volumes of religious and cultural manuscripts, with their gold leaf and gilded lettering, were incinerated so that the precious metal could be poured off and harvested from the ashes. This made good sense. Unable to read and in no sense multiculturally aware, the sea robber may have been fearful of magic spells in the strange black tracings on the page, but he certainly valued gold.

Archaeology indicates that life of a sort continued at Lindisfarne once the raiders had gone on their way. The surviving monks no doubt gave a decent burial to those of their brothers slaughtered by the barbarians, tidied up their ruined buildings and set about the business of restoring lost treasures, supposing they had the inventive genius and the technical capacities needed. For their part, the cottagers in the lee of a ravaged minster would return to work their land and possibly replace torched wattle and daub homesteads. Given a good growing season and good crops the material impact of the disaster would fade soon enough. 'For the ordinary person in Britain', to follow Julian Richards, such raids 'may have had little impact'. But ordinary people rarely leave much of interest. And whether or not such raids had much or little impact on them, the Viking age in general had a catastrophic impact on the general cultural life of the Anglo-Saxon kingdoms.

The eighth century has been called the 'age of the minsters', as it was also the flourishing time of the emporia, at home and abroad – London and Alcuin's York in England, Dorestad in Frisia. The merchant centres diminished almost to extinction during the ninth century and many of the great churches disappeared (the first abbey at Peterborough was destroyed in the 870s). This coincided with an upsurge in Viking incursions.

The invaders, raiders and origins

Early contacts of the Scandinavian homelands with Western Europe and the Mediterranean involved trading in the traditional products of the region, such as amber, skins, furs and, no doubt, slaves. It has been argued that Sutton Hoo and some of the objects found there indicate links between the East Anglian dynasty and Sweden from the very beginnings of the Anglo-Saxon period. *Beowulf* tells of a raiding expedition from southern Sweden to the lands of the Rhine basin dated to the sixth century. In the fifth century Swedish settlements on the island of Gotland were reaching across the Baltic. Here, in the region of Stockholm and in parts of Denmark, huge finds of Islamic coins running into the thousands testify to vigorous exchanges, whether by way of war or of trade in the ninth and tenth centuries.

Of course, the prime military secret of the sea rovers' success was the long double-ended ship that they used, with dragon-headed prow and (sometimes stern) posts. Developed over centuries, it had evolved by the eighth century into one of the most beautiful of human artefacts, as is clear from the famous Gokstad ship. This was an open long boat, clinker built (that is, with overlapped planking, secured with iron nails), upwards of 45 feet (14 m) long and powered by a square-rigged sail and some forty oarsmen.

For the victims a Viking raid was terrifying enough, even without the Hollywood-style horned helmets of tradition. If they wore helmets at all, and hardly any have been unearthed by archaeologists, these were most probably conical in shape, like those shown on the Bayeux Tapestry. The raiders struck fear wherever they went and, thanks to England's many rivers, whose meandering reaches were navigable to the shallow-draft dragon ships far inland, were often able to achieve near total surprise – especially when they were able to seize horses. Grave goods in Danish burial sites often include stirrups and harness fittings, suggesting that Danish Vikings at least were experienced horsemen, capable of hard riding across country. In 860 a 'great pirate force' crossed the Channel from raiding in Francia and appeared before the West Saxon capital of Winchester, which lies 12 miles (19 km) inland. Winchester was saved from the sack by a combined force drawn from the counties of Hampshire, under its ealdorman Osric, and Berkshire under Ealdorman Æthelberht. The raiders sailed back to their interrupted campaign in Francia.

The Vikings' reputation has been sanitized over the past thirty years or so, and attention has turned to their home lives and trading activities in Dublin, York or Scandinavia. From an English point of view they represented a murderous marauding banditry. Back home they were those adventurous seafaring heroes bringing back wealth and honour to their communities. Silver hoards more than 100 pounds (45 kg) in weight have been found buried in the Viking homelands. Why is not obvious. One supposes that enemy raids were not to be feared here! Maybe, in the absence of bank vaults, burial was the only solution. Julian Richards, in his *Blood of the Vikings*, intriguingly suggests that 'maybe it was just simply showing off, burying so much wealth being the ultimate way to demonstrate to your neighbours that you had silver to spare.' One thinks of the 'potlatch' ceremonies among the Kwakiutl Indians of the Northwest Pacific coast of North America, in which great quantities of wealth, measured in blankets, are disposed of in competitive status displays; in another type of potlatch valuable sheets of copper were actually 'destroyed' when sunk out at sea.

The origin of the term 'viking' (generally spelt with a capital 'V') is debated. One theory derives it from the southern stretch of the Oslofjord, known as the Vik, and the supposition that the first 'Vikings' came from there. According to another view, it was used in the Scandinavian homelands to describe (usually) young 'pirates', who went 'a-viking' for a season or two in search of adventure and riches, under a captain or chieftain of a ship or flotilla. For as long as the leader was successful his followers gave allegiance, very much as a household warrior did to his lord. As always the point of view is vital. In the villages and fjords to which they returned laden with wealth and treasures, the term denoted adventurous young tearaways, violent perhaps but above all heroic members of the war band, a credit to the homeland. Their victims, possibly prejudiced, did not share this view. For a start, profit and plunder were the purpose of their ventures, not heroism. The raiders preferred to operate from a fortified encampment from which they could pillage and terrorize an unarmed (it was to be hoped) population and to whose protection they could return should fighting men come on the scene. In the words of Patrick Wormald, the Vikings, if not actually mad, 'were probably bad and certainly dangerous to know'.[2] In any case the victims had various words for their oppressors: 'heathen', 'pagans', 'North men', even 'Danes' were just a few.

In a famous entry for the reign of King Beorhtric (*d.* 802), the *Anglo-Saxon Chronicle* speaks of the first of 'the Danish men who sought out the land of the English race'.[3]

Perhaps the terminology hardly mattered, since in both the English Danelaw and French Normandy the raiders did eventually settle in conquered territories. Little wonder if Frankish and English chronicles tended to view the Vikings or *Nortmanni* as a scourge from God as punishment for the failure of their societies to live according to his precepts. Did not the Old Testament warn 'Out of the north shall an evil break forth upon . . . the land' (Jeremiah 1:14)?

The northern world: Ireland, Isle of Man, Orkneys

The Vikings' countries of origin are not always clear, though the 'Vikings' of Russia came from Sweden, while the colonizers of Iceland towards the end of our period, and from there to Greenland and then on to 'Vinland', the Scandinavian colony on the mainland of North America, were mostly Norwegians and of Norwegian descent. The same is true of the Scandinavian populations of Ireland, the Orkney and Shetland Islands, the Hebrides, the Faroes and the Isle of Man. Excavations in the 1990s by a team from the University of York at the village of Tarbat, on the north-east coast of Scotland, revealed smashed sculpture and charred building rubble together with sword-hacked skeletal remains, all of which together pointed to a religious site – a Pictish monastery probably – sacked by Vikings.

Ireland soon came under attack. The written sources record Vikings raiding no fewer than fifty sites, but one assumes many more places suffered without benefit of memorial. For the general memory endured. Written in the twelfth century, the *Cogadh Gáedhel re Gallaibh* ('Wars of the Irish with the Foreigners') keened over the depredations of 'this ruthless, wrathful, foreign, purely pagan people . . . upon the suffering folk of Ireland . . . men and women, lay and priest, noble and base, old and young . . .'[4] Sometimes, regrettably, it seems that Viking followed in the footsteps of Christian. The rival kings of the island and their war bands traded rapine and slaughter with an even hand, recruiting 'the foreigners' as mercenaries both on land and sea. Between the 840s and the 940s the monastery at Clonmacnoise in the heart of Ireland was ravaged six times by the Vikings and eleven times by Christian cohorts.[5] Expelled from Ireland in 902, the 'foreigners' returned in 917; lured by slave trading, the Scandinavian presence was reestablished on the river estuaries at Dublin, Wexford, Cork and Limerick.

In Britain, too, slavery was endemic. In the west 'stock' was acquired in raiding among Welsh princes, in tribute paid by these princes to 'foreign' raiders, by princely claimants sometimes allied with the slaving fleets,[6] and from cross-border raiding between England and Wales. In the 1060s and 1070s Bishop Wulfstan of Worcester campaigned long and hard to stop the slave trade from Bristol to Ireland.[7] From the late ninth century Anglo-Saxon wills contain instructions about the freeing of the testator's slaves, while the Lichfield Gospels contains some such texts in Welsh for the early tenth century. Apparently the powerful Wessex dynasty of Godwine profited from the trade in the eleventh century.

The European dimension

From the 780s or 790s, when three shiploads of sea raiders landed on the south coast and pillaged into Wessex, to 1016, when Cnut of the royal house of Denmark became king in England, the country was subject to sporadic attacks of plunder and settlement of greater or lesser intensity from 'Viking' sea rovers. The period of the attacks can be divided between the 'First Viking Age', from about

780 to about 900 and the 'Second Viking Age' from the 980s onwards. This chapter deals with the first, chapter 11 with the second. During that first age England shared a common fate with the coasts of Scotland and the Isles, the kingdoms of Ireland, the territories of the Carolingian empire and its successor states, and the river networks of Russia from Novgorod to Kiev and from west to east. According to the early twelfth-century *Povest Vremennykh Let* ('Account of Years Gone By'), also known as the *Chronicle of Nestor* or *Kiev Chronicle*, which covers events in the land of Rus from the 850s to the 1110s and is the only European vernacular annals to match the *Anglo-Saxon Chronicle* in scope, the country owed its name to a Scandinavian people under their leader Rurik. Invited in by the feuding citizens of the northern emporium of Novgorod to sort out their differences, Rurik extended his influence southwards to found the city of Kiev.

In Western Europe things were bad enough in Charles the Great's later years for the emperor to order the construction of a fleet of ships to patrol the coast north of the Seine estuary against the pirate shipping there. Warfare amongst his descendants and the decline of Frisian sea power in the ninth century opened the way to worse depredations. From the 830s to the 880s we find records of raids into the Low Countries (the great emporium of Dorestad was sacked as many as four times in the 830s alone), into Provence, down the Gironde and Garonne to Bordeaux and up the Dordogne, up the Loire as far as Orléans, up the Seine to Paris and beyond, raids into Picardy as far as Amiens, and up the Rhine as far as Cologne.

Did these raiders, one wonders, sometimes enjoy the tacit approval of their own authorities, so to speak – rather like the English privateers of Queen Elizabeth, who robbed the Spanish treasure fleets lumbering back across the Atlantic with their plunder from the Amerindian civilizations? In the 830s we find King Harthacnut I of Denmark assuring the Carolingian emperor Louis the Pious that he would execute the ringleaders of a Viking band that had been raiding in Francia the previous year. At this time the pagan Danes and Danish Vikings did not necessarily observe undertakings made to Christian rulers – no doubt, like later Christian crusaders in dealings with Muslim powers, they did not regard pledges made to non-believers as binding. Louis's son Charles the Bald tried to buy off one war band, only to find its leader making a deal with another. The *Anglo-Saxon Chronicle* comments on certain of these raids, notably in northern France, in some detail (though it has much less to say about the Viking presence in the northern Isles and Ireland). The *Annals of St Vaast*, compiled at the monastery near Arras, fill out a harrowing picture of ramparts in ruins, people led off for slaves, houses in flames:

> Along the open streets the dead are lying – priests, laymen, nobles, women, youths and little children. Everywhere tribulation and sorrow meet the eye, seeing Christian folk [killed or] brought to utter ruin and desolation.[8]

By strengthening old Roman forts or building new forts and combining *pagi* or districts in the area, the counts of Flanders would lay the basis of their power as protectors in the region.

Reports by European chroniclers tell of rapid raiders switching pressure points at will, their flotillas banking well up the river courses, delivering warrior troops that seized horses and rode and looted at will across country. If superior forces arrived the raiders quit the region and in the last resort would retreat back to their ships and depart for some other land – only to return once an army had been disbanded and the territory was defenceless again. The Winchester–Francia pattern noted at the head of this chapter was typical. The ideal defence was attack, with a standing army at the ready, fortified defence positions and, ideally, a specialized fleet standing by. This was precisely the defensive formula Alfred the Great of Wessex was to adopt, as we shall see in the next chapter.

The Wessex front

King Beorhtric of Wessex (786–802), who, it will be remembered, had been married to the notorious Eadburh of Mercia and was almost certainly a client king to her father Offa, was followed on the throne by King Ecgberht, described as the eighth bretwalda by the *Anglo-Saxon Chronicle*. By 830 he had extended the sway of Wessex northwards to the Humber and eastwards into Essex. The triumph was brief. Not only did Wiglaf of Mercia claw back his position but in mid-decade Ecgberht (who died in 839) confronted a new danger – a seaborne attack by Viking raiders on the Isle of Sheppey in the Thames, the first such since the death of Beohrtric's reeve at Portland some forty years before. After Sheppey, thirty-five shiploads descended on the coast of Somerset; the king 'held the place of slaughter'. Two years later a great pirate 'ship army' came to Cornwall and found eager allies among the local British. Once again the West Saxons were victorious under their king, crushing the combined force at Hingston Down on the Cornish side of the Tamar river. For the next thirty years Ecgberht's son and grandsons faced almost annual fire-fights against such coastal incursions from what the Chronicles variously call 'heathen men' and Danes. Southampton, Winchester, London were just some of the places to suffer.

In 851 a force of 350 ships sailed into the Thames estuary, sacked London and put to flight a Mercian army under King Beorhtwulf. He was succeeded by Burgred. The same year Æthelwulf of Wessex and his two eldest sons won their famous victory over the Danes at Aclea, possibly in Surrey, and then a great sea victory off Sandwich. This raised the king's stock on the Continent and two years later, in alliance with Burgred of Mercia, he won a great victory over the Welsh. But the Viking threat was relentless. Before Æthelwulf's death in January 858 the raiders had over-wintered on the Isle of Sheppey in Kent and pillaged at will in East Anglia. Over the next two decades, in the words of Richard Abels, to whom much of this account is indebted, the struggles of his sons 'were to be ceaseless, heroic, and largely futile'.

In 860 raiders sacked Winchester before moving northwards to the Berkshire Downs, trawling the countryside with fire and sword for plunder. The men of Dorset and Berkshire under the command of their ealdormen were ready for them as they headed back to their ships, slowed down by loot-laden pack animals. Those raiders who stood their ground were cut to pieces; the rest, according to Asser, 'fled the place of slaughter like women'. Wessex had been the victim of an overspill from Viking activity in the basin of the River Seine. A major pirate expedition had set up its headquarters on the Isle d'Oissel, dangerously near to Paris. Charles the Bald had come to a deal with another company of pirates operating along the Somme to pay them well if they would turn gamekeeper and deal with the Oissel company. Having taken hostages, the Somme Vikings took time off across the Channel while he raised the cash from his hapless subjects.

The Battle for England

In 865 the men of Kent promised money to a force that had landed on the Isle of Thanet, but the enemy exploited the truce to overrun the entire eastern part of the kingdom. In that same year a number of Danish sea armies led by Ivar the Boneless and his brothers Halfdan and Ubba, joined forces seemingly for a massed campaign against England. They wintered in East Anglia 'and were provided with horses', the *Chronicle* records. It dubbed this new force the '*micel hæðen here*', 'great heathen army' or 'raiding army'. Sir Frank Stenton, the doyen of twentieth-century Anglo-Saxon studies, saw 865 as a turning point: a time when what had been uncoordinated bands of raiders coalesced into an army in the formal sense of the word with a thought-out strategy of conquest.

For more than a decade major forces ravaged the country from York to Wessex.

During this period two of the great historic kingdoms of the Angles, Mercia and Northumbria, were removed from the map as independent Anglo-Saxon states to be replaced by the Viking territory or 'kingdom' of York and a region of effectively autonomous communities subject to Danish law in the eastern half of England. For this region of 'Danelaw', the depredations of the raiders were such that virtually no charters survive from the pre-Scandinavian invasion era. Only in the kingdom of Wessex and the Lordship of Bamburgh in the extreme north did Anglo-Saxon sway hold. It hardly seems too much to describe the late ninth century as the age of 'the battle for England'. The winning of this battle would occupy most of the reign of Alfred the Great of Wessex, at this time a serious-minded but warlike teenager, who was to become king in six years time.

In the spring of 866 the great army headed first for York. We do not know why they made this rather surprising switch of target away from the heartlands of England. Scandinavian legend was to claim that it was to avenge the memory of Ivar's father, the legendary Ragnar Lothbrok, tortured to death at York some years earlier. Though why, if that were so, the army did not sail direct to the city and its emporium the previous year is left unexplained. It may be relevant that Northumbria's neighbour, the British kingdom of Strathclyde, was at this time coming under attack from the Norsemen of Dublin and Man.[9]

At all events the army was tidying up the old Roman defences of York by November 866 and the following spring faced an English force, led by the two current contenders in Northumbria's seemingly interminable civil conflict, momentarily united against the common foe. There followed a bloody and protracted battle among the ruinous structures of Roman York. The Northumbrians, we are told by the *Peterborough Chronicle*, did great slaughter there but when their two 'kings' fell, surrounded in death by loyal companions, the rest came to terms. The English kingdom of Northumbria was, bar a couple of puppet reigns, at an end.

That autumn the army marched south into Mercia where they prepared to winter in Nottingham. The Mercian king Burgred appealed to his brother-in-law Æthelred of Wessex for help but the combined English forces were unable to force the issue and the army was able to retreat on York and winter there. The following year, 869, the army marched south from York, following a Roman road for part of the route to make winter camp at Thetford in East Anglia. In November the men of East Anglia under their king, Edmund, went out to Hoxne to fight the heathen. But the Danes had the victory, killed the king and conquered the land. In such bald words the *Anglo-Saxon Chronicle*, it seems, would mean to tell us that Edmund died in battle. Alfred's biographer Asser, writing some twenty years after the event, took that to be the case. King Edmund of the East Angles, he wrote, died fighting fiercely with a great part of his army. This was the fitting death for a Christian hero king in the tradition of St Oswald and many another. Edmund's hagiographer, writing more than a century later, has it otherwise – as does tradition.

From the evidence of his coinage Edmund had reigned for some years. A generation after his death, commemorative coins were being struck to 'Saint' Edmund. A further fifty years on, during his stay at Ramsey Abbey (985–7), the Franco-Flemish monk Abbo of Fleury wrote his 'Passion of St Edmund'. He had the story from St Dunstan, who in turn had heard it from Edmund's armour-bearer, 'a very old man'. According to him, rather than be the cause of the shedding of Christian blood by giving battle, Edmund chose martyrdom. Like Jesus Christ he was mocked by the Danish soldiery; like St Sebastian he was shot full of arrows. John Blair tells us in *The Church in Anglo-Saxon England* (2005) that by the early eleventh century Europe's kings were being urged to emulate the suffering Christ, not Christ in majesty.

Alfred: Warlord against the Danes

After Hoxne the army laid waste the country round about and
utterly destroyed the abbey of Medeshamstede/Peterborough,
killing the abbot and all its monks and bringing 'to nought what
had once been mighty'.[10] The site would remain a wilderness landscape for the best part of a century. The following year, led by
Halfdan, Ivar's brother, the army crossed over into Wessex and made
its base at Reading, a well-provisioned and strategically placed royal
vill. King Æthelred and his brother Prince Alfred raised an army and
marched on Reading, while Æthelwulf the ealdorman of Berkshire
led the shire levies against a Viking foraging party and defeated
it. But a few days later the main Viking army defeated the full West
Saxon force and Ealdorman Æthelwulf was killed. A native of
Mercia, his body was rescued from the battlefield and taken back to
his home town for burial. The two royal brothers barely escaped
with their lives – and yet they rallied their forces again. In January
871 on the chalk ridge at Ashdown on the Berkshire downs, possibly near Streatley, they avenged the humiliation with a resounding
victory. The West Saxons attacked in two forces, Alfred leading the
first charge up the hill, 'like a wild boar', at the enemy shield wall;
his brother King Æthelred had remained to hear the end of mass in
his tent, before coming up with the main body to deliver the decisive blow. Halfdan's brother 'King' Bagsecg and five Viking jarls
(earls) were among the dead. Yet two weeks later Alfred and
Æthelred were defeated 'in open battle by the Danes at Basing'.

Alfred came to the throne with the death of his brother Æthelred
in April 871. He had reason to be apprehensive. Recurring warfare
was sapping the kingdom's manpower; the enemy by contrast could
expect reinforcement with every new fleet. Early in May he was in
action near the royal vill of Wilton, in the heart of historic Wessex.
Towards the end of a hard-fought day, the enemy turned as if in
rout. It was a feint. The English broke ranks in pursuit and were

defeated. The young king had failed to win victory in his first general command. As in their dealings with Frankish rulers, the Danes were able to enforce a cash payment as the price of peace. They pulled back to winter in London in Mercian territory.

In 875 Halfdan with a part of the raiding army went north from Repton and wintered on the River Tyne. The other part of the army under 'King' Guthrum and two others marched from Repton to Cambridge. (That summer the *Chronicle* records a sea victory against seven ships' companies.) At this period the defence of Wessex depended on land forces called to the king's service in response to an actual threat, and the muster took time. The Danes, being in an almost permanent state of war-readiness, could strike without warning. In early autumn 875 they were able to march virtually unopposed halfway across West Saxon territory to occupy the royal burh of Wareham in Dorset. Bounded by rivers and with its halls and outbuildings protected by palisaded defence works proper to such a site, it was an ideal base for Viking operations against the surrounding countryside, and its capture was a telling demonstration of the kingdom's vulnerability. Such sites were hardly castles in the Norman sense, but rather a kind of fortified premises against outlaws and robbers; any attempt to breach them attracted a scale of penalty or *burgbryce* in the law code of King Ine.

Alfred assembled his army and laid siege. The Danes gave their pledge, sworn on a ring sacred to the god Thor, to abandon hostilities; Alfred gave hostages as surety for his good faith. Evidently Thor did not hold his devotees bound by any oath sworn to unbelievers. Breaking the oath and slaughtering the hostages, the enemy made good their escape from Wareham and struck south to Exeter. They evidently anticipated the arrival of reinforcements from a fleet coasting down the Channel. When it was wrecked by storms off the Dorset coast, they found themselves encircled at Exeter with no escape. Again the Vikings swore oaths, but this time they kept them – for the time being. They crossed back into Mercia, where they made Gloucester their base and where their client king Ceolwulf made over part of the kingdom to them.

Wessex was still under dire threat. Guthrum ruled in East Anglia and controlled Mercia. No help could be expected from the distant north where the Anglian royal houses were split by now meaning-less rivalries and the Vikings of York dominated the old kingdom of Deira. After decades as raiders, the Scandinavian invaders were settling in as colonialists. And Guthrum, now the sole commander of Viking forces operating south of the Humber, still had Wessex in his sights.

Soon after Twelfth Night and the Feast of the Epiphany, 6 January 878, and taking advantage of the long Christmas holiday, he led a large army into Wessex and, according to the *Anglo-Saxon Chronicle*, 'rode over [the kingdom] and occupied it'. Specifically, the Viking army seized the heartland royal vill and estate of Chippenham. The mead hall where King Alfred had but lately caroused with his courtiers, his ealdormen and household thegns was now the property of such of those Viking war bands who were not harrying the English population. Many of those, we are told, 'fled across the sea'. Many also, among the landowners, submitted to Guthrum as their lord. The situation was dire indeed. If Alfred could be caught and killed the Vikings would have little difficulty in finding a puppet as they had in Mercia and the age of the inde-pendent Anglo-Saxon kingdoms in England would be over.

In these dark days the heroes were not at first Alfred the king and his companions, but men of Devon, king's thegns and their house-holds, under the local ealdorman, who routed an attack by a force of some twenty-three ships launched from a winter base in Dyfed in south Wales. The defenders were able to fall back on the earth-work of Countisbury Hill, a former British hill-fort. They slaugh-tered more than 800 of the enemy, killed their leader and captured the fabled 'Raven Banner' of Ragnar Lothbrok.

At this time Alfred, his family and a little party of retainers and household thegns were on the run among the marshes and woodland wastes. While Guthrum lived in his halls and off his food rents, the king lived more the life of an outlaw and marauder – to the Vikings, little better than a terrorist. In the spring he established his base of operations on the Isle of Athelney in Somerset, a low eminence above the surrounding marshlands, little more than 350 yards (320 m) long and barely 50 yards (46 m) wide, and accessible only by punt and hidden paths. The name, literally 'nobles' island', suggests a favourite haunt for hunters and wild fowlers, and no doubt for the king himself in his youth. With approaches camouflaged and fortified as best as possible, it offered a precarious refuge from which he and his men could sally out, raiding for supplies, harassing the enemy, reconnoitring his positions and keeping in touch, one supposes, with a network of partisans. At least one other West Saxon notable followed his lord's example, for we are told that Æthelnoth, the ealdorman of Somerset, headed a group of resistance fighters in the wooded country of Somerset and helped with the defences of Athelney. Here, about 880, Alfred would found a monastery as part of the fortified complex defended at its approach by 'a very strong fort . . . of most beautiful workmanship', built most probably under his direction.

For all involved this must have been a time of intense planning, logistical preparation and coordination of effort. In view of the triumphant victory with which the year was to be capped, it is testimony to the deeply motivational leadership of which King Alfred was capable. It was also the time of national myth and legend. Three stories, all reported generations later and each calculated to trigger useful responses, either suggest PR of conspiratorial genius or embody a genuine national sentiment. In one, the fugitive king snatches a roadside lunch with a poor beggar, who turns out to be St Cuthbert. The anecdote associates the West Saxon leader with Northumbrian tradition. In another the king and his assistant, disguised as wandering minstrel and *jongleur*, entertain the Danish camp with fooling and songs and in the process overhear essential military intelligence. Minstrel perhaps, but the harp as an emblem of monarchy reaches back to King David and the Bible. Significantly we are told two generations later that Olaf Sihtricson, Norse king of York, seeking intelligence before the battle of Brunanburh, spied upon the camp of Alfred's grandson Æthelstan disguised as a minstrel and indeed received largesse for his singing from his unwitting enemy.

Finally, the most famous of all: the story of the cakes. Mentioned in the tenth century, it was only fully recorded in the twelfth-century *Annals of St Neot's*. Nevertheless, it has the ring of truth. We find the king seated by the fire in a swineherd's hut 'preparing his bows and arrows and other instruments of war'. The housewife has set some loaves, or griddle-cakes, to rise by the fire and comes in to find them burning while her visitor sits by, day-dreaming, unaware. The wretched woman berates him, 'little thinking that this was the king, Alfred, who had waged so many wars against the pagans', and who was now pondering the country's drastic plight. A king on the run always makes good copy and, because there is no mention of his great sword, a badge of high birth and the emblem of the hero, his anonymity is believable. It is also one of the few reports about Alfred that does not reach us through a document written by him or a member of his circle.

In the seventh week after Easter 878, Alfred and his followers rode to 'Ecgberht's Stone' (probably a traditional rendezvous point) on the edge of Salisbury Plain and Selwood Forest; here he was joined by 'all Wiltshire and Somerset and that part of Hampshire this side of the sea'. The term may have been meant to exclude, as Asser believed, those men of Hampshire who had fled overseas 'for fear of the pagans', but there seem to have been deserters from other parts of Wessex. Perhaps 'the sea' referred to was not the English Channel but Southampton Water, which divides coastal

Hampshire between east and west. Presumably only forces and their leaders contactable by agents operating out of Athelney would have had news of the muster. After just one day at the assembly point Alfred led his army northwards and just two days later they were facing the 'whole army'. Guthrum occupied a defensive position, probably on the Iron Age hill-fort of Bratton near the village of Edington. The West Saxons advanced with the morning light, shield to shield.

The shield wall or *getruma* used by Scandinavians and Anglo-Saxons alike was, as the name suggests and as it was to be used at Hastings, a natural defensive formation but, like the Roman *testudo* (the Latin word Asser uses) or 'tortoise', could be used on the march. Alfred had also deployed it offensively at Ashdown, advancing only when the wall had been 'formed up in orderly manner' (*ordinabiliter condensata*).[11] Lines in the song of the *Battle of Brunanburh* indicate that in the contest between sword and buckler a poorly seasoned lime-wood shield might be hacked through by a well-tempered blade, and it was in any case desperate work to keep the line as comrades fell to right or left, felled by the sword or 'killed over the shield by spear' or arrow, for the Bayeux tapestry shows shield men wielding spears. At the Battle of Maldon in 991 Ealdorman Byrthnoth required his men to hold their shields properly to form the 'war hedge' and it is clear that shire levies must have received training if they were to join professionals in this specialized battlefield technique.

At Edington Alfred's men drove the enemy from the field after hard fighting and pursued the fugitives to a fortification presumed to be Chippenham. Not all the enemy found refuge in time and, again according to Asser, Alfred killed men, horses and cattle that he found outside the fort. After a siege of just fourteen days Guthrum capitulated. In the treaty that followed he offered hostages; Alfred offered none. Guthrum agreed to accept baptism, taking the Christian name Æthelstan, with thirty of his chief men. Alfred stood as his sponsor and the new converts wore their white

baptismal robes for the following eight days. This was an impressive
ceremony of submission by any measure. Even so it has been
pointed out that Guthrum was now accepted into the circle of
Christian kings. If he had accepted Christianity, however, presumably many of his followers were still pagans. From the terms of the
agreement it seems that Guthrum and his band were now a permanent element in the new political geography of England.[12] He had
agreed to leave Wessex and withdraw to his lands in East Anglia; in
fact he fell back only to Cirencester, just over the border in Mercia.
It was not until a full year later that he finally withdrew to East
Anglia, where he settled and 'shared out the land'.

The following year another force rowed up the Thames beyond
London as far as Fulham on the Mercian side of the river. If it had
been intended to join up with Guthrum and deliver a deadly blow
to the Anglo-Saxon presence its leaders thought better of the idea.
The fleet made its way back down the Thames and throughout the
880s its army campaigned in the lands of Francia.

The Danelaw

In the winter of 872 Burgred of Mercia was forced to negotiate a
peace deal with the Danish main force now at Torksey in Lindsey.
Late the next year, a detachment of the army had rowed down the
Trent, past Nottingham, and seized Repton in Derbyshire, the great
Mercian royal minster, burial place of kings and fortified residence.
Here they proceeded to fortify three and a half acres (1.5 hectares)
with ditches and a 130-metre semicircle of earthworks that incorporated the Anglo-Saxon church and used the river as the base of
the 'D'. With this as their base they raided the surrounding countryside. After a reign of twenty-odd years Burgred abandoned the
rearguard defence against the barbarian invaders and fled England;
two years later he died in Rome, where he was buried in St Mary's
church in the English *borgo*.

And yet, suggests John Blair, perhaps these pagans 'recognized the cultic and symbolic prestige of their victims' holy sites'.[13] Excavations led by Martin Biddle at Repton revealed not only the camp bounded by the Trent and its earthworks, but also Scandinavian-style graves from the 870s, including skeletal remains of a Viking chieftain of high rank buried with an amulet and a Thor's hammer pendant. The body was close to the relic crypt of the church and surrounded by the remains of 250 other young male bodies in what is now the vicarage garden. At the village of Ingleby nearby there is a site of cremations, indicating pagan rites, and on the hillside fifty-nine barrows.

The increased level of raiders and invaders from the mid-860s onwards produced changes in the human geography of eastern England across the regions we know as Yorkshire, Lincolnshire, the East Midlands and East Anglia. Scandinavian and specifically Danish place names are numerous, but their occurrence is sporadic. So the extent and depth of the changes is difficult to estimate. Even burial practices, though diverse, are not conclusive. We find inhumations with and without grave goods: sometimes in church grounds, sometimes in specially raised barrows, as at Heath Wood Ingleby; sometimes Anglo-Saxon style swords feature in apparently Scandinavian graves. These and other factors may simply indicate the influx of a conquering elite imposing name changes on a sub-jected population. If there had been a large movement of peasant farmers from Denmark into lands cleared by a 'Great Army' or by warlords, then one would expect some trace in the archaeological record. So far there are few Viking grave sites, whether of great men or lesser folk, and nothing like enough to support the thesis of a massive, or even substantial, population shift across the North Sea.

In the absence of archaeological back-up another avenue of research for what one might call the missing ethnic factor has been tried in the form of extensive DNA trialling nationwide. Even here, it appears, the results are inconclusive. So, whatever it was that the 'Danish men' featured by the *Anglo-Saxon Chronicle* sought in the lands of the English race, it does not seem to have been what Germans of a later age called *Lebensraum* ('living space').

But they left their mark on the social institutions. Where the English divided their shires into hundreds and measured their tax assessments by hides, the people of the Danelaw, whether conquered English peasantry or ethnic Danes, tended to work in 'wapentakes' (apparently from Old Norse *vápnatak*, meaning a 'taking [i.e. counting] of weapons') and 'carucates' (a measure of ploughland). A local assembly where assent was signified by the brandishing of arms fits well with one's image of the invaders.

Above all, the Danelaw was just that, a territory where Danish, not English, law and customs could be expected to apply, particularly with regard to land rights. However, uniformity was hardly to be expected. Viking war bands were essentially ships' companies each under its own ship's master or commander. As the time of raiding passed and the time for settlement came it was surely organized by the military leaders, whose voices were no doubt decisive when it came to decisions as to the details and the distribution of property.[14]

Danelaw was never a political entity with a fixed boundary. When King Alfred and Guthrum signed their treaty, one part of Danelaw, that part where Guthrum ruled, comprising parts of modern Bedfordshire and Hertfordshire, the whole of Essex, Cambridgeshire and East Anglia, was pretty well demarcated. Any Englishmen who lived here were awarded the same compensation rights or wergilds to buy off feud vengeance as Danes of equal status.

North of these territories lay the lands of the Five Boroughs (Leicester, Nottingham, Derby, Stamford and Lincoln), which were Danish strongholds conquered by Alfred's son Edward the Elder and his sister Æthelflæd. The area of Northumbria controlled by Viking York, or Jorvik, was fully independent of English control for the best part of fifty years, though subject for a time to the Vikings of Dublin and later the Norwegian prince Eric Bloodaxe. A map to show England at the time of the Danelaw can hardly represent reality. A line drawn diagonally across the country from London up to the region of Chester awards a huge swath of territory to the customs of the incomers. In fact the whole area is best understood in terms of a scatter of separate regional communities, each with its own roots back to the English past and a ruling stratum sharing for the most part a common Danish inheritance.

East Anglia is a case in point. The cult of Edmund the Martyr was fostered, indeed may have been launched, by Danes ashamed of the perpetrators. There are signs that Guthrum/Æthelstan, who ruled for a decade after his treaty with Alfred, may have 'gone native', that is to say may have identified himself with the traditions of English kingship following his conversion. It is also suggested that the Danish ruling stratum conformed to the religion of the surrounding population inspired by their leader's example. Archaeological evidence of the cult of St Edmund is provided by commemorative coins struck in the king's name by East Anglian mints from the 890s to the 910s. They may mark a genuine gesture of atonement for any atrocity of 869/70 or, as Julian Richards has proposed, be part of a policy to mollify smouldering English resentment and pacify any thoughts of rebellion.

Viking York

In the following decade a raiding army was ravaging the banks of the Tyne and doing battle with the Picts and the Britons of Strathclyde. Their leader, Halfdan, then descended on York once more and with no effective rivals to his lordship distributed this region of Northumbria among his followers. That year they were 'ploughing' and fending for themselves, the *Chronicles* tell us. This was settlement in progress and, as if to point up the significance of the annal, someone has added at this point in the Peterborough

Chronicle a Latin note to the effect that in this year too Rollo, founder of the duchy, invaded Normandy and ruled there for fifty-three years. Halfdan is generally credited as the founder of Viking York.

To many in the north of England surveying the scene in the 860s, the battle of England must have seemed lost. After 867 the venerable city known to Alcuin by its Roman name of Eboracum, seat of England's northern archbishops, a great home of learning, and northern Europe's first post-Roman 'city of culture', would be renowned as Jorvik. Until 954 the region of old Northumbria between the Humber and the River Tees witnessed the fluctuating fortunes of a succession of Viking leaders or rulers of a territory of uncertain and shifting boundaries, now generally known as the 'kingdom of York'. Noting that contemporary sources never use the term, David Rollason has observed in his *Northumbria 500–1100* (2004) that there is no evidence that Halfdan's conquest inaugurated a Viking or indeed any form of kingdom. In terms of cultural continuity he considers that 'the Viking kingdom of York' is perhaps better understood as the revival of the separate southern identity of Northumbria (between the rivers Tees and Humber), namely the old kingdom of Deira.

For a time Guthred of Viking Dublin held sway, to be followed by three shadowy figures until, about 899, it acknowledged a ruler of the house of Wessex. In that year Alfred died, leaving the crown to his son Edward. But Edward's cousin Æthelwold challenged the succession and looked for allies where he could find them, even among the national enemy, the Vikings. York opened its gates to him and may even have recognized him as king. Why, if York had a well-established line of Viking kings, it should accept a West Saxon malcontent is unclear. From there, he went into Essex with a fleet of ships and was soon recruiting men among the East Angles and raiding into Mercia and Wessex. The sequence of events is confused but the turmoil in the Wessex dynasty could have boiled into a civil war that, because the national enemy was now involved, could have overturned the burgeoning English state. As it was, although Æthelwold lost his life at the Battle of Holme (Holmesdale) in 902/3 the Vikings 'held the field of battle'. Eight years later at Tettenhall, near Wolverhampton, Halfdan II of York and two other 'kings', Eowils and Ivar, were killed, but in what sense the title meant anything more than war chief is not clear. In 937 Æthelstan of Wessex crushed a combined army of Vikings and others at Brunanburh, but when he died two years later Olaf Guthfrithsson re-established a Dublin Viking monarchy there and extended the kingdom's hegemony back over the 'Five Boroughs'. It was ephemeral. His successor Olaf Sihtricson was soon ousted (943/4) by Edmund of England, and returned to rule in Dublin. Norse rule in York had barely a decade to run. It was spent in rivalry between Sihtricson and a member of the Norwegian royal house, Eric, called Bloodaxe. For a Viking to earn such a sobriquet clearly called for something exceptional. Briefly king of Norway, Eric is said to have killed a number of brothers. Fittingly he was ousted by a half-brother and driven into exile. A sea raider among the Scottish Isles before coming to York, Erik, the last Viking ruler of York, was driven from the city by the English king Eadred in the mid-950s.

In the forty years before Eric seized the place we hear of six more warlords who held sway in Deira. Of these, Olaf Sihtricson, who held power in York for two brief periods, was also a 'king' of the Dublin Vikings and the Dublin connection recurs more than once. But it is hard to believe that men such as these, including Bloodaxe himself, were rulers of a calibre to make York 'one of the great cities of the Viking world'.

Perhaps, Professor Rollason has proposed, we should see York as 'essentially an ecclesiastical city ruled by its archbishops, comparable to Trier or Cologne'. Wulfhere, the archbishop ejected by Halfdan, was restored to office only six years later, perhaps precisely so that he would direct the governance of the region. In such a context the superb Coppergate helmet, war gear with a seemingly incongruous Christian inscription, might be read as emblematic of the entwined sinews of secular and ecclesiastical power. In 1069 the Normans of the post-Conquest garrison, as befitted their Viking ancestry, set a fire that destroyed the great York library. Maybe, Rollason surmises, the archival evidence that could have confirmed the hypothesis of a church-led administration also perished in the flames. Whoever actually ran the place, Viking York was highly prosperous despite the Byzantine and bloody power politics that absorbed its 'kings'.

Archaeology has revealed the construction of substantial defence works, such as the strengthening of the dilapidated Roman fortifications. Excavations from the 1970s in the Coppergate district uncovered the presence of a major commercial and craftworking centre in the fork at the confluence of the Ouse and Foss rivers. By about 900 there was a grid pattern of long narrow plots divided by wattle fences and built up with post and wattle structures, running back from open shop fronts on the street line. Some fifty years later a large rebuilding project replaced these structures with houses, workshops and occasional warehouses built of robust oak squared uprights clad in oak planking. Archaeology reveals that York was importing honestones from Scandinavia, pottery perhaps with wine in it from the Rhineland, even silk from the Far East. Its workshops were turning out leather goods, wooden household vessels, textiles and grave slabs and other stone work in the region's own characteristic 'Jelling' style of decoration, incised in double outline animal motifs. Furnaces and stocks of ore, crucibles and other equipment testified to working in iron, copper and precious metals. There were jewellers working in (imported) amber, shoemakers and skate makers among other artisans. Wells, drainage channels and purpose-built latrines complete the picture of a well-planned new business quarter. Coppergate was part of a much wider piece of town planning, but York was a thriving emporium before the Scandinavian settlement. Elsewhere in the city, for example at Fishergate, there are indications of merchants' quarters laid out in the late eighth century and the presence of Frisian traders.

The York mint was busy in the early decades of the tenth century producing coins for the Anglo-Saxon king Æthelstan, who occupied the place for a time in the 930s, and for the Viking Olaf Guthfrithsson, the last but one Scandinavian 'king' of York. Moneyers were part of the social elite and descendants of these Norse artisan dynasties were still at work in the time of William the Conqueror.

North by northeast and the province of St Cuthbert

It seems the Vikings quickly converted to Christianity. The cemetery of the 'Viking' period under the present York Minster shows uninterrupted Christianity at the heart of the city. To the northwest, Northumbrian hegemony over the Britons of ancient Cumbria, a region that in addition to the modern county of that name embraced districts along the northern bank of the Solway Firth in Dumfriesshire, modern Scotland, was disrupted and supplanted by raiders from Viking Dublin and also from Norway. In the tenth century a shadowy succession of rulers, beginning with Owain (c. 915–c. 937) and called the kings of the Cumbrians, is occasionally mentioned by northern sources.

Any account of the confused and shifting events and peoples in this northern part of England, based as it is on fragmentary chronicle references, disputed place name evidence and isolated archaeological finds, must largely be speculation, though there are some tempting allusions in sagas and bardic literature. The name 'Cumbria', related of course to the Welsh cymry, proclaims its British origins, but who these tenth-century kings of Cumbria might be is not clear. One theory starts from the fact that its northern neighbour, the British kingdom of Strathclyde, with its fortress of Alclyde (Dumbarton), was annexed by the kings of the Scots; it proposes that they used their new province as the base for further expansion southward. On this thesis, the title 'king of Cumbria' should be seen as the designation for the Scottish sub-kings of Strathclyde. The names of Owain's successors, Dunmail (Donald), expelled by the English king Edmund in 945, and Malcolm, who died in 997 and was perhaps also the ruler known as 'king of the Britons of the North', certainly have a Scottish ring. With the death of another Owain (Owain the Bald) in 1018 the Strathclyde Cumbrian regime was absorbed by the kings of the Scots. The situation would be contested for generations by border warfare that seems to have determined that British Strathclyde should remain Scottish, and British Cumbria remain English.

An alternative thesis argues that the king of Cumbria was not the Scottish king of Strathclyde under another name but rather an independent British ruler. According to this view, the British population submerged by the original Anglo-Saxon conquests was liberated by the collapse of Anglian Northumbria to reassert its identity under its own line of kings. Central to the debate are the numerous place names in the area of undoubtedly British origin. Were they planted in southward expansion from Strathclyde in the tenth century or were they in fact survivals from the pre-Anglian conquest period? The expert jury is still out, though a layman might suggest that Scottish kings of Strathclyde would hardly name captured or newly founded settlements in the language of their own subject British population.

The situation in the region northwards from the Tees to the River Tyne is a little easier to unravel. It would come under the sway of the monastic community of St Cuthbert. Rich in lands gifted by King Guthred, whom they believed owed his peaceful throne to their intervention, in 875 the community had set off with its patron's corpse from Lindisfarne in search of more secure premises.

Its peregrinations, first to Norham in Cumbria, then to Crayke and eventually to Chester-le-Street, became woven into the tapestry of the community's tradition. The brethren of St Cuthbert, far from being a 'band of ragged exiles clinging to their precious burden', were in fact 'rather, a prosperous religious corporation responding to political change by making a series of planned moves between estates which they already owned'.[15] After twelve years of peaceful prosperity (883–95) at Chester-le-Street, the bishop and community made their final move to Durham. Thus the core of the later palatinate and the powers of its prince bishops was planted in the huge estates acquired by followers of the humble saint in the wake of the Viking invasions. They reflect the territories of the former kingdom of Bernicia south and north of the Tyne. North of the Tyne in the early 900s we find a dynasty of earls ruling from the former royal palace of Bamburgh: the *Annals of Ulster* calls the first of them 'king of the North Saxons'. They held their lordship up to the Norman Conquest, as we note in chapter 12.

8

THE WESSEX OF ALFRED THE GREAT

It was the Wessex of Alfred the Great that prevented Anglo-Saxon Christian civilisation from being submerged by what one might call pagan 'cultural norms'. The Battle of Edington of 878 was the decisive turning point for England – some would say for Christian Europe. Others have argued that the survival of the English language itself could have been in jeopardy. But no serious historical commentator would contest that had Wessex gone under, so would the kingdom of the English or, as Alfred came to call it, 'the kingdom of the Anglo-Saxons'.

When he first used the term, in a charter of 885, the idea of a united kingdom even of the West Saxons was still comparatively new, as was the family in power. Alfred's kin could show descent from Cerdic (it was a condition of the kingship); they also claimed *Beowulf*'s Scyld Scefing among their ancestors, who in turn descended from Sceaf, a supposed fourth son of Noah. Apparently Alfred kept a little handbook by him with a genealogical note on West Saxon kings. On the other hand, his grandfather Ecgberht was the first of their branch of the dynasty to occupy the throne. In fact, one biographer of Alfred suggests that Ecgberht's background was 'essentially Kentish', his father apparently 'among Kent's last independent kings' before the old kingdom became a sub-kingdom or province of Mercia. Following Ecgberht's defeat of Mercia at

Ellendun in 825, Mercian hegemony in southern England was broken. Ecgberht's son Æthelwulf now led an army down into Kent and expelled its last king, Baldred, so that it became the great eastern province of the West Saxon kingdom.

The old rivalry of Wessex with Mercia was fading. About 852–4 the Mercian king Burgred (852–74) had married Æthelswih of Wessex, Alfred's sister, following a successful joint campaign with Wessex against the Welsh. Then about 867 Alfred's brother Æthelred effectively inaugurated a monetary union by adopting the Mercian type of lunette penny. A common currency based on coins minted exclusively at London and Canterbury now circulated from Dover to Chester and from Exeter to Lincoln.[1]

The making of a king

Alfred was born between 847 and 849 at Wantage in Berkshire, according to Asser, the youngest of the five sons of King Æthelwulf (839–58) by his wife Osburh, who died when he was still a boy. She was of noble birth and through her father could claim part-Jutish ancestry – 'useable' antecedents for a prince who would one day rule in Kent. With four brothers ahead of him there must have been doubts that he would in fact become king. Was he originally intended for a career in the church? He was declared heir only at age fifteen.

Yet his public life began early: aged six he was witnessing charters and participating in the activities of the court. He was soon learning the business of the hunt, the handling of weapons and the beginnings of horse mastery. He was also hanging around the falconers in the royal mews, where he no doubt learnt the English manner of carrying the falcon on the left wrist and, in handling, of grasping the bird across her back to reduce the danger of injury from flapping wings.[2] As a father, Alfred would insist that his children, and the noblemen's sons sent to be fostered at his court, learn to read and write in English and Latin before they mastered the manly skills associated with the hunt. For literature was a passion – a passion that extended as much to the courtly epic and the min-strel's lay as to the history and philosophy and the Psalms that he himself would translate. A famous anecdote, which his biographer Asser presumably heard from the king himself, tells how Alfred's mother promised a beautiful book of English poetry to whichever of her sons could first understand and recite it. The boy, who could not yet read, took the volume to his tutor, had him read it aloud, memorized it and claimed the prize. It no doubt came easily, for he was already memorizing the lays and epics declaimed in his father's mead hall. Later Alfred, the scholar king, evidently prided himself also as a worthy lord in the heroic manner. Dishop Wulfsige of Sherborne, wishing to flatter the king, used the language of the epic scop to hail him 'the greatest treasure giver of all the kings . . . ever heard of'.

Rome and Alfred

Simon Keynes has shown that references in a manuscript in Brescia confirm that Alfred twice visited Rome as a boy. On the first occa-sion, in 853, it would seem he was sent as a harbinger of a visit planned by his father; the pope, we are told, 'decorated him, as a spiritual son, with the dignity of the belt [*cingulum*] and the vestment . . . customary with Roman consuls'.[3] The boy was to remember the impressive ceremony as a royal consecration. Æthelwulf's victory over the Vikings at Aclea in 851 was still being feted in Europe in the *Annals of St Bertin* at Troyes. Two years later the boy prince returned, this time as part of his father's entourage. Together with 'a multitude of people', they were received with great honour by Pope Benedict III – Alfred as the spiritual son of the papacy, Æthelwulf as a warrior against the heathen and bearer of lavish gifts to St Peter, among them a gold crown four pounds in weight, a fine sword bound in gold, four luxury 'Saxon bowls' and much else, including largesse for the citizens of Rome.

Returning from Rome in 856, Æthelwulf and Alfred visited the court of the West Frankish ruler Charles the Bald. Evidently, a marriage had been arranged between Charles's daughter Judith, a girl aged about twelve, and Æthelwulf, now a man in his fifties. Perhaps because he knew kings' wives were not treated with special deference in Wessex, perhaps to give any child she might bear added status, or perhaps simply because it was becoming standard practice in West Francia, Charles insisted that the bride be consecrated queen during the marriage service. Archbishop Hincmar of Reims, expert in ritual, officiated at the ceremony. That spring, Danish raiders had penetrated to the heart of France and ravaged Orléans and in August a large force rowed up the Seine to within a few miles of Paris. Charles, possibly accompanied by his English royal guest, led an army against them and did great slaughter but failed to drive them from their fortified base. They were to return.

Arrived back in Wessex, Æthelwulf found himself faced by a general rebellion led by his eldest son Æthelbald. The cause is unknown. Maybe the heir was worried by the new queen's consecration ceremony. He need hardly fear a second wife as such, but the nubile youngster now installed was a full queen, sanctified by the church. Any son of hers might take priority over him. Æthelwulf retired with his young spouse to Kent. A charter dated November 857 suggests the kind of problems Wessex had to fear from Æthelwulf's Continental interests: it is a confirmation of a gift of lands at Rotherfield, Hastings, Pevensey and London to Saint Denis, the great monastery outside Paris; in other words the 'export' of substantial revenues.

When his father died the following year, Æthelbald neutralized any threat from Judith by marrying her (marriage with a stepmother, not unheard of in pagan practice, does not seem to have caused any technical problems for the church, though it scandalized Bishop

Asser). King Æthelwulf had maintained the domestic prestige of the monarchy left him by his illustrious father (a tenth-century archbishop of Trier who was proud to trace his descent from Ecgberht of Wessex). He also assured the ascendancy of his house in Kent so that minsters there turned to him for protection, rather than the archbishops of Canterbury. Indeed by the end of the century Alfred, his son, was able to appoint his own candidate to the see. He had a better than average record against the Vikings and he had promoted the standardization of the coinage carried forward by his sons. By his marriage into the Carolingian dynasty he had increased its standing abroad. Yet by his will he confirmed the division of the kingdom, leaving Kent and the eastern dependencies (Surrey, Sussex and Essex) to Æthelberht and Wessex, along with the former British territories of Dumnonia and Cornwall, to Æthelbald (who was to be followed by Æthelred and Alfred in the West).

On Æthelbald's early and childless death in 860 the surviving brothers agreed that Æthelberht should succeed to the kingdom as a whole, with the prospect of Æthelred and Alfred to follow. Five years after this Æthelberht, too, died childless. Again Alfred ceded the entire succession to his brother Æthelred. When he too died in 871, Æthelred left a baby boy. It was out of the question to have an infant on the throne during these times of Danish raiding and Alfred succeeded as sole king. There would be problems when the baby, Æthelwold, grew to manhood (see page 263).

We must assume that the consular installation ceremony at Rome coloured Alfred's entire life. He conducted a similar ceremony for his four-year-old grandson, Æthelstan, son of Edward. The child was invested 'with a scarlet cloak, a belt set with gems and a Saxon sword with a gilded scabbard'. To some present it seemed like a secular consecration. For Alfred one imagines there were powerful associations with the duties of a Roman consul, which he translated in Anglo-Saxon as *heretoga* (i.e. 'leader'). He saw himself as championing civilization against the forces of pagan barbarism.

He saw, too, comparisons between Wessex and himself facing the
Danes and Rome under barbarian attack centuries before, then
yielding to the impious rule of Theodoric the Ostrogoth (*d.* 520),
the heretic Arian Christian. Theodoric's chief minister was
Boethius, a Roman Christian of ancient patrician family who for
unknown reasons was arrested on treason charges. In prison awaiting trial (he was executed in 524) Boethius wrote *On the Consolation
of Philosophy*, which Alfred was to translate lovingly. In his view of
history Boethius had been a model champion of the moral way
withstanding a violent and unrighteous usurper. Similarly he, under
threat from the pagan Danes, was a just man, like Boethius, suffering
for a righteous cause. He ascended the throne conscious that the
aura of a Roman authority was about him and as consciously prepared to defend the Christian Roman legacy in his kingdom of
Wessex against the pagan invaders. His new 870s coin types from
the London mint show 'design elements deliberately and carefully
copied' from Roman models.[4]

Biography and history

The *Vita Alfredi Regis Angul Saxonum* is a Latin account of the 'Life
of Alfred King of the Anglo-Saxons' from his birth, through his
accession in 871 and up to the year 887 – that is twelve years before
the death of its subject and almost twenty years before the death of
its named author, the Welsh monk-bishop Asser (*d.* 908/9). About
half the text is a Latin translation of texts of the *Anglo-Saxon
Chronicle* covering the years between 851 and 887. The single
known manuscript of the *Vita*, made about the year 1000, was
destroyed in 1731 by a fire in the Cotton Library in Westminster;
various transcriptions and editions made before that time provide
the basis of modern editions of the book. Alfred had called Asser to
the West Saxon court to be his tutor in Latin, the lessons beginning
on St Martin's Day, 11 November 887. He became a valued royal

confidant and divided his time between the court and his monastery in St David's. He rose in the West Saxon church to become bishop of the rich see of Sherborne and received rich gifts, such as a most valuable silken robe. So it was that the biography of the English king renowned for promoting the English language as a vehicle of history and scholarship came to be recorded by a Welshman writing in Latin. But then Asser was heir to the old British tradition of Latin scholarship reaching back to the time of Gildas. He depicts the king more as saint or pope. James Campbell observed that 'Asser [wrote] with the zeal of the well rewarded'.

The idea for the project may have been inspired by the 'Life of Emperor Charles the Great' (*Vita Caroli*) written by the German churchman Einhard, who in turn had studied under Alcuin. But there are differences. Asser, writing in England, uses many AD dates, Einhard only one; Asser has anecdotes from his subject's childhood, Einhard none; Asser lays stress on the importance of the *carmina Saxonica* ('Saxon songs') in Alfred's upbringing. No such vernacular frivolities feature in Einhard.

Inevitably the Bible (particularly the Jewish Old Testament) provided themes for Christian monarchy. The inauguration of Saul as king of Israel, the example of Solomon as judge and law-maker, the decrees of God himself in the Ten Commandments were all seen as models. But even in military matters the 'Good Book' could seem relevant. When he read that 'King Rehoboam dwelt in Jerusalem and built cities for defence in Judah' (II Chronicles 11:5) Alfred would surely have found confirmation for his 'burh' building programme. Asser himself had an excellent command of the detailed Latin military terminology for defensive war and battlefield manoeuvres. Possibly he had read *De rei militaris*, the military treatise by the late fourth-century Roman patrician Vegetius and 'the most heavily used of all classical texts in Western Europe from the 5th to the 15th century'[5] that according to David Hill, was known in England. Even the Venerable Bede seems to have based his description of the rampart raised by the Romans against the Picts on it.[6] Perhaps Alfred too was familiar with it: Vegetius had much to say on the need for good intelligence gathering, the decisive importance of terrain and the correct use of reserves, all aspects of warfare in which Alfred was expert.

We do not know why Asser, who seems to have begun work in 893, ended the biography when he did, and there are factors that have led people to question whether he in fact was the author. The most extended argument for this thesis in *King Alfred the Great* (1995) by Professor Alfred P. Smyth. At the moment, though, the balance seems to be in Asser's favour. For just one example, Asser's book draws on texts that would have come naturally to a Welsh scholar, such as the 'Old Latin' version of the Bible, which was displaced in England by St Jerome's 'Vulgate' text a good fifty years before Alfred came to the throne but was still in use in Wales.[7]

The *Anglo-Saxon Chronicle* (or, better, *Chronicles*), is a series of annals purporting to record events from the year 494 to 1154. It has been said that 'Anglo-Saxon history would be virtually impossible to write without it.'[8] Being Europe's only vernacular chronicle of such detail over such a long stretch of time, it has been and is still subject to intense and critical scrutiny (see chapter 9). Probably inaugurated under the aegis of King Alfred, its origins are in fact unclear. The hand of the first scribe has been dated to the very end of the reign. Up to that point, together with the regnal list and genealogy as preface, it is a panegyric to the dynasty's conquest of southwest Britain followed by its triumph over the Danes. Whoever the compiler was, he could probably rely on 'back-up knowledge' of the oral traditions among his audience. If we add Alfred's law book, which records also the laws of King Ine, we have the testament of a dynasty as notable in the arts of peace as successful in the arts of war.

The value of the *Chronicles* to the royal house of Cerdic becomes obvious if we look at the other powerful kings and dynasties mentioned in its annals. None of them, not even the kings of Mercia, present us with the same sense of root or of destiny. Moreover, by its coverage, albeit selective, of other kingdoms in the land of the English 'Angelcynn' the *Chronicle* does have the aspect of a 'national' chronicle. While there is no direct evidence of Alfred's personal involvement, it is hard to believe that he was not associated with the enterprise. At the very least, Alfred's encouragement of learning and his deep sense of history support the supposition. After all, he did make additions to Orosius' Old English translation of world history. What is more, the first part of the *Chronicle* manuscript, which runs from 494 to 891, was written in the kingdom of Wessex, very possibly in Winchester, Alfred's favourite town. This record of the Anglo-Saxons and their success against the Danish 'Great Army' may well have been intended as morale-boosting 'propaganda', as we are told it was placed in Winchester, presumably in the Old Minster, attached by a chain to a reading desk. Moreover, it appears that copies were being sent out to the large churches of Wessex about the year 892 at the time of renewed Viking raids.[9]

This 'Winchester' Chronicle also covers many Continental events during Alfred's reign and not only events relating to Viking incursions into Europe, where England did have a common interest with the Frankish lands. There were at this time a number of Frankish monks in the fortified monastery founded by Alfred at Athelney, who no doubt kept up with their contacts in Francia and could have been the source of such information. Athelney input could also account for the Chronicle's well-informed coverage of local Somerset news. This combination of the local, the national and the international adds to the perennial fascination of the source.

It may be that almost all the sources regarding Alfred's reign 'originated with either Alfred himself or his immediate entourage' or, as another scholar somewhat acidly remarked, that 'We hold that Alfred was a great and glorious king in part because he tells us he was.'[10] But if the king was 'telling the tale', was he not also perhaps telling the truth? In any case there were Continental precedents for royal propaganda programmes. Einhard's *Vita Caroli* is an obvious parallel and the *Royal Frankish Annals* was straight propaganda for Charles's dynasty. Given the severity of the Danish Viking threat it would not be surprising if Alfred had a 'profound sense of dynastic insecurity' and turned, as has been suggested, to Frankish 'experts on kingship'.[11] We can assume that the *Chronicle*'s principal target audience was not posterity but rather Alfred's contemporaries; his aim, to rally them to take pride in the West Saxon royal house and support it in the struggle against the national enemy.

Apart from perhaps St Boniface, there is no Anglo-Saxon about whom we know more. The youngest of five brothers, it was noteworthy that he came to the throne at all. His sexuality seems to have been more or less normal for a king, with at least one illegitimate child credited to him by rumour. Unusually for a monarch of his time, and laughably by twenty-first century social convention, he valued personal chastity and prayed for some painful disease to inhibit his lusts. As a young man he did suffer from an extremely painful complaint, possibly haemorrhoids, possibly Chrohn's disease, which seems to have recurred throughout his life. It hardly hampered his achievement. A king who could read was remarkable; one who authored books was unheard of elsewhere in western Christendom before the millennium.

For Patrick Wormald, Alfred was the 'translucent mind of Old English authority',[12] for Bishop Wulfsige, as we saw, the greatest of treasure-givers. The quality praised is that of the heroic war leader and Alfred was certainly that; but the context, the bishop's preface to a translation commissioned by the king, is that of cultural patronage. For Alfred, recruits for the war against ignorance demanded the same kind of largesse as warriors against terror raids. In his own translation of Boethius the king claimed to have no interest in money or power for their own sakes but only as means to his job of administering his kingdom 'virtuously'.

The birth of the 'Anglo-Saxon' idea and cultural renewal

In the 870s Burgred, ruler of Anglian Mercia, had been expelled by the Danes. He made an English king's pilgrimage to Rome, where he died. He was followed by Ceolwulf, who gave hostages to the Danes and whom the *Chronicle* considered a mere puppet, though he issued a joint currency with Alfred. Nothing more is heard of him after 880 and Alfred placed Mercia under the rule of Æthelred, as ealdorman.

By adopting the style 'king of the Anglo-Saxons', Alfred clearly made a statement of unity within the Angelcynn. In the mid-870s coinage minted by Alfred in London had already represented him as 'king of the English' or as 'king of the Saxons and Mercians'. Such changes heralded 'a new and distinctive polity' and a combined effort to restore the glories of Anglo-Saxon culture. The reign's unparalleled output of vernacular literature was obviously the result of 'a conscious policy' carried through by the king and a small group of advisers and doers, to generate texts and see to their dissemination.[13]

The programme owed much to outside help, including the presence at Winchester of Continental Europeans – initially Fulco of Reims, and then the Frankish scholars Grimbald of St Bertin (proposed by one scholar as the man who suggested the *Anglo-Saxon Chronicle*) and John the Old Saxon (presumably from Saxony) – and the books they brought with them. But there were Welshmen, too, as well as the Franks, Frisians, Irishmen, Bretons and even Scandinavians, all drawn by the king's reputation for generosity. And, of course, Mercians such as Wærferth, who translated Pope Gregory's *Dialogues* at the king's request, and Plegmund, possibly Cheshire-born and described by Asser as a man of great learning. Alfred named him as one of those who, along with Asser and Grimbald of St Bertin, helped him with the translation of Pope Gregory's *Liber regulae pastoralis* ('Pastoral Care'), the handbook for bishops that was the foundation for Alfred's cultural reform programme. Alfred was to appoint Plegmund as archbishop of Canterbury. During a long reign (890–923) Plegmund would officiate at the coronation of Alfred's son Edward the Elder in 900 at Kingston upon Thames (it was here that Edward's grandfather Æthelwulf had been formally acknowledged as heir to his father, Ecgberht), and reorganize the church in Wessex, a preparation for the extensive church reforms later in the tenth century.

In his preface to the *Pastoral Care*, Alfred famously deplored the decay of learning and modern historians have commented on the 'atrocious quality' of, particularly Kentish, surviving charters, although Kent was not typical. English cultural life was certainly at a low ebb – even the transmission of Bede's works from this period depends heavily on manuscripts preserved on the Continent. The outflow of talented scholars probably meant a shortage of Latin teachers in the early ninth century with a consequent impact on later generations of clergy.[14] And Alfred may have been exaggerating so as to shock people into action.

The preface presents his plans for cultural and literary reform. A copy of the translation is to be sent to all bishops, for the 'cure of souls' is the beginning of wisdom. In former (i.e. pre-Viking) days, he reflects, men had come to England in quest of knowledge; in his day the country had to send abroad for help. Latin was in deep decline. Important books must be translated from the Latin into English. While peace prevails young men of free birth and apt ability should learn to read English and, those who could, Latin as well, since learning was not to be a clerical preserve. A school was to be set up in the royal household for his sons, young nobles being fostered and some boys of non-noble rank.

Alfred believed it was his duty to God to revive the kingdom of the English in learning and devotion and rally his people to the good fight against the heathen. The programme of historical writing, religious education and literary productions had its part to play by boosting the dynasty and recruiting the energies of his subjects to the common good. The most famous part of the programme, the translation from Latin into English of those books 'necessary to know', was unique in Christendom. Even Ireland, with Europe's other tradition of vernacular writing, had 'no parallel for the translation into the vernacular from Latin, such as was the hallmark of Alfred's reform'.[15]

The intervention of Continental scholars was a just payback for the Anglo-Saxon contribution to the Carolingian Renaissance. (There are indications that Alfred first considered Grimbald instead of Plegmund as archbishop of Canterbury.) After all, its central figure Einhard had been educated at Fulda, founded by St Boniface, and then graduated to study under Alcuin. But Alfred's English revival was not sympathetic to the contemporary Carolingian ethos of grandiloquence. No doubt England did not have the money and resources to match those of Charles the Bald, that 'Carolingian renaissance prince'. But the real difference lay in the contrasting personalities of king and emperor. The sumptuous bibles and psalters created for Charles glorified the monarch and distanced him from his subjects. Alfred's books, much more modest and workmanlike, were meant for circulation among courtiers and clergy as part of a dialogue between king and subjects.

Fittingly, it seems almost certain that the famous Alfred Jewel, the most familiar object from the period, was part of an *aestel*, a reading aid. Originally it seems a pointer was fitted in the gold animal head to be used, somewhat like the cursor on a computer screen, to locate the point in the text where attention was focused, much as the *yad* is used in Jewish synagogues to this day when reading the Torah. Depicting a figure with large staring eyes that may be meant to symbolize the sense of sight, and bearing the legend AELFRED MEC HÆT GEWYRCAN ('Alfred had me made') picked out in gold filigree, it was found in the marshes at Athelney, site of the king's retreat and monastic foundation, and is indeed a charismatic icon of the Alfredian age. There seems no doubt that the sponsor of the piece was King Alfred the Great, though some have suggested it might have been intended as a pendant.

Four such objects survive of different types. All make striking use of unusual materials, such as, in the case of the Jewel, 'recovered' rock-crystal, that is a pre-existing piece of crystal shaped for a Roman jewel and reused.

As beautiful as it is, the famous jewel is perhaps outdone in sophistication by the Fuller Brooch, a silver and niello ornament of complex iconography relating to the five senses and product of a highly intellectual court circle.

The practicalities of government and a reform programme

Because virtually nothing remains above ground, it is hard to realize the impact that Alfred's building programme must have had. In addition to the fortified burhs springing up the length and breadth of the kingdom, contemporaries wondered at 'the royal halls and chambers marvellously constructed of stone and wood'.

Government needed tools and resources. By the nature of his office a king was a figure of opulence in dress and of wealth in land. Alfred viewed riches as essential tools of the king's trade. A kingdom, if it is to flourish, must be peopled with fit and capable subjects to discharge the functions of war, prayer and labour; and the king (the ring-giver) needs the wherewithal to reward them with weapons, lands, drink, victuals and luxurious gifts if he is to keep their loyalty and service. The significance of such a list fills out when we realize that a 'weapon' might be a sword such as that Alfred bequeathed to his son-in-law Ealdorman Æthelred, which was valued at 3,000 silver pennies, enough to purchase more than 100 oxen or 300 acres of land.[16]

Much was indeed demanded. Nobles were required to lead their followers to the king's wars; to help him in the administration of public order; to mobilize the work forces on roads and fortifications and generally in the running of the kingdom. Some were charged with additional responsibilities as senior royal officials or 'ealdormen'. At first a kind of prefect in a sub-kingdom of Wessex, the ealdorman was the principal administrator of a shire from the time of King Ine. The high standing of men such as Ceolmund, ealdorman of Kent, or Wulfred of Hampshire, equivalent to a bishop in rank, was signalled by their wergild: 1,200 shillings as they were noble, and another 1,200 shillings as they held office. By 970 there were certain ealdormen (after *c.* 1020 the term gave way to 'earl' from the Danish *jarl*) with responsibility for many shires – regional governors in effect. They were however, always royal appointees and not, like French *ducs* and *comtes*, regional territorial dynasts.

In the *Pastoral Care* Alfred describes St Peter as receiving the 'ealdordom' of the Holy Church from God, which is as much a comment on the king's estimation of his own standing as on that of an ealdorman. Alfred describes the king on great occasions as seated 'on a high seat, in bright raiment', surrounded by thegns wearing ornamented belts and gold-inlaid swords.[17] The most celebrated lawsuit in Anglo-Saxon legal records concerns a man's loss of standing at law because of his conviction for the theft of a ceremonial belt. Perhaps the king had in mind the meeting of his witan convened to approve the will that excluded his nephews from the succession in favour of his son Edward.

Alfred relied on the council of his ealdormen and, of course, of his senior churchmen, but he might well consult less exalted but nevertheless important people, such as Beornwulf, the town-reeve of Winchester. A royal servant such as his 'horse thegn' or marshal could be in a position of influence: the king's own mother had been the daughter of his father's famous butler Oslac. Alfred divided his staff into three groups, who served at court for one month alternating with two months at home. Those in residence had their appointed sleeping quarters: those allocated to the royal chamber apartments might be the king's drinking and hunting companions and have their place in the great hall; others were relegated to sleeping 'on the threshing floor' in the barn. Then there would be noblemen's sons being 'fostered' in the royal household, and the household warriors. Outside the immediate entourage, royal officers in the country at large, and also prominent local landowners or 'king's thegns', could claim to be of what a later age would call the king's 'affinity', that is to have a special connection with the king. He communicated with them by sealed letters and the messengers could expect handsome lodging. At grassroots level the presence of kingship in a locality resided in the king's reeves, to whom a traveller or merchant in a district made his first report; they were agents of the king's interest in his estates, and among the villagers and local thegns, and were men of note.

The counsellors he summoned most regularly to advise him were accorded a status of respect as his *'witan'*, though their meetings never achieved the formalized standing of an institution of government suggested by the later (essentially Victorian) coinage 'witane-gemot' ('wisemen's meeting'). Compared with the quasi-imperial court of this grandson Æthelstan, Alfred's seems to have comprised rarely more than two or three bishops, four ealdormen and eight or so king's thegns, or ministers.[18] In earlier times nobles did not only hold land in their own right, but could be awarded 'loan-land', to use the term Alfred used, by the king in gratitude for services, which would revert to him on their death. The church by contrast had established the principle that lands granted to them by noble patrons or by the king himself could be secured by written charter to the recipient in perpetuity. By the late 700s the principle of 'bookland' was established for secular landowners too. The terms of his charter would probably require him to take armed forces to the king's army and mobilize labour for the king's works (see below), but the land could now remain in his family. At the practical level, Alfred's cultural programme (the term is hardly too strong) required an extraordinary amount of scribal activity based on his own and other groups of clerics, most of whom would have learnt their trade copying charters. After all, much administration was via letter, and some 200 charters survive from the ninth century for Wessex and Mercia. In the less polished examples scribal errors could creep in, which once prompted unjust suspicions of forgery (though some forgeries do exist). Some, notably those of the West Saxon type of the 830s–870s, remind us that beyond the bustle and sophistication of Winchester lie meetings of king and counsellors in shire towns, with the local reeves in attendance.

No doubt the network of book scribes was based on a 'headquarters' staffed by experts in the production and multiplication of bound manuscripts and where (surmises Michael Keynes) master copies were kept. He has identified a team of six: five of varying skills A, B, C, D and E ('the rather superior scribe'), who did the work while a sixth scribe, X, 'hovered behind them keeping track of their work'. The distribution network comprised various copyists at fixed points for the further duplication of exemplars. The preface to the *Pastoral Care* tells us that 'Alfred translated me into English' and then 'sent [the exemplar] south and north to his scribes (*writerum*) . . . to produce more copies [to be sent] to his bishops'. We know that at least ten bishops received copies in the 890s and can assume that they had further copies made for their parish clergy.[19]

Today the generally accepted canon of Alfred's literary work comprises the *Pastoral Care*, Boethius' *Consolation of Philosophy*, St Augustine of Hippo's *Soliloquies* and the first fifty of the prose versions of the Psalms. To these four works, which it is felt share characteristic features of style and vocabulary, the prefatory material to the laws is also added. While he almost certainly did not make the translation of Orosius it seems reasonable to suppose that it dates from his reign and may have been composed as part of his programme. Although Alfred had his children taught to write, he himself probably dictated his manuscripts and, for translations, may have dictated a first draft, to be worked up by a group of scholarly assistants.[20]

However it was done, we feel the presence of a vigorous and sympathetic imagination. When the writer of the Old English book of reflections loosely based on Augustine's *Soliloquies*, which is cast in the form of a dialogue between Augustine and Reason, compares himself, as a researcher in the groves of scholarship, to a forester going out to select timbers suited for his new structure of learning and his assistants to axemen following up with wagons, it is hard not to think of the architect-king supervising work for a new burh. Elsewhere a striking passage expounds trust in divine revelation in terms of the trust accorded to a secular lordship, when Reason asks

> Have you not a lord [the emperor] whom you trust in all matters better than yourself? . . . and do you think that the Emperor, the son of an emperor, is wiser or more truthful than Christ the son of God?[21]

There is nothing mechanical or hack about Alfred's English prose works, which are among the very earliest of the genre. It is a sophisticated style derived from the rhetorical devices of Latin models and deploying the typical patterns of Anglo-Saxon verse, alliteration and wordplay.

Alfred loved the dialogue as a literary form. A foundation text in his programme was the *Dialogues* of Pope Gregory (an exchange between Gregory and his friend Peter the deacon). It was followed by Alfred's own adaptation of Boethius. Conceived as a dialogue between the author and Lady Philosophy, the book became one of the most popular of the Middle Ages and its devotion to wisdom

immediately seized Alfred's imagination. The king's version, inter-
nalized as a dialogue between Wisdom and the Mind, creates an
authorial person called 'Boethius', who is the victim of a tyrant king
and invites us to see the world from his perspective.

The Church, the junior partner?

Alfred strongly associated the church with the governance of his
realm but it seems he was the dominant partner: indeed the balance
of power between church and court seems to have shifted in
favour of the king so that 'the reign of Alfred should be put in a
context of major constitutional change'. By the 790s the church in
England had acquired immense wealth, both in treasure and in real
estate: in Kent, for example, more than 30 per cent of all the landed
wealth seems to have been in the hands of the clergy. Monasteries,
it seems, were everywhere. By 800 there were almost thirty in the
Worcester diocese alone. Senior clergy were pivotal figures: the
archbishop often dominated the synods even when the king was
present and Archbishop Wulfred of Canterbury (805–32) struck
coins bearing his name alone. But as the ninth century advanced,
thanks in part to the Viking raids, the church's grip was loosened
and many religious estates passed into lay control. Alfred gave the
huge see of Sherborne to Asser without papal intervention, and
after the Welshman's death King Edward the Elder would divide it
into three sees.[22]

  Disposable land was an essential tool of kingcraft – the currency
in which the great men who served a king in peace expected
payment, as well as the traditional inducement to attract warriors to
his following in the days when warfare among the English kingdoms
had ensured a supply from among the defeated. For Alfred this
course was not open, but on occasion it seems he would appropriate church lands recovered from defeated Vikings.

Justice under law

The administration of law was grounded on the oath of an oath-worthy man solemnly given before God and accepted as valid. Charged with a crime, a man acquitted himself not by a trial on evidence but by giving his own oath and finding oath-helpers to bear out his statements and claims and his good faith. To lose one's oath-worthy status was to risk falling out of the law and be at the mercy of anyone with a claim against one's property or a grudge. But the powers of law enforcement were limited and in the most extreme crime, that of murder, the maintenance of order depended on the enforcement of a code of vendetta or feud supervised by the king according to strict rules of compensation based on the scale of wergild (or 'wergeld') payments. The laws of King Alfred, which also incorporate those of his predecessor King Ine, are represented by the stately '*domboc*' ('law book') set down in about 893. They have been described as 'the product of deep thought, intensive research, and great political vision',[23] an expression of ideological aspirations perhaps, rather than practical guidance for judges.

Legislation was not necessarily promulgated by the king in written form and judgement was validated more by the word of the king (*per verbum regis*) than by any text. In a celebrated case Alfred delivered judgement by word of mouth while washing his hands in his private chamber. The king, however, seems to have conceived law as a written text, for he remarks in his preamble that he had 'ordered to be written' (*awritan het*) many of the laws that his forefathers observed, and how he had not presumed to set down in writing many of his own. His code survives in just six manuscripts, the earliest of them dating from 925–50.

Alfred considered an ability to read English an essential requirement for a man in authority if he were to make sound judgements. Cases determined in local assemblies by ealdormen or reeves were to be referred to the king if they were disputed by the litigants. He was liable to intervene at random if he considered any judgement unfair and would order the judge to apply himself forthwith to 'the pursuit of wisdom' at risk of losing his job. The reading might be records of legal cases heard, or more likely it meant reading in 'those books that it is necessary to know'. For 'wisdom' in Alfredian terms, as described by Asser, was that which taught a man to care for truth and seek the common good rather than his own personal advantage. Rather than lose the king's favour, illiterate ealdormen, reeves and thegns would apply themselves to the mastery of the unfamiliar discipline of reading and learning, following, if need be, the king's advice to find someone to read books aloud to him 'by day and night, at any opportunity' – the very way Alfred the boy had memorized the poetry book offered by his mother.

Alfred's London

London comprised the old Roman *civitas* within the walls, the 'burh' of the *Anglo-Saxon Chronicle*, and the extramural settlement, the port of Lundenwic, which had a population of about 5,000 and covered some 148 acres (60 hectares) on the north bank of the Thames, running westward from Chancery Lane to Trafalgar Square. The first recorded Viking attack here is in 842, the second about 851: coin hoards have been unearthed for the first date at the Middle Temple and for the second a 'purse-hoard' of Northumbrian coins was found near the Royal Opera House. Other hoards have been unearthed near Waterloo Bridge (872) and within the city walls, dated to 880. Found in the early 2000s it contained coins of the special London Monogram type, which Alfred probably issued to mark his resumption of control of London after Ceolwulf's departure. Then for the year 886 the *Anglo-Saxon Chronicle* records '*gesette Ælfred cing Lundenburh*', in other words he occupied Roman London and made it habitable again. In this year, too, 'all the English people who were not in captivity to the Danes submitted to him'. By 893 and again in 895 the 'citizens' (burgwara) of London were sufficiently numerous to mount a body for effective military action. In 898 the king presided over a meeting, attended by among others his son Edward, the archbishop of Canterbury, Bishop Wærferth of Worcester and Ealdorman Æthelred of the Mercians and his wife, Alfred's daughter Æthelflæd, that confirmed the 'instauration' of the borough and the establishment of a grid plan of streets between what is now Thames Street and Cheapside. Digs in the early 2000s revealed just such market streets running off a central spinal thoroughfare. The archaeology indicates that from 900 onwards the main business and residential quarters were within the city walls. In other words, by the end of Alfred's reign, London had 'entirely changed its shape and focus'[24] away from the Aldwych Strand back into the Roman walled city.

Preparations for the return of the heathen and defence of the realm

For much of the 880s the Viking raiders were harrying the northern lands of West Francia so that, in the lament of the chronicler of St Vaast, 'the Christian folk [were] brought to utter ruin and desolation.' These same years saw the kingdom of the West Saxons engaged in public works programmes and military reorganization. Three English kingdoms, Northumbria, Mercia and East Anglia, had been removed from the map. Alfred planned a system of defence round his borders and land. His plans rested on the known tactics of the enemy, best practice overseas and antecedents in the English tradition.

Asser writes of 'the cities and towns that he restored, and the others he built where none had been before . . .', though he does not claim that Alfred was the first to build such towns and fortifications. In the 1970s archaeologist Martin Biddle, excavating the 'Roman' burh of Winchester, revealed rectilinear street patterns adapted to military defence and trade. The basic pattern comprised a main street, with parallel back streets linked at right angles to the high street by side streets, and a perimeter boulevard running round inside the wall. Similar planning has subsequently been detected in other Alfredian foundations such as Wareham, Wallingford and Oxford. It is argued that such sites stand at the beginning of the continuous history of the medieval English town. The once flourishing cross-Channel trade of early ninth-century Hamwic was a thing of the past when Alfred came to the throne, probably in part because it was an undefended site. Thanks to him and his new urban developments, however, a vigorous internal market was to spring up.[25]

The Viking raiders generally avoided battle. Their preferred tactic was to seize some defensible site as their base of operations and plunder the surrounding region before the English could mobilize forces and then to retreat behind the fortifications until the English should disperse – or they made good their escape under cover of night. It is probable that Alfred knew of the fortified bridges that Charles the Bald had built on the River Seine and similar defensive works, though they were hardly more advanced than the fortified burhs known in eighth-century Mercia.

The basic text here is the Burghal Hidage. It gives a list of some thirty 'burhs' (defended settlements or fortifications), each with its own garrison and established around Wessex, Sussex and Surrey in such a way that no place of importance was more than a day's march from the nearest and that every navigable waterway, Roman road or major track way penetrating Wessex was commanded. Even the best landing beaches were accessible from a garrison in a burh. The system was reinforced by army tracks (*herepaths*) skirting estate boundaries for the muster of local contingents. Some burhs seem to have been intended as towns from the start, others were emergency forts, hurriedly thrown up as part of a crash building programme. Quite apart from the actual construction, huge quantities of gravel, flints and timber had to be shifted on site before work could begin, calling for high logistical capacity and administrative skills. It has been estimated that labour on the defensive banks for the burh at Wallingford alone would have required more than 120,000 man hours.[26]

The actual labour force would be recruited at the expense of local landowners, as indicated above, under the convention known by historians as the 'common burdens', apparently first established by the Mercian king in the mid–eighth century, when monks were obliged to fulfil it, much to the horror of St Boniface. The so-called 'trinoda necessitas' (or, as Eric John proposes, 'trimoda . . .'; or 'three mode necessity'), required those liable to supply work on bridges, fortifications ('burhbot') and troops for the levy. Alfred exploited the system as fully as possible and after him it was stretched to embrace ship-building.

The 'Hidage', based on the hide, an ancient unit of land considered sufficient to support one peasant family, designates the number of 'hides' assigned to each burh for its structural maintenance and defensive manning. A formula specifies that one man was to go from every hide and dictates the length of wall that such a force was expected to defend. Altogether the document calls for some 27,000 men to be employed in the maintenance and defence of the forts. One man from each hide; the idea seems simple enough but recruiting and managing men in such numbers could only have been done by thegns who commanded the loyalty of the men and already took services from their land.

Maybe Alfred's programme of town fortifications, which perhaps included the late Saxon work on Exeter's Roman wall, was also coloured by childhood experiences in Rome. In 846 a Saracen fleet had sailed up the River Tiber and attacked the city; the residents at the foreign schools – Franks, Saxons, Lombards and Frisians – helped defend the fortifications. After the raid a high wall, completed in 852, was built round the basilicas of St Peter's and its vicinity; the area enclosed was known as the Leonine City. The postern gates were surmounted by an inscription recording its builders, among them the Posterula Saxonum. Nearby, hostels housed the Saxon community in a compound known as their *burh* (*borgo*). No doubt the inscription over the Saxons' postern had been pointed out to Alfred and his father on their visit to Rome in 855, along with accounts of deeds of prowess by the school's trained bands back in 846.[27]

The other essential element in the defence strategy was the creation of a standing army. Alfred reorganized the kingdom's military resources, starting from existing West Saxon military traditions of the 'fyrd' or army. The West Saxon fyrd was not a levy *en masse* but a mobilization of king's men and their retainers – the king's following arrayed for battle with, in summer, local territorial forces from the shires. This meant landowners and their personal followings led by ealdormen, reeves and local king's thegns, operating either as divisions in the king's army or as local defence forces. Raising these forces as need arose took time, and by the time they had arrived on the scene the enemy was probably gone. Alfred ordained that the force be divided in two, one half active for military service while the other remained to work on the land; he doubled the length of the service, probably from forty to eighty days, establishing in effect a fighting force available through most of the campaigning season. These seems to have been a standing elite that amounted to a King's lifeguard: no king of Alfred's line fell in battle, despite their exposed position of command fighting at close quarters in the middle of the shield wall.[28]

In the autumn of 892 famine threatened in northeast Francia. The Vikings made their way to Boulogne, where the Franks provided them with 250 ships so that they could cross the Channel 'in one journey, horses and all'. These were heterogeneous war bands of diverse allegiances under an experienced leader like Hæstan, who came 'with eighty ships in the mouth of the Thames, and built himself a fort at Milton'. In that same season 'the other host' was at Appledore. Wessex was ready. In the 870s the raiders had campaigned through the heartlands more or less at will. Now a yet larger force made hardly any serious penetration of the frontiers. After a faltering start, the Alfredian defence system worked, in the words of Richard Abels, 'precisely as planned'. The enemy was able to land because there was an uncompleted burh on the Lympne. They set up fortifications under the watchful eyes of an army in the field and the new, year-round garrisons of the burhs. In land, instead of towns and settlements open to attack, they would find garrisoned burhs fortified with earth banks and pal- isades, proof against storm assault. To lay a siege now meant being attacked from neighbouring garrisons or the field army division of the fyrd. To leave the garrison in place was out of the question. From Maidstone Alfred could monitor the enemy through pickets along the Downs while patrols could pick off raiding parties. Alfred's ability to maintain his troops in the field proved decisive. However, his physical distance from the centre of military action in 893 meant that the exploits of his son Edward as field army com- mander, recorded fifty years later in the chronicle of Ealdorman Æthelweard but unmentioned by the official chronicle, may have seemed more dramatic.

Alfred had designed his system of burhs not so much to prevent conquest as to minimize the possibility of raiding. As a result he was able to fight Vikings simultaneously on the east, west and north frontiers of the kingdom. His son Edward was able to use the system for aggression, conquest and settlement.

A king's navy

King Alfred ordered the building of a fleet of ships – it seems that his son Edward had about a hundred in 910 – England's first royal navy. The ships were to be built to a new design that he stated 'could be most serviceable'. They were commanded and crewed by Frisians and English, although the actual ship designs owed nothing to Frisian example. The *Chronicle* reports they were twice as long as the Danes', were faster and, having more freeboard, steadier in the water. This presumably offered a firmer fighting platform in hand to hand combat: during an encounter in 882 two ships' companies were slaughtered, whereupon two more surrendered. As with the system of burhs, Wessex arranged for the financing of its ships. Specific estates thought capable of raising the necessary funds were designated 'ship sokes' and each was required to provide a warship and provision its crew.[29]

Thanks to demonstration sailings by Edwin and Joyce Gifford in the mid 1990s of half scale models built after ten years' research, we have a good idea of how Alfred's longships may have performed. Built in the Sutton Hoo manner (a vessel unearthed at Graveney in Kent, dated to about 900, indicates that Alfred's naval architects may have been aware of that tradition) but with up to 60 oars, they 'could have carried a complement of 140 men at speeds of up to 12 knots when sailing and 7 knots under oar'. Since Alfred's coastal burhs were rarely more than 25 miles (40 km) apart, the Giffords estimated that squadrons could have reached any stricken beach within two hours of receiving the alarm. Given the improved signalling facilities and coastal fortifications we may have another part of the explanation for the decrease in Viking successes. The Anglo-Saxon state put high store on its naval defence. According to William of Malmesbury, King Edgar (957–75) patrolled the coasts of Britain on the look out for pirates on an annual basis. His account indicates that Edgar maintained three fleets, one each on the east and west coasts and one in the north. Presumably each flotilla returned to its home waters under its own commander once it had sailed its stretch of coastline. Admittedly it is highly improbable that the king regularly circumnavigated Britain, but it was hardly less impressive that he was reported to have maintained a standing navy.

At his death the *Chronicle* said that while he lived 'no fleet however flaunting of itself was able to win booty in England.' Writing in 1996, M. Strickland argued that the navy was 'the arm to which the Anglo-Saxons attached great, if not supreme significance'.[30] Indeed, the English may have set a trend. A longship found at Hedeby in the late 1990s, with space for sixty-four oars, suggests that Alfred's model found imitators.[31]

A warship could make a spectacular gift to the king 'who had everything'. Bishop Ælfwold of Crediton (later the see of Exeter) bequeathed a longship of 64 oars to Æthelred II. Earl Godwine gave a great ship to Edward the Confessor. Emperor Henry III asked England for a flotilla of ships to support him in his campaign against Count Baldwin V of Flanders.

Threnody of triumph

Alfred, king of the Anglo-Saxons, died on 26 October 899, aged either 50 or 51, after a reign of twenty-eight years – a momentous epoch in the history of England. By holding the line against the Viking Danes, Alfred prevented the establishment of a pagan power on one of the pillars of European civilization. Triumphant in the field, he structured a national defence in depth, organized the reform of the demoralized clergy as leaders of a programme of education, commissioned or himself carried through translations into English of major works of history and philosophy, and almost certainly inaugurated the *Anglo-Saxon Chronicle*.

His reputation seems to have faded somewhat after his death. No other English king bore his name. But it was he who brought Wessex and West Mercia through the decades of danger. There was little likelihood of his subjects following the fashionable reinvention of Vikings, begun by gallery curators in the 1970s, as over-aggressive traders and salesmen pressing their wares on somewhat unappreciative customers.

Archaeological digs from the 1960s on may have revealed new dimensions of this Viking trade, but they have also heightened awareness of Winchester as the 'traditional' capital of Wessex; by identifying Alfredian towns and fortifications on the ground they have also substantiated Alfred's activities as defensive strategist. Ealdorman Æthelweard, the king's distant kinsman who died a century after him, dubbed him 'the Magnanimous', 'unshakable pillar of the people of the west a man full of justice, active in war, learned in speech and, before all, instructed in divine learning . . .'[32]

Later generations took as given the platform of the Anglo-Saxon kingdom Alfred had rescued and upon which they built the kingdom of England. Comparisons are often made between Charles the Great and Alfred the Great, so it is worth noting that whereas the successors of Charles, the Carolingians, fragmented his empire, Alfred's successors strengthened the ties that united his kingdom and created an English 'empire' in Britain. Whether because of childhood memories of public inscriptions in Rome, or because he knew of the Latin-literate public policy of Carolingian Europe, or, more probably, because of his own passion for learning, Alfred profoundly believed that exploitation of the power of the written word, above all the 'Englisce' written word – whether in charters, the Guthrum treaty, the law code, the *Chronicle* or the translations of those books 'needful to know' – was indispensable to good government. In the words of Simon Keynes,

> Soldier, law-maker, statesman, educator, and scholar, not to mention
> ship-builder . . . all were . . . inseparable [from] his determination to
> discharge the responsibilities of his high office for the good of his sub-
> jects and in the service of God.[33]

9

LITERATURE, LEARNING, LANGUAGE AND LAW IN ANGLO-SAXON ENGLAND

Bede wrote in Latin, Europe's language of learning, and pre-Conquest England produced many other fine Latinists whose work will be mentioned. But the chief theme of this chapter is English and its pioneering achievement as Europe's first vernacular to evolve from the oral tradition into a fully articulate vehicle for all the categories of high civilization – literature, learning, law, administration and historical writing. Thus a language that begins to emerge as a distinct branch of the Germanic group about the fifth century would outmatch even Old Irish and Welsh in the range of its applications, as well as proving their equal in the glories of its literature. The tradition was on an upswing even as it was blotted out. To judge from the surviving manuscripts, the decades before Hastings saw a surge in the number of books produced in the vernacular.[1] Many were older titles but the quantity indicates an increase in the reading population.

In addition to the *Beowulf* manuscript itself, as many as 300 manuscripts and texts survive, despite a tragic fire in the year 1731 that consumed much of the great collection of medieval manuscripts assembled by Sir Robert Cotton (1571–1631), a founder member with William Camden of the original Society of Antiquaries. One of the manuscripts destroyed was the epic fragment known as the

Battle of Maldon, an account of a heroic defeat at the hands of Danish raiders during the reign of Æthelred 'the Unready' (see chapter 11). Shortly before the great fire David Casley, deputy keeper of the collection, had made a careful line by line copy of the manuscript fragment. Thanks to him we have what scholars consider a sound version of this masterpiece of alliterative Old English verse, the last in the Germanic heroic tradition and, in short, the culmination of the spirit of *Beowulf* itself. Other superb poetry includes the old heroic poem *Widsith* and one commemorating the great victory at Brunanburh found in the *Chronicle*. Of the prose there is, of course, the *Chronicle* itself, the English language law 'codes' of most of the Anglo-Saxon kingdoms, translations of scholarly texts and books of the Latin Bible texts, such as the interlining of the Latin text of the Lindisfarne Gospels with an English translation, the issue of government writs in the language of the people, and even word games or 'riddles' written in English. We start with the poetry.

Old English poetry

The characteristic verse idiom in Old English poetry comprises the measured line divided into two balanced half-lines, each with a minimum of four syllables, in which syllable length and stress are swung together by alliterative patterns. Such alliteration, which seems ideally adapted to declamation in an oral tradition, is to be found in other early Germanic languages. The Anglo-Saxon poet attempting Latin verse met with problems of metrical versification that did not confront his Continental counterparts for whom the Latin language was still a living tradition. Aldhelm, England's earliest poet in Latin, produced some fine work in the language, but equally from time to time deployed his native alliterative idiom in the language of the church.

According to a story that was still going the rounds four hundred years later, Aldhelm, a Wessex nobleman and first bishop of

Sherborne (705–9), was wont to take his stand on a bridge at a river crossing near his church, harp in hand, and sing to his congregation hurrying homewards after mass, hoping to hold their interest in things spiritual with words from scripture tagged into popular songs. Aldhelm in his minstrel mode reveals a world where the vernacular tradition of the *gleomen* or *scops* (minstrels) was shared as part of a common culture by noble, churchman and commoner.

The *scop* (pronounced 'shop', with a short vowel sound), a bardic minstrel who might be in regular service with one lord or travel from one mead-hall court to another, was the guardian of the ancient Germanic oral tradition. Writing about AD 100, the Roman historian Tacitus knew of the Germans' 'old songs' (*carmina antiqua*). According to the *Beowulf* poet, the din of carousing and banqueting daily shook the walls of King Hrothgar's Heorot Hall. We may have a hint of the effect from the writings of Adelard of Bath, a twelfth-century English scholar and musician at the court of Henry I's Queen Matilda, who was descended from the old English royal line. According to Louise Cochrane, Adelard recalled how once, when he was playing the stringed *cithara* before the queen, a little boy among the courtiers became so carried away by the rhythm of the music that he enthusiastically waved his arms about, making the company laugh out loud. Anyone who has heard performances of medieval minstrel music will know the pulsating and rowdy rhythmic effects possible on early stringed instruments.

Presumably the hubbub subsided when the *scop* swept his lyre, which since the time of Homer down to the histrions (epic ballad singers) of the Balkans has been the instrument of the bard, to begin his 'clear song'. Among the treasures revealed at the Prittlewell excavation were the shadow remnants of such an instrument imprinted in the earth. Instrument-builder Zachary Taylor lovingly and meticulously recreated the ancient lyre. The original must have been highly valued for Taylor discovered it had been fractured at some time and painstakingly repaired with gold and silver rivets.

Its musical quality was surely much diminished but, like Philadelphia's Liberty Bell, cracked beyond restoration, its aura was irreplaceable. The 'clear song' might be the bard's version of a traditional lay, a section of an epic featuring the deeds of ancestors of those present, or an ode improvised to celebrate the occasion.

We know something about the life of the *scop* from a poem that survives as part of a tenth-century collection called the Exeter Book. Named after its fictional author, *Widsith* (literally 'wide [or far] traveller') tells of visits to the mead halls of heroes and kings of the pagan past (from the fourth to the sixth centuries), and of the rich gifts the poet was given. It refers to Offa of Angeln, claimed as an ancestor by the great eighth-century king of Mercia, and Widsith was also at the court of Eormanric, king of the Ostrogoths (Ermanaric, who ruled vast tracts of modern Ukraine in the 370s), who gave him a precious arm-ring. Widsith presented it to his own lord, who in turn conferred lands upon him.

The tone of the *Widsith* poem is distinctly upbeat. By contrast, the forty-two lines of *Deor*, also about a *scop*, are a lament for the loss of a lord's favour, the poet's dismissal from court and the loss of his lands. He recalls the misfortunes of legendary figures from the Germanic past and reflects in a stoical refrain that, just as their troubles passed, so will his. Like *Widsith*, *Deor*'s lament is a glimpse of the aristocratic Anglo-Saxon lifestyle; both remind us that the bardic verse central to the cultural life of the warrior nobility belonged to a largely oral tradition, of which only a fragment survives in the literary record. And central to the imaginative life of such traditions is the performance in the present, which relies on the memory, the skill and the inventive genius of an unlettered artist with words.

Noble (whether literate or non-literate) and peasant shared common cultural conventions (as we shall note, there is good evidence that many nobles were literate, from the late eighth century onwards at least). The villager, too, had his feastings, though not perhaps to match the mead hall. As the evening advanced the harp (perhaps that of some more prosperous farmer) began to circulate and any member of the party who could not provide a song, accompanied or not, was poor company indeed. One of the best-known stories in Bede tells how a farm-hand called Caedmon became a poet. Because he was no singer he would get up and leave the table as he saw the harp on its way. One night, having quit the feast as usual and tidied out the animal byre, he curled up on the straw and went to sleep. He dreamed that a man stood beside him and called him by name: 'Caedmon, you shall sing a song for me about the Creation of all things.' Inspired, the illiterate labourer improvised a poem that told how 'the Lord of Glory . . . [made] . . . Middle Earth for men, to be their mansion.'[2]

Bede quotes a snatch of the song in a Latin version, and then explains that he can only give the gist of it because poetry 'cannot be translated literally from one language into another without losing much of its beauty and dignity'. The remark is a measure of the standing of the English language in Bede's world, but more so of Bede himself. Outside the British Isles, it would have been unheard of for a Latin-literate cleric to accord equivalence of status to a work in the vernacular. But then Bede was not only in the Anglo-Saxon tradition, he also, we are told, wrote English devotional poetry. Caedmon's original Anglo-Saxon is to be found added on to Latin manuscripts of Bede's great *History*, copied shortly after his death. Impressed by the peasant poet, St Hild of Whitby, that great lady, invited Caedmon to join her community and he became, in effect, the house specialist hymn-writer. Once a passage of the Latin scriptures was explained to him, he could produce a moving and delightful English song. Many lay people were converted to 'heavenly things' as a result.

Conversely, many Anglo-Saxon churchmen hankered after the Old English, and therefore pagan, secular tradition. The church synod of 747 fulminated against monasteries that encouraged 'versifiers and harpists' to visit, as well as priests who delivered their sermons in the manner of a scop delivering an epic. Perhaps such priests were only doing their best to make Christianity 'relevant to contemporary concerns'. Presumably St Aldhelm at least would have approved.

For even bishops were not immune to the charms of the vernacular tradition. The Exeter Book, copied about 975 and the largest collection of Anglo-Saxon poetry to have survived, is so called because it was donated to Exeter's cathedral library in the eleventh century by Bishop Leofric. Of Cornish extraction, despite his English name, Leofric was educated in Lotharingia and became chaplain to Edward the Confessor in exile in France. He returned with the king in 1041 and was appointed bishop of Cornwall, where his family had an estate at Tregear, and Devon. He reconstituted the region's two sees, at St Germans and Crediton, as one at the Benedictine monastery within the burh of Exeter. Under him the Exeter cathedral library was noted for its scriptorium and ranked fourth in size in England after Canterbury, Salisbury and Worcester.

The Exeter Book opens with three poems concerning the life of Christ, including the *Ascension* by a poet whose name, Cynewulf, appears in runic characters in three other Old English poems. One of these, *Elene*, in the collection known as the Codex Vercellensis, is an account of the finding of the True Cross by St Helena, mother of Emperor Constantine the Great and traditionally associated with Britain.

Most of the Exeter Book poems are religious but, in addition to *Widsith*, there are a few outstanding pieces, lyrical or elegiac in mood, that can reach across the centuries to stir the reader today, when family breakdown and exile affect so many lives. In *The Wife's Lament* a woman tells of her misery and grief at being separated from her husband to satisfy the honour of his kin, while in *The Husband's Message* a man begs his wife to remember her former vows of love and join him overseas where he has found a new home.

Two other poems are more ambitious in theme and so more profound in their effect. Later hauntingly adapted as a radio play, *Seafarer* almost anticipates elements of the story of the Flying Dutchman, as it tells of a seemingly endless trek across dark and hostile wastes of sea, through wind-blown ice sprays and the cries of seabirds. It laments 'the mead hall and the laughter of men' that symbolize the good life of the soul in this world – the world that the poet has lost. *Wanderer*, explicitly the lament of an exile, regretting the happiness of the life that is gone and bemoaning the cold and friendless present, is a reflection on the state of the Christian soul resistant to the mercy of God in this transient world. Both poems interweave the realities of the quotidian and the spiritual life; in both the world of the poet is the world of lordship and loyalty. In *Wanderer*, indeed, the real plight of a friendless but above all lordless man seems almost to outweigh the allegorical spiritual plight of a soul without God. These two works offer us a glimpse of that wanderlust that brought the Anglo-Saxons to England in the first place, and led many to venture overseas to the Continent. As in the minstrel life of *Widsith*, the setting is the aristocratic world of the *Beowulf* poet. It is a world where the queen presides over the feasting of the warriors and even serves them at table. *Judith*, the text of which survives in the *Beowulf* manuscript, is a verse adaptation of the apocryphal *Book of Judith*, which tells how a beautiful Jewish widow slew Holofernes, commander of an Assyrian army, and so ensured the defeat of the invaders. As the Old English poem develops the story, whereas the original was a widow who disarmed her enemy with her beauty and cut off his head as he lay asleep, the patriot heroine of this poem is a warrior virgin triumphant in battle. Pauline Stafford suggests it may have been a tribute to the warlike Æthelflaed, Lady of the Mercians, a star of the next chapter.

Finally there is a collection of 'riddles' – poems, mostly short, designed for social entertainment in mead hall or refectory. Perhaps Aldhelm's Latin short puzzle poems or *enigmata* hold the key.

Somewhat bookish and intended as exercise texts for the teaching of poetic forms, they were, he said, modelled on joke verses
extemporized in late classical times as entertainments at drinking
parties. Other churchmen, including an archbishop of Canterbury
and St Boniface, were inspired by Aldhelm's example to pass an idle
hour composing such word games, though they rarely produced
results to divert a party of serious drinkers – even if Boniface did
send the cathedral monks at York two tuns of wine for 'a merry day
with the brethren' (see chapter 5). The Exeter Book vernacular
riddles describe everyday objects in allusive, sometimes opaque,
lines demanding to be deciphered. In Anglo-Saxon England, what
had pleased the ancient Romans became – in that jewelled world of
swords, shields and goblets – a crafted form of entertainment where
those objects and many others asked a festive audience to guess their
names. As well as mundane, the object of a riddle could be serious:
as likely a book of the Gospels as a weathervane, a shield, animals
or birds. Number 55 muses on the paradox that the Cross, once the
punishment of thieves, is fit to be adorned in gold and jewels.
Sometimes they remind us of Robert Frost's dictum that poetry
begins in delight but can end in wisdom. And sometimes they don't!
Number 54 concerns the churning of butter – in which the serving
man is 'one moment forceful . . . the next . . . knocked quite up,
blown by his exertion'.[3] Some 700 years later Henry Purcell was
setting drinking 'catches' that might have caught the occasional
mood 'down Exeter way'. One thinks in particular of the footman
and scullery maid assembling a kitchen broom: he, called John, with
'a thing that is long'; she, called Mary, with 'a thing that is hairy'.

The Vercelli Book, despite its scholarly Latin title of Codex
Vercellensis, is another Old English manuscript held in another
cathedral library, this time that of Vercelli in Piedmont, where it was
discovered in the 1820s. Apparently in English use in the eleventh
century, although written in the tenth, it could have been in the
baggage of one of the party that accompanied Bishop Ulf of

Dorchester, one of Edward the Confessor's Norman appointees, when he attended the church council in that city in 1050. The anthology comprises prose (a life of St Guthlac and twenty-three homilies) and poetry, including the complete text of *The Dream of the Rood*, fragments of which are found carved on the Ruthwell Cross (see chapter 3).

The fragments of a poem inscribed on a cross in the seventh century written down in a tenth-century manuscript encapsulate the basic problems of dating most Anglo-Saxon verse. The age of a manuscript in which a work survives is not, evidently, a guaranteed indicator of even the approximate date of composition. Things are further complicated by the fact that the poems we have survive as the result of chance events and are isolated copies made in transmission stretching over generations, probably across dialect boundaries and in any case exploiting archaisms of language for poetic effect. It may well be that the oldest of the long poems are those on biblical themes, notably the *Genesis*, *Exodus* and *Daniel* in the so-called Junius Manuscript, now in Oxford's Bodleian Library (MS. Junius 11). Bede noted these very biblical themes as ones that Caedmon sang about, so Junius 11 was once known as the 'Caedmon manuscript'. It is in any case a remarkable production, evidently designed from the start as an illustrated book, the text written first and blanks left for illustrations. The project was never completed but more than fifty line drawings by two artists depict such scenes as God the Creator enthroned above Chaos before the Beginning of the World.

Old English Prose

Anglo-Saxon England [provides] the leading example of a vernacular culture worthy of the name in the whole of western Europe. French and German did not achieve a like status of literary quality and use till the twelfth century, whereas Old English had [before that time] reigned for hundreds of years.[4]

And nowhere in western Europe does another national tradition, not even the rich vein of Old Irish and Middle Irish literature, with its annals such as the *Annals of Ulster*, have a documentary source to equal the *Anglo-Saxon Chonicle* for extent and detail. From the opening sentence of the Genealogical Preface to the (Ā) manuscript commonly known as the Parker Chronicle ('In the year of Christ's Nativity 494, Cerdic and Cynric his son landed at Cerdicsora with five ships'), to its last, the election in 1154 of William of Waterville to be abbot of Peterborough Abbey, as recorded in the (E) manuscript commonly called the Laud Chronicle, the various versions of the *Anglo-Saxon Chronicle* provide an almost unbroken sequence of annals over a span of 660 years. From the 890s the writers are sometimes contemporaries of the events they describe: we are told, for example, that Abbot William 'has made a good beginning' and, with the writer, hope that 'Christ [may] grant that he end as well'.

But the *Chronicle* (perhaps '*Chronicles*' is better, as there are a number of different copies and independent variants) tends to favour the house of Wessex, not surprisingly, if indeed the so-called 'common stock' of the various texts originated in the late ninth century at the instigation of King Alfred (see chapter 8). Between 892 and 975 copies were made and continued at various centres – Winchester up to the year 1001, Canterbury, Abingdon, Worcester and Peterborough – which vary in local emphasis and material. For example, at some time in the eleventh century the Winchester copy (sometimes known as the Parker Chronicle after Archbishop Matthew Parker of Canterbury) was moved to Canterbury, and its new continuators inserted various items relating to Kentish history for earlier years. There are various fragments of other versions and some passages are in Latin. But these are a small percentage of the whole. It has been described as

a diary whose entries were made year by year instead of day by day . . .
There are many years for which no entries were made at all . . . and

[many] . . . which record the barest details of battles and of the succession of kings and bishops. But at other times . . . the *Chronicle* expands into a full and detailed narrative of enthralling interest and of the highest historical value.[5]

As an ordered presentation of a sequence of events it compares poorly with some of the Continental Latin annals and there are times when it breaks away from the strict historical narrative in digressions that, if published together, could make a varied and fascinating anthology. For the year 755 [757] a dramatic account of a murderous attack by elements hostile to King Cynewulf of Wessex on his royal love nest has been called the first short story in English. There are incisive pen-portraits, including one of William the Conqueror, and snaps of reportage like the slaughter of monks at Glastonbury in 1083. The *Chronicle* even includes one of the pinnacles of Anglo-Saxon poetry, a majestic fragment commemorating the military epic of the victory at Brunanburh (937). But it is, before all, an evolving work of English prose. A recent analysis has proposed that its many scribes aimed at a style with a hidden numerological element patterned on contemporary theories of structures seen to lie behind the Biblical writings.[6] To the Anglo-Saxons themselves, one imagines, more important than the *Chronicle* were the various Biblical texts available to them in their own language for centuries. The first of these biblical translators was the Venerable Bede himself. At his death he was working on an English version of St John's Gospel and we know from one of his letters that he had provided English translations of basic texts such as the Lord's Prayer to priests who had no Latin, so that they could teach them to their congregations.

Ælfric, a distinguished scholar born about 950 and as prolific as Bede, wrote mainly in the vernacular. In him Anglo-Saxon prose achieved its zenith of stylistic beauty and clarity of expression. Sometimes he adapts rhetorical devices from classical Latin authors

to great effect; at others his flowing prose rhythms follow the alliterative verse patterns of Anglo-Saxon verse. He influenced writers
of Old English well into the twelfth century.

Ælfric was educated at the monastic school in Winchester, under
Bishop Æthelwold. When he was about twenty he was sent as an
instructor to the monastery at Cerne Abbas in Dorset and then, in
1005, appointed as abbot of the newly founded minster at Eynsham,
Oxfordshire, where he spent the rest of his life. The foundation was
new, but its buildings were on a site settled since the Bronze Age –
possibly a place of traditional sacred associations. He wrote a Latin
grammar in English, which aimed in part to explain Old English
and was also a handbook to the speaking of Latin. This *Colloquy*
takes the form of conversations between the teacher and his pupil,
a monastic novice, and various lay people such as farm-workers,
hunters and merchants. One suggestion is that it might have been
intended as a sort of play, to be acted by the children of the cloister.
Ælfric's very lively dialogues tell us a good deal about the life in early
eleventh-century England and also about the man himself – obviously an alert observer, fascinated by the world about him. He also
wrote many books in English and sermons based on the writings of
the Church Fathers, among them Bede. He wrote in English, he
tells us, because other writers in that language often contained errors
that could mislead 'unlearned men' who could not check the Latin.
One of his 'Catholic Homilies' is an Easter sermon about the presence of Christ in the bread and wine of the communion service.
The debate had been running in Latin theological texts for more
than a century and continued well after Ælfric's time. A formulation
of the Roman Catholic doctrine of 'transubstantiation' (a term first
used in the twelfth century) was given in the documents of the
Counter-Reformation Council of Trent (1545–63). According to
John Godfrey, in his book *The Church in Anglo-Saxon England*, 'it is
impossible to square Ælfric's teaching with that later defined by the
Roman Catholic Church' and just three years after the final session

of Trent a 'modern English' version of the Easter sermon was published with the approval of Anglican bishops, though it is equally
difficult to make it 'square' with the Anglican Article concerned
with the doctrine. Be that as it may, it is hardly surprising that the
Post-Reformation Protestant church in England cherished what
they called 'A Testimonie of Antiquitie', written by an Englishman
in English. Perhaps of more interest to us is the fact that Ælfric
tackled such abstract and elusive concepts in his native tongue at all.
No doubt he felt, in his awkward Anglo-Saxon way, that a central
article of Faith enjoined on all Christians should be explicable in the
language of the believer.

Another matter of great importance to him was the question of
the plight of the Christian soul in the afterlife, awaiting the Day of
Judgement or Doomsday. Debate on the matter went back at least
as far as St Augustine of Hippo in the fifth century. Related questions were the meaning of 'Paradise': was it to be identified [typo-
logically] with the Garden of Eden as an equivalent of heaven, as
St Augustine had held, or was it a location distinct from both Eden
and heaven. In touching on such matters, Ælfric was working in a
tradition of Anglo-Saxon theology stretching back to Bede's Latin
'Vision of Drythelm' and other ideas of an 'interim paradise', which
fed into the formulation of the doctrine of Purgatory in the twelfth
century.[7] Ælfric produced at least forty lives of saints and planned
an English version of the Old Testament (part translation/part commentary), of which the first seven books were completed.

Although prompted by a request from a West Saxon aristocrat for
an English translation of the book, it was turned out as a sermon-
writer's reference crib, written in the end, like all but one of Ælfric's
works, as a text to aid his fellow clerics, above all the ill-educated
parish clergy. This tradition stretched back to Alfred and his conviction that a well-grounded clergy was the life-blood of a vigorous church and that, in turn, was the guarantee of a vigorous and
healthy nation. Such a view of the role of the church seems bizarre

in today's secular Britain, but in the tenth century it was received wisdom throughout Europe. The difference was that in England the church establishment respected its front-line troops, the parish priests, and that, while many bewailed their lack of Latin (as no doubt Peter Cook's E. L. Wistey would have done), others in typically English fashion not only offered them a helping hand through the difficulties of the alien language used by the church, as Ælfric did in his *Colloquy*, but also took immediate practical steps to instruct the priests in a language they could understand – their own.

The exception among Ælfric's programme of texts for priests was a biblical treatise designed as a layman's guide to the Old and New Testaments. A long preface addresses the thegn (with estates near Fyncham) who had prompted the book and who apparently had been pestering him for yet more English books. One glimpses an educated reading public among the higher ranks of Anglo-Saxon society and indeed Ealdorman Æthelweard (*d. c.* 998), the man who had commissioned Ælfric's Bible version, and was the author of the Latin *Chronicon*, based on the *Anglo-Saxon Chronicle* (see chapter 5). Claiming descent from King Alfred's brother Æthelred I, he wrote the book for his German cousin, abbess Matilda of Essen, about the year 980. He praised their ancestors' skill in turning books from the ornate Latin tongue into English, so that not just scholars but any lay person who may read it could, in a measure, hear the 'tearful passion' of the book of Boethius brought to life in their own language.

After 1066 the writing of English continued for some time. As we have noted, the Peterborough version of the *Chronicle* was kept up until 1154: for the best part of ninety years this great Benedictine house on the edge of the Fens, last shrine of the arm of St Oswald, continued its record of national events in the language of the subject people. Of the other five versions extant not one runs later than 1070. The Peterborough continuation, kept up with annual entries to 1136, and intermittently thereafter, seems almost like a gesture of defiance to the alien regime.

The English allegiance was evidently very strong at the abbey. In 1066 Abbot Leofric (nephew, by the way, of Earl Leofric and his wife Godiva of Coventry), went with Harold's army to Hastings, dying a week after the battle. The monks immediately elected an Englishman named Brand as his successor – and intrepidly paid homage to Edgar the Ætheling of the royal house of Wessex as the next king. Eventually William angrily agreed to Abbot Brand's installation but imposed on Peterborough the highest rate of military levy on its income of any abbey in the kingdom. With the death of Brand in 1069, the Norman king imposed a Norman abbot, Thuroldus of Fécamp – 'more a man of war than a man of god'. And yet as late as 1098 the monks of Peterborough were still petitioning to be allowed to appoint an Englishman. Then on the night of 4 August 1116, the Eve of the Feast of St Oswald, a fire destroyed most of the abbey buildings, including the library, and consumed the old *Chronicle* manuscript. Some five years later the work of restoring the text began. The decision to undertake this work is surely significant. The story of Old England was by now an antiquarian's memory, but the abbot of St Augustine's, Canterbury, was approached for the loan of a Kentish Chronicle (now lost). Thus Peterborough could be brought up to date for the eleventh century and then the Chronicle was continued by various scribes for the next half century. Admittedly there may have been motives other than pure antiquarianism and patriotism at work. The updating scribe for the earlier periods took the opportunity of inserting various entries that (we have seen) notably favoured the abbey!

The language of Old English

While King Alfred's charters called him King of the Anglo-Saxons in the later part of his reign, he called the language that he spoke and wrote *Englisc*; the Latin scholars of the realm called it *lingua Anglica* or *lingua Saxonica*; we, today, call it Anglo-Saxon or Old

English. Along with Old High German, Old Saxon and Old Frisian it forms a sub-group of the Indo-European family of languages (the ties with Old Frisian were so close that some scholars talk of an Anglo-Frisian language). The differences between the language spoken by the original invaders and that of the English subjects of William the Conqueror were considerable and there were also important differences between three broad dialect areas: Kent, East Anglian and Saxon. The most notable was West Saxon, which, having some features and loan words from Anglian and other dialects, became the principal literary language of the surviving collections of Anglo-Saxon writings, both prose and verse. We do not know when *Beowulf* was first declaimed in some noble mead hall, nor how long an oral tradition preceded the *Beowulf* manuscript through which it came down to us, but that manuscript is in the West Saxon literary language. The *Anglo-Saxon Chronicle* shows the evolution of that language from Early up to Late West Saxon, the form used by Ælfric.

Compared with the West Saxon legacy, the literary survivals from other dialect areas are meagre indeed. Among them is the mid-tenth century Late Northumbrian version of the text interlined between the stately lines of the Latin of the Lindisfarne Gospels, 'the oldest surviving translation of the Gospels into the English language'. Maybe so, but was there not perhaps some antiquarian aesthete among the community of St Cuthbert at Chester-le-Street who fumed, necessarily in silence, at the insult offered to the majestic calligraphy by the somewhat spidery hand of Brother Aldred? We know the translator's name because he himself records it, eager, it would seem, to associate himself with the genius of the illuminator, Bishop Eadfrith, now dead more than two centuries. Aldred was hardly a model of the monastic virtue of humility (after all, the bishop had not seen fit to record his own name in the holy book), yet but for him one genius of the western artistic tradition would still be anonymous.

It seems the Anglo-Saxons introduced runes to Britain (their alphabet of some thirty plus characters is larger than that of Old Norse, which appears about 800). Even so it survives in only a few inscriptions, such as the poetic fragment of the *Dream of the Rood* on the Ruthwell Cross in Dumfriesshire. The Latin alphabet in the elegant script brought to England by the Irish missionaries of the early seventh century was more usually employed both for English and Latin works. Was the art of writing in Old English invented by an Italian cleric in the early seventh century? A few runic characters were taken over for sounds for which the Romans had no letter. Thorn (þ) and eth (ð) were used for the *th* sound in *think* and *then*, and a third letter called wynn, confusingly similar to the Latin *p*, for the 'w' sound. There were a few other characters including '7', an equivalent of the ampersand for the Old English 'and'.

The study of the evolution of both literary style and fashions in handwriting is an academic specialization all of its own. For example, if we look at the 'Parker' manuscript of the *Anglo-Saxon Chronicle*, we find that the long first section, which starts with the year 494 and ends in the year 891, is written in a single hand. The records for the next 180 years down to the last entry in 1070 are made in a succession of hands, more or less contemporary with the events they describe, which makes it possible to trace the changes in official script and the introduction of new vocabulary. As to pronunciation, refined comparative studies of variant patterns of spellings and mis-spellings led one scholar to the conclusion that they were probably the result of dictation and, moreover, the result of a 'Welshman dictating to an English scribe'.[8]

Runic characters, it is believed, were originally devised for engraving on wood. If so they take us back to what one might call the prehistory of book production. As is well known, both the English word 'book' and the German word *Buch* share a common root with the word for the beech tree (*Buche* in German). What is perhaps not so generally remembered is that the Latin word *liber*, 'a book' (French *livre*), has as its primary meaning 'the inner bark of a tree; from the use of this in writing'.[9] Thus the ancestors of Caesar appear to have used the same basic writing support as did the ancestors of Bede. However, their Mediterranean alphabet was utterly different from the Norse script, even though this in fact originated in the south. The decision, taken presumably about the year 600 in Kent, to render the language of the newly converted Germanic peoples of Britain into written form, for recording in Roman style the Laws of King Æthelberht, meant devising a written alphabetic equivalent of Anglo-Saxon. This in turn 'involved the transformation of sound into writing and required informed decisions on spelling and grammar'.[10] Some clerics may of course have taken the trouble to master runes and there is some evidence for familiarity with the runic script among the lay educated classes of society. Runic inscriptions are found on a few Anglo-Saxon coin issues and there are runic signs scribbled in the margins next to some of the Exeter Book riddles, as if intended as clues to the solutions. But at a time when, as Robert Runcie observed, 'everyone wanted to be Roman', the Latin alphabet was bound to prevail.

Latin: learning and literature

Anglo-Saxon men and women of letters produced a wide range of works in Latin, the language of the Church and Continental officialdom. In fact, it was one specialized item in this category, namely 'the Latin land charter (technically, diploma) and the associated vernacular documents dealing with land and property', that, in the words of Susan Kelly, provided 'the primary and most accessible record of the interaction between early Anglo-Saxon society and the written word'.[11]

Compared with the veil of printed matter – books, newspapers, public notices, advertisements, DIY instructions, football programmes, legal documentation, etc. – through which we tend to see our world, in Anglo-Saxon England even an educated layman or woman could pass from one year's end to the next with barely sight of a page of script. And when one did confront the written word it was more likely to be a land deed, or perhaps a relative's last will and testament, than a book of verse or a page of history. Few if any outside the church read for business or pleasure. There were (worldly) churchmen too, one suspects, for whom documents of law might hold greater treasures even than Holy Writ. For 'unlike its Italian models which originated in lay society . . . the early Anglo-Saxon diploma is essentially an ecclesiastical document' drafted in a bishop's or monastery's scriptorium.

We know from original documents attested in Kent, Surrey, the kingdoms of the Wicce and the West Saxons that by the early 600s churchmen were looking to this form of (written) instrument as a guarantee of ownership of land or other property made over to them or their organizations by pious donors. The first charters are dated in the 670s; before that such grants might be written at the back of Gospel books. In addition to 300 single-sheet parchment sheets, original charters in contemporary script, we have some 1,200 later copies for attesting to such transactions in the Anglo-Saxon period. Typically drafted on behalf of the beneficiary rather than the donor, such a charter would record a grant from the king or other lord to an individual cleric or layman wishing to found or endow a monastery. Grants of land to an existing foundation could be similarly confirmed. The recipient organization certainly treasured such evidences of property to Christ or their tutelary saint as the lord of their community. The document was sometimes stored upon the high altar of the church or even bound into a Gospel book. It seems that some Gospels were bound with blank endpapers ready to receive anticipated charter texts. Since the vast majority of the lay population can be considered as living in a preliterate society, the question as to what weight such documents actually carried inevitably presents itself. What legal force could they have in the secular world?

The property hand-over was accompanied by ceremonies and rituals that might involve, for example, an actual sod cut from the land in question. Such rituals themselves conferred recognized traditional authentication on the deed of transfer. Where a diploma or charter had been drawn up it featured as part of the ceremonies and itself remained a potent symbol of the event and thus of the ownership of the property in question by the owner of the diploma. As late as the 1970s the present writer can remember collaborating in a similar kind of ritual, in the somewhat embarrassed privacy of a country solicitor's office. Following instructions, he placed his forefinger upon a little red disc attached to a document and uttered the words, 'I deliver this deed as my word and bond.'

When we come to look at literary works written in Latin, Aldhelm of Sherborne, a somewhat older contemporary of Bede's and whose poetry and *enigmata* we have mentioned, was the first and remained one of the most prolific authors. Born apparently in the 640s, some five years after Birinus had first preached Christianity to Wessex, by the time he was fifteen the building of the first church at Winchester had begun and Penda, the pagan king of Mercia, had driven out the Christian king of Wessex and had himself been killed in battle. Before the boy was twenty, Theodore had taken over as archbishop of Canterbury in Kent and established the cathedral school. Here Aldhelm spent several years as a student before moving back into Wessex to become abbot of Malmesbury. The early Christian years were surely rollercoaster times for the new faithful.

Aldhelm was no Bede. In place of the limpid clarity of the historian's Latin his prose tended to extravagant (an unfriendly critic has said 'pompous') conceits, recherché coinages and elaborate grammatical constructions, though at its best it was highly influential on later writers. The anonymous *Liber monstrorum*, a diverting and instructive book of monstrous creatures, both human and animal, from legends about the natural world and, above all, classical literature, owes much to his style. Its authorship cannot be confidently attributed but the work is probably of English origin and by the ninth century was widely diffused throughout Europe.[12] His output was voluminous and varied: a long treatise on virginity (*De virginitate*), in verse and prose versions; a verse travelogue through Cornwall and Devon (the British realm of Dumnonia), a lengthy letter-cum-treatise to its king, Geraint, on the Roman manner of calculating Easter; a letter to the Northumbrian king, Aldfrith; numerous dedicatory verses or *tituli* for new churches and altars, which he called *Carmina ecclesiastica*; and technical treatises on poetics and numerology. He was widely read in the Anglo-Saxon world, both in Britain and on the Continent, but he never matched the universal appeal of Bede. Accessible in style and clear in exposition, Bede's writings including the *History*, despite its English theme, were studied throughout most of continental Europe almost from the moment they left his writing table.

The laws of England in English and the uses of literacy

The laws of England's kingdoms were expressed in the language of England's kings. There were varying writing styles. 'West Saxon minuscule' (830s–870s) differs from the minuscule practised at Alfred's court in the 890s – and the late ninth-century charters can be said to stand for a growing tradition of lay literacy in ninth-century Wessex.

Even in government business, documents never threatened to displace word of mouth, but the written word was nevertheless widely used for utilitarian or practical purposes in the ninth century, and often in the vernacular. King Alfred refers to a lord's 'written message and his seal', as though it were commonplace to make one's will known to the thegns by this means, but we also know that he commonly communicated with his 'judges' through his 'trusted men', who would report by word of mouth. A written message was, of course, also more discreet – one bishop tells a correspondent that he has taken the trouble to convey his meaning by letter (*per letteras*) 'so that it may not be[come] . . . known to many'.

The king's trusted men themselves also used sealed documents, as we know from surviving seal matrixes – a typical example, inscribed with the words 'Sigillum Ælfrici' ('Ælfric's seal'), shows a man brandishing a sword (probably as much an emblem of lineage as of power). It certainly seemed quite natural to King Alfred, who believed that a healthy kingdom rested on Christian subjects ready and prepared to follow the sometimes unexpected, even unfamiliar, message contained in holy scripture, to illustrate his point by using an analogy involving the readiness of a local reeve or ealdorman to follow the unknown intention represented by a lord's writ (*ærendgewrit*) and his seal. According to James Campbell, Alfred's law code, including as it does the laws of Ine, amounts to 120 items; and that number, being the number of years in the life of Moses, the great biblical lawgiver, was considered sacred. Indeed this target number was so important that we find two or three seemingly unrelated provisions grouped in single numbered clauses: one, for example, deals with the law on killing a pregnant woman, the ratio between fine and restitution, and the fines for theft of gold, horses and bees.

English was used for sermons by prelates as well as by village priests. Wulfstan, later archbishop of York and who Latinized his name as Lupus (Latin for 'wolf'), made his name when bishop of London (996–1002) with apocalyptic sermons on the Coming Days. They would have been in tune with the times as the year 1000 approached. A French tract 'Concerning Antichrist', written in Latin, was well known and nowhere so more so than in an England beset by recurrent Danish invasions. Cannier than many another millenarian, Wulfstan was not insistent as to the exact year. Recalling an ancient prophesy that after a thousand years Satan would be 'unbound', he went on: 'A thousand years and more is now gone since Christ was among men in a human family and Satan's bonds are loosed and the time of Antichrist is at hand . . .'[13]

In the early 1000s English law-making was largely in the hands of Bishop Wulfstan. Only the End of the World could explain why God had allowed the kingdom that the kings of Wessex had so painfully laboured to build in His name to fall into its present parlous state. Not for the first time, but perhaps with a special sense of urgency, he proposed Sunday trading laws, that people 'eagerly' desist from markets on that day and treat the Sunday Feast as befits it. For Wulfstan (d. 1023), who wrote laws for King Æthelred as well as Cnut, the overarching imperative was to apply the mandates of heaven to human society. People should honour God, hold to one Christian Faith, and abandon all heathen rites. For him the law of King Edgar was the model. In the 'Winchester' code he drew up at the behest of Cnut it was cited almost in full, as were salient points from the laws of Alfred, Æthelstan and Æthelred.

Wulfstan was one of the most influential stylists in Old English, idiosyncratic, florid and elaborate, but also one of the most thoughtful, as may be seen, for example, in the work known as the *Institutes of Polity*. He was a 'social idealist' whose aim was to engineer a reformed social order: in a preamble to a law code he spoke of the English as one people under one law. But he stirred his contemporaries above all as a preacher and moralist of passion and power. His famous 'Words of the Wolf to the English' (*Sermo Lupi ad Anglos*) was a declamation against sin, but also a passionate plea to his countrymen for repentance. One senses, from the law preamble just quoted, that under the pressure of the Danish threat people, perhaps especially in the Danelaw territories, were defecting back to pagan practices to placate the old gods of their invading kinsmen. In his famous sermon, Wulfstan reminded his listeners that a 'councillor' called Gildas had written that the Britons of those days had so angered God by their sins that He finally let the army of the English (Wulfstan used the word *here*, the common term in his day for the Danish raiding army) conquer the land from them. He warned his own contemporaries that they should seek to come to terms with God. The English had acquired their land even when pagans through the sins of the Britons and they could as easily lose it to another pagan people. Indeed, for Wulfstan his fellow Englishmen were more at fault than had been the Britons because, he said, they, like the ancient people of Israel, had been favoured by a special covenant with God.[14]

Whereas on the Continent late Roman bureaucracy and the use of Latin continued under the new regimes of invading barbarian lords, in England spoken Latin seems to have disappeared and the imperial bureaucracy to have collapsed, as a result, in the words of Susan Kelly, 'Latin was remote from the secular side of society.' This presumably is one reason, among others, for the adoption of the vernacular as a vehicle for legal documentation. Another may be that the process of law-making or, better, the business of law promulgation was different from the way we understand the process. Patrick Wormald distinguished in technical terms between *lex scripta* and *verbum regis*, between 'written law' and the 'word of the king'. It has been argued that it was the word (*verbum*) rather than the actual written text that gave it the force of law.[15]

The first English laws, those of Æthelberht I of Kent, were promulgated at very nearly the same time as Italian churchmen were introducing Latin literacy into England (see chapter 2). Kent had close ties with the Merovingian court at Paris; surviving Merovingian written law is in Latin. But if it was the word of the king that gave force to the law and if the laws that he spoke were the traditional rulings of the people, then, if they were to be written down, ways had to be found of writing the English language.

Indeed the relationship of the English language to royal law does not seem to have been a straightforward business of promulgation and application. Following the concept of *lex scripta* and *verbum regis*, even King Alfred's great code may have 'represented more of an attempt to express the king's ideological aspirations than to provide the judges with a practical work of reference'. Even in the tenth and eleventh centuries it may be that what counted was not the written 'code' but the king's oral pronouncement. (In a celebrated case, as we have noted, judgement was given by the king by word of mouth while washing his hands in his private apartment.) Thus 'legislation was not formally promulgated *by the king* in written form and those who produced the texts were doing so on their own initiative.' Often, it seems, 'the actual recording in writing was left in a surprisingly casual way to ecclesastics and individual or [even] local enterprise.'[16]

The language of administration: officialese

The fact that the English clerical bureaucrat came to use his own language, in preference to the idiom of imperial or papal curia, did not make his practice any less effective than elsewhere in Europe. Across the Continent, the ninth and tenth centuries witnessed the development of legal formulations and documents relating to land tenure and land grants. In England, too, the Latin diploma or charter, pioneered by church proprietors to protect their rights, was increasingly adapted to secular requirements. Unlike *folcland* (land held by traditional rights), which was liable to the render of various rents and dues and was subject to the normal claims of succession by the kindred, *bocland*, which was held by charter or 'book', could be disposed of at will by the landowner and book holder. The charter, generally drawn up in Latin, identified the territory and guaranteed its owners right to alienate it while the document itself 'could be transferred together with the land to a new owner'. This being England, by the early 800s 'charter scribes [were regularly including] a detailed boundary clause in English', so that the charter, or *boc*, was on the way to becoming a true written record standing independent of any physical ceremony or token as a conveyance of right and definition of territory. The encroachment of the vernacular into the domain of the law may have been a measure of declining standards of Latinity, but it would surely have been a welcome development for the English landowner. As the ninth century advanced English legal documents multiplied – agreements of all kinds, leases and wills. Of the fifty-eight wills to survive from this period, fifty-three are in English. An example dated between 832 and 840 has a Kentish reeve named Abba making elaborate disposal of his lands and bequeathing a sword – a reeve had military as well as civil duties.

In addition to the wills we have records of more than a hundred leases, no doubt only a small fraction of those drawn up. These documents were mostly in Latin but with key passages, and almost always the date, rendered in English and mostly in the form of a chirograph. An ingenious solution to the problem of making reliable copies before carbon paper or photocopier, such a document carried the text of the agreement in duplicate or triplicate on a single sheet, with the word CYROGRAPHUM printed in large letters in the space(s) between the copy texts. The parchment was then cut through the word CYROGRAPHUM and each party to the agreement given one of the parts. In case of dispute the copies could be compared and matched along the join to validate their authenticity. It seems that chirographs were regularly appealed to: sophisticated English secular society was quite comfortable with the use of documents – and English language documents at that. The language was used as a teaching medium as well as by the royal government for its writs and laws, and of course by the religious establishment. Often religious texts have English equivalents jotted down for difficult Latin words. The approach is the typical English way, pragmatic. No doubt church people should know their Latin, but the priority was for them to know the meaning of what they were doing and saying.

A pioneer vernacular

It was not just that the English habitually used their own language in literature of all kinds; it seems they introduced the notion to others. It would certainly catch the imagination of the country's invaders – at least in the second generation. The first effect of Hastings and its aftermath was the destruction of the English clerks' tradition. Apart from Coleman's *Life of Wulfstan*, the revered bishop of Worcester who remained in office until his death in 1095, and the Peterborough continuation of the *Anglo-Saxon Chronicle*, 'Old English book production came to an end . . . [the] finest manuscripts, high-status books, were treated as plunder and sent abroad.'[17]

But there were those among the Continental incomers impressed by England's literary culture. The Flemish monk Goscelin of St Bertin, who had settled in England in 1058 in the household of the bishop of Ramsbury and Sherborne and ended his days some time after 1107 in the community of St Augustine's Abbey, Canterbury, made his own notable contribution with a number of Latin hagiographies of English saints, such as King Edgar's daughter Eadgyth of Wilton (*d.* 984), singing the praises of the abbey where she spent her life. During his years as an itinerant writer he lodged as a guest at other great English houses, including Ely and Winchester. For him, it was the Normans who were the barbarians.

A sign that change was in the air came with the bilingual Latin/English version of the *Anglo-Saxon Chronicle* compiled at Canterbury (possibly by Goscelin) about the year 1100, presumably for the Norman churchmen of all ranks who were flooding into English institutions, at the expense of native clerics. Then, some time in the 1140s, Geoffrey Gaimar, possibly a native of Normandy, produced a 'History of the English' for Constance, the French wife of a Lincolnshire landowner, Ralph Fitzgilbert. The settler popula-tion, though mostly retaining family and family lands in the home country, was developing a taste for the history of the conquered people and cultivating an interest in the days of Good King Edward and his ancestors. Gaimar's ambitious project was in fact a verse translation of the story of their past – in short, of the *Anglo-Saxon Chronicle*. It was, of course, not written in the language of its subject, which, after all, was a conquered people, but nor was it written in Latin, the natural choice for a Continental writer on a serious theme. No, with his verse *L'Estorie des Engleis* Geoffrey produced the earliest historical work in the French language. Paradoxically his work, so innovative in the history of French literature, appeared in the decade that the *Anglo-Saxon Chronicle*, kept up in English since the 890s, was coming to an end.

Anglo-Norman writers achieved a number of other literary 'firsts' in French. Philippe de Thaon, through his *Cumpoz/Comput* (a calendar/chronology of the church year) and his allegorical works on animals and precious stones (lapidary), pioneered the use of the language in science-related topics. Benedit, a talented poet, produced one of the first saints' lives in French with his *Vie de Saint Brendan*. The French vernacular drama called the *Jeu d'Adam* ('The Play of Adam'), the first mystery play with French dialogue throughout, though with stage direction in Latin, survives in just one copy found in an Anglo-Norman manuscript. The play itself may actually have originated in England. Even in defeat, England seemed to encourage the spirit of innovation in others.

10

THE HEGEMONY OF WESSEX THE ENGLISH KINGDOM AND CHURCH REFORMS

'The creation of the English kingdom through conquest is the primary theme of the first half of the tenth century.' So wrote Pauline Stafford in her book *Unification and Conquest* (1989, p. 29) and, despite continuing reassessment of the balance between Wessex, the Viking lordships in the north and the remnants of Mercia, East Anglia and the other English kingdoms, it seems a safe generalization. Writing in 2003, M. K. Lawson speaks of the 'obvious scale of the forces deployed by Edward the Elder in the reconquest of the Danelaw', comparing it with the sheer extent of his father's military measures, in terms of manpower, ships and fortress construction. He also points out that, though the sources are scant, we must assume the presence of an 'array of refined and important details' in logistics and command structure. It all led to the success of the West Saxon dynasty's 'audacious attempt to persuade the English people at large of its leadership.'[1] As never before, the royal court of Wessex/England developed as the focus of patronage seeking, of factional rivals and agenda pushers, whether secular or clerical: in short, of political activity. The nobleman looking for grants of land or influence in local affairs, or a royal judgement favourable to a client, attended the peripatetic household of the king as much as possible. Here too came the bishop or abbot eager to promote reforms in the English hierarchy or initiate a building programme. As the royal house of Wessex extended its hegemony, so royal assets in both lands and patronage increased and the pull of the court became ever more powerful. During this period, too, more than one queen found suitors for her patronage, often in church matters.

Edward the Elder and Æthelflæd of Mercia: consolidators of England

When King Alfred died in October 899 leaving his kingdom to his son Edward (known to history as Edward the Elder to distinguish him from a descendant), the upper reaches of English society must have sensed change in the air. For one thing, the comparatively recent title 'King of the Anglo-Saxons' seemed to be becoming standard usage. For another, Edward chose Kingston upon Thames in Surrey to hold his consecration – the first of the royal house of Wessex to do so. Exactly why he made the decision we do not know, but Kingston, near to the old Kentish lands and the once Mercian city of London, may have seemed more suited for a kingship wider than Wessex.

The new reign opened dramatically with an attempted coup that won support among the enemies of Wessex and for a time seemed to threaten Alfred's line. It was led by Æthelwold, the son of Alfred's elder brother King Æthelred I, cousin of the new king and representative of the senior line. He was undoubtedly 'ætheling', that is a 'throneworthy' member of the royal house. Indeed, according to a strict succession by primogeniture (i.e. descent in the senior male line) it was he, and not his uncle Alfred, who should have become king on the death of his father back in 871. He had been a baby then; now a man in his early thirties, he was bent on making good his claim. With a body of supporters, he seized the royal manor of

Wimborne – the place where his own father lay buried. The bid failed. Edward, with a force of mounted levies, encamped against the barricaded manor house. His cousin refused to yield and made his escape under cover of darkness. According to the *Anglo-Saxon Chronicle*, he 'came to the host in Northumbria', that is to the Viking 'kingdom' of York where he may even have been acclaimed king (see chapter 7).

In 902–4, we are told by a northern version of the *Chronicle*, Æthelwold 'came hither from oversea to Essex' with a large fleet. Does this mean he sailed south with York Vikings, or that he had crossed over to Denmark and recruited supporters there? Either way, he and a substantial body of allies, both Danish and English, ravaged westward into Mercia, 'seizing all they could' before returning 'east homewards'. The loyalist 'Wessex' *Chronicle* naturally calls him 'prince'; a northern source speaks of him as 'elected king', and he was presenting himself as rightful king of Wessex. He would have offered those who followed him booty from the lands in Mercia and Wessex holding 'disloyally' for his cousins Edward the Elder and Æthelflæd, Lady of the Mercians. The East Anglians may even have considered him as the true continuator of their royal line. According to the *Annals of St Neot's* he was called 'king of the Danes', while the annalist also called him 'king of the Pagans'.

Compared with its account of Alfred's reign, and in particular of the tensions among his brothers prior to his succession, the *Chronicle* is very detailed for these years and the revealing account of the 'rebellion' of Æthelwold lights up the English political scene 'as by a lightning flash'.[2] Nothing in the annals for Alfred's reign could have led us to expect this. For a fateful moment the Norns, the three sisters of Norse myth who control men's destiny, toyed with the thread of his family line – should they break it? In 903 King Edward fought a major battle against the raiders somewhere in Cambridgeshire. Many great men fell on both sides, among the Danes 'their king Eohric and prince Æthelwold who had incited him to this rebellion'. Among the fallen there was also a possible claimant to Mercia. Although the following year 'the host from East Anglia' and 'the Northumbrians' forced Edward to come to terms, without Æthelwold the main threat was over.

In fact, Edward had now secured his position in the English kingdoms; he next trounced the Northumbrian Danes and thereafter proceeded to entrench his supremacy south of the Humber. A new Northumbrian raiding army in search of reprisals was caught between Wednesfield and Tettenhall in Staffordshire on 5 August 910 and went down to a crushing defeat that left three Danish leaders dead on a field of slaughter held by the English.

An essential partner in Edward's extension and consolidation of the Anglo Saxon kingdom was his sister Æthelflæd, wife of Æthelred of Mercia. She had always taken an active role with her husband in the military affairs of western Mercia. The two were responsible for the translation of the bones of Northumbria's St Oswald southward into Mercia. Following Æthelred's death in 911 after a long illness, during which she had been the effective power in the land, she continued to complement her brother Edward's tactics. For William of Malmesbury she was 'a woman of great determination'; for Pauline Stafford, writing in 1983, Æthelflæd, the Lady of the Mercians, was the virtually independent ruler of Mercia from 911 to her own death 918 and a great 'warrior queen'. We are told that she led her forces into battle and on occasion, it is believed, commanded the army on horseback

She expanded the network of burhs and continued to strengthen existing ones to serve as defensive and offensive pressure points against the Danish presence in eastern Mercia and the North. The section of annals known as the Mercian register, in the B, C and D manuscripts of the *Chronicles*, tells how after her husband's death she built fortresses at Bridgnorth, in Shropshire, at the important centre of Tamworth and then at Stafford. She sent an army against the Welsh that captured the wife of the king of the Brecon region, 'won the borough called Derby' and took Leicester 'by peaceful means', receiving the allegiance of the majority of the Danish forces there. In the year of her death and 'the eighth year of her rule over Mercia as . . . rightful lord [sic]' she seems to have won recognition for a time as 'Lady of the people of York'.[3]

Devised by Alfred as a defensive measure against invaders, the burghal system began to be adapted by his children as a tool of conquest and consolidation as they recovered the English position in the lands of the Danelaw. The new 'burh' towns became centres for royal administration and trade so that by the 950s, it has been said, 'a burh was defined more by its mint and its market than by its ramparts.'[4] From the start, artisans and merchants were encouraged to settle in these walled settlements, which would in time provide the preconditions for a market economy.

Worcester was a case in point. In the 880s, responding to a petition by 'their friend' Bishop Wærferth and with the approval of King Alfred, Ealdorman Æthelred and his wife Æthelflæd ordered the building of a burh at Worcester 'for the worship of god and the protection of all the people'. In return the noble patrons would receive the bishop's prayers and half of all his revenues from the market or street stalls. Since the church seems to have met the bulk of the costs in erecting the fortifications, it earned its concessions.

The burhs also evolved as a vital armature of the Anglo–Saxon state – centres from which the king's officers presided over their region and made the royal presence felt throughout the kingdom. The great men were obligated in the king's service to mobilize the workforce necessary for the maintenance of the burhs and the defensible market town soon emerged as 'central to England's political structure'. The point was fully demonstrated in the decades following the Norman Conquest. The Normans, eager to control and exploit that structure of centralization, demolished whole quarters of old English towns and burhs to make room for royal castles.[5]

The royal team of siblings, the Lady Æthelflæd and King Edward, made a logical division of labour. She looked after the western frontiers against the Welsh and the northwest against the incursions of Irish Vikings via Cheshire and Lancashire while at the same time making probing attacks into the northern Danelaw beyond Watling Street. Edward combated the Danish warlord kings in East Anglia and the east Midlands with the aim of extending West Saxon hegemony in those regions. Contemporaries could have viewed the same events as old-style Wessex and Mercia pursuing traditional interests under two rulers happy to cooperate.

The two royal establishments had not merged into a single court. We find a Mercian source describing the combined military forces as 'English', but to all intents and purposes Æthelflæd was a sovereign head of state, a unique position for a woman in the Europe of her time. After her death in 918 a group of Mercian nobles supported the succession of her daughter Ælfwyn as 'Lady'. Edward may have felt threatened by the burgeoning success of his sister's 'dynasty': he consigned his niece to a convent and took direct control in Mercia.

About this time, according to the Winchester *Chronicle*, the Welsh kings submitted to Edward at a great meeting at Tamworth, the historic seat of Mercian kingship and far from the border with Wales. Two years after this, with the West Saxon king's rule now virtually undisputed south of the Humber–Ribble line, the *Chronicle* tells us that the rulers of north Britain, among them Ragnald, 'king' of Viking York, the lord of the Strathclyde Britons, and Constantine II, king of Scots, and the English lords of Northumbria independent of York, acknowledged him as their 'father and lord' at a great assembly in the Derbyshire Peak District on the frontiers between Mercia and the lands of Scandinavian York. As the West Saxon conquest of the Danelaw territories advanced with the extension of West Saxon power, the heterogeneous nature of the local administrations revealed a general lack of political solidarity among the Danish settlers.

King Edward died in the summer of 924 at Farndon on Dee, near Chester in Mercia. He left five sons and six daughters, the offspring of three partners. Of these the eldest boy was Æthelstan, who was of middling height, slim build and flaxen hair and with remarkable piercing blue eyes. He had been fostered at the Mercian court of his aunt Æthelflæd and had probably fought under her command, but his legitimacy was in question. It seems the dead king had meant that he should rule in Mercia, while Alfweard, his younger brother but the oldest legitimate son, should take the ancestral kingdom of Wessex. The prince, however, outlived his father by barely a fortnight and was also buried at Winchester. Æthelstan, with Mercian support, took over in Wessex as well and was consecrated at Kingston upon Thames, as his father had been, despite the claims of three legitimate half-brothers. But the consecration took place in the year following Edward's death. The opposition party at Winchester had contended that although he was the child of Edward's first union, his mother Ecgwyna was a woman of low birth, little better than a concubine, and that the prince was to all intents illegitimate. Æthelstan's party by contrast claimed she had been the 'noble concubine of his father's youth'. It was not uncommon for a prince to take such a partner before he was considered of marriageable age: as Pauline Stafford explains, 'such concubines were usually of high birth'.

William of Malmesbury would describe Ecgwyna as 'an illustrious lady', and she did have a daughter who was accepted in marriage as his queen by Sihtric, the ruler of York. Perhaps she was not of the highest rank, but even the bastard daughter of a powerful king may be acceptable as spouse to a lesser. The Welsh prince Llewellyn 'the Great' ap Iorwerth (d. 1240) was happy to marry Joan, the illegitimate daughter of John of England. Moreover, William had reason to be loyal to Æthelstan's memory since the king had handsomely endowed his abbey and the royal tomb was still to be seen there. It was also claimed that the patriarch of the dynasty, his grandfather

King Alfred, had inducted him in a ceremony recalling his own consular 'consecration' when a boy at Rome.

Æthelstan: 'ruler of the whole of Britain' and kinsman of Europe (924–939)

The title comes from an inscription found in the Coronation
Gospels, which King Æthelstan received from his brother-in-law
Otto the Great, the German emperor, on Otto's accession in 936
and later presented to Canterbury Cathedral. In full the title reads
'*Anglorum basyleos et curagulus totius Bryttannie*'[6] – note that Æthelstan
uses the term *basyleos*, the Greek word for 'king' but by his day used
by the Byzantine emperors. By 937 Æthelstan was recognized as
king throughout England, both Angelcynn and Danelaw, from
Northumbria to Kent. By this time, too, he had forced homage from
the king of Scotland and many Welsh rulers. In 930 at Nottingham
he had presided over what in British terms was a truly imperial court
attended by many English notables, two archbishops, three Welsh
under-kings and six Danish jarls. Among the business Æthelstan
conducted was a grant of lands north of Preston – this was the exercise of effective power. In 927 he established direct rule over
Scandinavian York and so became the first king to rule all the lands
of the English. In later campaigns he drove the Welsh back beyond
the Wye and established the River Tamar as the frontier with the
West Britons, in other words the Cornish. In 934 Æthelstan led a
joint sea and land force against Scotland.

The mixed, if impressive, auguries at Æthelstan's succession heralded an astonishing fifteen-year reign of major law codes, of preparations for currency reform and of military triumph. In 937, in the
most important victory by a king of England between the death of
his grandfather and Hastings, Æthelstan routed a coalition of Olaf
Guthfrithsson, king of York and Dublin, Constantine of Scotland/
Alba and Owain of Strathclyde, together with warlords from the

Hebrides and the Danelaw, at the Battle of Brunanburh. It was the culmination of a conflict originating in the 920s when Ragnald, the Norse leader from Dublin, had defeated the Danes of York and the English lords of Bamburgh. Brunanburh made Æthelstan the most powerful of Britain's rulers. His court was a magnet for English nobles from all over the country, and Welsh rulers, kings in their own world, resigned themselves to the status of *sub regulus* ('under ruler') in the eyes of the mighty West Saxon.

In his Latin *Chronicle* Ealdorman Æthelweard recalled that the English remembered Brunanburh as 'the great war'. After Brunanburh, the Vikings in the north of England seemed for a time a spent force. (The Vikings on the Isle of Man may have kept the title 'king' until 1266 but caused no serious trouble in England's affairs.) The *Annals of Ulster* recorded Brunanburh as a 'lamentable battle' in which several thousands were killed among the Norsemen and that Æthelstan, 'king of the Saxons', won a great victory. For all that, the actual site of the engagement is not known, although Paul Hill (2004), after an exhaustive discussion, concludes that the most likely candidates are Bromborough in the Wirral and Brunenburh in Yorkshire. He also notes that the English army included jarls from the Danelaw and Scandinavian mercenaries and that the great Anglo-Saxon poem on the battle recorded in the *Anglo-Saxon Chronicle* for the year 937 shows strong influence from the skaldic techniques of Norse epic poetry. For Henry of Huntingdon, writing in the twelfth century, the poem despite all its 'strange words and . . . language' offered a memorial 'of this nation's deeds and courage'. The 'nation' of which this post-Conquest historian writes is a *'patria . . .* a fatherland . . . created not by the Norman conqueror but by his English predecessors.'[7]

For all its Norse elements it is a vibrant hymn to an English victory and echoes with the world of *Beowulf* and the *scop*. Standing by King Æthelstan, 'lord of warriors and ring-giver of men . . . upon the fateful field . . . was his brother Prince Edmund'. As the field grew dark with the blood of men, exults the poet, 'the sons of Edward . . . triumphant in war' drove their enemies back to Ireland, back to Scotland, back to Wales. Never, since the Angles and Saxons invaded across the ocean from the east to win a kingdom for themselves, as old books tell, had there been such slaughter in this island by the sword. This allusion to the *adventus Saxonum* (the invasion across the ocean) is almost unique in Old English literature.

Æthelstan's policy towards the English regions and provinces that still had a measure of independence was clear. Allies like Mercia or English Northumbria were due for absorption. As a fostered courtier at his aunt Æthelflæd's Mercian court, Æthelstan had been sitting ringside when his father took over power there on her death in 918. He himself had similar intentions towards the rump English kingdom of Northumbria if only to counterbalance and eventually, one supposes, oust the Viking overlords there. He encouraged the spread of the cult of the great northern patron St Cuthbert in Wessex. The treasury at Durham Cathedral still holds a sumptuously embroidered stole that the king presented to the shrine of St Cuthbert in 934 and which was commissioned, or more probably worked in person, by his step-mother Queen Ælflæd.

Æthelstan not only fixed the English–West British boundary at the Tamar, he expelled a Cornish enclave in Exeter, beyond the river, and held his quasi-imperial great court in the city in 928 and 935. With the marriage of his sister to Sihtric, the Viking lord of York, he asserted claims to Wessex hegemony in the old territories of Northumbria. Two years later, by expelling Sihtric's brother Guthfrith he established himself as king of all the English, as he was to remain until his death in 939. Yet for all his glory historians have sensed something sinister behind the reign. A remarkable number of his kinsmen found a premature or violent death in suspicious circumstances. Years later, the chronicler Symeon of Durham charged him with arranging the death of his half-brother Edwin, who was sent into exile in Flanders and drowned at sea.

While, remarkably for a king, Æthelstan never married, he was the best-connected ruler in the Europe of his day through marriages he arranged for his sisters or half-sisters. Edward the Elder left no fewer than nine daughters, of whom Eadgifu, the second born, had become queen of Francia by her marriage to Charles III of West Francia (ruled 892–922, d. 929). In 922 Charles was ousted in a dynastic struggle and incarcerated by his enemy, the Lord of Vermandois, but Eadgifu had escaped across the Channel to England with their baby son Louis. Thus, with a Queen of France in exile as a half-sister and her son the pretender to that disputed crown, when Æthelstan came to the throne in 924 he already had a personal connection with one corner of continental European politics.

His dynastic diplomacy would not have disgraced the Habsburgs. In 926 Eadhild married Hugh the Great, the Count of Paris, and far and away the most powerful man in West Francia (roughly modern France). Born about 938, their son Hugh Capet would be elected king of France in 987. Æthelstan married his sister Eadgyth to Otto of Saxony in 930. The initiative came from Otto's father Henry the Fowler, elected king of Germany by the nobles of Franconia and Saxony, though not recognized by Swabia and Bavaria. He needed a 'good' marriage for his son and heir to boost his standing and the approach testifies to the high recognition of the Anglo-Saxon kingdom on the Continent. It seems to have been believed that the royal family was descended from St Oswald of Northumbria (see chapter 8). Envoys went between the two courts and Æthelstan sent two of his sisters for the young duke's approval. It is supposed that the duke, later emperor as Otto I, chose the prettier. But while Eadgyth was apparently considered without parallel for her virtue by the English, and while Hrotswitha of Gandersheim, noblewoman and royal intimate, nun and imperial eulogist, praised her charm, regal bearing and her 'radiant goodness and sincerity of countenance', beauty as such does not feature anywhere on the inventory. Given that he married two other sisters into the ruling houses of

Aquitaine and Burgundy, it was fitting that *The Annals of Ulster* should dignify him with the appellation of 'roof-tree of the dignity of the Western World'.[8]

In the spring of 936 a deputation arrived in England to escort Æthelstan's now fifteen-year-old nephew, Louis d'Outremer ('from Oversea'), back across the Channel to be crowned in Laon Cathedral by the archbishop of Reims, as King Louis IV of West Francia. His English mother went into retirement at Notre-Dame, Laon. With one aunt married to the most powerful man in France and another to the king of Germany the young monarch might have expected a smooth ride. Unfortunately the half-English king of France was not properly submissive. He moved his court to Laon, away from the overbearing presence of Uncle Hugh in Paris, and then intervened in the region known as Lothringen (roughly modern Lorraine), which angered the nobles of East Francia. Uncle Æthelstan may have lent diplomatic or moral support. But Louis proved adept at European manoeuvring and came to terms with both his European kinsmen; his career seemed in the ascendant when he died, just thirty-three, in 951.

English connections with Germany continued through the cult of St Oswald well into the Middle Ages, as did more practical links, too. In the 990s Archbishop Egbert of Trier was proud of his English name and liked to boast of his descent from Ecgberht, king of Wessex in the early 800s. It seems that the archbishop was instrumental in the appointment of the English-born Leofsige as abbot of Mettlach on the bank of the River Saar. Praised by a modern German scholar as a 'Renaissance man' ('*Renaissancemensch*') before his time, Leofsige was noted as a physician, was something of a versifier and as a patron was responsible for one of the oldest structures in the modern Saarland, Mettlach's octagonal Alter Turm ('Old Tower'), built as a funerary chapel for St Leodwin.[9]

To the people of his day Æthelstan was a model of kingship: victorious in war; lord of kings; focus of Europe's most illustrious royal kinship; rich in the wealth of this world and, more noteworthy still, in the wealth of the spiritual world. He was renowned as an expert collector of relics. When Hugh the Great sent to petition for the hand of the king's sister in marriage the embassy, headed by Baldwin Count of Flanders, the king's uncle by marriage, was laden with treasures of incredible worth − gemstones and exotic perfumes, horses with golden harnesses. But far above these was the sword of Emperor Constantine the Great, the almost conventional opulence of which was as nothing when compared with a simple iron nail set in the sword's pommel, for this was one of the nails used at the Crucifixion of Jesus Christ. Nothing in Christendom could exceed the value of this, except for the spear with which the centurion had pierced the side of Christ as he hung upon the Cross or a portion of the Cross itself.

These were fitting gifts for a connoisseur of the numinous, one whose agents trawled Europe for relics much as the Getty Museum today does for works of art. In thanks for a favour Æthelstan had granted, a Breton church sent 'relics, which we know you value more than earthly treasure'; in return the king distributed largesse from his hoard of holy treasure to monastic communities, with a prodigality to match the open-handedness of Hrothgar, 'ring-giver of men', from the ancient hall of pagan Heorot.

In the age of the itinerant royal household, when monarchs must travel their kingdoms to consume the food renders due from their subjects, the imperial court of Æthelstan on the move would have been an impressive sight indeed, though for the localities through which it passed back and forth, from Colchester to Winchester, Tamworth to Exeter, it must have been a serial nightmare of organization. When there were subject kings paying court or an arch-bishop or two, each with their own retinues, numbers might swell to as many as a thousand to be fed and housed, whether billeted on the locals or in tents and pavilions pitched for the few nights stay before the move on.

Literate and evidently also of artistic taste, Æthelstan, who claimed the scholar Aldhelm among his spiritual ancestors (he commissioned his tomb) and patronized his young kinsman Dunstan, the future archbishop of Canterbury, died at the height of his power to be succeeded by his brother Edmund, and in turn by their younger brother Eadred. Æthelstan is said to have fathered an illegitimate daughter.[10]

Dynasty

Edmund, who ruled from 939 to 946, was the first king to succeed to the rule of all England, thanks to the heroic reign of his predecessor – but it was an uncertain inheritance and he spent most of his time fighting to make it good. Although he had fought at Brunanburh, he would find it a short-lived triumph. First his brother's death and then the resurgence of Olaf Guthrithsson of York destabilized the results of victory. In 940 the archbishops of Canterbury and York arranged a peace at which Watling Street was agreed upon as the boundary between Danish/Norse and English territories. In fact, shortly after that Edmund was able to recover the region of the Five Boroughs, a success celebrated like that at Brunanburh with a poem, albeit a short one in the *Anglo-Saxon Chronicle*; Edmund also received the submission of the Welsh prince of Gwynedd. In the last year of his reign he even enforced a momentary English authority on Strathclyde. He died a violent death, stabbed to death at his royal vill of Pucklechurch as he intervened in a brawl trying to save a court official. There were many suspicious dynastic deaths in the tenth century; Edmund's was certainly murder, though there is no evidence it was premeditated.

The nine-year reign of his successor, Eadred (*d.* 955), was marked by his eventually successful struggle to force the Danes of York to acknowledge his supremacy. The changes in his fluctuating authority are reflected in various regnal titles in successive charters, which twice designated him as 'king of the Anglo-Saxons, Northumbrians, pagans and Britons' and as 'king of the English'. Probably of equal importance in the eyes of the king (nearing forty, it has been suggested, at his succession and subject to severe illness from about 950), was the move towards church reform inaugurated with his encouragement by his chief councillor, Dunstan, abbot of Glastonbury. A man of 'forceful personality', Dunstan was driven from court on the death of his royal patron.

The new king, Eadwig, was either immature, lascivious and in thrall to a noblewoman set on marrying him to her daughter, or he just wanted to free himself of the domineering churchman. Possibly, of course, he was merely a victim of gossip. He was certainly young, little more than fifteen at his accession and, if we are to believe the scandal, sexually liberated in advance of what the twenty-first century normally expects from the tenth. Dunstan's biographer, at least, credited the king with a taste for incestuous troilism, reporting that the churchman had to drag the recently consecrated monarch back to his coronation feast from a bedroom session with mother and daughter. Dunstan was ordered into exile, which he passed in Flanders, and Eadwig married the lady (i.e. the daughter). Later the church ordered the couple to separate on the grounds that the match was within the prohibited degrees of consanguinity. It has been suggested that Eadwig and his bride could trace a common descent from King Alfred. Two years into his reign as king of the English, he faced insurrection in Mercia and Northumbria and was succeeded there as king by his brother Edgar. From this power base Edgar succeeded to the crown of Wessex on Eadwig's death in 959. He 'discarded two wives as his needs and aspirations changed', notes Stafford.[11]

Ælfthryth, Edgar's third partner and mother of the ill-fated Æthelred II 'Unraed', displaced Wulfthryth (possibly a concubine), who in turn had displaced Edgar's first wife, the mother of Edward (later king and 'Martyr'). The king's marital status was sufficiently confused, even at the time, for some to hold that his third partnership was in fact adulterous. Both in England and on the Continent, kings inclined towards serial monogamy and the distinction between wife and concubine was essentially a question of dowry; it assured the wife of a measure of economic independence. The concubine, like a wife, might give her consent to the liaison but consent could be given in secret and in the last resort this, the vital element in a marriage from the church's point of view, might depend on the word of the king. On repudiating Wulfthryth, Edgar made her abbess of Wilton, and here their daughter Eadgyth (St Edith) was to live an exemplary life of humble devotion, refusing all attempts to persuade her to accept a position as abbess.

Known as '*pacificus*', which may be interpreted as 'the peaceable' or the 'peace-maker', Edgar, who was inaugurated as king probably at Kingston upon Thames about the year 961 and died in 975, certainly pacified his country with stern, possibly harsh rule. It is also true that there was no attack on his realm from either land or sea throughout the reign. In 973, a year of high ceremonial, he was rowed in state upon the River Dee at Chester by some eight lesser kings – Scottish, Welsh, British and Scandinavian. This may have been the culmination of one of the patrols of England's coastal waters that Edgar was said to captain. (see chapter 8). Whit Sunday that same year, the king's thirtieth, also witnessed his quasi-imperial consecration at Bath in an order of service (*ordo*) devised by St Dunstan that consciously invoked the Biblical concept of priestly intervention in the proclamation of King Solomon. The text on 'Zadok the priest and Nathan the prophet' has featured in every coronation up to that of Elizabeth II in 1953.

In a short poem the Parker *Chronicle* celebrates the king as valorous in deeds of war and notes the date as almost one thousand years since the days of the Lord of Victories, i.e. Jesus Christ set firmly in the tradition of warlords. Two years later different versions of the *Chronicle* lament the death of the king, 'friend to the West Saxons and protector of the Mercians', in whose reign, they recall, no raiding host had been able to win booty for itself. Edgar, King from 957 to 975, claimed supremacy of rule in Britain; in England his reign saw major organization of local government by shires, reorganization in church life and reform in the coinage. It firmly established the idea of a single English state.

Church, state and reform

With the arrival of Theodore of Tarsus as archbishop of Canterbury in 669 and his organization of the ecclesiastical structure, the English kingdoms got used to the idea of a supranational allegiance embracing the whole of their part of the island of Britannia. This combined with the emerging concept of an over-kingship, expressed in the Anglo-Saxon word 'bretwalda', to prepare the way for the idea of a geographical unity occupied by the ethnic unity of Angelcynn, in a country that Cnut would call *Angla lond* even though it was by then occupied by a mélange of ethnicities, such as Danes, Norwegians and British as well as Anglo-Saxons. The tenth-century Vikings of Dublin, on becoming Christian, distanced themselves from the Irish church to affirm allegiance to Canterbury.

Since the time of Bede the Angelcynn had recognized themselves in the Latin term *gens Anglorum*, which derived ultimately from the usage 'Anglii', adopted by Gregory I. Once the decision had been made at Whitby to adopt Christianity, the still strong current of Celtic Christianity and Irish traditions would eventually flow into a common channel of establishment religion. The distinction that apparently seemed important in 662 in some sense faded. This meant that saints from various *provinciae* or kingdoms came to be venerated as the common spiritual ancestry of the entire English nation. So Saints Chad and Cedd, trained by Aidan of the Irish/Celtic tradition at Lindisfarne on Holy Island, became venerated as the founding fathers of Christianity in Mercia and East

Anglia, and those two patriarchs of Northumbrian Celtic tradition, Cuthbert and King St Oswald, found devotees and patrons of their cults across Southumbria. Even Wilfrid of Ripon, that most northern of saints, came to have a shrine at Canterbury.

No doubt the rituals and creeds of the Roman church's tradition, the authority of its bishops and the local allegiances built on England's evolving parochial structure knitted the Christian church into the fabric of English life. Whereas in the eighth century the founding and endowment of religious buildings had been largely the business of kings and nobles, John Blair has noted that 300 years later such patronage was increasingly the work of people of 'middle-ranking' status. The actual local church building was treated as community property in a way that modern parish clergy might envy, though clergy at the time could have mixed feelings on the subject. Pastoral letters complain of thoughtless behaviour in church, careless talk, eating and sometimes excessive drinking – the building was clearly a popular venue! In the Canons of Edgar, priests are warned not to carry arms on the premises – certainly not in the altar enclosure. But at the deep level of magic where pagan and Christian blend, the English saints – some of Irish antecedence, others, like Wilfrid, with Roman allegiance – provided a structural network, like the rafting laid down to receive the foundations of a fenland abbey, for the church in England and in the community as 'nodes and links in a network which connected royal power to local piety over most of [the country]'. To this we can add the conviction of Anglo-Saxon churchmen that saw themselves and their compatriots as 'a people of God, a new Israel'. For such an elite, 'whose predecessors had passed through the desert of the Viking invasions', the long tenth-century vernacular poem based on the book of *Exodus* would have been full of resonance.[12] Sadly for them, many would live to see the return of the wilderness years with the renewal of the Danish raids after the reign of Edgar the Peaceable.

The monastic revival

About the year 950 an upheaval began in the English church that would last for the next thirty years as reforms were introduced that would reshape monastic life and so the cultural life of the country at large. This followed reforms heralded on the Continent by the founding of the abbey of Cluny in 910 and most powerfully expressed in the monasteries of Flanders and Lotharingia/Lorraine.

The English reform was managed by three men: Dunstan (924–88), a Somerset man, from a rich landed family with estates near Glastonbury; Æthelwold (?905–84), Winchester-born and in his youth at the court of Æthelstan; and Oswald (*d.* 992), son of a rich family of Danish descent; all three were subjects for important near-contemporary biographies. Less prominent but nevertheless important was Oda, archbishop of Canterbury from 942 to 958 and Oswald's uncle.

Dunstan spent his early years at Glastonbury exploring a library still rich in classical as well as ecclesiastical texts and, so said the envious, too interested in the pagan texts for the good of his soul. Being bright, he naturally had enemies. A copy of the works of the Roman poet Ovid, then at Glastonbury, now in the Bodleian Library in Oxford, contains a finely drawn monumental figure of Christ with the monk Dunstan crouching at his feet. A note on the page tells us it was drawn by Dunstan himself and there are claims that he designed metalwork. In addition he was renowned as a singer and musician and seems to have exploited the effect of the aeolian harp (the sounds caused by the wind blowing through the strings of a free-standing instrument). Versatile, gifted and well born, he was prominent at the court of King Edmund and entered the church only at the urgings of an uncle, Ælfheah, bishop of Winchester. About 943 the king appointed him abbot of Glastonbury and it was now that Dunstan inaugurated a new era in English church life, rebuilding the monastery and introducing a revised Rule of

St Benedict. Some time later Æthelwold joined Dunstan at Glastonbury, before going on at the request of the new king, Eadred, to reform the dilapidated monastery at Abingdon.

During these years Archbishop Oda had explored the reform movement on the Continent, already some four decades old, with a visit to the abbey of Saint-Benoît-de-Fleury, which held relics of St Benedict and was a hub of the reforming movement. At the same time Dunstan, who had been forced into exile by King Eadwig, was a refugee guest at the newly reformed monastery of Ghent in Flanders, while the third member of our reforming trio, Oswald, had made his way to Fleury at the suggestion of Oda, his uncle.

After the hiatus of Eadwig's reign, the reform movement resumed under Edgar from 959. Dunstan was installed at Canterbury where he seems to have devoted himself to the affairs of the archdiocese rather than general monastic reform. However, Æthelwold, installed as bishop of Winchester in 963, and Oswald, now bishop of Worcester, pushed things along with vigour. At Winchester the monks in charge at both the Old Minster and the New Minster were unceremoniously expelled, possibly with violence, on the orders either of the king or, as one of his acolytes was later to claim, by Bishop Æthelwold. The same happened at other houses under his control. He then began the resettlement, so to speak, of church territories deserted since the Viking raids of a century or so before, notably in the Fens and East Anglia. Not only were the buildings in ruins or completely razed – at Peterborough sheep grazed the foundations – but both there and at Ely and Thorney the lands of their former endowments had mostly been expropriated. Æthelwold refounded all three and ensured their future endowments. All were to revive and extend their influence with sister houses.

Today the saint, in his lifetime seemingly tough and unloved, is remembered for the important customary for the reformed monastic life, the *Regularis Concordia*, that he compiled and above all for the majestic and exquisitely adorned manuscript he commissioned, the Benedictional of St Æthelwold. The *Regularis* drew on mostly Continental models for its rule, but it also made provision for election procedures that in England tended to favour monks above secular clergy and, in acknowledgement of the encouragement the reformers had received from King Edgar, enjoined that prayers be said for the monarch and the royal family. With his Benedictional, Æthelwold oversaw the production of the acknowledged masterpiece of the Winchester school of illumination.

One Fenland abbey, the great house at Ramsey, was indebted to St Oswald for its foundation. The community had been inaugurated as a dependency of the see of Worcester at Westbury on Trim near Bristol. But now, with land granted by Ealdorman Æthelwine of East Anglia and interested help from Fleury in the person of the renowned scholar Abbo, he set up a major teaching centre there.

The making and giving of law

Discussions of Anglo-Saxon law-making are liable to be dogged by the question of the extent to which the law books were actually used as legal texts and to what extent they were, rather, statements of principle or records of traditional provisions. According to Patrick Wormald, it seems that there is no instance of a judgement in which a law book was actually cited. An act from the reign of King Edgar (*IV Edgar*), however, carries an instruction that what 'is made known in this document' shall be written in 'many documents', and these are to be sent to two named ealdormen who in their turn shall send them in all directions, so that the measure 'may be known to both poor and rich'. As always, the paucity of surviving records means that it is difficult to be certain of the conclusion to be drawn. It is the only act with such explicit instructions as to procedure. Are we to assume that it was standard procedure that many other documents now lost would confirm. Or, just the reverse, is it the only one to survive because very few such acts were issued? In any case, Ælfric commented 'One thing is the ordinance which the king commands through his ealdormen and reeves; quite another is his own decree in his own presence.'[13]

In his chapter 'Royal Government and the written word', to which this section is heavily indebted, Simon Keynes noted that King Edgar commanded that Sundays be observed as a solemn festival from Saturday noon until dawn on Monday 'under pain of the fine that the law book (*domboc*) prescribes'. While he adds that 'we may not have the dog-eared copies that the judges actually used', it seems pretty obvious that tenth-century law-makers could rest easy that when they issued laws judges, that is those presiding over public courts, often ealdormen, would have easy access to written codes where they were recorded, though probably not as an enduring frame of reference. The important thing was always the king's 'oral decree', what he actually said. Professor Keynes proposes that it was a basic function of tenth-century law codes, at least, 'to assist in the process of bringing knowledge of the king's decrees into the localities'.

In the act referred to above, known as the *Wihtbordesstan*, Edgar made a ruling that would prove of fundamental importance decades later, namely that the Danes of his kingdom should follow 'such good laws as they best prefer'. It was surely this that led the Danish king Cnut to promulgate the observance of the laws of King Edgar. For his English subjects, Edgar provided that they should observe the provisions that he and his 'wise men . . . have added to the judgements (*domum*) of my ancestors'. The code is particularly stringent on the matter of theft and the disposal of stolen goods and describes a complex strategy, especially on cattle rustling, and prescribes extremely brutal punishment (*steor*) for English offenders.[14]

The previous chapter looked at the use of the English language in the law and officialese; here we turn to more specifically tenth-century legal technicalities and particularly in relation to land.

A celebrated case shows the use of written evidence of title, whether diploma or charter. In a sheet of parchment addressed to King Edward the Elder and now held in the archives of Christ Church, Canterbury, Ealdorman Ordlaf explains how an estate in Fonthill, Wiltshire, came into the possession of the bishop of Winchester, and how at one point in the dispute a former owner had produced a written document 'that was duly read and found to be in order'. In fact, Ordlaf himself abandoned his suit, for, although a dispute could turn on the possession of a diploma or other type of document, at this time the written word was just one among various modes – witness evidence or oath – of establishing or maintaining one's right. The admissibility of written material in a court of law or other tribunal was still a matter for debate, perhaps in the same way as certain types of forensic evidence and phone tap records are today. In code *I Edward* (of King Edward the Elder) there is a specific injunction to all the king's reeves that 'judgements should be made in accordance with the law books (*dombec*) and "compensations paid as has been previously written",' which clearly implies that the regime was in the habit of issuing written injunctions to its officials on the ground.[15]

With the reign of Æthelstan the use of the written word in the proclamation and enforcement of the laws seems really to have taken off. The so-called *Ordinance of Charities* is written injunctions from the king specifically to his reeves. Three out of his six codes are in the first person. And there is evidence that the king's ordinances could be available to officials of the shire court in written form – the Grately decrees (*II Æthelstan*) are referred to in one source as a *scriptum*, for example, as is the code *III Æthelstan*.

The coinage of the Anglo-Saxon kingdom

We have seen something of the development of the coinage under King Alfred; here we can trace it further. Up to the 850s England had half a dozen mints or so situated in or near the major seaports for Continental trade, though we have seen that archbishops of Canterbury might mint their own coins. The second and third quarters of the ninth century, with the mounting number of Viking incursions, saw a dramatic debasement of the currency both in England and on the Continent. The fineness of the English penny was restored by Alfred in a major monetary reform, which has been recently dated to *c*. 875–6, that is even before the victory over the Danes at Edington of 878. There is evidence to suggest that the king minted coins in 874 at London, the principal Mercian mint from the seventh century, and that the Winchester mint was established (or re-established?) in the 870s during the replanning of the city, dated to this period by archaeologist Martin Biddle. Alfred implemented his second and last currency reform about 880, adjusting the weight of the penny and introducing a new denomination, the round halfpenny.

With Alfred, followed by Edward the Elder, the network of mints was extended and deepened, apparently in step with the programme for the creation of defended burhs, though unfortunately few of their coins carry any mint signature. In the later 920s and early 930s there was a sharp rise in production, as a result perhaps of increased silver supplies from Viking Northumbria and the Irish Sea area, or possibly from increased production by Welsh mines. During the reign of Æthelstan (924–39), when the number of mints south of the Humber grew to about 40 nationwide, it became common to name the mint. No fewer than twenty-five moneyers operated in Chester alone, at least seventeen of them concurrently.

The first instance of the portrayal of a king's crowned head on the coinage, as opposed to a chaplet, wreath or helmet, comes in the reign of Æthelstan.[16] The Grately code, given at Grately in Hampshire as *II Æthelstan* in the late 920s, contains the earliest piece of Anglo-Saxon legislation to refer to the administration of the coinage. It specifies that there is to be one coinage over all the king's dominion; that moneyers are licensed to operate only in towns; and that any found breaching this rule, or guilty of false moneying and unable to clear himself by the ordeal shall have the hand that committed the offence struck off and set on the mint. The code details the number of moneyers to be licensed in various centres: seven in Canterbury, for example, comprising four for the king, two for the archbishop, one for the abbot; in Rochester one for the king and one for the bishop; London eight; and Winchester six. There would also be a dozen or more in other named boroughs: Exeter was an important mint continuously from the reign of Alfred, Oxford from the reign of Æthelstan to the end of the period and in the east the importance of Lincoln as a die-cutting centre and mint was exceeded only by York.[17]

The practice of naming the mint lapsed for the most part until the early 970s when King Edgar seems to have made it obligatory. As Mark Blackburn notes in his work on the Grately code and the coinage on which much of this section is based, this means that it is possible not only to date the great majority of coins of the late ninth century and the early tenth, and to date them to specific periods within reigns, but also to suggest regions in which they were struck, in some cases identifying the actual mints.[18] Moneyers, who were highly regarded as craftsmen, were appointed by the crown. For the best part of a century, from 973 to 1066, the national coin-types were changed every six years or so and all money had to be brought in and reminted. The succeeding types varied in weight in a way that suggests a systematic monetary policy. During this period there were at least forty and perhaps as many as seventy minting places in England and there was hardly a village south of the Trent that would have been more than a day's walk from one of them. In medieval terms the Anglo-Saxon state operated a monetary system that was exceeded in its complexity and controls only by the Byzantine empire.[19] In fact, the English king's monopoly of minting rights was almost unique in Europe and the enforced integrity of the coinage respected at home and abroad. For generations, sterling was the currency of choice in much of northwestern Europe, where many mints copied the designs of the English coinage.

The English state

When King Alfred sought to administer his kingdom he was working within an old system of lordship, of courts and territories. In the twelfth century William of Malmesbury wrongly believed that Alfred had invented the hundreds and tithings of England; nor does it seem that he gave any new shape to the West Saxon shires whose origins date back long before his day. But by getting boroughs built and garrisoned, whether or not with market-friendly street plans, as excavated at Winchester, he opened the way to England's urban future. The shiring of England was largely a tenth-century programme. 'The creation of many of the midland shires', it has been said, 'cannot have occurred much earlier than the reign of Edward the Elder or later than that of Æthelred II.'[20] It is reasonable to suppose that much of the work was done in the reign of King Edgar. It was well done. When British local government was reorganized in 1974 just three of England's historic shires were dissolved: Cumberland, Westmoreland and Rutland, all three 'Johnny-come-lately' post-Conquest creations.

The basic, all-purpose tool of Anglo-Saxon administration, evolving at least from the reign of Alfred, was the administrative letter or 'writ'. It was adopted and adapted for instructions to reeves, directives to ealdormen, and announcements in the shire court of land transfers, grants of privilege and official appointments. The document known as *VI Æthelstan*, although related to the king's business in requiring every reeve to exact a pledge from his shire to observe the king's peace, was issued in the name of the bishops and reeves of the 'peace guild of London'. Given that the language of the people was the common means of communication in all official as well as social contexts, it is not surprising to find that the use of messages in written form was not confined to the royal government.

The king's writ, then, authenticated by his seal, was a simple and effective means of conveying the royal will nationwide and of instructions to regions and individuals. The evolution of this brilliant tool of Anglo-Saxon administration during the transition from English to Norman is detailed by Richard Sharpe in his fascinating article (2003). He contrasts it with the large-format diplomas, written in an imposing script and in ponderous Latin, although, a significant detail this, breaking into English for the practical specifics of the boundary markers if a piece of real estate was the matter in hand. In the vernacular from the start, the *gewrit* uses an informal script even though, thanks to its seal, it was every bit as authoritative as the diploma. A kind of hybrid, the writ charter, first found in the reign of Æthelred II and in English up to the year 1070, opened with a general address to the *thegnas* summoned by the sheriff; later this official is to be designated subordinate to the *comes* (count), the Latin equivalent of the earl. As to the document itself, it was issued by the king at the request of the beneficiary, who paid for it, to be read aloud in the shire court. Up to 1066 it was, of course, read in English; for the next four years in English with a French translation, and then from 1070 onwards in Latin with translations into English and French.

The use of written documents was not, of course, unique to England, but the idea of using the vernacular in government always had been. In the opinion of Elton, there was nothing to match the writ – characteristically brief, concise, exact and highly authoritative. After the Conquest, once the English bureaucracy had trained its replacements in the mechanics of government, writs were turned into Latin. 'The central organization built up by the Normans and Angevins – and by them bequeathed to later ages – grew upon those little scraps of parchment with their pendant seals.'[21]

Queens, questions of policy and an ominous intervention

With the death of Æthelstan, the ageing dowager Queen Eadgifu, widow of Edward the Elder, had used her position at the courts of her sons Edmund and Eadred to push the interests of her favourite reformers. She helped advance Dunstan and Æthelwold, bishop of Winchester. Queen Ælfthryth, third wife of her son Edgar, would occupy a similar position in court religious policy, her support going especially to Bishop Æthelwold. She used her influence with the king to settle land disputes in favour of Winchester and to cooperate in the foundation of her nunnery at Wherwell.

When Edgar died two court factions would face each other. On one side were supporters of Edward, the son of his first wife, led by Dunstan, archbishop of Canterbury, and the ealdorman of East Anglia; on the other stood Æthelred, championed by his mother Ælfthryth, patron of Æthelwold, bishop of Winchester, and who in addition could call upon her relative Ælfhere, ealdorman of Mercia, and probably on her brother Ordulf, a substantial lord of southwest England. Edward was the older claimant but his mother had not been consecrated Queen, whereas Ælfthryth had been consecrated with her husband at the time of King Edgar's 'imperial' coronation at Bath in 973. A century earlier the Carolingian princess Judith had been anointed queen on her marriage to King Æthelwulf. This had apparently been the first time Wessex had known a full queen in the technical, consecrated sense. Had she had sons their 'throne worthiness would have been superior to that of their younger brothers'. So, more than a century later, Æthelred's party now argued that he enjoyed a privileged status by virtue of his mother's coronation, though at that time she was a wife of eight years standing and her son probably about five years old.

The ritual used for the queen recalled the ceremony used in West Francia when coronation was part of a queen's marriage, so

Ælfthryth received a ring as a sign of faith and, as the bishop poured the oil on her head in the presence of the great nobles, he blessed and consecrated her for her share in the royal bed. The crown used was considered the crown of eternal glory and it is tempting to think that we may have a sight of the actual headpiece in the depiction of the crowning of the Blessed Virgin Mary as the Queen of Heaven in the sumptuous Benedictional of St Æthelwold, Ælfthryth's favoured churchman.[22]

Thanks to the vagaries of royal partnership rules, King Edgar 'pacificus' left two sons contesting his crown, each abetted by a court faction (and the younger by an ambitious mother). When the successful older son of King Edward was set upon and murdered at Corfe in Dorset in May 979, as he rode to visit his young brother Æthelred. The body was buried without ceremony. Few people doubted that Queen Ælfthryth was involved. The murderers were members of her household; the young king was dragged from his horse at the gates of her estate. Although regicide was considered a particularly heinous crime by the monastic reformers who had long been prominent in government, the killers were never brought to book.

In fact, the monastic restructuring and other church reforms under King Edgar had offended some churchmen and, perhaps more important, had encroached on aristocratic preserves and property interests. Edgar's death had been followed by attacks on the properties of the reformed monasteries by rival court factions. Whatever the politics behind the crime, the surviving boy-king Æthelred does not seem to have been as grateful as his mother expected. There were rumours that she had beaten him about the head with a candlestick, outraged at his ingratitude.

11

DANISH INVASIONS AND KINGS ÆTHELRED 'UNRÆD', CNUT THE GREAT AND OTHERS

Writing of Edward the Confessor, his modern biographer Professor Frank Barlow observed, 'He was the son of a warrior king.' That warrior king was Æthelred II. Commonly pigeon-holed as 'the Unready', Æthelred saw a good deal of action in the second half of his long reign. The English and their great men generally recognized him as 'lord' of their land in the old-fashioned sense of warlord and ring-giver. In the last year of his life, at war with the Danish pretender Cnut, an English army raised by his warlike son Edmund, called 'Ironside', refused to take the field when it was learnt that Æthelred would not be there to lead them.

Nine or possibly twelve years old when he came to the throne, Æthelred would reign for some thirty-eight years, the ninth longest in the history of the English monarchy since the time of King Alfred. It was the best part of a year before the remains of Edward, soon to be called 'the Martyr', were given a decent burial at the nunnery of Shaftesbury. Thus as a result it was not until May 979 that Æthelred was consecrated at Kingston upon Thames, in the presence of the archbishops of Canterbury and York and ten bishops. The Abingdon version of the *Chronicle* says that 'the councillors of the English people' rejoiced at the event; but it also speaks of the appearance of a red blood cloud in the sky the same year. Later people reckoned the reign was ill-omened from the start. The king's name, '_Æthel-ræd_', literally 'noble-counsel', was common among English king lists; but given the many disasters of his reign, particularly in his last years, some wit after his death could not resist adding the by-name '_Unræd_' ('ill counsel', rather than 'unready', though he would often seem that as well).

While most accepted Queen Ælfthryth was complicit in her stepson's death, she seems to have had support from the powerful ealdorman of East Anglia, and also Ealdorman Byrthnoth of Essex. The year 980 saw the first Viking raid in nearly a century, though few seem to have heeded the omen – court intrigue was doubtless more absorbing. In any case the big occasion for that year was the rededication, in October, of the building known for many decades as the Old Minster at Winchester. Even as late as 984 the death in August of that year of the dominating figure of Bishop Æthelwold would probably have seemed more significant than the renewal of harassment by the Norsemen.

Æthelred, a young man of handsome face and stylish appearance, took as wife Ælfgifu, a lady of noble birth who was apparently the daughter of Thored, earl of Northumbria. The match may have been thought to offer valuable goodwill for the Wessex dynasty in that distant and prickly province and the king gave land to the community of St Cuthbert at its church in Chester-le-Street. Friends would be needed in the face of what were now annual Danish raids, whether by fleets returning from the Scandinavian homeland each new raiding season or by a force that, once established, remained in an English base.

The raiders expect support from their Norse kinsfolk in Normandy. Æthelred sought the good offices of a papal envoy in diplomatic approaches to Richard of Normandy. In summer 991 a large fleet appeared off the coast of Suffolk and sacked the trading port of Ipswich before working its way down the Essex coast to the

Blackwater estuary. There on 10 or 11 August, at Northey island near Maldon, stood England's senior ealdorman, Byrthnoth of Essex at the head of his household warriors and the local fyrd, crying the defiance of a loyal liegeman: 'This is Æthelred's land.' In his early sixties, he was a man of heroic stature, more than six feet tall. With holdings in ten shires, after his lord the king he was England's second or third most important layman. The 'Battle of Maldon', the epic poetic fragment that tells of the battle against the *wicinga*, reads like an eyewitness account.

The two forces face one another across a channel, which can be crossed only by a causeway. Byrthnoth rides up and down the lines to supervise the dressing of the shield wall. Then he dismounts to fight among those companions he knew to be most loyal'. The Vikings, who will first have to face opposition as they cross the causeway and then deploy from the narrow bridgehead, offer to be bought off. But Byrthnoth rebuts their bid; in fact he forces a battle. He orders his men to pull back and allow their enemies to cross the causeway. He seems bent on a hero's death. Is it a culpable miscalculation? Is it pride, as the poet claims? Or is it, as has been suggested, a sacrificial tactic to deplete the raiders as far as possible, rather than let them off unscathed to ravage elsewhere? A truly heroic calculation.

There follows the roar of battle, with ravens circling overhead waiting for the carrion corpses of the fallen warriors. We hear Byrthnoth urging on those companions who would win glory from the Danes ('*Denon*'). We see him wield his golden-hilted sword; we hear him pray to the 'Lord of Hosts for grace to his spirit' as he is hacked down by a foeman. His companions Ælfnoth and Wulfmaer fall at the side of their lord, but others, spearmen, desert him. Godric, who had received many a fine horse from his ring-giving lord, now leaps on that lord's horse and rides away on the rearing steed. Others, recognizing the horse, think it is Byrthnoth himself who is in flight and they too flee. The rest, rallied by Dunnere, 'a simple yeoman', fight on. Edward the Tall breaks out through the shield wall to avenge in noble death his treasure-giving lord. Heroic, maybe, but surely a gesture of despair: once an Anglo-Saxon shield wall began to break up, as at Hastings, seventy-odd years later, the end was in sight. An old retainer, Byrhtwold, delivers the final threnody: 'Here lies our lord, the great man in the mire . . .' No one can abandon the battle game now – all are doomed to die. As strength falters so courage must grow. Like Dunkirk an epic reverse, like Dunkirk long remembered, the poem, with its named participants, was surely intended for bardic performance at court or in the great man's hall. And yet, in the words of Roberta Frank, there must have been among the English 'ordinary men aching to get back to their ploughs and puddings'. The battle was worthily celebrated on its millennium in 1991. Donald Scragg's *The Battle of Maldon* came out in that year and the poem exists in more than 45 editions.

For the poet, the battle embodied noble traditions from a heroic age still felt to be part of the present. But reality locked in with Byrthnoth's shocking death. Up to this time the establishment had discounted Viking nuisance as sporadic and small scale. Maldon forced a rethink. It was Archbishop Sigeric of Canterbury, the *Chronicle* tells us, who in the reign of Æthelred decided on the first payment to the 'Danish men' of a 'tax' because of the terror they brought. The next year the raiders defeated a fleet from East Anglia. It was the beginning of a pattern.

In 994 Sigeric apparently paid a tribute to the Danes to save Canterbury Cathedral from being torched. We first hear of him as a monk at Glastonbury under the patronage of St Dunstan. A brilliant career lay ahead. Appointed archbishop in 990 he made the journey to Rome to receive his pallium from Pope John XV. He won recent media attention when, as reported in the *Sunday Times* of 14 November 2005, Romano Prodi, the former president of the European Commission, planned to activate a tourist pilgrim route, dubbed the 'Via Francigena' ('Way of the Franks'), stretching for 1,200 miles (1,930 km) and supposedly 'founded by Sigeric'. In fact, starting with Wigheard in 667, no fewer than nine English arch-bishops and seven English kings travelled to Rome, but Sigeric stands out because a contemporary travelogue of his route survives. It records seventy-nine stages of the journey and twenty-three churches he visited, among them Reims, Lausanne, Pavia and Lucca. Whether modern pilgrims will be entertained to lunch by the pope, as Sigeric was by John XV, may be doubted. Sigeric, however, was a great prince of the church: he bequeathed seven costly wall hangings emblazoned with white lions to Glastonbury, sufficient to cover the wall surface of the old church when they were brought out every year on his anniversary.

The wealth of the realm

Maldon marked the beginning of decline for a generally fortunate aristocracy. The great inaugural celebrations at Ramsey Abbey on 8 November 991, presided over by Archbishop Oswald of York, its spiritual founder, and Æthelwine, ealdorman of East Anglia, its wealthy lay patron, reflected the glory days of ostentatious magnificence. The event is described by Oswald's biographer Byrthferth. Luxury and opulence everywhere met the eye; while music of great elaboration assailed the ear as the choir and cantors sang antiphonally and, no doubt, in early polyphony. With this style of singing in two or more parts European art music was already sig-nalling its breach with the monophonic traditions of the rest of world music. Part and parcel of the revolution was the mechanistic apparatus of the organ and keyboard. By this time almost every important Benedictine abbey in Europe had such an instrument. Inspired by the liturgical revolution at Cluny, the service of God was to be conducted with the kind of splendour in liturgy, vestments and music to be expected in the service of a great lord. But while the scops and scalds of the mead hall would remain true to the bardic monophonic traditions, Ramsey had a fine organ.

The monks of Ely recovered the body of Ealdorman Byrthnoth after the battle for the solemnities of a great funeral. The church dazzled with ornaments (Byrthnoth himself had donated two gold crosses). At Winchester the reliquary commissioned by the king for the remains of St Swithun was made of 300 pounds of refined gold ornamented with silver and precious stones. England at this time was a treasurehouse to its Danish plunderers. 'The evidence for the wealth of England in this period is various and extensive . . .', in cash as well as treasures, for it seems that 'early eleventh-century English kings could raise larger sums in taxation than could most of their medieval successors.'[1] Following the endowments of monastic reforms the ecclesiastical establishment was also immensely rich. The celebrations at Ramsey were followed by a sumptuous drinks party, as was the approved custom, at which the mead and wine were dispensed most freely. Drawn from warrior stock, great churchmen were as much at home in the mead hall as in the sanctuary and, when occasion required, on the battlefield. Twenty-five years later, the abbot of Ramsey and his predecessor in office both fell fighting in the army of Edmund Ironside against the Danes at the Battle of Assandun.[2]

It was a time when the English were becoming acquainted with the use of the word 'Englalond' to describe their homeland. It was a land where the elite kin groups of church and state formed, as we have noted, an extended network or cousinship usually linked with the royal family by blood, marriage or by fosterage at court; where the peasantry, as elsewhere in Europe, was largely oppressed (the penalties for theft were savage, on a par with shariah law), but where, and this was unusual, we may detect the beginnings of a middling sort of people who in a later age would be called 'the gentry'.

For a hundred years, since the time of King Alfred, the idea of society as divided into three orders, those to fight, those to pray and those to labour on the land, had been common in England, as on the Continent.[3] But it was becoming as misleading as it was simplistic. The growth of the 'ceorl' grouping of small gentry-style farmers may be connected with the splitting up of great estates and associated with the creation of new parishes and new parish churches. It evidently came to carry weight in the community of the realm. In 1027, when Cnut issued a letter for proclamation in shire courts throughout the kingdom, he addresses it in English to 'the whole race of the English, whether nobles or ceorls'.

Following Maldon, a tribute or *gafol* of 10,000 pounds was paid to the raiders. Still larger payments, in money and in gold and silver would be made in subsequent years. The amount of bullion disbursed is a testimony to the great wealth of England; the quantities of silver coinage are a clear demonstration of the power of the English state. Coin hoards in Scandinavia, accumulated as the proceeds of plunder, have provided numismatists with some of their best resources for studying and demonstrating the sophistication and effectiveness of the monetary system of the Anglo-Saxon state. The estimated figures run into millions of items. In the reign of Cnut, in the view of numismatist Michael Metcalf, one issue alone (the Quatrefoil) may have run to as many as 40 million coins.

Two years after Maldon a much larger English army was put to flight (rumour said that the leaders were Danish sympathizers). Then in 994, on the Feast of the Nativity of the Virgin Mary (8 September), a large fleet under the command of Olaf Tryggvason of Norway and Swein Forkbeard the Dane, among others, sailed against London. According to the Peterborough *Chronicle* the citizens repelled the attack, to the astonishment of the enemy, thanks to the protection of the Virgin. For this humiliation the Danish army wreaked a terrible vengeance on the country and coasts from Essex to Hampshire, 'taking their horses' and riding inland wherever they would. They made winter camp at Southampton and were provisioned with supplies from the whole kingdom of Wessex.

The government agreed a treaty by which yet more money and bullion were handed over. Olaf, however, now accepted baptism (994) as a Christian in a ceremony at Andover, with King Æthelred standing sponsor, and moreover gave his oath never to return to England as an enemy. He kept it too, the chronicler notes in surprise. Perhaps that was because this Viking oath to the Christians was pledged by one who was now a fellow Christian. Olaf went back to Norway to make good his position as king there. Swein, it seems, had already returned to Denmark with the same objective.

Even in these extreme conditions the Anglo-Saxon civil administration of reeve and local collectors was able to meet the demands for supplies to the raiders from central government. More problematic, surely, is the total failure throughout these decades of the Alfredian strategic defence measures of garrisoned burh and standing army units to deliver effective protection. The mid-990s, it must be said, were a time of comparative peace. Perhaps a substantial body of the Danish army settled on the Isle of Wight as a mercenary force in English pay. Then, in the years running up to the millennium, large-scale raids were reported up the Bristol Channel, against the coasts of south Wales and Devon, back to Dorset, up to the Thames and riding through Kent. In the year 1000 they crossed over to Normandy and then they were back harrying southern Wessex. An attempt to buy them off with the largest payment yet, 24,000 pounds, might have had some effect but for the notorious events on St Brice's Day, 13 November 1002. In a gesture of desperation, certainly 'ill-advised' while negotiations were yet going on, Æthelred ordered the killing of all 'the Danish men who were among the English race', described in a royal charter as 'sprouting like weeds amongst the wheat'.

The St Brice's Day massacre may have decided King Swein to return to the English theatre of operations. We find him campaigning in the West Country the following year. Aimed against those Danes 'in England', the wording of the decree presumably excludes the population of the Danelaw. And it certainly excluded any raiders encamped on the Isle of Wight; to massacre *them* would have required an army. No, the target must have been those Danes in England west of the Danelaw, presumably second-generation, gradually integrating into English communities – or possibly the Danes paid off that summer who had not gone home or 'ceased their evil doing'. At Oxford, Danes fleeing for sanctuary had broken into the church of St Frideswide: the citizenry burnt it down about their heads. Later it was claimed there had been a Danish plot against the king to 'ensnare' his kingdom. Swein of Denmark would do just that. Meanwhile Æthelred found himself facing a demand for compensation from the minster of St Frideswide's.[4] It was a royal edict that had sanctioned the outrage.

Of all the woes to trouble King Æthelred, top of the list must have been Normandy. Treaties with the ducal house could not be made to stick. An attempted naval invasion of the duchy ended in futility. Then the death of his first wife opened the door to diplomacy by dynastic marriage. In the spring of 1002 the princess Emma, daughter of the late duke, Richard I, and sister of the present ruler, Duke Richard II, came to England and, with the newly conferred English name of Ælfgifu, became its queen, her most frequent title in Æthelred's Latin charters being '*conlaterana Regis*', '[she] who is at the king's side'.[5]

The marriage was surely loveless. Admittedly Æthelred had already fathered ten children by various wives or concubines and had three more with Emma: the eldest, Edward, became king in due course as 'the Confessor'; his brother Alfred was to die in the succession struggle following their father's death; and a daughter, Gode, married a count of Boulogne. But within months of the wedding the king authorized the massacre, with consequences that, in Norman eyes, were 'shocking even to pagans' – it is unlikely that Emma would have differed from that opinion. Towards the end of her long life (she died in 1052) Emma/Ælfgifu would commission

an account of her life and times from a Flemish monk, evidently one
of her close circle. At the time of the composition of *Encomium
Emmae Reginae*, which roughly translates as *In Praise of Queen Emma*,
Æthelred had been dead close on thirty years and she had in any case
also married his successor Cnut, also dead. Even so it seems a notable
fact that it makes not a single mention of her English husband.

In 1006 the Danes attacked in still greater force, arriving off
Sandwich and delivering raiders to ravage at will through the counties, as was their wont, with their base on the Isle of Wight. The
next year they sailed away, the better off by 36,000 pounds paid as
tribute, to add to whatever they had looted the previous season.
It was a respite. Why now and not earlier we do not know, but at
this point the government ordered the building of warships. The
bureaucracy went into action; funds were raised with the usual
efficiency, with one ship funded from every 310 hides. Just two years
later (1009) a fully equipped 'ship army', some one hundred vessels
in number, was riding at anchor off Sandwich. But the national
effort was sabotaged. When a certain Brihtric of Mercia laid charges
against 'Prince Wulfnoth the South Saxon', apparently one of the
fleet commanders (and perhaps father of the future Earl Godwine),
Wulfnoth detached a squadron and raided along the south coast.
What follows is a remarkable tale in which corruption, betrayal and
administrative fecklessness would seem to have played their parts.
The upshot was the destruction of eighty ships, wrecked in a storm
and then torched on the beach by order of the commander himself.
The king and his ministers abandoned their squadron and 'took
themselves home' while the crews took the ships to safe haven in
London. The ship levy was discontinued. Within weeks the first
Danish fleet in three years was back outside a defenceless Sandwich.
Its commander was Thorkell the Tall, who was to be involved in
English affairs for more than a decade.

For the best part of two years the host ranged unrestrained
through the hapless shires. Now, if ever, the royal regime and the

king himself earned their reputation for bad decisions ('*unraedas*') and for belated payments of *gafol*, made only when great damage had been done. Even after it was paid 'for all this truce and peace they travelled . . . in bands and raided and roped up and killed our wretched people.'[6] Then in 1011, thanks to treachery, raiders broke into Canterbury, 'that [now] wretched town from where . . . first came to us Christendom and bliss', and seized Ælfweard, the king's reeve, the bishop of Rochester, various other senior churchmen, scores of lesser clerics and Archbishop Ælfheah himself.

For months they hauled him about with them at the end of a rope until a ransom should be paid. But Ælfheah refused to permit any such payment. This angered them greatly and one evening at Greenwich, drunk on 'wine from the south', they seem to have staged a mock trial at their '*hustings*' or 'house court'. There, despite the reported intervention of Thorkell the Tall himself,[7] the archbishop was pelted with cattle bones and finished off with a blow from the butt of an axe. The feast day of Canterbury's first martyred archbishop (often known as St Alphege), so honoured with the approval of St Anselm, is on 19 April.

The *Chronicle* gives the impression that treason and faction ruled at court, but the author was writing after Æthelred's reign, with the bitterness of hindsight. In 1009, so the Peterborough *Chronicle* tells us, Æthelred at the head of an army managed to intercept the raiders trying to regain their ships. Everybody was ready to attack, but Ealdorman Eadric stopped the action, 'as it always was'. This Eadric Streona, appointed ealdorman of all Mercia in 1007, seems to have been the moving spirit in a palace revolution the year before. The chief victims were Ælfhelm the Mercian, ealdorman of Northumbria, who was killed while out hunting as a guest of Eadric in an ambush set up by his host, and Ælfhelm's two sons, blinded on the king's orders while guests at the royal vill of Cookham, Berkshire.[8] Both incidents outraged the primal laws of hospitality, but both are too easily believable of the court of Æthelred.

At about the same time as he was created ealdorman in Mercia, Eadric Streona was given the hand of the king's daughter Edith in marriage. Described by Simon Keynes as 'a convincing villain', he was at the heart of the royal councils for ten years; by 1012 he was recognized as at the head of the rigidly observed hierarchy of the royal ealdormen of King Æthelred, but five years later he was killed on the orders of King Cnut and his body left unburied outside the walls of London. In the intervening years he features in the murky and confused events that ended with the triumph of Cnut over the English champion Edmund Ironside. Eadric, it would appear, was 'a most notorious traitor' to both.

Relief of a sort seemed in sight for the English in 1012. On payment of a tribute of 8,000 pounds the raiding army dispersed and a substantial force under Thorkell the Tall, at his base in Greenwich, agreed to take service as mercenaries under Æthelred, who in his turn agreed to feed and clothe them – and, as it turned out, to make them an annual payment. Regularized as an annual levy on land, the army tax (*here geld*), later called danegeld, continued to be levied until 1051 when it was temporarily suspended. Given its centralized administration, galvanized by Alfred and streamlined by the reforms of his tenth-century successors, England had always been pirate-friendly when it came to collecting *gafol* or tribute. Now the system proved able to deliver Europe's first effective system of nationwide public taxation since the collapse of the Roman empire in the west. The last 'danegeld' as such was raised under Henry II in 1161. Insofar as taxation may stimulate economic activity by the need to recreate the wealth lost and by the recirculation of the revenue raised within the economy, then, notionally, danegeld could have brought benefits; but they were surely marginal! 'If the Chronicle is to be believed then English and Anglo-Danish kings raised at least £272,147 in gelds between 991 and 1018 . . . [and] . . . much of the bullion went to Scandinavia.'[9]

Thorkell provided little protection. In 1013 King Swein of Denmark invaded. He received submissions from East Anglia to Mercia, from Lindsey and the Five Boroughs, from Earl Uhtred and all Northumbria. He took his ships up the River Trent to Gainsborough, leaving them in the charge of his son Cnut. It was presumably here that the prince met Ælfgifu of Northampton, daughter of Ealdorman Ælfhelm, who bore him Swein, later king in Norway, and Harold 'Harefoot', to be Harold I of England. The Danes were said to have a form of marriage by seizure, in which the forcible taking of a woman was then legitimized through a payment, a sort of ransom. According to Pauline Stafford, Danish marriage at this time was monogamous, but concubinage was practised and the result could be close to polygamy.

King Swein continued his victorious progress, crossing over Watling Street from the Danelaw, taking hostages, from Oxford for example, and doing 'the greatest evil a raiding army could do'. He went south to Winchester and then back towards London, where Æthelred and Thorkell, his mercenary captain, were safe behind the fortifications. The actual mercenaries seem to have been still at Greenwich – where they remained! Swein did not press a siege, instead he and his army swung down into the West Country, making camp in King Edgar's 'imperial' city of Bath. He received the submission of all the western thegns. Leaving the Londoners suspended in their now isolated defiance, he returned to Cnut and the ships. All the country accepted him as 'full king', whereupon the Londoners submitted.

After having plundered at will for five months, Swein naturally demanded payment and compensation for his trouble – so as naturally did Thorkell for his mercenaries. After keeping Christmas on the Isle of Wight, King Æthelred was permitted to make his way into exile with his brother-in-law in Normandy. Emma had already gone, escorted by the abbot of Peterborough while the æthelings Edward and Alfred were escorted overseas by the bishop of London.

Never actually crowned, Swein Forkbeard was to all intents and purposes king in England when he died on 3 February 1014 with the fleet at Gainsborough. His body was taken for burial to York.[10] The fleet, Swein's chief advisers and Cnut's war band elected Cnut as king. Presumably the Danelaw concurred.

The reign of Æthelred Unræd still had two more troubled years to run. But this is perhaps the time to review something of the state of England away from the battle fronts. During this time legislation became notably more exhortatory in tone and ecclesiastical in content. Where earlier codes had 'let every moneyer . . . guilty of . . . striking false coin . . . be slain,' we find 'let one . . . shun . . . false weights and measures . . . and let all be eager for the improvement of money everywhere in the land.' Victorian historians saw in this mildness of tone evidence of a regime in despair under the recurrent incursions of Danish invaders. But the change may well be in part due to the style of Wulfstan 'the Homilist', archbishop of York, active in Æthelred's government and noted for his florid style of sermonizing.

Behind the *Chronicle*'s long pages of despair and horror, the charters, the laws and the coinage tell a different and more positive story. Before his messy martyrdom at Greenwich, St Ælfheah's career had been one of creative work. In the tenth century, that miracle age of pioneer church organ-building in Europe, the best-known account is of the organ at Winchester; it was said to require twenty-four men, and more, to operate the foot bellows and was audible a mile away from the cathedral. There are those who question the accuracy of the details and doubt the possible musicality of the apparatus – but it was surely some Wurlitzer and it was apparently largely the achievement of Ælfheah.

He was abbot of Bath at the time of King Edgar's coronation there (973) and was consecrated bishop of Winchester in October 984. He continued St Æthelwold's various works to beautify the city's churches. For the past four years, for example, work had been in progress at the New Minster, at King Æthelred's expense, on a tower 115 feet (35 m) high, topped by a golden weathercock. Each of its external registers was carved. The first was devoted to the Virgin, who was depicted surrounded by the lords and citizens (*principes et cives*) of the heavenly Jerusalem, a great queen within the court.

Religion could be the mainspring of political action. In 1009, the response of King Æthelred and his advisers in council at Bath to the advent of Thorkell's army had been to promulgate a national three-day programme of prayer, fasting and barefoot processionals. It was not the prescription of nursery-minded cowards, nor of a cynical religious elite looking to manipulate a backward peasant populace, but the response of a government, a millennium away from us, believing that national security be found in group penitence and supplication to a concerned god. Regrettably, salvation was not delivered.

When Swein Forkbeard died and Cnut was proclaimed his successor, King Æthelred was in Normandy. Æthelstan, his eldest son by his first wife, seems to have been lying low in England, possibly in company with his younger brother Edmund. The English decided to call back Æthelred on condition he govern them better than before, and he agreed on condition that they behave with greater loyalty. He returned in the summer of 1014 and raised an army to challenge Cnut, who abandoned allies from Lindsey and East Anglia and departed for Denmark, leaving behind brutally mutilated hostages on the beach at Sandwich.

Briefly the English royal family seemed to be back in business: the king with his heir at his side, their Danish enemies leaderless. Suddenly, in the morning of 25 June 1014, Prince Æthelstan received his father's permission to make a will. Its bequests embody the ideal of a warrior lord in his mead hall – a war trumpet, a drinking horn and a number of swords of ancient and honourable provenance, one of which, the sword of King Offa of Mercia, he willed to his brother Edmund. Æthelstan was already desperately sick and died later that day. He was buried in the Old Minster, Winchester. The following year the kingdom would have to face the return of Cnut. But the moment of harmony had passed.

There were divisions in the English camp. Most people reckoned that Eadric Streona was all powerful at court. Thus, when Edmund opposed Eadric's interests over the lands of the rich widow Ældgyth, it could be interpreted as disloyalty to his own father. Her husband Sigeferth had been killed, his lands confiscated and she had been imprisoned on the king's orders. In 1015 Edmund freed the lady from her house arrest, married her and appropriated the family lands in the east Midlands in the region of the Five Boroughs 'and the people [i.e. the people who mattered] all submitted to him.' He had the lady, but he also held the historic sword of Offa – a potent talisman for the Mercian English.

Meanwhile Cnut was receiving submissions including from Wessex and the Mercians under Eadric. An army raised by Edmund refused to fight when Æthelred did not come to lead it – was this perhaps due to the influence of Eadric? But Edmund had the support of Uhtred of Northumbria in a campaign through Cheshire and the northwest Midlands, 'Eadric's Mercia' so to speak. Like Eadric a royal son-in-law, Uhtred has been described as 'quite simply the most important man in the north of England'.[11] He also was the enemy of Eadric Streona, who was siding with Cnut. When the Dane succeeded in occupying York, however, Uhtred agreed to a meeting in one of his manor halls to make his formal submission. He was murdered in his own hall for his pains, almost certainly with Cnut's connivance. Beside the earl, forty of his followers were slain by a rival northern magnate, Thurbrand 'the Hold', in a bloodbath that started a sixty-year feud. Edmund's cause had lost a powerful friend. He headed for London to join his father.

Æthelred, by now in his mid-fifties, died in London on St George's Day, 23 April 1016. It had been a long reign and for the most part inglorious. Wulfstan the Homilist recorded harrowing sights of thegns watching listlessly while their womenfolk were serially raped by Danish raiders, and of ordinary citizens so terrorized that they made no attempt to intervene as crowds of their fellow countrymen and women were driven shipboard into slavery by just three or four seamen. Gossip later claimed that Cnut's sister had run a profitable trade in the export of English girls as slaves to Denmark.

London held off the enemy and the citizens and such notables as were there chose Edmund to succeed; they may even have had him crowned king. An assembly at Southampton elected Cnut king. All that summer, inconclusive battles and manoeuvrings saw the advantage tip first one way then that. Edmund threw back a Danish siege and found reinforcements to defeat another one. A contemporary German source mentions a report of 24,000 coats of mail being held in London.[12] It appears that Queen Emma/Ælfgifu remained, sharing in the 'heroic resistance that was remembered in the North'.[13] At Otford Edmund defeated an army led by Cnut himself, which persuaded Eadric Streona to come back on side. In October the English king summoned yet another army 'of all the English nation', among them the force led by Eadric Streona. On 18 October 1016, at the battle of 'Assandun' in Essex, either at Ashingdon or Ashdun, Streona and his people swapped sides once again. Cnut won the encounter but Edmund recouped his forces. After more campaigning in the West Country, Edmund was able to conclude a treaty at Alney, Gloucestershire, that agreed a division of England by which he became king of Wessex while Cnut held Northumbria, Mercia and presumably East Anglia. It was a notable outcome for the house of Cerdic. In February 1014 the uncrowned Swein Forkbeard the Dane died acknowledged king throughout England. By late 1016 his son had been forced to concede the heartland kingdom to the native claimant. King Edmund Ironside had raised levies time after time in many shires and forced the invader to terms. But on 30 November he died, possibly of a lingering battle wound. Perhaps his half-brother, the boy-prince Edward (later the Confessor) had fought in his last battle. Christmas that year we hear of him in Ghent.

No source at the time of Edmund's death suggested foul play, but some sixty years later there was a rumour going the rounds in Germany that he had been poisoned. Later still, Gaimar's *Estorie des Engleis* (c. 1150) names Eadric Streona. It is not so much the bizarre mode of assassination – shot with an arrow up the anus, presumably up the down vent of a cantilevered first-floor privy – that's intriging here as the fact that, more than a century on, the fate of the last full-blooded Englishman to rule the country was still of interest. Edmund left two sons who found exile in Hungary: Edward, to whom we shall come later, and Edmund. Cnut was said to have made a pilgrimage to his rival's tomb at Glastonbury and to refer to him as his 'brother': good theatre, perhaps by someone who liquidated Edmund's brother Eadwig.

About this time, an assembly of English notables in London renounced any allegiance to Edmund's sons, proclaimed amity between the Danes and the English and swore loyalty to Cnut. In addition foreigners were to be permitted to live in peace and the official celebration of the Feast of Edward 'the Martyr' was promulgated. Thus the murder of his half-brother came back to haunt Æthelred Unræd even in death. His entire reign was impugned and his descendants utterly discredited also by association. Cnut's inauguration, by contrast, tied the Danish conqueror directly into the traditions of English kingship by the honour he did to the Martyr.[14]

Cnut confiscated English estates with which to reward his followers; it was the normal pattern in the tradition of the gift-giving war leader. He made his most powerful ally, the chief Norwegian magnate Eirik, earl in Northumbria, and Thorkell the Tall earl in East Anglia. Clearly a great power in that province or earldom, he may for a time have considered challenging Cnut himself, but Thorkell's English career was ended by banishment. There was nothing to match the root and branch dispossession of the

Anglo-Saxon establishment that followed 1066. The overthrow and death of Eadric Streona was a necessary security precaution against a threat waiting to materialize. Thanks to that famously efficient English tax-raising bureaucracy Cnut was able to pay off followers with immense silver handshakes that sent them happily back to their home territories set up for life. By 1018 most of the fleet was dispersed and agreement had been reached, 'according to the laws of Edgar', between the English and their new master.

By now Cnut had also done as much as he could to scotch the snake of a dynastic comeback. Ironside's infant children in faraway Hungary were hardly a threat. Æthelred's sons by his Norman queen Emma/Ælfgifu, the teenage Edward and the boy Alfred, were by now ensconced in Normandy and offered no immediate danger, although they could be useful little stalking horses if a Norman duke should one day want to challenge the Viking king in England. In July 1017 Cnut married their mother. According to the lady's biography, written under her direction some twenty-five years later, things were not quite so simple. An acid allusion to the children of Ælfgifu of Northampton states, 'It was said the king had sons by another.' Emma tells us that she refused even to become betrothed without a promise that if she bore a son he and no other would rule after the king. The marriage was celebrated 'to the joy of the people' and was soon to be enriched by the birth of a son, Harthacnut, whom, according to Emma's apologia, the royal couple 'kept ever with them as the future heir to the kingdom.'

It was a revolution of dynasty; quite unlike the Norman revolution fifty years later, the new Danish regime wanted an accommodation with the English. By marrying the widowed queen, the conqueror consolidated the bond of amity. The church consecrated at Assandun to celebrate Cnut's victory also honoured the English dead. In June 1023, in a great ceremony of national reconciliation, the Danish court moved to expiate the murder of Archbishop Ælfeah of Canterbury by drunken Danish soldiery twelve years before. The relics of the martyr were translated from London to Canterbury and the cortège was met at Rochester by Queen Emma and the infant Prince Harthacnut. From there they accompanied the jubilant crowds on the road to the metropolitan cathedral, where the Queen presented gifts at the new shrine. Danish standing in Canterbury received a boost. Londoners were probably seething – it has been suggested that the saintly relics were in fact moved out of the city under armed guard and under cover of darkness. Cnut wanted stable community relations. It was not for nothing that the new regime was to be run 'according to the laws of King Edgar'. After all, those laws had specifically been prepared to concede a measure of legal autonomy to his Danish subjects.

Cnut and the business of government

Under Cnut the units of authority formerly known as ealdordoms came to be called earldoms. For the last fifty years before the Norman Conquest the big three – Wessex, Mercia and Northumbria – were in the hands of Cnut's appointees, or their descendants. The names can still awaken echoes. 'Old' Siward of Northumbria features in Shakespeare's *Macbeth*; Leofric of Mercia was husband to Godiva of Coventry. A pious lady, rich in her own right and a munificent patron of churches, she is above all remembered for the ride she made through the market-place of Coventry, naked save for her long golden hair, at the challenge of her husband to have him free the townspeople of all tolls.

Godwine is remembered as head of Anglo-Saxon England's most famous family and father of its last king, Harold II. We are told that Cnut favoured him because of his eloquence, a man 'profound in speech' according to the biographer of Edward the Confessor, probably somewhat orotund, a little pompous perhaps, but what the eighteenth century would have called 'a man of bottom'. Godwine was probably the son of thegn Wulfnoth, *cild* of Sussex, but although of minor English noble birth his rise to power came under the new Danish dynasty. His wife, Gytha, sister-in-law to Cnut, bore him six sons, Swein, Harold, Tostig, Gyrth, Leofwine and Wulfnoth, and three daughters, of whom Edith was to become queen of England. By 1018 he had been appointed an earl in England south of the Thames, but it was as a result of his prowess in Denmark in the suppression of rebellion in 1019 or 1022–3 that Cnut advanced him higher. Some would say too high and blame Cnut's faulty judgement for making Godwine the over-mighty subject of Edward the Confessor's reign.

An earl was expected to preside at the shire courts in his jurisdiction, though it appears that royal representatives (*legati*) were regularly present. These royal legates or observers frequently had judicial functions and were active in Northumbria as well in southern shires. From the time of Edward the Confessor we find that local administrative responsibilities devolve increasingly upon the sheriff, who might be appointed by the earl in whose place he stood but often by the king. An earl could be expected to lead the local armed forces of the shires, though here again the intervention of the centre was important, since the king had overriding powers concerning the *fyrd*. Traditionally a man's military equipment (*heregeatu*, literally 'war gear') had been supplied by his lord; it was the physical sign of the link between lord and man in this warrior society. At the man's death it was to be restored to the lord. The convention persisted down to the Conquest and, though it became in effect a form of death duty, 'heriot', as it was known, was still rendered as weapons or other military equipment, varying according to the man's rank. Cnut's law code issued in the early 1020s listed an earl's heriot as eight horses, together with a sizeable arms, including four swords, and sufficient gold to fit out four troopers and their attendants. With high status went great power in their locality. But English earls, unlike continental courts, remained royal appointees. Witness lists of royal charters reveal that even the most powerful, even the earls of Northumberland, were in frequent attendance at the royal court.

The response of the Æthelredian state to its ordeal appears at best 'inadequate' and much given to exhortation, with law codes almost pleading with the population to be good. But a similar tone can be detected in Cnut's legislation. Like Alfred himself, these later legislators believed that a right relation with God was fundamental to good government. The spirit of the age saw the terrible afflictions of the Scandinavian terror raids as just punishment of a sinful people; society should purge itself of its guilt and such penitence could and should be regulated by law. Cnut adopted the public role of good, penitent Christian. On his regular visits to Wilton nunnery he always dismounted in respect of the place. The monk of Saint-Omer, author of Queen Emma's *Encomium*, who witnessed the king's actions 'with his own eyes' as he passed through Saint-Omer on pilgrimage to Rome, saw in him a near saintly figure, the friend to churchmen, a 'co-bishop to the bishops'.

Where Alfred had his cakes, Cnut had the tide. The story of the king seated on the seashore, the wavelets lapping at his feet as he fails to stop the incoming sea, derives from two twelfth-century chroniclers. Apparently Cnut staged this demonstration of his powerlessness against the forces of nature to silence some sycophantic courtiers. It seems entirely plausible for the hard-headed ruler of a sea-borne empire.

That empire was funded, as we learn from M. K. Lawson, Cnut's recent biographer, by the wealth of the pre-Conquest English state. No reign better illustrates, he observes, not only the wealth of that state but also the capacities of its 'comprehensive administrative system'. They weighed heavily on taxpayers. The records show cases of landholders dispossessed in favour of others better able to pay and churches cashing in or melting down plate or other valuables to raise the money. We have already noted the huge sums raised simply to pay off the invader's army, even before the English started to fund his

Scandinavian expeditions (an estimated 47 million coins of the quatrefoil type, presumably to pay the £82,500 the *Chronicle* reports
handed over in 1018). But England's advanced coinage operation,
with mints in production at sites throughout the country seems to
have had a practical impact on the expansion of Denmark's money
economy under Cnut. During this reign the country witnessed an
innovation when pennies began to be produced in Denmark at four
or five royal mints. The Scandinavian contact with England through
Cnut seems probably to have contributed to the evolution of the
royal writ in Norway.[15] And Cnut could also draw on the renowned
artists of his Anglo-Saxon kingdom to bolster his fame, as when the
scriptorium at Peterborough was commissioned to produce an illuminated Psalter to be sent to the church at Cologne.

For England the reign seems to have been the first great era of tax
and spend – abroad: it brought little of benefit at home. Even the
king's renowned visit to Rome could bring little extra prestige to the
country, given that many of its kings had made the trip before and
that for some 150 years it had tendered a unique annual alms payment
to the Holy See. Known as the Romescot or *Romfeoh* (more popu-
larly as Peter's pence or hearth penny), it seems to have originated in
ad hoc donations by eighth-century kings of Wessex and Mercia, and
had been formalized in the ninth. By the reign of Cnut, the collection of the penny-per-household levy had been regularized at traditional provincial collection points to be paid by midsummer's day.

In so far as the Danes, having conquered the country, were no
longer invading it, one could presumably say that Cnut's conquest
brought peace – though not, it seems without heavy policing by
garrisons of *huscarls* (royal household troops). The church, it is true,
generally sang his praises and with good reason. Almost certainly a
baptized Christian when he arrived in England, he may have grown
into a man of genuine piety. He was a lavish donor of lands and precious artefacts. Besides endowments to the 'Danelaw' abbeys of Ely
and Ramsey, he also endowed the shrine of St Ælfheah (Alphege)

at Canterbury. It was said that later in life, he walked five miles barefoot to the church of St Cuthbert at Durham. Of course, such gifts
were calculated. In what may have been his last charter of endowment, to Sherborne Abbey, he prays that his benefactions may ease
his way to the heavenly kingdom. He died at Shaftesbury, in the
homelands of Wessex, on 12 November 1035. He was buried in
the Old Minster at Winchester, to be joined seventeen years later
by Emma/Ælfgifu, his wife.

Some lucky beneficiaries certainly had reason to bless the memory
of King Cnut. Further than that, to the nation at large, the legacy was
scant and dubious. As with the Norman Conquest, just thirty years
later, 'the immediate effect was a vast dispersal of English wealth
abroad.' Whereas there was none of the wholesale destruction for
which the Normans were to be responsible, 'architectural reminiscences of the Danish conquest and rule are non-existent.'[16] The
rivalries between the three great earldoms that, thanks to Cnut,
became dominant in the nation's affairs were to cause much trouble
in the next reign and his ramshackle Nordic 'empire', bar a few
trading concessions, brought little benefit to England.

Just one of the kingdoms of King Cnut the Great (in Danish,
Knud den Store; in Norwegian, Knut den Mektige), the country
seems to have bankrolled his Nordic empire. It was a measure of
Cnut's statecraft that he manipulated 'Englalond's' fine governmental machine without the permanent dispossession of its governmental and aristocratic elite. He did replace Æthelred's ealdormen
and from 1018 to 1023, apart from Godwine and a small number of
new English king's thegns, he relied principally on Nordic earls and
thegns in the upper reaches of his administration. But after 1023 he
promoted more loyal English followers. On at least three occasions
English troops followed his banner in wars in Scandinavia. In 1028
they helped him assert his overlordship in Norway with King
St Olaf the Good or 'the Stout'. There his English consort Ælfgifu
and her son Swein ruled for a time but they were driven out by the

Norwegians in favour of the dead Olaf's son, Magnus I, and were forced to flee to Denmark.

At home, the English saw war on only one occasion, when in 1027 Cnut made a foray into Scotland to enforce the submission of Malcolm, king of Scots. This same year he made his famous pilgrimage to Rome, reviving a tradition of earlier kings of Wessex, and was received by Pope John XIX. He also attended the coronation of Emperor Conrad II. Negotiations between the two monarchs would benefit English merchants with toll reductions and some years later Cnut's daughter Gunnhild would marry Conrad's son Henry (the Emperor Henry III), though Cnut never matched King Æthelstan's continental dynastic networking. At his death he was followed in Denmark by Harthacnut, barely sixteen years old. The boy was promoted by his mother Emma to succeed Cnut in England but opposed by the Londoners who supported Harold, his son by Ælfgifu of Northampton. In 1037 Harold won general recognition.

Cnut's marital status certainly left a few puzzles at his death. For Pauline Stafford, in her book *Queens, Concubines and Dowagers* (1983), it was a clear example of polygamy. Ælfgifu, his English wife, had borne him both Harold and Swein before his politically useful marriage to Emma/Ælfgifu of Normandy, his predecessor's widow; recognized as full wife from the start. For Stafford the two women are to be considered 'simultaneous wives' though with different 'spheres of influence'. The church seems to have made little protest over the arrangements during Cnut's lifetime (given the benefactions it received that is, perhaps, not to be wondered at), though after his death the perspective may have shifted.

Disputed successions

Though half English by birth and 'acknowledged as full king over all England', Harold was apparently not popular. And his birth was an issue. Scandal, no doubt assisted by Emma, also claimed that he was illegitimate, not just because he was not Cnut's son by the Englishwoman, but because he was not her son at all: since Ælfgifu of Northampton was unable to have children, she had had the child of a serving maid smuggled into her bed. Such was the story detailed in the *Encomium*. The question of bastardy may have been a factor at the back of the mind of Archbishop Æthelnoth of Canterbury when, with a dramatic gesture, he refused to hand over the coronation regalia (crown, sceptre, anointing ampula, etc.) and forbade Harold or any bishop to remove them. Harold took the throne nonetheless – even though Harthacnut had been accepted as king by Godwine and Wessex. Æthelred's sons by Emma, Edward and Alfred, were in Normandy.

In the last years of the Danish ascendancy in England, according to the Norman chronicler William of Jumièges, the Norman Duke Robert, nephew of Cnut's queen Emma, came to look upon her sons by the long-dead Æthelred of England as his brothers. They had after all spent most of their lives among his people. It seems he even assembled an invasion fleet on their behalf, though it was scattered by gales in the Channel. As early as 1033, we find Norman charters that accord Edward the title of 'king' in England.

Meanwhile, Harold marched on Winchester where Emma had claimed control of the royal treasure hoping to hold the fort for her son, Harthacnut of Denmark. In fact, Harold, called 'Harefoot', was able to seize the greater part and assumed the rule. His cause was supported by Leofric, earl of Mercia and his wife Godiva, the Londoners, a group of Northern lords and his mother Ælfgifu of Northampton, who held great feasts to win friends and influence important people. But the party of her great opponent, Hathacnut, king of Denmark and Queen Emma's favourite, was the man who would soon prove the most important in England, and whose faction the Godwine of Wessex led.

Neither Edward nor Alfred seems to have been considered. Some time in 1036 both arrived back in England, perhaps summoned by a letter purporting to be from their mother at Winchester, perhaps attempting invasion. Norman sources tell us that Edward made a landing on Southampton Water but was forced to retire by the local levies while Alfred, crossing over from the region of Boulogne on the Channel coast, probably somewhat later, was intercepted by men of Godwine's household who took him to King Harold; it was said he was blinded and died of his wounds. Some of his followers were blinded, others sold into slavery.

An assembly of great men at Oxford decided that England should be divided between Harold as king of Mercia and Northumbria, and Harthacnut as king of Wessex. A new coinage was struck in both names, but from the second year of the issue Harold's name came to dominate, even appearing on coins struck at Winchester where Emma was still ensconced with Harthacnut's supporters. In 1037 Harold drove them from the city and finally became king of all England. Edward had made good his return to Normandy while, two years into her second widowhood, his estranged mother was into her second exile, this time at Bruges with Count Baldwin of Flanders and his 'royally born' wife Adcla. But Emma would soon return. Harthacnut lingered in Denmark until he came to terms with Magnus of Norway in 1039 and, with ten ships, sailed for Bruges. Following Harold's death on 17 March 1040, Emma sailed from Flanders with Harthacnut. Their fleet was solemnly welcomed by Earl Godwine, who made him the present of a splendid warship manned by eighty elite warriors fitted out with valuable weapons and wearing gold armlets.

In his brief reign Harthacnut won a reputation for brutality. When men of Worcestershire killed two of his tax collectors, the king dispatched a force to ravage the county, kill the male inhabitants and burn down the city. Kings were permitted to take such punitive action: in the twelfth century, for example, Louis VII of France authorized action in Champagne in which hundreds of people died, murdered in the streets or burnt alive in the churches where they had sought refuge. Harthacnut did not go to these lengths, but maybe his officers were excessive. The city was duly burnt and pillaged, large tracts of the shire plundered by the troopers, and if few men were slaughtered it was because most had fled in good time.

In the following year Harthacnut invited Edward back from Normandy. He himself was perhaps already ailing. At any rate, Edward took 'some kind of oath as king' and, according to the *Encomium*, belittled his own claims in favour of his half-brother. Harthacnut died of convulsions at a wedding feast on 8 June 1042. Edward, 'the Confessor' to be, now made a secure entry on the English scene. It was his turn to receive a warship from Godwine, the great courtier. Still more magnificent than Harthacnut's, it carried 120 men, had a gold-embroidered purple sail and a 'golden dragon at the prow . . . that belches fire with triple tongue'. (Was it what the Byzantines called a *siphonophore*, that is fitted with a Greek fire flame-thrower?) According to Godwine's supporters, Edward owed his throne to the earl's intervention with the English magnates. Edward, though, had long regarded himself as true king and had been named as such in charters issued in Normandy during his exile.

Briefly, after a lifetime in the corridors of power under Harthacnut and for a time under Edward, Queen Emma may have exercised real power. Named as *mater Regis* ('king's mother') and invariably placed next after the king,[17] she features in many charter witness lists. In 1043 her son Edward moved against her. She was attacked without warning at Winchester by the earls Godwine, Leofric and Siward, and deprived of untold treasure in gold and silver. All her lands were taken into the king's hands and he returned to her only enough for her needs. The reasons are unknown, though rumours were rife: she had refused reasonable request to yield the land; she had been hard on her son; she had been having an affair with Bishop Stigand, her spiritual adviser, who was deprived of his see at Elmham at this time. Years after her death, a story was going the rounds in Canterbury that she had been offering to fund an invasion of England by Magnus of Norway.

Emma died on 6 March 1052 in Winchester, about seventy years old. King Edward arranged for his mother to be interred next to her Danish warrior husband Cnut in the church of St Swithun, the Old Minster. She was the first queen to be buried there. She was also the first queen since Alfred the Great's Æthelswih to be buried with her husband. Nunneries were the normal place of retirement for widowed queens, and the normal place of their burial. Emma/Ælfgifu's death was still commemorated in the later eleventh century and the house where she had lived was still identified as hers in the twelfth.

Hard woman, hard world

Emma of Normandy's life reads like a feminist metaphor for a woman's frustration in politics. The *Encomium Emmae reginae* ('In Praise of Queen Emma'), written about 1041 and which she almost certainly commissioned and may well in part have dictated, reads as the anonymous CV of a great talent woefully underused. A frontispiece, not a common feature of books at this time, depicts the queen in royal regalia seated upon a throne, an early example of a secular figure seated in majesty, with the kneeling author at her feet presenting the volume into her hands. Behind him stand her two royal sons, the half-brothers Edward, son of Æthelred, and Harthacnut, son of Cnut. The kneeling author is presumably of no interest to anyone, except perhaps himself, but the trio of royals represent the tense up-to-the minute story of English politics in the pages that follow, told very much from Emma's viewpoint. The information on the English scene is no doubt provided by her and so we may assume that the narrative reveals how the people it deals with were viewed by her and her party.

Her antecedents, she boasts, lie with a victorious people that wrested the province of Normandy in Gaul (echoes of imperial Rome) from the Franks and their prince. Rich in wealth and lineage, beautiful and wise, the most outstanding woman of her day, she is now a famous queen. As if to validate her vaunted wisdom, the *Encomium* opens with a general survey of Denmark before her birth to explain the decision by Swein, father of Cnut, to invade England in 1013. More than a praise text, though it was that, the book urges the claims of Harthacnut, her son by Cnut, as the next king of England. Emma was no mere wife or bedfellow but a fit companion for a warrior monarch in the true Viking mode:[18] a woman familiar with war at sea as well as on land; a lady as at home with the warrior band as in the mead hall; above all, a worthy 'consort in his *imperium*'.

For fourteen years she was the wife of Æthelred, king of England. The fact is suppressed by the *Encomium* and the sons of that marriage, Edward (later 'the Confessor') and Alfred, barely mentioned. The *Encomium* was meant to influence the future, through a version of the past that met the questions of the present. It was aimed at her sons, and more widely at the great men of the English. It was a political work, from a political woman in the thick of politics[19] – but politics in a man's world. When the son she had backed for the crown died and the son she had dispraised (some said wished dead) succeeded, retirement from the scene was all that was left.

For England the legacy was more serious. In 1038 that favourite son had struck a deal with Magnus of Norway that if either died childless the other would succeed to his kingdom. In 1042 Harthacnut died – and was succeeded by Edward. Preoccupied by threats to his crown, Magnus was never able to follow up his claim. In 1066 his son and heir Harald Hardrada invaded England and helped ensure that King Harold II was in battle at Stamford Bridge, 250 miles away from the beaches of Pevensey Bay, when William of Normandy was preparing to disembark his invasion force there. No doubt Emma of Normandy would have approved.

12

EDWARD THE CONFESSOR, THE CONQUEST AND THE AFTERMATH

Edward was crowned king at Winchester on Easter Day, 3 April 1043. He had been exercising the powers of the kingship for ten months since the death of Harthacnut in June 1042 and may have been joint king since 1041. A contemporary saw a man in his late thirties, tall above the average and to be feared in his rage. He was passionately addicted to hunting with dogs – English hounds were renowned throughout Europe – and had inherited an impetuous streak from his father. He was half Norman by birth and spoke Norman-French as fluently as, if not more so than, English. His entourage comprised Bretons as well as Normans and the Lotharingian Herman, whom he appointed bishop of Sherborne. His most influential councillor, Earl Godwine of Wessex (according to Robert Fleming 'a parvenu'[1]), had been raised to power by Cnut the Dane. The earl's Danish wife, Gytha, far more distinguished than her husband, had been the great king's sister-in-law and Edith (i.e. Eadgyth) his half-Danish daughter, was shortly to become Queen of England. The family had connections with Ireland (possibly trading in slaves to that country) and Queen Edith would prove a fluent Irish-speaker, as well as mistress of various other languages. There was nothing about the vigorous and cosmopolitan court of this Edward of Wessex and England, third of his

name since Alfred the Great, to suggest the milksop image history
sometimes associates him with as 'Edward the Confessor'.

Just months after his coronation, in November 1043, Edward
moved in company with the three great earls, Godwine, Leofric of
Mercia and Siward of Northumbria, against his once-powerful
mother Queen Emma/Ælfgifu and her adviser Bishop Stigand,
ensconced at Winchester, home of the kingdom's treasury. The next
year Edward had his Norman counsellor, Robert, abbot of Jumièges,
appointed bishop of London (in 1051 he would move him to
Canterbury). It seems he aimed to use churchmen to counterbalance
the influence of the lay advisers already in place. Equally he acted
with royal assurance as he wished, banishing a kinswoman of Cnut's
and her family, and then a powerful Danish magnate. He even over-
rode Earl Godwine in one vital matter by refusing support for
Denmark, which was then under attack from Magnus of Norway. In
fact, Godwine was probably right: Magnus had a claim on the
English throne, as we know, and had he overrun Denmark England
would have been next in line. Magnus died in October 1047, but
the danger did not die with him.

That same year Edward banished Swein, the eldest son of Earl
Godwine, because he had abducted and raped the abbess of
Leominster, in the Welsh marches. This was a direct confrontation
with the mighty dynasty. Swein Godwineson, for five years earl of
Herefordshire, as well as Oxfordshire, Gloucestershire, Somerset
and Berkshire, was in local rivalry with Ralph of Mantes, Earl of
Worcester, a French nephew of the king's, who now displaced him
in his earldom, along with their cousin Beorn. The following year
Swein was back in the king's favour, but almost at once he breached
the king's peace, this time with the murder of Earl Beorn, from
what motive is still unknown. He was declared '*nithing*' [of
absolutely no account or social standing] by the king. (Three years
later, he was to make the extravagant penance of a barefoot pilgrimage to Jerusalem.) Yet, after a further brief exile in Bruges with

Count Baldwin of Flanders, the impetuous and twice-exiled Swein was once again restored to the king's grace.

For much of his life Edward had been in the exile zone between England, Flanders and Normandy. Tostig Godwineson, another exile on the run, would marry the Count's daughter, Judith. Orderic Vitalis claimed that in April 1066 he actually visited the court of William of Normandy (a cousin by marriage) to offer him assistance in his invasion of England, before going north to join the Norwegian king. But in general we know little of the bargains, deals and understandings that were currency among the players – only that the throne of England seemed to be perennially in the hazard. Had not Edward himself won it against the odds? Earl Godwine had been a power in the land long before Edward arrived from exile. For Edward the royal court must sometimes have seemed a luxurious form of house arrest with Godwine's daughter, Queen Edith, the turnkey. Between 1050 and 1052 Edward would manoeuvre for a break-out.

The challenge that failed

Quite apart from anything else, his dynasty needed an heir. Married in January 1045 and at least fifteen years the king's junior, the talented and solicitous young queen seems to have been a major figure in the protocol and ceremonial of the court. She controlled that department of the royal treasury dedicated to the visual presentation of the dignity of the king. She saw to it that '[he was] arrayed in garments of splendour' and had the throne adorned with gold-embroidered mantling. In her fascinating book *Queen Emma and Queen Edith*, Pauline Stafford mentions five goldsmiths listed among Edith's servants, one of whom, Leofgeat, held land in return for the service of producing *aurifrisium*, presumably the same luxury product as the London guild of silk women was famed for in the later Middle Ages. The queen also provided him with a staff encrusted with gold and gems for his everyday use and directed the smiths to hang his saddle and horse trappings with golden birds and beasts. (Any collector of antique horse brasses must surely get the picture . . . at the bottom end of the market!) The goldsmiths who worked for her and the king included a certain Theoderic, who with his wife held lands in Oxfordshire, and a German, Otto, who married an Englishwoman and held properties in Essex. Edith excelled as a mistress of the wardrobe and director of ceremonies. It was almost certainly she who would commission the King's *Life* (*Vita Edwardi Regis*), which often reads like a eulogy of the Godwine family. But she had yet to produce children.

Any move against the queen inevitably entailed a move against her family and, of course, her father. Next to the earl and the king the most powerful man in the kingdom was the archbishop of Canterbury. The huge wealth, extensive lands and great powers of patronage that went with the primacy made for contentious politics. In October 1050 the archdiocese fell vacant with the death of Archbishop Eadsige. Godwine, as lay lord of Kent, was adept at encroachments on the property of the see and had hopes that the electors, the monks who ran the cathedral, favoured a kinsman of his. Strictly speaking, the election of archbishop required papal approval, but this had usually followed automatically on the wishes of the lay ruler. However, church reform was in the air. The German-born Pope Leo IX, though himself appointed by Emperor Henry III at the end of a period of church decline, was not the man to approve a courtier's puppet at Canterbury and during his reign (1049–54) he did much to re-establish the authority of Rome. And Godwine faced another obstacle – King Edward was keenly interested in church matters. The year before he had sent Duduc, bishop of Wells, a learned Saxon appointed by Cnut in the 1030s, Wulfric, abbot of St Augustine's, Canterbury, and Abbot Ælfwine of Ramsey to the synod at Reims presided over by Leo: this was the first time a pope had left Italy in 300 years. In 1050 other English churchmen were dispatched to the papal council at Rome and Bishop Ulf of Dorchester, one of Edward's Norman appointees, attended the council at Vercelli in northwest Italy. (Did he take the Codex Vercellensis with him?) By contrast William of Normandy, who extracted papal support for his conquering raid into England, never permitted any clergy of his to attend papal councils.[2] Edward had received papal permission for certain reforms and, famously, built the great minster or collegiate church of St Peter's to the west of London. With the exception of the contemporary cathedral built by the German emperors at Speyer on the Rhine, this building, later known as Westminster Abbey, was the largest church built north of the Alps since the fourth century.

Edward's acceptance of reforms in the church marked royal compliance with papal wishes beyond anything seen in England for centuries. For years, one man had been both archbishop of York and bishop of Worcester. When Ealdred of Worcester became archbishop of York in 1062, Rome insisted that such plurality, the holding of more than one see by one man, should end and Wulfstan succeed him in Worcester. Edward concurred.

In 1050 Edward's candidate for Canterbury was Robert of Jumièges, since 1044 bishop of London. Robert departed for Rome to receive his pallium. On his way he is supposed to have negotiated an alliance between the twenty-three-year-old Duke William of Normandy and King Edward; later Norman writers were to claim that at this time Edward nominated the duke his heir to the English throne. Robert was also a tough defender of church property against lay predators and an advocate of general church reform. Pope Leo approved as much as Earl Godwine objected. Robert also provoked Edward's hostility towards Godwine by allusions to the death of Prince Alfred, the king's young kinsman reputedly murdered on the earl's orders. On his return from Rome in the summer of 1051 Robert's devotion to reform heightened: he now refused to consecrate the king's own candidate as bishop of London.

The king had further trouble in store. Plenty of people in England resented the French/Norman presence at court. A visit from his brother-in-law, Count Eustace of Boulogne, triggered a crisis. On his way to embarkation, the count and his retinue were badly mauled in the streets of Dover. The cause of the fracas was naturally contested, but an assault on a guest of the king was an assault on the dignity of the king himself and Edward ordered Earl Godwine to punish the citizenry by sending in armed men to sack the place. Godwine refused. This made him popular with the people but not with the king. Summoned to account for himself, Godwine called up his sons Swein, back from exile, and Harold, who ordered their household warriors to assemble. The king summoned Earl Leofric of Mercia and Siward of Northumbria with their men to meet with his councillors at Gloucester, along with Ralph of Mantes and his men. Two armies, one royalist and the other potentially a rebel force, were now mustered in the region of Gloucester. Civil war seemed possible but was averted for the time being. The D *Chronicle* records that there were men on both sides who considered that conflict 'would be a great piece of folly', since battle between the 'noblest in England' would open the country to attack from its enemies and 'cause much ruin among ourselves'.

By his refusal of the king's order Godwine might be guilty of contumacy and it was agreed he should stand trial in London. The two forces began the march to that city, but the rebels began to melt away and Earl Godwine looked to make his peace with the king when Edward outlawed Swein. Using as his messenger Bishop Stigand of Winchester, reckoned one of Godwine's party, Edward replied that the earl could have peace when he restored Prince Alfred to him. The king's distrust and hostility could not be made plainer: apparently he still held Godwine responsible for his brother's death. Equally obvious was that Stigand, if willing to carry such a message, had switched his allegiance.

England's most powerful family was in disarray. The earl himself, his wife and their sons Swein and Tostig took ship from their port of Bosham for Flanders. Harold sailed for Ireland. The whole family was declared outlaw, except of course for Queen Edith. On the king's orders she was sent to the nunnery at Wilton; Robert of Jumièges even felt able to recommend divorce. Her removal from the royal presence was logical, both as a member of a disgraced family and as a royal consort who had not produced an heir. Later it was said that she had been accused of adultery, too, though had proved her innocence in the ordeal of fire, walking unharmed over red-hot ploughshares.[3] Her humiliation did not last long. Her family were planning their return.

The king ordered a fleet to stand by at Sandwich and alerted coastal commanders. Godwine's fleet was intercepted as it made its way from Flanders to England. Although Harold was able to join up with his father, gales scattered both royalist and rebel forces. But the Godwine family regrouped and in mid-September, 'the sea covered with [their] ships and the sky aglitter with weapons', thanks to their opponents' inertia they crossed 'the Kentish sea' and were able to establish themselves on the south bank of the Thames, threatening the king's party of loyal earls and its French supporters in the city. But the Englishmen's hearts were not with the king. Edward realized that he could not rely on the Londoners' support against England's chief noble dynasty. Robert of Jumièges and the French bishops of Dorchester and London, together with the rest of the French party, had to force their way out against the hostile citizenry. It was a Godwine triumph. The entire Godwine party was declared innocent of all crimes with which they had been charged and their lands and honours were restored. On the advice of his councillors Edward gave Godwine the kiss of peace, Queen Edith was returned to court and the king was obliged to accept a huge loss in authority and prestige. Godwine's enemies were outlawed.

Some of the French/Norman refugees from the events of 1052 fled to Scotland, always ready to fish in England's troubled waters and the court of King Macbeth (1040–57). Malcolm Canmore, son of Duncan, the king whom Macbeth had defeated and killed in battle near Elgin, was in exile in England where he found an ally in Siward, Earl of Northumbria. The earl twice invaded Scotland in Malcolm's cause, with the approval of Edward, and English levies were prominent in the army that Malcolm himself led to victory over Macbeth to become king as Malcolm III (*d.* 1093). He established the Scottish monarchy through which James VI of Scotland and I of England traced his descent. Macbeth and his wife Cruoch suffered character assassination in the version of history encouraged by Malcolm's descendants. (Not surprisingly, when Shakespeare came to write his *Macbeth* for performance before James VI and I about 1606 he followed this tradition.)

While the historical Macbeth could hardly have been a figure of the towering complexity of his tragic namesake, neither was he the murderer of his predecessor. Shakespeare's Edward, on the other hand, was 'gracious England', and had 'the most miraculous' power to cure 'people all swollen and ulcerous' (*Macbeth* IV, 3). The ability to cure the unsightly disease of scrofula, a tuberculosis of the lymph glands, was attributed to Edward from an early period, as it was to the Capetian kings of France, his contemporaries. Shakespeare has Malcolm reporting that Edward left 'to the succeeding royalty . . . the healing benediction'. James I himself offered the healing gesture and his granddaughter Queen Anne was the last British sovereign to do so. (In France Charles X, reigned 1818–30, still performed the practice.)

The Godwine family in the ascendant

After 1052 the Godwine influence was paramount in England. Although Swein died while returning from his pilgrimage and Earl

Godwine himself collapsed of a seizure in the king's banqueting hall in April 1053, the family remained the arbiters of English affairs. Harold smoothly succeeded to the earldom of Wessex, though he diplomatically surrendered his position in East Anglia to Ælfgar of Mercia, Earl Leofric's son. When Siward of Northumbria died two years later, however, the all-powerful family asserted its absolute ascendancy. Siward's son was deemed too young to succeed his father and Leofric of Mercia was clearly too old to combine the two great earldoms. Mercian influence in the north was utterly excluded when his son Ælfgar was sent into exile and lost part of his earldom to Gyrth, one of the younger Godwine scions. (For a time, the embittered Ælfgar allied with the Welsh prince Gruffudd of Gwynedd) Northumbria now went to Tostig, Queen Edith's favourite brother. The Northumbrians themselves seem to have considered him as the king's representative, not as an imposed territorial lord, though they were to find his rule offensively strict. The great families of Anglo-Saxon England were not provincial in the sense that the French nobility commanded provincial power bases; their personal estates were scattered in relatively small units, not held in large blocs, and they, like their lands, were integrated into a wider, essentially nation-wide whole.

When Earl Leofric of Mercia at last died in 1057 he was succeeded by his son Ælfgar but Gyrth Godwineson became sole earl in East Anglia. That year Ralph of Herefordshire also died. Together with a number of other French lords settled by English policy in these Marcher territories, he had developed his earldom as a Marcher lordship using mounted troopers to harry and pursue Welsh raiders and building strong points with castles, Norman style, rather than building burhs in the English manner. But in the autumn of 1055 he and his fellow Marcher lords went down to a crushing defeat at the hands of the northern Welsh prince Gruffudd ap Llywelyn of Gwynedd and Powys. Early the following year an English force under Leofgar, the newly appointed warrior bishop of Hereford, was dealt with just as summarily. On Ralph's death, Harold Godwineson took his earldom and its problems; the remaining brother, Leofwine, was accommodated with an earldom from the southeastern shires. By 1060 Mercia was the only English earldom not controlled, in the king's name, by a member of the house of Godwine.

The contradictions in Tostig's image are exemplified by his activities in 1061. Unpopular though this West Saxon courtier might be in Northumbria, he felt confident enough in his governorship not only to campaign into Wales in support of his brother but also to continue to be absent from his post for the best part of a year while he led an embassy to Rome in company with Ealdred, the newly appointed archbishop of York. They travelled down the Rhine, presumably by way of Cologne and Mainz, devoutly visiting all the shrines on the route. Passionate in his politics, Tostig was also pious in his religion and is recorded with his wife Judith of Flanders as a patron in the *Liber Vitae* at Durham in letters of gold.

It was the view of the family's eulogist in the *Vita Edwardi* that, 'When briefly joined in peace', Tostig and Harold seemed as England's 'mainstays'.[4] At court the family's presence was felt in the person of Queen Edith as the king pursued his passion for hunting and increasingly concerned himself with ecclesiastical matters; later she may even have hoped to influence the succession. She certainly amassed wealth and land. At Edward's death only the royal estate, Earl Harold and Archbishop Stigand outdid her personal holdings. The Domesday Book shows her with property scattered across England from Old Wessex to the eastern Midlands, the dower portions of the queens of Mercia, the bulk of these in the little territory of Roteland, known from the 1150s as the shire of Rutland. (It was 'reformed' away in 1974 but, thanks to local lobbying, restored some twenty years later. It would appear that the East Mercians are a determined breed!)

In the last ten years of his reign Edward presided over a kingdom prosperous within its borders and more or less holding its own against its Celtic neighbours. Malcolm III of Scotland, who owed his throne to English help, made a courtesy visit to the English court at Gloucester in 1057, though that did not stop him from making inroads into Northumbria in the following years. As to Wales, the late 1050s and early 1060s were years of Welsh ascendancy. It was not until 1063 that the situation was adjusted. In the spring Gruffudd managed to weather a punitive expedition led by Earl Harold. Tostig marched down from Northumbria and joined forces with Harold, who burnt the palace at Rhuddlan. Their successful campaign in the Marches forced the Welshmen to sue for peace and traitors killed their own charismatic prince. His head and the beak of his raiding ship were brought to Harold, hostages yielded up and tribute paid.[5] A century later, standing stones were still to be seen along the border recording Harold's numerous victorious engagements.

At this time Harold was just forty: England's greatest landholder, her richest man and most powerful royal minister. The Anglo-Norman historian Orderic Vitalis (writing in the 1120s) recorded him as tall, well built and noted for his eloquence, courage in battle and affability to his supporters. His partner, the beautiful Edith Swanneck, was a rich woman in her own right with extensive land-holdings in the east of England. They had five children and if their liaison did not conform entirely to the church's requirements they formed a formidable and loyal couple. A man of great consequence in the nation's affairs since his early twenties – his eastern earldom had covered much of East Anglia, Essex and Cambridgeshire (including Huntingdonshire) – Harold was also a person of con-ventional piety. For example he was a keen and discriminating col-lector of relics and a great patron of religious establishments. The abbey of Peterborough was a favourite and, much to its disadvan-tage, Abbot Leofric was with Harold at the Battle of Hastings. By contrast, the small religious community of Waltham Holy Cross greatly benefited from the beautiful stone church that Harold had built for them, much to the approval of King Edward. Harold apparently had a special devotion for the cult of the Cross, like other English nobles at this time.

Like them too he seems to have visited Lotharingia and been much impressed by the religious reforms going forward there, and to have been a connoisseur of fine manuscript illumination. He may even have visited Rome; he is certainly known to have been in Saint-Omer in November 1056, when he witnessed a charter there for Count Baldwin V of Flanders, his brother-in-law. Of his other visits to the Continent, the one to Normandy, when he is supposed to have pledged his oath to William to support him as successor to the English crown, should in the view of Professor Frank Barlow, in his recent book on the Godwine dynasty, be dated to the year 1064 – if it ever took place at all. It certainly features dramatically on the Bayeux Tapestry but, Barlow argues, the detail 'must be viewed with caution'. There is no mention of this visit in the *Chronicle* and he considers the later English sources that do mention it, such as Eadmer, are merely 'refashionings' of the Norman version of events. He points out that there are differences as to where the ceremony took place – at Bonneville-sur-Touques according to William of Poitiers, at Rouen according to Orderic Vitalis – while the Bayeux Tapestry specifies no location. From the start, the Norman apologists claimed, Edward wanted William to be his heir but, Barlow observes: 'There is no good evidence that Edward ever or consistently regarded William as his heir.'[6] Even so it was central to William's case for papal support in his invasion plans and one wonders whether the papal curia would have credited a total fabrication. And the Bayeux Tapestry unequivocally depicts Harold in Normandy.

Whoever actually made the famous piece of needlework (the question is discussed in Appendix A), it was surely commissioned as a record of the Norman version of how the crown of England was acquired by the duke of the Normans. It follows the account in William of Poitiers of how Harold visited Normandy on a mission from King Edward with instructions to confirm his oath, first made during William's visit to England in 1051–2 along with the other English magnates at that time, to accept William as the next king of England. He was wrecked off the coast of Ponthieu in Picardy and seized by the local count, who ransomed him to Duke William. While the duke's guest, Harold joined him in his military campaign against Conan fitzAlan, count of Brittany – which features extensively in the Tapestry. The earl's mission, we are told, was to convey to William that King Edward had designated the duke his heir to the English crown. William had his English visitor swear to support him as king and then had the cloth removed from the table on which he had placed his hand – to reveal a cache of saints' relics beneath!

Back in England Harold, as head of the house of Godwine, faced trouble from the Northumbrians angered by the harsh administration of his brother Tostig as earl of Northumbria. Scandal darkened the last weeks of the dying king. The Christmas court of 1065 was in uproar at the death, most said the murder, of the northern magnate Gospatric, who like Tostig had been at court for the festivities and was a known enemy of the earl. Such a breach of the king's personal peace rocked the foundations of established order; worse still, another rumour accused the queen of having set it up.[7]

Northumbrian loyalties were divided between the Anglian lords of Bamburgh, of whom Gospatric was one and who were dominant north of the Tyne, the church community of St Cuthbert at Durham, and the predominantly Scandinavian aristocracy of Yorkshire. Tostig's appointment as earl in 1055 had brought rough but effective, and hence contested, rule. He and his wife Judith of Flanders were renowned for their generosity to St Cuthbert, including the donation of a large crucifix, covered in gold and silver and accompanied by images of the Virgin Mary and St John. Tostig had identified the ringleaders as the house of Bamburgh and had two of its members murdered at York while under safe conduct.

The rebels, among them Yorkshire thegns, declared Tostig out-law and invited Morcar, younger son of Ælfgar of Mercia, to be their earl.

They marched south to ask the court to authorize the appoint-ment. In a sense it was a vindication of Tostig's rule since it seems his brief had been to bring the northern region into line with the rest of the kingdom.[8] Harold met them at Oxford and agreed their demand. King Edward rubber-stamped the appointment; Tostig was forced into exile, with no support from his brother.

Some regarded this quarrel as responsible for the collapse of the Godwine family fortunes. Harold, ignoring his 'Danish marriage' with Edith Swanneck, now married Morcar's sister: their son would no doubt have succeeded to the throne had Harold won at Hastings.

The last Anglo-Saxon reign

Harold was crowned king of England in Westminster Abbey on 6 January 1066, the day following the death of King Edward. The great church had been dedicated some ten days earlier on 28 December as the king its patron lay dying. Preparations for the forthcoming ceremony must surely have been under discussion. It was certainly hasty; some could say unseemly. But Bishop Wulfstan of Worcester, who prophesied to the king disaster if the country did not mend its debauched ways, did not level the charge of perjury against Harold. There were other candidates, most strongly Edgar Ætheling, grandson of Edmund Ironside, as well as William of Normandy. But there is no evidence that either had a party of sup-porters in England. It seems that Harold had right on his side when he claimed that the dying king had named him his successor, and the council had acclaimed him. Why should they do otherwise? Norman influence had been strong enough in the first half of the Confessor's reign; with the ruler of the duchy on the throne of England, their position as English magnates would be parlous.

The 'E' version of the *Anglo-Saxon Chronicle*, written in the scriptorium of Peterborough Abbey, whose abbot Leofric was with the English army at Hastings, records straightforwardly that 'Earl Harold succeeded to the realm of England, just as the king had granted it to him and as he had been chosen to the position.' The twelfth-century English historian John of Worcester would confirm this and even William of Poitiers believed that the dying Edward had nominated the earl his heir. John also tells us that Harold was crowned by Archbishop Ealdred of York. Norman sources, however, claimed that the coronation had been conducted by Stigand of Canterbury, who had received his pallium of office from Benedict X, whose reign ended after just nine months when he was expelled by reformers and declared anti-pope. Pope Alexander II, sponsor of the invasion of England, did not of course recognize Stigand. The Tapestry tellingly depicts his ambiguous position – he stands to one side of the enthroned King Harold, not wearing his pallium but displaying it to the spectator. Evidently he had not conducted the coronation. Interestingly, Stigand was not replaced at Canterbury until 1070.

Harold's nine-month reign was largely occupied with preparations against invasion. The country's fabled wealth was mobilized for war, the mints striking thousands of pennies bearing the new king's head at more than forty sites from Romney in the south to York and Chester in the north. The Welsh threat had revived under new leaders. But more serious was the fact that Tostig, determined to recover his position in England, had made common cause with the Norwegian king, Harald Hardrada, the most renowned warrior of the time, who was now ready to prosecute the claim dating back to his grandfather's deal with King Harthacnut. (In Harald's opinion, even Edward the Confessor had been an intruder, let alone the Godwineson now in place.)

And then, of course, there was the relentless build-up of William of Normandy's invasion forces along the Channel coast. All summer

Harold held his troops on stand-by in the southern counties with ships in readiness at Sandwich and off the Isle of Wight. There are hints that he may have 'raided the Norman coast at some time during the summer'. Week after week the wind blew from the north, making it impossible for William to launch his troop trans-ports. In the first week of September the supplies provisioned for the English troops on standby ran out 'and the men were allowed to go home, while the fleet returned to London.'[9] But if the winds hampered the Normans they favoured the Norwegians and in September news reached Harold that they, with Tostig and a fleet of some 300 ships, had sailed into the Humber estuary and marched upon York. Edwin and Morcar led the forces of Northumbria against the invaders and were routed on the banks of the River Ouse, 'south of York'. (The twelfth-century chronicler Symeon of Durham sites the battle at Fulford.) By forced marches that were a tribute to his army's discipline and fitness, Harold arrived to face the enemy at Stamford Bridge on 25 September. The fighting lasted the best part of the daylight hours; the invaders were crushed, both Harald and Tostig met their deaths, as did a great proportion of their troops both 'Norwegians and Flemings'.[10] Harold gave quarter to the survivors. Figures vary as to the slaughter. According to the *Anglo-Saxon Chronicle* 'the very great raiding army' arrived in 300 ships and, after their defeat, returned in 24 ships. John of Worcester gave the figures as 500 and 20, respectively. According to Orderic Vitalis a mountain of whitened bones was still to be seen on the battlefield in the 1120s.[11] Harold's triumph was brief. The winds in the Channel had changed. On 28 September the fleet from Normandy crossed the narrow seas and William was able to land his invasion force unopposed at Pevensey. The duke himself stumbled and fell and, to avert the omen, a quick-thinking lieutenant let it be known that the duke wished to embrace his new kingdom.

Raising his army had presented problems for William too. It is not clear that his vassals owed him service outside the duchy. From outside, Eustace of Boulogne was his principal ally but he also recruited soldiers from Brittany, Maine and even Aquitaine. He was able to hire mercenary archers and crossbowmen. It seems that the building of the fleet and troop transports did not begin until after news of Edward's death reached Normandy. He seems to have sailed with a fleet of between 500 and 700 ships. His delayed sailing played in his favour in so far as Harold was in the north of England during the vital days that the Normans crossed the Channel. This gave them time to deploy from the old Roman fort at Pevensey to Hastings.

The Battle of Hastings

Again Harold of England traversed his kingdom, he and a number of his troops no doubt on horseback. By 7 October he was in London. There a family conference is said to have ensued and, among other things later tradition tells us, his mother urged him not to fight and his brother Gyrth proposed that he, not Harold, should command the army because he was an oath-breaker.[12] Contemporary English sources say nothing about the oath and the story is first found in Orderic Vitalis, who may have had in mind the oath supposedly sworn to William in 1051/2.

It seems that Harold spent the best part of a week in London assembling an army. One presumes this entailed dispatching writs for the raising of levies through the southern counties, for we are told that men came in as he rode through Kent and Sussex. The chronicle of Abingdon Abbey records that the thegns owing duty to the abbey fought at Hastings and as we have noted Abbot Leofric of Peterborough was there, presumably with the men at arms owing service to the abbey.

William of Malmesbury records that the night before the battle the English were carousing. Supposedly the English thought the Normans must be priests because they lacked the flowing

moustaches of true warriors; and the Normans thought the English
a womanish bunch with their combed and pomaded hair.[13] If Wace
is to be believed the Normans' battle cry at Hastings, the semi-Latin
'*Deus aïe!*' ('With God's help') was answered by the Anglo-Saxon
cry '*Ut!*' ('Out!')

On 14 October Harold took up position on a hill ridge at Senlac
some seven miles (11 km) from Hastings and prepared to engage the
enemy – even though other English forces were on the road to
rendezvous with the royal army. Accounts of the battle are piecemeal and confused. M. K. Lawson (2003) tends to accept one source
formerly discounted, the *Carmen de Hastingae Proelio* ('Song of the
Battle of Hastings') by Guy, bishop of Amiens. It begins by comparing William to Julius Caesar and many of the sources make classical allusions. There is a much disputed account of how Taillefer, a
juggler, threw his sword into the air in front of the French lines and
killed an Englishman who rushed forward against him.

Harold's battlefield position was well chosen, as it seems
Duke William was unable to turn either flank. Accounts speak of
ditches, one of them large and well concealed, which suggests
that the English position extended with field defences beyond the
ridge. Later pro-English chroniclers report the inadequate size of
the English force. As to numbers, Lawson comments, 'How large
a "large" army may have been there is no way of knowing.'[14]
William of Poitiers, on the other hand, speaks of the 'immense size'
of Harold's army with reinforcements from Denmark, while the
'D' text of the *Anglo-Saxon Chronicle* reports Harold as assembling
a 'great host' (presumably swelled by local shire levies), which the
Normans attacked 'before his people were set in order' ('*ær his
folc gefylced wære*'). Had they been delayed by the preparation of the
field defences? Was the shield wall still being marshalled? Was it
because the local levies were still being mobilized into the
main army? Or was it because they had been carousing the night
before?

William of Poitiers speaks of indiscipline, recording that the English forces three times left their sound defensive position, the third time to be surrounded and cut down by those it thought in flight. The English fought under Harold's banner of 'The Armed Man' ('*homo armatus*'), worked in purest gold apparently, which was sent to the pope after the battle as spoils of victory. This was appropriate since Pope Alexander II seems to have sent William the banner that his people fought under, 'the standard of St Peter the Apostle' as Orderic Vitalis called it. The English shield wall held against repeated Norman cavalry charges and arrow fire. Towards the end of the day the Norman foot fell back in what proved a tactical feint. The shield wall broke; the enemy returned to the attack. The English faltered and then tried to flee. Many were cut down as they ran. Accounts of the battle are scant and confused. According to the *Carmen* the Normans were already stripping the bodies of the dead when Harold was seen on the ridge of the hill still fighting. When four Normans attacked and killed him one speared him through his shield; one hacked off his head; one split his entrails; a fourth hewed off his thigh. William ordered that Harold's corpse be buried on the seashore.

At the end of the day Harold's brothers Gyrth and Leofwine and many of the Anglo-Saxon nobility lay dead on the place of slaughter. The pro-English twelfth-century historian William of Malmesbury is among those who records the tradition of Harold's death by arrow shot. Apparently the English army only abandoned the fight as reports of the king's death spread through the ranks. An arrow shot, whether in the eye or not, seems probable. Harold's prowess was such, men said, that he could overthrow a horse and its rider with a single blow, so that no one could approach near enough to kill *him*. Discounting the legends that he survived the battle (they are explored in Appendix B), death by arrow shot (whether in the eye or not) seems probable.

Resistance

Like Waterloo, Hastings, it seems, was a near run thing. The length of the battle from morning till dusk indicates evenly matched opponents, whether or not there was an imbalance in numbers. Had he fought out the day to a stalemate, with nightfall Harold would still have been king of England and William looking to bivouac in hostile country with a bleak prospect for the morning. As it was, the English defeat was total, and the systematic rape of the southern counties stubbed out immediate resistance. But resistance there was.

After a week spent on a savage punitive expedition to the south and west of London, William paused at Berkhamsted in Hertfordshire to receive the leading citizens of London, Edgar the ætheling, Archbishop Ealdred of York and the earls Edwin and Morcar, and accept their hostages and allegiance.

Three months after his coronation in Westminster Abbey on Christmas Day 1066, William left England for Normandy and was attending to business in the duchy until the following December. There were local uprisings in many parts of England but they were not coordinated. Unrest in the southwest, however, was more serious. William may even have had reason to believe that its aim was to put Godwine, Harold's son by Edith Swanneck, on the throne.[15] Aged perhaps eighteen at the time of Hastings, he held property in Somerset. The other great old-regime landowner in the region, with large estates in Devon and Wiltshire as well as Somerset, was the young man's grandmother, Gytha, wife of the old earl and matriarch of the Godwine dynasty, presumably now in her sixties. Exeter, a dower city of her daughter Queen Edith, was the chief rebel centre and it was here that William directed his energies in early 1068. After heavy initial losses the new king took the place after an eighteen-day siege. Gytha and her entourage made good their escape and in due course she arrived at Saint-Omer with sufficient bullion and other treasures to see her through a comfortable retirement away from the hazards of court politics and attempted comebacks.

Meantime, towards mid-summer 1068 Harold's brothers and his son Godwine, who had crossed over to Ireland where the family friend King Diarmait of Leinster had helped fit them out, appeared in the mouth of the River Avon with 'a raiding ship army' and plundered the countryside. The citizens of Bristol fought them off, so they took their loot back to their ships and went up into Somerset before returning to Ireland. The next year they returned with more than 60 ships, landing on the coast of north Devon. Again they were driven back with the loss of many of their best men, this time by the Breton count, the Conqueror's earl in the district.[16]

In the summer of 1069 a Danish fleet commanded by King Swein II found safe anchorage in the Humber. Even from the records that survive it is clear that England was seething with discontent after Hastings; the explosion came in the north. It was William's Norman appointee as earl of Northumbria who set the torch to the brushwood. The men of the Durham region surprised him inside the stronghold there and killed him and the 900 men with him. The arrival of the Danish fleet sparked a rising in York. By 20 September the city was lost, Yorkshire was in rebel hands and the entire Norman project in England in jeopardy. Within days the seventeen-year-old Edgar the aethling had arrived in the city, marching south from his exile in Scotland. Since Hastings Edgar had managed to keep out of William's way while receiving various embassies of support, notably from Brand, the new abbot of Peterborough, 'because the people there thought he ought to become king.' He had made his way to the court of Malcolm of Scotland, along with his Hungarian mother Agatha and his sister Margaret, who, much against her will, was obliged to marry the Scottish king.

York received the ætheling with jubilation. But William stormed north, retaking York as the ætheling escaped back to Scotland.

William celebrated Christmas in its smouldering ruins; he continued northwards to the River Tees through the lands of St Cuthbert
and the Lordship of Bamburgh. News came of further risings in
Cheshire and Wales. William drove his army southwest across the
Pennines in the depths of a bitter winter. Desertification, death and
rapine followed him. The harrying of the North that ensued
brought the practice of the punitive expedition to the nadir of
horror. Fifteen years later the Domesday commissioners were
noting 'laid waste' against village after village of the region, entry
after entry.

With the country in turmoil, 'the English people from the Fens'
had flocked to Swein of Denmark, thinking his army was planning to occupy the region. At about this time the monks of
Peterborough heard that one of their tenants, Hereward of Bourne,
was marching on the abbey because he and his men had heard that,
with the death of Abbot Brand, the Conqueror had handed the place
to the Norman soldier/churchman Turold of Fécamp. In what followed the once 'golden borough' crashed to 'wretched borough',
plundered of its treasures by foes and friends alike, claiming to save
them from the alien invaders. Pirates, we are told, sailed up to the
minster wharf and tried to break in. When the monks resisted the
attackers set fires. They then plundered the abbey of its gold, from
the crown on the head of the crucified Christ hanging on the rood
screen to many other crosses and gold and silver ornaments of all
kinds, as well as precious manuscripts. Even the talismanic arm of St
Oswald was carried down to the ships and, with the rest of the booty,
taken off to Ely – supposedly for safe-keeping away from the depredations of the Normans.

There Hereward, known to history and legend as Hereward the
Wake, joined by Earl Morcar of Mercia and Bishop Ælfwine of
Durham, held out with hundreds of desperate rebels, their hope
fixed on the Danish fleet in the face of news of King William's
progress. Ely Abbey, on its island among the fenland marshes, was

well suited for a stronghold, but as at Alfred's Athelney resistance could not be indefinite.

By the spring William had flayed his rebel kingdom back to obedience. In a campaign that historian David Douglas rated 'one of the outstanding military achievements of the age', he was once more master. At this point the Danes came to terms with the Norman king and sailed away to Denmark, with much English booty in their holds. Now, too, the leaders of Ely's lost cause made what peace they could while Hereward made good his escape into the half-light between legend and history. The Conqueror is said to have pardoned him and he supposedly crossed over to France. There, according to Geoffrey Gaimar, the French historian of the English, writing his *Estoire des Angleis* for the wife of a Norman lord in Lincolnshire, Hereward was run to ground and murdered by a party of vengeful Normans. It is fitting that the end of his story, whether true or fiction, should be penned so near to Hereward's home territory. Anglo-Saxon England's last real, if faint, hope was Edgar the ætheling, Ironside's grandson, who had been named king in October 1066 by the English bishops and the remnant of the nobility: he survived to join the armies of the First Crusade, where, as a man in his early forties, he would strike a contemporary as 'handsome in appearance; liberal and noble in eloquence.'

Aftermath and rebirth

According to the *Vita Edwardi Regis*, as he lay dying Edward, indicating the queen, had said to Harold: 'I commend this woman with all the kingdom to your protection.' The *Chronicle* explicitly states that 'Harold succeeded to the realm of England, just as the king had granted it to him and as he had been chosen to the position.'[17] If true it was the first time such a bequest had been made to one not of the royal line. Reports of the deathbed scene come from witnesses who were, by definition, Harold's supporters. However, one

Norman source tacitly accepts that the deathbed nomination was made, by charging Harold with perjury for accepting it. As to his sister, the dowager queen Edith, a *Chronicle* entry for the year 1076 tells us that the Lady Edith, dowager to King Edward, passed away at Winchester seven days before Christmas and the king had her body brought to Westminster with great ceremony and buried beside her lord. She was the first queen to be buried there, just as her brother was the first king of England to be crowned there.

The Normans called Harold an oath-breaker and perjurer. But from an English point of view William, the illegitimate descendant of pirates, with no share in the blood royal, who had not been chosen by the councillors or people of the realm and whose claim to be the nominated successor had been superseded by the dead king's nomination of Harold, could be considered as openly planning a war of usurpation and conquest against the lawfully anointed king of one of Europe's ancient Christian kingdoms. The pope's blessing was essential, and for that blessing to be given 'Harold the Perjurer' was an important bogey-man. After 1066 some religious establishments deleted the Godwine name from their lists of benefactors.[18]

As R.H.C. Davis has stated:

> The most interesting fact about the Norman Conquest is what made it so complete . . . Apparently . . . England received a new royal dynasty, a new aristocracy . . . and virtually a new church, as the result of one day's fighting . . .[19]

In fact the picture was not quite that simple. But the total defeat of the English at Hastings made a reversal of the decision virtually inconceivable.

Hastings shattered the English army, and William subdued the kingdom by terror. Quite apart from the horrors to come in the north, from the day after Hastings until the week before their master's coronation William's soldiery, drawn from Brittany, Picardy, French Flanders and other regions of northern France by the lure of booty in England, carved a swath of devastation across southeast England. But the leading members of this 'joint stock enterprise', as his army has often been called, expected more than casual loot: they expected to be rewarded with land.

The pope, the patron of William's war, enjoined penances on the army. After the coronation, William issued a writ in English to the bishop and citizens of London (who had been spared the punitive rampage), greeting them as friends, proclaiming his wish that they should continue to enjoy the laws that had governed them in King Edward's day, and promising to protect them from injury. There now followed a systematic suppression of native English culture that in the emotive rhetoric of our own day would be called cultural genocide.

First, there was the suppression of the language and literature. Secondly, there was the dismantling of the vibrant spirituality of the Anglo-Saxon church tradition and the destruction of many of its buildings.

> The organized wealth of southern England was in the hands of the con-
> querors and they celebrated their triumph in stone . . . nowhere else in
> Latin Christendom was so much built in so short a time . . .[20]

By dint of 'unfortunate conflagrations', combined with ordered demolitions, within fifty years of the conquest Old English cathedrals and minsters had been levelled to the ground, in most cases to be replaced by Norman-style buildings, built under Norman contractors, even using stone from Norman quarries. It was a highly profitable rebuilding programme in which the native participation rarely amounted to more than forced labour, which first demolished its own historic structures and then raised, 'to the glory of God', the 'great churches' of the conquerors. The architectural glories of England's Norman/Romanesque architecture are, like the ruined castles that still line the heritage trails, perpetual monuments to an historic act of cultural cleansing.

In addition there was spiritual vandalism. A particular feature of Anglo-Saxon religious life had been its exceptionally developed cult of the Virgin Mary. (Modern scholars tend to accept that the cult of the Virgin Mary at Walsingham probably began in the last years of Edward the Confessor.) Certain of the Marian feast days, including the Presentation [of Christ] in the Temple and the Conception of the Virgin, seem to have originated at Winchester in the 1030s. From there they found their way to Canterbury, where they were entered in the liturgical calendar of the archdiocese. One of the first acts of the new Norman archbishop Lanfranc, who finally succeeded Stigand in 1070, was to reform the calendar and abolish many of the old feasts of the Anglo-Saxon Church, among them these Marian celebrations. Elsewhere, such as at the great abbey of Abingdon, which in the time of Æthelwold had been adorned with an altar table of gold and silver and texts in silver decorated with precious stones, treasures were destroyed or dispersed after the Conquest.[21]

William had made various land grants before his return to Normandy in February 1067. In his train went a number of aristocratic English hostages to be paraded through the streets of Rouen as part of the spoils of victory. According to the chronicler William of Poitiers, 'these long-haired sons of the North, with their almost feminine beauty' made something of a stir.

For William, acceptance as the lawful heir of Edward the Confessor was of critical practical consequence. He had acquired an exceptionally well-run country. The basic unit, the shire, was in the hands of an administrative team that was 'literate, active and continuous'. Here the assessment and collection of levies were organized on the basis of a sort of land register. The sheriff, instructed by writ, was responsible for implementing such instructions. His court was the place where local disputes were settled and local big men could be enlisted in support of the king's business. Only when England's sheriffs and their staff were satisfied that the alien ruler now in place was duly vested with the authority of a king of the English would they willingly discharge their functions. Their collaboration was essential to ensure the continued services of skilled Anglo-Saxons as scribes in his court writing office (or chancery) and as local officials in the shires and boroughs, to ensure the smoothest possible completion of the conquest, at least until a sufficient number of Frenchmen had been trained to replace them. The shire court lies behind the success of the Norman settlement.

A Norman granted land by the king need only present himself before the court with a sealed writ to that effect. If inspected and found authentic it was then read to the assembly. The leading men of the shire, thus made witness to the royal will in the matter, were duty bound to see it implemented. The alien intruder had to be duly informed of the lands that were now his and assisted, if need be, in taking possession of them. Not all the beneficiaries were best pleased. Orderic Vitalis tells us that while some were astounded by the extent of the lands awarded to them, others complained about 'domains depopulated by war'. ('*Tant pis* to you', any Anglo-Saxon with a smattering of Norman French might no doubt have been heard to mutter.)

Yet when it suited him William was scrupulous in paying respect to the old ways. At a famous trial held on Pinnenden Heath in Kent in the 1070s, Æthelric, bishop of Selsey, 'a man of great age and very wise in the law of the land' was brought on William's order in a wagon to the place of the trial so that 'he might expound the ancient practice of the laws.'

In his 1966 essay, 'The Norman Conquest', R. H. C. Davis assumed that at first the Normans would have had to live like an army of occupation, 'living, eating and sleeping together in operational units . . . and . . . exploiting their estates as absentee landlords for the time being'. But castles of various types soon encroached like a malignant rash across the English landscape, to enforce obedience. The simplest type comprised an earth mound (the motte) topped by a palisaded enclosure, or possibly a wooden tower, sur-rounded by a ditch and a palisade enclosing an outer compound, the bailey. Designed as protection for the henchmen of an alien warrior brigandage intent upon becoming a 'nobility', it was a constant menace to the subject countryside and a standing humiliation to its people whose forced labour had raised the structure. Stone-built keeps (donjons) replaced the first emergency timber towers. That the French name for a tower rising skywards was transmuted into 'dungeon' in the language of the conquered population to signify the dank and dreadful pit at its base, the domain of torment and sewer rats, recalls realities of the Conquest years that are rarely touched on. But the Normans had a hidden advantage. Many ordi-nary English may have felt that the invaders were sent as a scourge from God for the nation's sins. After all, the pope in Rome had, for reasons known to himself, blessed the alien banners.

The more adventurous among the conquerors might take advan-tage of the general confusion to add to their holdings. Some 'manipulated' the suitors at the shire courts to make false returns in their favour. For example, Rochester Cathedral under its Anglo-Saxon bishop suffered for years at the hands of a Norman sheriff named Picot. He claimed that the cathedral's manor of Freckenham in Suffolk was in fact royal demesne and as such under his manage-ment – and kept the profits for himself. In due course, however, the old English bishop was succeeded by a Norman and he persuaded King William to have a shire court convened to give judgement as to 'whose the land ought to be'. Eventually the new bishop tracked down the Englishman who had managed the cathedral estates in the Confessor's time and he confirmed that the manor had indeed belonged to the king.

King William was as interested as anyone to discover the exact location and value of the grants of lands he had made and whether any of his followers had seized more than allotted to him. Confident in the Rolls-Royce administration of his new kingdom, he ordered an inventory of England and its landholders – Domesday Book. The first question posed about any manor was 'Who held it in King Edward's time?' If the answer did not match the one expected, in other words if the present occupier was not the one to whom the king had awarded the lands of the Anglo-Saxon lord named, then he could expect trouble. Many *clamores* or complaints came before the Domesday commissioners, some revealing attempted encroachments on the king's land and then it could be the Normans' turn to suffer. A certain Berengar, charged with invading the royal demesne land, found himself 'in the king's mercy' – he became so ill that he was unable to attend the official hearing.

Before the Conquest it had become common practice for the great monastic houses to keep detailed records of their estates, tenants' rents and so forth; lay landowners may have followed the same practice. The machinery of the sheriff's court was essential to the Domesday inquests but such estate records, as we saw in the case of Freckenham, must have provided invaluable back-up material:

> The Domesday survey brought the Norman Conquest to a conclusion by examining all the details of the ruthless spoliation, and approving them only when they had been done with authority . . . It made the Norman settlement permanent.[22]

English heritage

The death in a hunting accident of the second Norman king, William Rufus, in the New Forest near Winchester on 2 August 1100 seemed ill-omened to contemporaries and still attracts conspiracy theories: the most lurid of these claim that he was the sacrificial victim of a pagan fertility cult, although more likely it was the result of a coup. On Friday 3 August, the day after the body was interred in the cathedral at Winchester, the assembled barons elected his brother Henry to be king. Having put a guard on the royal treasury, still housed in the old West Saxon 'capital', Henry rode for London, its English citizenry ranked below only the bishops and the Norman baronage in their influence on national affairs. That Sunday he was consecrated as Henry I by the bishop of London before the altar in Westminster Abbey 'and all the people in this land submitted to him'. Barely three days after one king's accidental death a new one is elected, consecrated and acclaimed.

By the terms of William the Conqueror's will Robert, the eldest son, had Normandy; to William went the newly acquired conquest of England; Henry received only money. William was unmarried and Robert away on the First Crusade. He was now on his return. Once he and William made their brotherly reunion Henry could kiss goodbye to the English throne unless it should become vacant – quickly. The timing and location of William's accident, an hour or so's ride from the kingdom's treasury, was certainly convenient.

At the consecration Henry solemnly pledged 'before God and all the people . . . to uphold the best of the laws upheld by any of his predecessors'. This was confirmed in a 'charter of liberties', which specifically committed Henry himself to maintain 'the law of King Edward [the Confessor]'. Intriguingly the text of the Latin document as we have it uses the vernacular word *laga* instead of the Latin *lex*.

For England's Norman conquerors the model for good government was to be found in pre-Conquest Anglo-Saxon England. The Confessor as Law-giver would be cited in many a post-Conquest text. Yet no laws actually issued by him have survived. The text known as *Leges Edwardi Confessoris* dates from about 1140 and is not an authentic record of any previous code. It is of course possible that Edward did make laws that are lost or that his reputation for justice rested on his judgements and pronouncements by word of mouth.

Henry sent a copy of his coronation charter to every shire; then he turned to the threat from his brother Robert. At length in September 1106, largely thanks to his English troops, he defeated his brother at the Battle of Tinchebrai in Normandy, and Robert became his prisoner for life. The English fought enthusiastically for their Norman king, not least because he had married into the English royal house, his wife Matilda/Edith being the great grand-daughter of Æthelred II.

During this reign there was something of a resurgence in things Anglo-Saxon. Although probably the son of a French father and an English mother, William of Malmesbury, who wrote his *Gesta regum Anglorum* following a request by Matilda/Edith that he compile an account of her ancestors, considered that Hastings had been a fateful day for England, 'our sweet country'. His contemporary John of Worcester, born, a contemporary tells us, of English parents and a par-tisan for the memory of King Harold, drew on Bede and other Anglo-Saxon sources to amplify the English content in his continuation of a 'Universal Chronicle' he worked on up to about 1140. In addition he also produced royal genealogies of the pre-Conquest kingdoms. The last of these 'Mercian-born' historians, Henry of Huntingdon, wrote his *Historia Anglorum* ('History of the English') in ten short books. It found a wider market. The abbot of Westminster made a premature move for the beatification of Edward the Confessor. Miracles claimed for the king included the story that Earl Godwine had choked to death on bread blessed by him, while attempting to prove his innocence of the mysterious death of Edward's brother, Alfred, years before (see the cover illustration of this book).

As a twelve-year-old, Henry I's son William had received the homage of England's Norman baronage and was presented as the ætheling to a gathering of English notables. He drowned in the wreck of the *White Ship* in 1120 but his sister Matilda, wife of Emperor Henry V (the third daughter of a king of England to marry into the empire since the accession of Æthelstan), continued the blood line. Years later Henry Plantagenet, her son by Geoffrey, count of Anjou, would become Henry II of England. Now the pro-motion of the Confessor's cult began in earnest as Henry, the first post-Conquest king to have the English blood royal in his veins, took up the cause. Pope Alexander III proclaimed the new saint in February 1161. In October 1163 Thomas Becket, the controversial new archbishop of Canterbury, presided over a dazzling ceremony at Westminster Abbey at which the saint's bones were installed in a new shrine.

Henry II's treasurer, Richard FitzNigel, wrote that he could no longer detect a difference between the king's English and French subjects. In London 'a considerable proportion of the aldermanic class remained English' and these great men of the city took high umbrage when the low-born Frenchman William Longchamp, bishop of Ely and chancellor to King Richard I, failed to address them in English. So, in the country's metropolis, a minister of the crown was now expected to speak the language of the governed and not of the government. In the early 1200s the barons who would force Richard's brother John to grant Magna Carta at Runnymede were appealing back to the laws of Edward the Confessor. The king himself looked to other English patrons, being buried at his own request in Worcester Cathedral, where his tomb is presided over by Bishop Wulfstan and Bishop St Oswald.

His son Henry III sought to honour St Edward by rebuilding his abbey of St Peter at Westminster and in 1268 had the Confessor's body solemnly translated to its new resting place behind the high altar, where it still lies; the discovery of the exact location of the Confessor's tomb by radar imaging was announced in December 2005. Henry named his eldest son Edward and on his crusade to Palestine in 1270–71 this Edward inaugurated the crusading Order of St Edward of Acre, yet another, if transitory, token of the Plantagenet cult of Englishness.

Edward was followed by his son Edward II and he by his son Edward III, who led England to victory against France in the Hundred Years War. His first-born son was also christened Edward, and this Edward, known to history as the Black Prince, also named his eldest boy after the Anglo-Saxon saint. But the line of Edwards was broken when the Black Prince and his eldest son both died prematurely young, and the Prince's second son Richard came to the throne. And yet it was Richard's reign that produced the most powerful testament of nostalgia for the old pre-Conquest monarchy in the magical painted panel known as the Wilton Diptych. Here we see King Richard II adoring the Virgin Mary, supported by St John the Baptist and the Anglo-Saxon royal saints, Edward and Edmund.

In the context of world culture the legacy of Anglo-Saxon England has been incalculable. The common era for the dating of the world's events is still the one adopted by England's first historian, the Venerable Bede. For the best part of five centuries the majority population of the southern half of Britain inhabited a society in which the vernacular language, mother of today's global language, was the norm in every walk of life. Then came conquest and, except among the aldermanry of the city of London, the habit of English among the nation's elite seemed lost. But although Latin and Norman French were to remain the principal languages of officialdom for generations, in 1263 we find the first 'certainly known governmental document in English issued after the reign of William I'; in this King Henry III proclaimed his willingness to abide by the terms of the Provisions of Oxford, forced on him by his barons five years before. The proclamation was copied to all the shire courts, in the language of the country[23] – as had been standard Anglo-Saxon governmental practice before the coming of the Normans.

APPENDIX I

THE BAYEUX TAPESTRY

Recent important publications and a new theory

At the time of going to press, the most recent work published on the subject was Lucien Musset's *The Bayeux Tapestry* (2005). This followed the commercial release in 2002 of *The Bayeux Tapestry Digital Edition*, devised by Martin Foys, and *The Bayeux Tapestry: Embroidering the Facts of History* (2004), edited by Pierre Bouet, Brian Levy and François Neveux, while in the summer of 2005 George Beech, emeritus professor of medieval history at Western Michigan University, Kalamazoo, published *Was the Bayeux Tapestry Made in France? The Case for St Florent of Saumur.*

Anyone who has walked along the Bayeux Tapestry in its display case in Bayeux will know the vigour and violence of the scenes, the tension and drama of the unfolding narrative, and the sense of frustration as it breaks off before the end of the story. We have seen Edward, king of the English, on his throne; Harold, king of the English, on his throne and how he arrived at it; Duke William of Normandy receiving Harold at his court; a long and mysterious episode showing them on campaign in Brittany; then we have followed the historic battle between the two: surely, after his death, which we have just seen, the pictures will lead us up to William, the new king of the English, on his throne with all the action accompanying such a climax. We do not know how much of the fabric is missing; also we cannot be certain as to the authenticity of all the surviving images. What we see today differs in some details from the way it looked when it was put on public display at Bayeux in the early 1700s. The most famous episode of all, the standing figure with an arrow apparently in his eye (supposedly King Harold at the moment of death), has been the subject of much controversy. The stitches and stitch holes that today represent the 'arrow' are probably later additions. And then perhaps it was a spear: it has even been suggested that King Harold is in fact the adjacent figure being felled by a swordsman.

There is no direct evidence of any kind as to the location of the workshop where it was made, as to who may have been the person who commissioned the work or the person or persons who planned and devised this masterpiece of design, or even to the date of its execution. At one extreme we have the suggestion that, because the work is generally sympathetic to the English, it was commissioned and made between October 1066 and the English rebellion of 1068–9: that is a maximum of two years for the discussion, planning, designing and actual manufacture of the artefact.

The existence of the work was first attested in the 1470s, when it was being hung in the nave at Bayeux Cathedral during the annual celebration of the Feast of Relics. This led to the supposition that it had been commissioned by Duke William's half-brother Odo, bishop of Bayeux, for the consecration of the new cathedral there in 1077. For the last five years of William's reign (1082–7) Odo was in disgrace, having been imprisoned by William for raising an army without permission.

In France it was long known as the *Tapiserie de la reine Mathilde* (Queen Mathilda's Tapestry, that is the Conqueror's wife) and presumed to have been the work of French craftswomen. Then the general opinion came round to the view that it was done by a team of Englishwomen, presumably nuns, at either Canterbury or

Winchester, though there is no trace of workshops at either place. However, the English were renowned throughout the Middle Ages for this craft and skill, particularly for their work in gold and silken threads, and such hangings are quite often mentioned in tenth- and eleventh-century England. Wills of the period commonly bequeath such items as 'a set of bed clothing with tapestry and curtain', 'a hall tapestry to Ælfwine' or 'a tapestry for a hall and tapestry for a chamber', while the twelfth-century chronicle of the abbey of Ely records a piece donated by the widow of Earl Byrthnoth of the Battle of Maldon, in the form of a hanging that depicted the heroic deeds of her husband.

Then, in July 2005, Professor Beech argued the case for the man-ufacture of the tapestry at an embroidery workshop operating from the late tenth century at the abbey of St Florent at Saumur on the River Loire. The workshop has long since disappeared and there are indeed few remains of the abbey itself. A fire devastated the work-shop in the 1020s, but it seems to have been restored and was again in production some years later. The historian of the abbey, writing in the later twelfth century, makes no mention of the manufacture of the famous tapestry; this is explained by supposing that, once finished, the great work would have been sent to the commission-ing patron, presumed to be William the Conqueror, for display 'somewhere in Normandy or England'; thus it need never have fea-tured in the holdings of Saumur. Unfortunately, the abbey's chron-icler makes no mention of any textile production of any kind at the workshop during the 1070s and 1080s, the very period when, Professor Beech believes, it must have been created. The twelfth-century chronicler offers a tantalizing hint of possible English con-nections when he speaks of *une reine d'outremer* ('a queen from overseas'), who apparently commissioned work at St Florent in the 1010s. This lady, argues Beech, must have been Emma of Normandy, queen to both Æthelred and Cnut and, coincidentally, the aunt of Duke William. But if St Florent's chronicler saw fit to mention, allusively, a commission from William's aunt 160 years in the past, why would he not mention a commission only 70 years before his time made by her nephew, the most famous figure in northern France during that period?

Professor Beech points to the close links between William of Normandy and the family of William, the abbot of St Florent. Rivallon, the abbot's father, was lord of Dol, the fortified town in Brittany that stood close to the duchy's frontier with Normandy. He allied himself with Duke William against his natural overlord, Duke Conan of Brittany, whose capital was at Rennes, when William raided into the duchy. That campaign occupies about 10 per cent of the length of the surviving tapestry and the siege of Dol features among its scenes. The lord of Dol and his family became favourites with the duke of Normandy.

Thanks to Duke William's lavish endowments of priories, churches and church land the abbey of St Florent was a major presence in the Norman church. Perhaps these were in payment for the great embroidery commissioned, Beech proposes, from the abbey workshops; he suggests that the extensive Breton sequence was included at the prompting of Abbot William. Certainly the tapestry displays intimate local knowledge of Brittany and Breton personalities.

There are similarities between figures, motifs and design elements to be found in the tapestry and in sculptures in churches and illuminated illustrations scriptoria in the districts of Poitou, Anjou and the Loire, in particular carvings of lions' tails in churches near Saumur. But there is no proof positive to support the thesis and there are numerous details that do not fit, as well as more general counterarguments. The design gives the impression that cavalry had been important on the assault on Dinant during the campaign in Brittany, but a French designer would know that castles rarely, if ever, surrendered as a result of horsemen charging their walls. In one scene the Anglo-Saxon name 'Gyrth' is spelled with the Anglo-Saxon barred 'Đ'; in the lettering of another there is a tell-tale slip where the text speaks of CASTELLUM AT HESTENG^{A}, using the English 'at' in place of the Latin 'ad'; elsewhere we find the use of the Anglo-Saxon ampersand '7'; and the general letterforms strongly suggest an English hand behind the design and workmanship. In terms of artistic influence as such, while there may be design elements that find echoes in the Loire valley, there are many more similarities with English art and design: Norman illumination of the time has been seen as a somewhat provincial version of the English art.

The tapestry was presumably commissioned to be hung in the great hall of a castle, possibly in England, and if the warrior bishop Odo was the patron then perhaps one of his. However, there exists what at first sight seems to be an early description of the tapestry that may cast doubt on such a suggestion. It is to be found in a long poem by Baudri, the abbot of Bourgueil near Tours, dedicated to Adela, wife of Count Stephen of Blois and daughter of William the Conqueror, and known as *Adelae Comitissae* ('To Adela the Countess'). It was written some time between 1096 and 1102 and contains a detailed description of the great chamber of the castle at Blois along with its decorations, specifically the series of wall hangings on various topics with subtitled scenes, presumably in the manner of the famous 'tapestry'. These are enriched with pearls and jewels and worked in richly coloured silks with gold and silver thread, says Baudri. Around the bed of the countess, he tells us, such a hanging depicts the life of her father, the duke-king William, from his birth, through his early struggles in Normandy to a speech in which he announces his claim to the English throne and his determination to make it good. A battle, clearly Hastings, is recounted with scenes described that are found on the Bayeux Tapestry. But the 'Adela' hanging continues the story after the death of Harold: the following morning William exhorts his army to leave the quest for booty until the war is won, and this too the 'Blois' wall hanging apparently depicts. Nothing is said about a coronation scene.

Could this be a description of the tapestry at Bayeux as we know it? That has nothing about his childhood or youth and nothing about his early struggles within Normandy against rivals for the duchy. It has no richly coloured silks or gold and silver thread – such luxury materials could no doubt have been robbed over the centuries but it hardly seems plausible that a piece of work more than 230 feet (70 m) long in its finished state would have been worked in gold thread. (Or maybe there was a second, luxury, version that is the subject of Baudri's poem.) And could a piece of such dimension be accommodated around the bed of the countess?

Lawson suggests that the entire description of the chamber, let alone the hanging, might be a fiction. The details of the battle could have been taken from contemporary written sources or from oral tradition – one of which has Harold hit by an arrow. In this case Baudri's poem can be seen in a tradition, stretching back to late antiquity, of poetic depictions of buildings and works of art, both real and imaginary.

For Professor Beech, Baudri's description of the 'Blois' hanging is potent evidence to support his contention that the Bayeux Tapestry was made at the workshops in the monastery at Saumur. It is to be explained not by the reason that Baudri gives, namely that he saw it in the chamber of Countess Adela, but that being resident at Bourgeuil he was able to see the piece as a work in progress at St Florent, across the river. It is indeed rather unfortunate that, if he did see the tapestry there, he did not see fit to mention the fact.

Quite a lot of the tapestry's existing stitchwork is not original. In part this is because there was a time when those in charge allowed visitors to remove small pieces as souvenirs (rather as the owner of Stonehenge hired out hammers to visitors so that they might take chippings). The artefact has been subjected to exhaustive study and laboratory analysis. But we shall presumably never know who designed the masterly narrative sequence or the composition of the individual scenes, whether man or woman, nor how the selection of the episodes came about.

The Battle of Hastings was an engagement that lasted an entire day and involved thousands, possibly tens of thousands, of men. Besides the tapestry we have the piecemeal evidence of scattered chronicle accounts and poems that may or may not have been available to the designer. He or she may, of course, have had access to other sources of information, now lost – and surely eyewitness accounts or veterans' reminiscences, whether skewed or reliable. No doubt what its patrons required was a decorative hanging that would justify the conquest of a Christian kingdom and show them in their hour of glory. Possibly the great work would form a backdrop or diorama to epic recitations of the battle by professional minstrels.

APPENDIX 2

THE DEATH OF HAROLD AND HIS AFTERLIFE?

The fact that there were resistance movements after Hastings and that none of them evoked the name of Harold is, presumably, the most conclusive proof, if any were needed, that he died on the battlefield. There were problems, it is true, about identification: the face of the body shown as his was so badly wounded as to be unrecognizable. There are differing traditions about the place of burial. It is said that his mother, Gytha, offered William the body's weight in gold to receive it for burial, which at least is a tribute to the fabled wealth of the Godwine family. The Conqueror refused and is said to have given instructions for the body to be interred on the seashore. In 1954 building excavations at Holy Trinity, Bosham, the coastal church featured in the Bayeux Tapestry and associated with the Godwine family, but taken into his private estate by the Conqueror, revealed an important tomb with the bones of a tall man with the head, the right leg and part of the left leg missing. These correspond to the dreadful wounds Harold was reputed to have sustained at Hastings. Bosham is certainly near 'the seashore', and it is tempting to see these bones as those of the last English king, hidden away by the victor safely under his control to avert the possibility of any popular cult. If this is right, the burial was certainly hushed up, for early tradition held that the body had been moved

from the battlefield and buried at Harold's foundation of Waltham
Abbey, where the supposed site of the grave was still pointed out in
the late twentieth century.

The church at Waltham Holy Cross had been a place of pilgrimage since the reign of Cnut, when it became home to a great flint
cross discovered in the vicinity of Glastonbury and, following
miraculous intervention, brought here. In 1060 Harold built a large
new church in honour of the cross and founded a college of secular
canons to tend the venerable object. If the church was his final
resting place, the canons seem to have been uneasy about the possibility of a popular cult developing. Anyway, they fostered legends
about the king escaping after the battle and travelling on the
Continent. Then about 1204 an anonymous writer at Waltham produced the *Vita Haroldi*, claiming to have his information from a
certain Sæbeorht who had been the king's servant during his last
years, passed in hiding near Chester.

Smuggled from the battlefield more dead than alive, so went the
story, Harold spent two years in hiding at Winchester recovering
from his wounds in the care of an Arab woman. (Presumably, the
superiority of Arab medicine at this time was testified to by returning crusaders.) Restored to health, he journeyed incognito through
Germany looking for support to recover his crown. Unsuccessful,
he continued his travels as a pilgrim, finally returning to England
where he took refuge in a cave near Dover. After ten years he moved
to Wales before settling at Chester, where he was associated with the
local hermit attached to the church of St John. The mysterious
stranger rarely left the hermit's cave and when he did wore a veil
over his face. When the hermit died the disguised king took his
place; he was said to wear a mail shirt next his skin. And so the last
native king of England ended his days an obscure recluse on the
marches with a country that in his young days he had harried to
submission. Some say that he revealed his identity shortly before his
death. In the thirteenth century it was said that a royal body was

unearthed in St John's, uncorrupted and wearing leather hose, golden spurs and a crown.

The historical Harold did have a link with Chester, in so far as his second wife, Alditha, sister of Earl Morcar, gave birth to their son Harold there. The association of the city with the Mercian earl and the dead king's family ties in with the rebellion in the area of 1069–70, so ruthlessly suppressed by the Conqueror. In his article 'The Cult of King Harold at Chester', on which much of the foregoing is based, Alan Thacker surmises that the *Vita Haroldi* was commissioned by the Augustinian community of Walthamstow Abbey (reformed by Henry II) to the glory of the divine cross, through describing the merits and virtues of its most celebrated worshipper. Whatever its provenance, the *Vita* is an interesting addition to the theme of nostalgia for Anglo-Saxon England in English thirteenth-century culture.

APPENDIX 3

ROYAL WRITING OFFICE OR CHANCERY?

Some have romantically dated the office of chancellor to early seventh-century Kent; many academics would debate the very existence of an Anglo-Saxon royal chancery. Others would apply the term, at least from the tenth century onwards, to the royal writing office of the kings of Wessex from the time of Alfred, that drew up charters of grants made to ecclesiastical establishments or other recipients.

Between 928 and 935 charters issued in the name of King Æthelstan seem dedicated to projecting the concept of the 'kingdom of the English'. Writing on the diplomas of Æthelred II in 1980, Simon Keynes concluded that the charters were produced not by the clerks of the recipients but by a royal writing office or chancery; however, there does not seem to have been a central record kept.

Latin-literate chaplains serving the royal court could be well rewarded. Under Edward the Confessor, the cleric Regenbald accumulated estates and enjoyed the legal status of a bishop. He was called 'Royal Chancellor' in the witness list of a charter dated of 1062 and was probably the man chosen by William I as his 'Chancellor'. However, the actual latin title *cancellarius* (chancellor) may not pre-date the Norman Conquest – the 1062 charter being perhaps a later forgery.

NOTES

Introduction

Sir Frank Stenton's *Anglo-Saxon England* (3rd edition, 1971) is considered an academic classic. After this, Peter Hunter Blair's *An Introduction to Anglo-Saxon England* (1956) is much respected; in the third edition (2004) the text was reprinted with a valuable and up-to-date bibliography. The richly illustrated *The Anglo-Saxons* (1991), edited by James Campbell, is both authoritative and a joy to the eye, with much photography of archaeological sites. Christopher Brooke's *The Saxon and Norman Kings* (1963) remains a stimulating analytical survey. *The Blackwell Encyclopaedia of Anglo-Saxon England* (1999, reprinted in paperback in 2004), edited by Michael Lapidge and others, is an indispensable reference work. *After Rome* (2003), edited by T. M. Charles-Edwards in 'The Short Oxford History of the British Isles' series is an authoritative overview of the early chapters.

1 Campbell, 'Late Anglo-Saxon State', 1994; cited in Campbell, *Anglo-Saxon State*, 2000, p. 10.
2 Charles-Edwards, *After Rome*, 2003, p. 24.
3 See Campbell, 'United Kingdom of England', 1995, p. 31.
4 Levison, *England and the Continent*, 1946, p. 93.
5 Godfrey, *Church in Anglo-Saxon England*, 1962, p. 221.
6 Elton, *The English*, 1994, p. 4.
7 Talbot, *Anglo-Saxon Missionaries*, 1981, p. 205.
8 Lapidge, 'Asser's Reading', 2003, p. 33.
9 Talbot, *Anglo-Saxon Missionaries*, 1981, p. 69.
10 Levison, *England and the Continent*, 1946, p. 83.
11 Campbell, 'United Kingdom of England', 1995, p. 31.

12 Gillingham, 'Britain, Ireland and the South', 2003, pp. 217–18.
13 Campbell, 'United Kingdom of England', 1995, pp. 31–5.
14 Mason, *House of Godwine*, 2004, p. 149.
15 Lawson, *Cnut*, 2004, p. 15.

Chapter 1 – Invaders and Settlers

Here, as for the next three chapters, the primary source is the Venerable Bede and his *Ecclesiastical History of the English People*, for which the edition of 1969 by Colgrave and Mynors may be considered standard. The contributors to *The Origins of the Anglo-Saxon Kingdoms* (1989), edited by S. R. Bassett, opened up valuable, sometimes controversial, new ideas on early Anglo-Saxon history for this section and chapter 2.

1 Orchard, 'Latin and the Vernacular Languages', 2003, p. 217.
2 See Lapidge, '*Beowulf*, Aldhelm, the *Liber Monstrorum* and Wessex', p. 311.
3 Hines, 'Society, Community, and Identity', 2003, p. 92.
4 For the development of these arguments see Ward-Perkins, *Fall of Rome*, 2005, and Heather, *Fall of the Roman Empire*, 2005.
5 Kabir, *Paradise, Death and Doomsday*, 2001.
6 *Bede's Ecclesiastical History*, ed. Colgrave and Mynors, 1969, p. 135.
7 Blair, *Church in Anglo-Saxon Society*, 2005, pp. 24–5.
8 Hawkes and Mills, *Northumbria's Golden Age*, 1991, pp. 4–5.
9 Allott, *Alcuin of York*, 1987, p. 18.
10 Wallace-Hadrill, *Early Germanic Kingship*, 1971, p. 21.
11 For this paragraph see Blair, *Church in Anglo-Saxon Society*, 2005, pp. 252 and 267.
12 Canon J. Higham, notes for Peterborough Cathedral Guides.
13 *Bede's Ecclesiastical History*, ed. Colgrave and Mynors, 1969, p. 49, n.
14 Hawkes and Mills, *Northumbria's Golden Age*, 1991, p. 265, citing Howe, *Migration and Mythmaking*, 1989.
15 Neuman de Vegvar, 'Travelling Twins', 1999.
16 Bassett, ed., *Origins of the Anglo-Saxon Kingdoms*, 1989, p. 63.
17 Reynolds, *Kingdoms and Communities*, 1984, p. 250.
18 Chaney, *Cult of Kingship*, 1970, p. 118.
19 Rollason, *Northumbria, 500–1100*, 2003, p. 62.
20 Ibid., p. 77
21 Blair, *Church in Anglo-Saxon Society*, 2005, p. 26.
22 Rollason, *Northumbria, 500–1100*, 2003, p. 6.
23 Ibid., p. 64.

24 Chaney, *Cult of Kingship*, 1970, p. 74.
25 Ibid., p. 11.
26 Talbot, *Anglo-Saxon Missionaries*, 1981, p. 231.
27 Chaney, *Cult of Kingship*, 1970, pp. 1–3.
28 Ibid., p. 3.
29 Gifford and Gifford, 'Alfred's New Longships', 2003, p. 282.

Chapter 2 – The Southern Kingdoms AD 600–800

J. M. Wallace-Hadrill's *Early Germanic Kingship in England and on the Continent* (1971) is essential reading, along with Bassett's *Origins of the Anglo-Saxon Kingdoms* (1989). Also recommended is T. M. Charles-Edwards *After Rome* (2003). For this and the next chapter D. P. Kirby's *The Earliest English Kings* (2000) and. Barbara Yorke's *Kings and Kingdoms in Early England* (1990) are recommended.

1 Charles-Edwards, *After Rome*, 2003, p. 128.
2 Blair, *Church in Anglo-Saxon Society*, 2005, p. 70, n.
3 Kelly, 'Literacy in Anglo-Saxon Lay Society', 1990, p. 58.
4 John, *Reassessing Anglo-Saxon England*, 1996, p. 18.
5 See Wallace-Hadrill, *Early Germanic Kingship*, 1971, p. 32.
6 Stancliffe and Cambridge, eds, *Oswald*, 1995, p. 27.
7 Higham, 'Dynasty and Cult', 1999, p. 104.
8 Campbell, 'United Kingdom of England', 1995, p. 35.
9 *Bede's Ecclesiastical History*, ed. Colgrave and Mynors, 1969, p. 50, n. 2.
10 Wallace-Hadrill, *Early Germanic Kingship*, 1971, p. 36.
11 Wormald, *Making of English Law*, 1999, p. 94.
12 Whitelock, ed., *English Historical Documents*, i, 1979.
13 Blair, *Church in Anglo-Saxon Society*, 2005, pp. 177–9.
14 See Wallace-Hadrill, *Early Germanic Kingship*, 1971, p. 85.
15 See N. Faulkner, 'Swords', *Current Archaeology*, 192, 2004, p. 550.
16 Ibid., p. 560.
17 Campbell, *Anglo-Saxon State*, 2000, p. xxviii.
18 Based on Swanton, *Anglo-Saxon Chronicle*, 1996, p. 54, notes.

Chapter 3 – Northumbria: The Star in the North

As will be apparent from the notes, this chapter owes much to David Rollason's *Northumbria 500–1100: Creation and Destruction of a Kingdom* (2003) and to *Northumbria's Golden Age* (1999), edited by

Jane Hawkes and Susan Mills and their collaborators. Also recommended are the titles by Kirby and Yorke, mentioned above under chapter 2.

1 Rollason, *Northumbria, 500–1100*, 2003, p. 64.
2 Charles-Edwards, *After Rome*, 2003, p. 37.
3 Stancliffe and Cambridge, eds, *Oswald*, 1995, p. 71.
4 Blair, *Church in Anglo-Saxon Society*, 2005, pp. 54–6.
5 Bede, *Ecclesiastical History*, II, 14.
6 Rollason, *Northumbria, 500–1100*, 2003, p. 100.
7 Stancliffe and Cambridge, eds, *Oswald*, 1995, pp. 80–81.
8 Ibid., p. 51.
9 Chaney, *Cult of Kingship*, 1970, p. 117.
10 Stancliffe and Cambridge, eds, *Oswald*, 1995, p. 100, citing E. Salin, *La civilisation mérovingienne d'après les sépultures, les texts et le laboratoire*, Picard, 1952.
11 *Current Archaeology*, 163, June 1999.
12 Attwater, *Penguin Dictionary of Saints*, 1979, p. 96.
13 Campbell, *Anglo-Saxon State*, 2000, p. 74.
14 Blair, *Church in Anglo-Saxon Society*, 2005, p. 284.
15 Kabir, *Paradise, Death and Doomsday*, 2001, p. 12.
16 Ibid., p. 149.
17 Rollason, *Northumbria, 500–1100*, 2003, p. 183.
18 Lang, 'Imagery of the Franks Casket', 1999.
19 Kendrick, *Anglo-Saxon Art*, 1938, p. 119, cited in Hawkes and Mills, eds, *Northumbria's Golden Age*, 1999, p. 1.
20 Talbot, *Anglo-Saxon Missionaries*, 1981, p. 155.
21 For a fuller discussion of Ruthwell and related matters see Hawkes and Mills, eds, *Northumbria's Golden Age*, 1999.
22 Brown, *Lindisfarne Gospels*, 2003.
23 Michelli, 'Lindisfarne Gospels', 1999, p. 357.
24 Rollason, *Northumbria, 500–1100*, 2003, p. 143 and, for the rest of this paragraph, pp. 144–6.

Chapter 4 – The Mercian Sphere

Here a special debt is owed to the contributors in *Mercia: An Anglo-Saxon Kingdom in Europe* (2001) under the editorship of Michelle P. Brown and Carol A. Farr. Ann Dornier's *Mercian Studies* (1977) is a classic and a useful survey is to be found in Ian Walker's *Mercia and the Making of England* (2000).

1 Blair, *Church in Anglo-Saxon Society*, 2005, p. 287.
2 Featherstone, 'Tribal Hidage and the Ealdormen of Mercia', 2001.
3 Bassett, ed., *Origins of the Anglo-Saxon Kingdoms*, 1989, p. 170.
4 Keynes, 'Mercia and Wessex in the Ninth Century', 2001, pp. 319, 322.
5 Swift, *Croyland Abbey*, 1999, p. 4.
6 Hodgkin, *History of the Anglo-Saxons*, 1935–9, I, p. 385.
7 Wormald, 'The Age of Offa and Alcuin', in Campbell, *The Anglo-Saxons*, 1991, p. 128.
8 Abels, *Alfred the Great*, 1998, p. 48.
9 Blair, *Church in Anglo-Saxon Society*, 2005, p. 274.
10 Keynes, *Councils of Clofesho*, 1994, p. 3, n. 14.
11 Ibid., p. 6.
12 Ullmann, *Short History of the Papacy*, 1972, p. 79.
13 For the potential military importance of these scholae, realized in the mid–ninth century under Sergius II, see the translations from the *Liber Pontificalis* by Raymond Davis, *The Lives of the Eighth-century Popes* and *The Lives of the Ninth-century Popes*, Liverpool UP, 1992, 1996. See also Nelson, 'Carolingian Contacts', 2001, pp. 136–7.
14 Lapidge and others, eds, *Blackwell Encyclopaedia of Anglo-Saxon England*, 1999, p. 106.
15 Brooks, 'Alfredian Government', 2003, p. 8.
16 Blair, *Church in Anglo-Saxon Society*, 2005, p. 257.
17 See the article by Gareth Williams and Gerard Spink in *Current Archaeology*, 194, 2004, pp. 56–7.
18 'A papal seal from Herefordshire' by Peter Reavill in *Current Archaeology*, 199, September 2005, p. 317.
19 The two foregoing paragraphs are heavily indebted to Cowie, 'Mercian London', 2001.
20 Keynes, 'Mercia and Wessex in the Ninth Century', 2001, p. 323.

Chapter 5 – Apostles of Germany

A useful collection of primary sources in translation is to be found in C. H. Talbot's *The Anglo-Saxon Missionaries in Germany* (1981), which comprises a selection of the letters of St Boniface; the life of the saint himself (*Vita Bonifacii*) by St Willibald; the Life of St Willibrord (*Vita Willibrordi*); the Life of St Lioba (*Vita Leobae*) by Rudolf of Fulda; the Life of St Sturm, Boniface's German assistant; and the *Hodoepericon* by Huneberc or Hygeburg of Heidenheim. The classic survey of the subject in English is still *England and the Continent in the Eighth*

Century by the German scholar Wilhelm Levison, published in 1946 but originating as the Ford Lectures delivered at Oxford University in 1943.

1 Ullmann, *Short History of the Papacy*, 1972, p. 66.
2 Levison, *England and the Continent*, 1946, p. 57.
3 Ibid., p. 58.
4 Bede, *Ecclesiastical History*, III, 13.
5 Levison, *England and the Continent*, 1946, p. 72.
6 Ayerst and Fisher, *Records of Christianity*, 1977, II, p. 55.
7 Talbot, *Anglo-Saxon Missionaries*, 1981, p. 39.
8 Ibid., p. 74.
9 Ibid., p. 47.
10 Levison, *England and the Continent*, 1946, p. 84.
11 Talbot, *Anglo-Saxon Missionaries*, 1981, p. 96.
12 Ibid., p. 99.
13 These paragraphs are based on Beckett, *Anglo-Saxon Perceptions of the Islamic World*, 2004, pp. 44–52, and the translation of the *Life of Willibald* in Talbot, *Anglo-Saxon Missionaries*, 1981.
14 Ayerst and Fisher, *Records of Christianity*, 1977, II, p. 58.
15 For all the above see Boniface's letter (Tangl 51) to Pope Zacharias for the year 742; Talbot, *Anglo-Saxon Missionaries*, 1981, p. 100.
16 Talbot, *Anglo-Saxon Missionaries*, 1981, p. 134.
17 Ibid., p. 118.
18 McKitterick, 'England and the Continent', 1995.
19 McKitterick, *Uses of Literacy in Early Medieval Europe*, 1990, p. 25.

Chapter 6 – Alcuin of York

An important recent source is *Alcuin of York* (2003), edited by L. A. J. R. Howen and A. A. MacDonald. In this chapter I have used the selected edition of Alcuin's letters in translation from the Latin by Stephen Allott in *Alcuin of York: His Life and Letters* (1987). This also contains excerpts from his 'The Bishops, Kings and Saints of York', of which the Oxford Medieval Texts published a full edition by Peter Godman in 1982. For the legends of St Oswald on the Continent, the standard reference is *Oswald: Northumbrian King to European Saint* (1995), edited by Clare Stancliffe and Eric Cambridge, notably the paper by Annemiek Jansen, 'The Development of the St Oswald Legends on the Continent'. D. A. Bullough's entry 'Alcuin' in the *New Oxford Dictionary of National Biography* (2004) is recommended.

1 Allott, *Alcuin of York*, 1987, Letter 69, p. 85.
2 Ibid., Letter 160, p. 156.
3 Compare Bolton, *Alcuin and Beowulf*, 1979, and Bullough, 'What has Ingeld to do with Lindisfarne?', 1993.
4 Campbell, ed., *The Anglo-Saxons*, 1991, p. 106.
5 Allott, *Alcuin of York*, 1987, p. 187.
6 Cited in Stancliffe and Cambridge, eds, *Oswald*, 1995, p. 161.
7 Elton, *The English*, 1994, p. 17.
8 Talbot, *Anglo-Saxon Missionaries*, 1981, pp. 189 and 190.
9 Ibid., p. 199.
10 Orchard, 'Latin and the Vernacular Languages', 2003, pp. 212–13.
11 Talbot, *Anglo-Saxon Missionaries*, 1981, p. 229.
12 Ibid., pp. 156–7.
13 Levison, *England and the Continent*, 1946, p. 98.
14 Abels, *Alfred the Great*, 1998, p. 73.
15 Campbell, ed., *The Anglo-Saxons*, 1991, p. 106.
16 Stafford, *Queens, Concubines and Dowagers*, 1983, p. 86.
17 Lapidge, 'Asser's Reading', 2003, p. 39.
18 Garrison, 'Social World of Alcuin', 1998, pp. 78–9.
19 Marenbon, *From the Circle of Alcuin to the School of Auxerre*, 1981.
20 Allott, *Alcuin of York*, 1987, pp. 8 and 40.
21 Garrison, 'Alcuin', in Lapidge and others, eds, *Blackwell Encyclopaedia of Anglo-Saxon England*, 1999.
22 Ullmann, *Short History of the Papacy*, 1972, p. 1981.
23 Cochrane, *Adelard of Bath*, 1994, p. 5.
24 Bullough, 'Alcuin', *ODNB*, 2004.
25 Garrison, 'Alcuin', in Lapidge and others, eds, *Blackwell Encyclopaedia of Anglo-Saxon England*, 1999, p. 24.
26 Robertson, *History of German Literature*, 1962, p. 18.

Chapter 7 – Viking Raiders, Danelaw, 'Kings' of York

The Danelaw (1992) by Cyril Hart and *Vikings and the Danelaw: Select Papers from the Thirteenth Viking Congress* (2001), edited by James Graham-Campbell and others, both carry fascinating essays on the subject. *Viking Empires* (2005) by Angelo Forte, Richard Oram and Frederik Pedersen, a survey of Scandinavian culture in general from the first century AD to the late thirteenth, appeared as this book was going to press. Of more interest from an Anglo-Saxon and British perspective is H. R. Loyn's *The Vikings in Britain* (revised 1994) and *Blood of the Vikings* (2000) by Julian Richards. David

Rollason's *Northumbria 500–1100* (2003) is the major contemporary survey of its subject and of special interest in its treatment of the 'kings' of York.

1   O Croínin, 'Writing', 2003, p. 170.
2   Keynes, 'The Power of the Written Word', 2003, p. 17.
3   Swanton, *The Anglo-Saxon Chronicle*, 1996, p. 55.
4   Richards, *Blood of the Vikings*, 2000, p. 78.
5   Ibid., p. 20.
6   Stafford, 'Kings, Kingships, and Kingdoms', 2003, p. 38.
7   Gillingham, 'Britain, Ireland and the South', 2003, p. 231.
8   Cited in Abels, *Alfred the Great*, 1998, p. 285.
9   Hunter Blair, *Introduction to Anglo-Saxon England*, 1956, p. 70.
10 *Anglo-Saxon Chronicle*, 'E' annal 870.
11 See Lawson, *Cnut*, 2004, pp. 164–6, for much of this paragraph.
12 Crawford, 'The Vikings', 2003, p. 57.
13 Blair, *Church in Anglo-Saxon Society*, 2005, p. 293.
14 Crawford, 'The Vikings', 2003, p. 61.
15 Blair, *Church in Anglo-Saxon Society*, 2005, p. 312.

Chapter 8 – The Wessex of Alfred the Great

There is a plethora of books to draw on. Of recent biographies, John Peddie's *Alfred: Warrior King* (1999) is admired for its handing of his military record; David Sturdy's *Alfred the Great* (1995) makes revealing comparative use of the actual texts of the *Anglo-Saxon Chronicle* relating to its subject. *Alfred the Great: War, Kingship and Culture in Anglo-Saxon England* (1988) by Richard P. Abels is a lucid account of the reign within its historical context. Alfred P. Smyth's *King Alfred the Great* (1995) is in danger of being dominated by his protracted argument that Asser's biography of the king was in fact the work of a forger. *Alfred the Great: Asser's Life of King Alfred and Other Contemporary Sources* (1983), edited and translated by Simon Keynes and Michael Lapidge, is on the other side of the debate. An important survey of Alfredian studies is provided by *Alfred the Great: Papers from the Eleventh-Centenary Conferences* (2003), edited by Timothy Reuter. Finally, of the many recent works of special interest, one would mention *The Defence of Wessex: The Burghal Hidage and Anglo-Saxon Fortifications* (1996), edited by David Hill and A. R. Rumble. A specialist study of particular interest is *Kings, Currency and Alliances: History and Coinage in Southern England in the Ninth Century* (1998), edited by Mark A. S. Blackburn and David N. Dumville.

1 Blackburn, 'Alfred's Coinage Reforms in Context', 2003, p. 205.
2 Cochrane, *Adelard of Bath*, 1994, p. 58.
3 Whitelock, ed., *English Historical Documents*: 1, p. 810.
4 Blackburn, 'Alfred's Coinage Reforms in Context', 2003, p. 207.
5 Foard, 'Field Offensive', p. 13.
6 *Bede's Ecclesiastical History*, ed. Colgrave and Mynors, 1969, p. 26, n.
7 Lapidge, 'Asser's Reading', 2003, p. 46.
8 Abels, *Alfred the Great*, 1998, p. 14.
9 Crawford, 'The Vikings', 2003, p. 56.
10 Wallace-Hadrill, 'The Franks and the English', 1950.
11 Keynes, 'The Power of the Written Word', 2003, p. 176.
12 Wormald, *Making of English Law*, 1999, p. 450.
13 Keynes, 'The Power of the Written Word', 2003, p. 175.
14 Kelly, 'Literacy in Anglo-Saxon Lay Society', 1990, p. 59.
15 O Croínin, 'Writing', 2003, p. 286.
16 Smyth, *King Alfred the Great*, 1995, p. 398.
17 See Abels, *Alfred the Great*, 1998, pp. 261, 268.
18 Sturdy, *Alfred the Great*, 1995.
19 For these paragraphs on Alfred's 'writing office', see Keynes, 'The Power of the Written Word', 2003, pp. 184–5, 193–5.
20 Bately, 'The Alfredian Canon Revisited', 2003, pp. 109–11.
21 Godden, 'The Player King', 2003.
22 Campbell, 'Placing King Alfred', 2003, p. 6.
23 Keynes, 'The Power of the Written Word', 2003, p. 192.
24 Keene, 'Alfred and London', 2003.
25 Based on Hill, 'The Origins of Alfred's Urban Policies', 2003, pp. 219–33.
26 Abels, *Alfred the Great*, 1998, pp. 203–4, 206.
27 Based on Hill, 'The Origins of Alfred's Urban Policies', 2003, pp. 219–33.
28 Sturdy, *Alfred the Great*, 1995, p. 152.
29 Mason, *The House of Godwine*, 2004, p. 12.
30 Cited in Lawson, *Cnut*, 2004, p. 133.
31 Gifford and Gifford, 'Alfred's New Longships', 2003, pp. 281–9.
32 Campbell, ed. and trans., *Chronicon Æthelweardi*, 1962, p. 51.
33 Keynes, 'The Power of the Written Word', 2003, p. 197.

Chapter 9 – Literature, Learning, Language and Law in Anglo-Saxon England

Essential here is Rosamond McKitterick's *The Uses of Literacy in Medieval Europe* (1990), with such chapters as 'Royal Government and the Written Word' by Simon Keynes and 'Literacy in Anglo-Saxon Lay Society' by Susan Kelly. *The Cambridge Companion to Old English Literature* (1991) by Malcolm Godden and Michael Lapidge is invaluable, while E. Temple's *Anglo-Saxon Manuscripts* (1976) is still basic. Patrick Wormald's *The Making of English Law* (1999) is a magisterial survey. For the fuller background, the best is probably *Learning and Literature in Anglo-Saxon England* (1985), edited by Michael Lapidge and Helmut Gneuss. As an introduction to the language itself, nothing can approach Bruce Mitchell's *An Invitation to Old English and Anglo-Saxon England* (1995). Michael Swanton's *Anglo-Saxon Prose* (revised 1993) and S. A. J. Bradley's *Anglo-Saxon Poetry* (1982) are comprehensive anthologies and the finest translation of *Beowulf* is the one by Nobel Laureate Seamus Heaney (1999).

1 O Croínin, 'Writing', 2003, p. 183.
2 Bede, *Ecclesiastical History*, IV, 24.
3 Crossley-Holland, *The Exeter Book Riddles*, 1980.
4 Elton, *The English*, 1994, p. 36.
5 Hunter Blair, *Introduction to Anglo-Saxon England*, 1956, p. 352–5.
6 Howlett, 'The Anglo-Saxon Chronicle and the Idea of Rome', 2003, p. 3.
7 Kabir, *Paradise, Death and Doomsday*, 2001, p. 183.
8 Cited by Lapidge, 'Asser's Reading', 2003, p. 41.
9 D. P. Simpson, *Cassell's New Latin–English, English–Latin Dictionary*, revised 1979.
10 Kelly, 'Literacy in Anglo-Saxon Lay Society', 1990, p. 58.
11 Ibid., p. 39.
12 Lapidge, '*Beowulf*, Aldhelm, the *Liber Monstrorum* and Wessex', 1982.
13 Wormald, *Making of English Law*, 1999, p. 451.
14 For this paragraph see ibid., pp. 462–4.
15 Keynes, 'Royal Government and the Written Word', 1990, pp. 228–9.
16 Loyn, *The Governance of Anglo-Saxon England*, 1987, cited by Keynes, 'Royal Government and the Written Word', 1990, p. 229.
17 Gillingham, 'Britain, Ireland and the South', 2003, p. 229.

Chapter 10 – The Hegemony of Wessex

Given the scant nature of the materials relating to England's tenth-century kings, 'biography' in the usual sense of the word is difficult. Recent works focusing on specific reigns are Higham and Hill's *Edward the Elder, 899–924* (2001) and Paul Hill on *The Age of Æthelstan* (2004), which gives much attention to the antecedents of the reign.

On religious life John Blair's *The Church in Anglo-Saxon Society* (2005) is essential if somewhat specialized reading here, as throughout the period, and John Godfrey's *The Church in Anglo-Saxon England* (1962) is a valuable general survey. For a general survey of the period Pauline Stafford's *Unification and Conquest:A Political and Social History of England in the Tenth and Eleventh Centuries* (1989) is recommended.

1 Wormald, *Making of English Law*, 1999, pp. 170–71.
2 Campbell, 'Placing King Alfred', 2003, p. 4.
3 *Anglo-Saxon Chronicle*, 'C'.
4 Abels, *Alfred the Great*, 1998, p. 218.
5 Gillingham, 'Britain, Ireland and the South', 2003, p. 215.
6 Brooke, *The Saxon and Norman Kings*, 1963, p. 120.
7 Campbell, ed,, *The Anglo Saxons*, 1991, p. 11.
8 *Annals of Ulster*, cited in Stafford, *Unification and Conquest*, 1989, p. 35.
9 Hare, 'Abbot Leofsige of Mettlach', 2004.
10 For much of this paragraph see Hill, *The Age of Æthelstan*, 2004, pp. 32, 35, 105.
11 Stafford, *Queens, Concubines and Dowagers*, 1983, p. 21.
12 For this paragraph see Campbell, 'The United Kingdom of England', 1995, pp. 39, 41.
13 Keynes, 'Royal Government and the Written Word', 1990, p. 243.
14 Wormald, *Making of English Law*, 1999, p. 126.
15 Keynes, 'Royal Government and the Written Word', 1990, pp. 235, 248–9.
16 Hill, *The Age of Æthelstan*, 2004, p. 121.
17 Ibid., p. 25.
18 Blackburn, 'Mints, Burhs and the Grately Code', 1996, p. 160.
19 Davis, *From Alfred the Great to Stephen*, 1991, p. 57.
20 Campbell, 'The United Kingdom of England', 1995, p. 38.
21 Elton, The English, 1994, pp. 47–8.
22 Stafford, *Queens, Concubines and Dowagers*, 1983, p. 133.

Chapter 11 – Danish Invasions and Kings

There are a number of important recent books here, including the study by M. K. Lawson, revised as *Cnut: England's Viking King* (2004), an exhaustive view of original sources by the leading authority in the field; Frank Barlow's *The Godwins:The Rise and Fall of a Noble Dynasty* (2003);

and Emma Mason's *The House of Godwine* (2004). Pauline Stafford's *Queen Emma and Queen Edith* (1997) is highly recommended, as is her 'The Reign of Æthelred II: A Study in the Limitations on Royal Policy and Action' (1978). Simon Keynes's somewhat specialist *The Diplomas of King Æthelred 'The Unready': 978–1016* (1980) opens up such documents as quarries for historical evidence. For a glimpse of the dramatic and sometimes sordid reality behind the politics, see Richard Fletcher's *Bloodfeud* (2003).

1 Campbell, *Anglo-Saxon State*, 2000, p. 160.
2 Ibid., p. 166.
3 Ibid., pp. 167–8.
4 For above see Swanton, *The Anglo-Saxon Chronicle*, 1996, p. 135, note.
5 Stafford, *Queen Emma and Queen Edith*, 1997, p. 224.
6 Based on Swanton, *The Anglo-Saxon Chronicle*, 1996, p. 135 ('E', sub anno 1010).
7 Attwater, *Penguin Dictionary of Saints*, 1979, p. 41.
8 Fletcher, *Bloodfeud*, 2003, p. 74.
9 Campbell, *Anglo-Saxon State*, 2000, p. 181.
10 Swanton, *The Anglo-Saxon Chronicle*, 1996, p. 144, notes.
11 Fletcher, *Bloodfeud*, 2003, p. 1.
12 Lawson, *Cnut*, 2004, p. 134.
13 Stafford, *Queen Emma and Queen Edith*, 1997, p. 225.
14 Ibid., pp. 226–7.
15 Campbell, *Anglo-Saxon State*, 2000, p. 8.
16 Gillingham, 'Britain, Ireland and the South', 2003, p. 215.
17 Stafford, *Queen Emma and Queen Edith*, 1997, p. 247.
18 Damico, *Beowulf's Wealtheow and the Valkyrie Tradition*, 1984.
19 Stafford, *Queens, Concubines and Dowagers*, 1983, p. 29.

Chapter 12 – Edward the Confessor, the Conquest and the Aftermath

Frank Barlow's *Edward the Confessor* (1970) is still the classic work on the king and the last years of Anglo–Saxon England. With *The Battle of Hastings, 1066* (2002), M. K. Lawson produced the definitive work on the battle. Mason's and Barlow's books on the Godwin(e)s (see previous chapter) are of course important in this chapter too. Ian Walker's *Harold: The Last Anglo-Saxon King* (1997) is a major and exhaustive study, while Ann Williams's *The English and the Norman Conquest* (1995) is basic in its field. In the post-Conquest age 'the Laws of Edward the

Confessor' were of recurrent interest, and behind this and all studies of Anglo-Saxon law looms Patrick Wormald's monumental and sometimes controversial *The Making of English Law: King Alfred to the Twelfth Century*, I: *Legislation and its Limits* (1999). Pauline Stafford's *Queen Emma and Queen Edith* (1997) gives body to the shadowy figure of Edith and her entourage.

1 Robin Fleming, 'Harold II', *ODNB*, 2004.
2 Gillingham, 'Britain, Ireland and the South', 2003, pp. 206–7.
3 Campbell, 'The United Kingdom of England', 1995, p. 36.
4 Stafford, *Queens, Concubines and Dowagers*, 1983, pp. 82 and 76.
5 Lawson, *Battle of Hastings*, 2002, p. 136.
6 Barlow, *The Godwins*, 2003, p. 67.
7 Ibid., p. 75.
8 Stafford, *Queens, Concubines and Dowagers*, 1983, pp. 97, 134,
9 Lawson, *Battle of Hastings*, 2002, p. 36.
10 Barlow, *The Godwins*, 2003, p. 98.
11 Ibid., p. 99.
12 Lawson, *Battle of Hastings*, 2002, p. 45.
13 Mason, *The House of Godwine*, 2004, p. 161.
14 See Lawson, *Battle of Hastings*, 2002, p. 160.
15 Walker, *Harold: The Last Anglo-Saxon King*, pp. 188–9.
16 Mason, *The House of Godwine*, 2004, p. 194.
17 Barlow, *The Godwins*, 2003, pp. 251–2.
18 Mason, *The House of Godwine*, 2004, p. xi.
19 Davis, *From Alfred the Great to Stephen*, 1991, p. 56.
20 Gillingham, 'Britain, Ireland and the South', 2003, p. 215.
21 Prescott, Andrew, *The Benedictional of St Æthelwold*, 2002.
22 Davis, *From Alfred the Great to Stephen*, 1991, p. 62.
23 Campbell, 'The United Kingdom of England', 1995, p. 37.

SELECT BIBLIOGRAPHY

In a 'Brief History' an exhaustive bibliography of the subject is neither possible, given the constraints of space, nor appropriate. What follows aims to give an idea of the range of works available as well as details of the works I have consulted.

Selected Primary Sources

The starting point must be the two volumes of *English Historical Documents*: i: *c. 500–1042*, ed. Dorothy Whitelock, 2nd edn, Eyre & Spottiswoode, 1979, and, covering the last generation of Anglo-Saxon England, ii: *1042–1189*, ed. D. C. Douglas and G. W. Greenaway, 2nd edn, Eyre & Spottiswoode, 1981. Together they constitute the most extensive selection available of documents of every kind, all in translation.

There are various editions of Bede's *Ecclesiastical History of the English People*. The English language edition by Leo Sherley-Price, Penguin Classics, 1955, has been reissued in a revised edition by R. E. Latham and D. H. Farmer (1990). For the Latin text, annotated and with an English translation on the facing page, the standard edition is by Bertram Colgrave and R. A. B. Mynors, OUP, 1969.

In the case of the *Anglo-Saxon Chronicle*, probably the most accessible is the edition by G. N. Garmonsway, Everyman's Library, 1953, revised 1972. The most recent annotated edition is that translated and edited by Michael Swanton, Routledge, 1996, revised 2000.

The best recent translation of Asser's 'Life of King Alfred' was published by Simon Keynes and Michael Lapidge in *Alfred the Great: Asser's 'Life of King Alfred' and Other Contemporary Sources*, Penguin Classics, 1983. Other contemporary biographies include the text and translation of the life of Queen Emma, edited by Alistair Campbell as *The Encomium Emmae Reginae*, CUP, 1949, reprinted with a new introduction by Simon Keynes, CUP, 1998; and Frank Barlow's *Edward the Confessor*, Eyre & Spottiswood, 1970, 2nd edn OUP, 1992. The *Life of St Wilfrid* by Eddius Stephanus and other basic texts by Bede may be found in *The Age of Bede*, translated and edited by J. F. Webb and D. H. Farmer, Penguin Classics, 1965, revised 1983. For the Anglo-Saxon missions in Germany, a wide selection of Boniface's letters as well as biographies of St Willibald and St Lioba and others appear in C. H. Talbot's *The Anglo-Saxon Missionaries in Germany*, Sheed and Ward, 1954, revised 1981. The standard edition of the Boniface letters in English translation is by Ephraim Emerton in *The Letters of St Boniface*, Columbia UP, 1940, reprinted with introduction by Thomas F. X. Noble, 2000). For Alcuin the most accessible text is probably the selection from the letters and 'The Bishops, Kings and Saints of York' in Stephen Allott's *Alcuin of York: His Life and Letters*, William Sessions, 1974, reprinted 1987.

There can be a temptation to regard 1066 as a cut-off point – before, everything was Anglo-Saxon; after, everything was Norman. Of course, we know this is not so. Domesday Book, the culminating achievement of Anglo-Saxon government, was produced twenty years after the defeat. The great visual primary source, the Bayeux Tapestry, is superbly reproduced in full and with an authoritative commentary in David M. Wilson's *The Bayeux Tapestry*, Thames & Hudson, 1985, revised 2004, while the Domesday book has been the subject of a magisterial facsimile edition.

Then there is what one might almost call a school of Anglo-Norman historiography. It is led by four writers, all writing in Latin, who it has been said 'brought to the study of the past a professionalism hardly equalled in England since the days of . . . Bede.' John of Worcester, whose chronicle was formerly attributed as by Florence of Worcester, and who may have been born as early as 1095 and died no later than 1143, based his work on various sources, including versions of the *Anglo-Saxon Chronicle*, and made numerous, sometimes extensive, additions to it. In addition we owe to him bishop lists for all the Anglo-Saxon sees, which are of great importance to the historians of the English church, and royal genealogies for the various kingdoms. He was probably at his most productive between about 1120 and 1132/3 and born (a contemporary tells us) of English parents. He was a clear partisan of King Harold and proud of his Anglo-Saxon past. William of Malmesbury (*d. c.* 1143), son of a French father and an English mother, and who considered Hastings a fateful day for England, 'our sweet country', was also a considerable Latin stylist and scholar during what is

known as Europe's 'Twelfth-Century Renaissance' of classical learning.
He was also a notable historian in the modern sense, using administra-
tive documents as well as many narrative sources and boasting that his
Gesta Regum Anglorum ('The Doings [i.e. History] of the Kings of the
English') was the first Latin history of the English since the days of Bede.
William also wrote the *Gesta Pontificum*, a history of the English church.
Henry of Huntingdon, the son of the archdeacon of Huntingdon and
an English mother, began his *Historia Anglorum* ('History of the English')
at the suggestion of Alexander, bishop of Lincoln. By the standards of
the day Henry's book, in ten fairly short books and in straightforward
Latin, with a number of battle scenes in verse, was light reading. It was
certainly very popular. Bishop Alexander also commissioned the
Oxford-based Welsh clerk Geoffrey of Monmouth to write a book on
the prophesies of Merlin, which, with its diverting tales of King Arthur
and under the sober-sounding title *Historia Regum Britanniae* ('History
of the Kings of Britain'), was to become one of the most influential
works of fiction in the history of Europe and Hollywood. Orderic
Vitalis (1075–c. 1142), born near Shrewsbury, was the son of a French
priest by his English 'hearth companion'. He wrote a *Historia Ecclesiastica*
('History of the Church') in which features his description of the Battle
of Hastings. Despite its title, the *Historia Novarum in Anglia* ('A History
of the Recent Events in England') by Eadmer (c. 1060–c. 1128) is largely
an account of Archbishop Anselm of Canterbury's role in those events
and carries anecdotes about the recent past as they touched on his
subject. It seems that Eadmer, the son of a rich English family impov-
erished by the outcome of the battle, had spoken with veterans of
Hastings.

Wace (b. c. 1110), a native of Jersey, then part of the duchy of
Normandy, is known for his *Roman de Rou* ('The Story of Rollo', the
first duke of Normandy), and the *Roman de Brut*, an unfinished verse
history of Britain. Important French historians for the later period
include William of Poitiers, writing before 1077, whose *Gesta Guillelmi*
('The Deeds of William'[the Conqueror]) was a considerable work of
classical Latin, and William of Jumièges, author of the *Gesta
Normannorum Ducum* ('Deeds of the Dukes of the Normans'), written
about 1070.

Books and Articles

Anonymous, 'New Saxon Horse Burial in Suffolk', *British Archaeology*,
    L/5 (1999)
—, 'The Origin of a London Dock', *Medieval Life*, v, pp. 14–25

Abels, Richard P., *Lordship and Military Obligation in Anglo-Saxon England*, British Museum Publications, 1988

—, *Alfred the Great: War, Kingship and Culture in Anglo-Saxon England*, Longman, 1998

—, 'Alfred the Great, the *micel hæthen here* and the Viking Threat', in *Alfred the Great: Papers from the Eleventh-Centenary Conferences*, ed. Timothy Reuter, Ashgate, 2003

Adam, A. J., *A Conquest of England:The Coming of the Normans*, Hodder & Stoughton, 1965

Ahrens, C., ed., *Sachsen und Angelsachsen*, exh. cat., Helms-Museum, Hamburg, Nov. 1978–Feb. 1979

Alexander, Michael, *Old English Riddles from the Exeter Book*, Anvil Press, 1980

Allott, Stephen, *Alcuin of York: His Life and Letters*, William Sessions, 1974, reprinted 1987

Attwater, Donald, *The Penguin Dictionary of Saints*, Penguin Books, 1979

Audouy, M., 'Excavations at the Church of All Saints, Brixworth, Northamptonshire, 1981–2', *Journal of the British Archaeological Association*, cxxxvii, pp. 1–44

Ayerst, David, and A. S. T. Fisher, *Records of Christianity*, ii, Basil Blackwell, 1977

Backhouse, Janet, *The Sherborne Missal*, British Library, 1999

Backhouse, Janet, D. H. Turner and Leslie Webster, eds, *The Golden Age of Anglo-Saxon Art, 966–1066*, exh. cat., British Museum, London, 1984 [published on the 1000th anniversary of St Æthelwold's death]

Barbaro, Alessandro, *Charlemagne: Father of a Continent*, U. California Press, 2004

Barlow, Frank, *Edward the Confessor*, Eyre & Spottiswoode, 1970

—, *The Godwins:The Rise and Fall of a Noble Dynasty*, Longman, 2003

Bassett, S. R., ed., *The Origins of the Anglo-Saxon Kingdoms*, Leicester UP, 1989

Bately, Janet, 'The Alfredian Canon Revisited: One Hundred Years on', in *Alfred the Great: Papers from the Eleventh-Centenary Conferences*, ed. Timothy Reuter, Ashgate, 2003, pp. 107–20

Bates, David, *William the Conqueror*, George Phillip, 1989

Battles, Paul, ' *Genesis A* and the Anglo-Saxon "Migration Myth" ', *Anglo-Saxon England*, 29, 2000, pp. 43–66

Beckett, Katharine Scarfe, *Anglo-Saxon Perceptions of the Islamic World*, CUP, 2004

Bede the Venerable, *Bede's Ecclesiastical History of the English People*, ed. Bertram Colgrave and R. A. B. Mynors, OUP, 1979

Beech, George, *Was the Bayeux Tapestry Made in France? The Case for St. Florent of Saumur*, Palgrave Macmillan, 2005

Blackburn, Mark, 'Mints, Burhs and the Grately Code', in *The Defence of Wessex: The Burghal Hidage and Anglo-Saxon Fortifications*, ed. David Hill and A. R. Rumble, Manchester UP, 1996

—, 'Alfred's Coinage Reforms in Context', in *Alfred the Great: Papers from the Eleventh-Centenary Conferences*, ed. Timothy Reuter, Ashgate, 2003, pp. 199–218

Blackburn, Mark A. S., and David N. Dumville, eds, *Kings, Currency and Alliances: History and Coinage in Southern England in the Ninth Century*, Boydell Press, 1998

Blair, John, *Anglo-Saxon Oxfordshire*, Sutton Publishing, 1994

—, *The Church in Anglo-Saxon Society*, OUP, 2005

Bolton, Whitney French, *Alcuin and Beowulf: An Eighth-century View*, Rutgers UP, 1979

Bonner, Gerald, David Rollason and Clare Stanclffe, eds, *St Cuthbert, his Cult and his Community to AD 1200*, Boydell Press, 1989

Bouet, Pierre, Brian Levy and François Neveux, *The Bayeux Tapestry: Embroidering the Facts of History*, Presses Universitaires de Caen, 2004

Bradley, S. A. J., *Anglo-Saxon Poetry*, Everyman's Library, 1982, reprinted 1995

Brooke, Christopher, *The Saxon and Norman Kings*, Batsford, 1963, 3rd edn, Blackwell 2001

Brooks, Nicholas, 'The Administrative Background', in *The Defence of Wessex: The Burghal Hidage and Anglo-Saxon Fortifications*, ed. David Hill and A. R. Rumble, Manchester UP, 1996

—, 'Alfredian Government: The West Saxon Inheritance', in *Alfred the Great: Papers from the Eleventh-Centenary Conferences*, ed. Timothy Reuter, Ashgate, 2003, pp. 153–74

—, *Church, State and Access to Resources in Early Anglo-Saxon England*, Brixworth Lectures, 2nd series, no. 2, Friends of All Saints' Church, Brixworth, 2003

Brooks, Nicholas, and Catherine Cubitt, eds, *St Oswald of Worcester: Life and Influence*, Leicester UP, 1996

Brown, Michelle P., *Anglo-Saxon Manuscripts*, British Library, 1991

—, Introduction, *The British Library Diary 2004: The Lindisfarne Gospels*, Frances Lincoln Publishers, 2003

Brown, Michelle P., and Carol A. Farr, eds, *Mercia: An Anglo-Saxon Kingdom in Europe*, Leicester UP, 2001

Bullough, D. A., 'What has Ingeld to do with Lindisfarne?', *Anglo-Saxon England*, 22, 1993, pp. 93–125

Cameron, A., and others, eds, *Dictionary of Old English* (Toronto, 1986–)
Campbell, A., ed. and trans., *Chronicon Æthelweardi, or The Chronicle of Æthelweard*, Thomas Nelson, 1962
Campbell, James, general ed., *The Anglo-Saxons*, Penguin, 1991
—, 'The Late Anglo-Saxon State: A Maximum View', *Proceedings of the British Academy*, LXXXVII (1994)
—, 'The United Kingdom of England: The Anglo-Saxon Achievement', in *Uniting the Kingdom? The Making of British History*, ed. Alexander Grant and Keith J. Stringer, Routledge, 1995
—, *The Anglo-Saxon State*, Hambledon & London, 2000
—, 'Placing King Alfred', in *Alfred the Great: Papers from the Eleventh-Centenary Conferences*, ed. Timothy Reuter, Ashgate, 2003, pp. 3–26
Cannon, Christopher, *The Making of Chaucer's English*, CUP, 2004
Chambers, R.W., *Beowulf: An Introduction to the Study of the Poem*, CUP, 1931, 3/1967
Chaney, William A., *The Cult of Kingship in Anglo-Saxon England*, Manchester UP, 1970
Charles-Edwards, T. M., 'Wales and Mercia, 613–918', in *Mercia: An Anglo-Saxon Kingdom in Europe*, ed. Michelle P. Brown and Carol A. Farr, Leicester UP, 2001
Charles-Edwards, Thomas, ed., *After Rome*, Short Oxford History of the British Isles, OUP, 2003
Clayton, Mary, *The Cult of the Virgin Mary in Anglo-Saxon England*, CUP, 1990
Cochrane, Louise, *Adelard of Bath: The first English Scientist*, British Museum Press, 1994
Cooper, Nicholas J., *The Archaeology of Rutland Water*, Leicester Archaeology Monographs, 6, 2000
Cowie, Robert, 'Mercian London', in *Mercia: An Anglo-Saxon Kingdom in Europe*, ed. Michelle P. Brown and Carol A. Farr, Leicester UP, 2001
Crawford, Barbara, 'The Vikings', in *From the Vikings to the Normans*, Short Oxford History of the British Isles, ed. Wendy Davies, OUP, 2003, pp. 41–65
Crossley-Holland, Kevin, *The Exeter Book Riddles*, Penguin, 1980, 2/1993
Damico, Helen, *Beowulf's Wealtheow and the Valkyrie Tradition*, U. Wisconsin Press, 1984
Davies, Wendy, ed., *From the Vikings to the Normans*, Short Oxford History of the British Isles, OUP, 2003
Davis, R. H. C., 'The Norman Conquest', *History*, LI, 1966
—, *From Alfred the Great to Stephen*, Hambledon & London, 1991

Dillon, Myles, and Nora K. Chadwick, *The Celtic Realms*, Sphere Books, 1973

Dolley, R. H. M., *Anglo-Saxon Coins: Studies Presented to F. M. Stenton*, Methuen, 1961

Dornier, Ann, ed., *Mercian Studies*, Leicester UP, 1977

Duggan, Anne J. (ed.), *Kings and Kingship in Medieval Europe*, King's College London Centre for Late Antique and Medieval Studies, 1993.

Dumville, David N., 'The Anglian Collection of Royal Genealogies and Regnal Lists', *Anglo-Saxon England*, 5, 1976, pp. 23–50

—, *Wessex and England from Alfred to Edgar*, Boydell Press, 1992

—, *Britons and Anglo-Saxons in the Early Middle Ages*, Ashgate, 1993

Eaton, Tim, *Plundering the Past: Roman Stonework in Medieval Britain*, Tempus Publishing, 2000

Elton, Geoffrey, *The English*, Blackwell, 1994

Farmer, D. H., ed., *The Oxford Dictionary of Saints*, OUP, 1978

Farrel, R. T., ed., *The Vikings*, Phillimore, 1982

Featherstone, Peter, 'The Tribal Hidage and the Ealdormen of Mercia', in *Mercia: An Anglo-Saxon Kingdom in Europe*, ed. Michelle P. Brown and Carol A. Farr, Leicester UP, 2001

Fell, Christine, *Women in Anglo-Saxon England and the Impact of 1066*, British Museum Publications, 1984

Fisher, D. J. V., *The Anglo-Saxon Age, 400–1042*, Longman, 1973

Fleming, Robert, 'Lords and Labour', in *From the Vikings to the Normans*, Short Oxford History of the British Isles, ed. Wendy Davies, OUP, 2003, pp. 107–32

Fletcher, Richard, *Bloodfeud: Murder and Revenge in Anglo-Saxon England*, Penguin Books, 2003

Foard, Glenn, 'Field Offensive', *British Archaeology*, 79 (November 2004)

Foot, S. ' "The making of angelcynn" English identity before the Norman Conquest', in *Transactions of the Royal Historical Society*, sixth series, 1996, pp. 25–47.

Forte, Angelo, Richard Oram and Frederik Pedersen, *Viking Empires*, CUP, 2005

Foys, Martin K., *The Bayeux Tapestry Digital Edition*, CD-ROM, Scholarly Digital Editions, 2002

Ganz, David, 'Book Production in the Carolingian Empire and the Spread of Caroline Minuscule', in *The New Cambridge Medieval History*, II: *c. 700– c. 900*, ed. Rosamond McKitterick, CUP, 1995

Garrison, Mary, 'The Social World of Alcuin: Nicknames at York and at the Court of Charlemagne', in *Alcuin of York: Scholar at the Carolingian Court*, Germania Latina III, ed. L. A. J. R. Houwen and A. A. MacDonald, Egbert Forsten, 1998

Gifford, Edwin, and Joyce Gifford, 'Alfred's New Longships', in *Alfred the Great: Papers from the Eleventh-Centenary Conferences*, ed. Timothy Reuter, Ashgate, 2003, pp. 281–92

Gillingham, John, 'Britain, Ireland and the South', in *From the Vikings to the Normans*, Short Oxford History of the British Isles, ed. Wendy Davies, OUP, 2003, pp. 203–32

Godden, Malcolm, 'The Player King: Identification and Self Presentation in Alfred's Writings', in *Alfred the Great: Papers from the Eleventh-Centenary Conferences*, ed. Timothy Reuter, Ashgate, 2003, pp. 137–49

Godden, Malcolm, and Michael Lapidge, *The Cambridge Companion to Old English Literature*, Cambridge, 1991

Godfrey, John, *The Church in Anglo-Saxon England*, CUP, 1962

Graham-Campbell, James, Richard Hall, Judith Jesch and David N. Parsons, eds, *Vikings and the Danelaw: Select Papers from the Thirteenth Viking Congress*, Oxbow, 2001

Gransden, Antonia, *Historical Writing in England*, I: *c. 550–c. 1307*, Routledge, 1974

Grant, Alexander, and Keith J. Stringer, eds, *Uniting the Kingdom? The Making of British History*, Routledge, 1995

Grant, Paula, *Aldfrith's Beowulf*, Felinfach, 1995

Guara, Scott, and David W. Parker, ed. and trans., *Anglo-Saxon Conversations: The Colloquies of Ælfric*, Boydell Press, 1997

Hadley, D. M., 'In Search of the Vikings', in *Vikings and the Danelaw: Select Papers from the Thirteenth Viking Congress*, ed. J. Graham-Campbell and others, Oxbow, 2001

Hamerow, H., *Excavations at Mucking*, II: *The Anglo-Saxon Settlement*, English Heritage Report, 21, 1993

Hare, Michael, *The Two Anglo-Saxon Minsters of Gloucester: The Deerhurst Lecture for 1992*, Friends of Deerhurst Church, 1992

—, 'Abbot Leofsige of Mettlach: An English Monk in Flanders . . .', *Anglo-Saxon England*, 33, 2004

Hart, Cyril, *The Danelaw*, Hambledon & London, 1992

Hastings, Adrian, *The Construction of Nationhood: Ethnicity, Religion and Nationalism*, CUP, 1997

Hawkes, Jane, and Susan Mills, eds, *Northumbria's Golden Age*, Sutton Publishing, 1999

Haywood, John, *Dark Age Naval Power*, Anglo-Saxon Books, 1991, revised 1999

Heaney, Seamus, trans., *Beowulf*, Faber and Faber, 1999

Heather, Peter, *The Fall of the Roman Empire:A New History*, Macmillan, 2005

Higham, N. J., *The Death of Anglo-Saxon England*, Sutton Publishing, 1997

—, 'Dynasty and Cult: The Utility of Christian Mission to Northumbrian Kings between 642 and 654', in *Northumbria's Golden Age*, ed. Jane Hawkes and Susan Mills, Tempus Publishing, 1999, pp. 95–104

Higham, N. J., and D. H. Hill, *Edward the Elder, 899–924*, Routledge, 2001

Hill, David, *Ethelred the Unready: Papers from the Millenary Conference*, British Archaeological Reports, British Series, 59, 1978

—, *An Atlas of Anglo-Saxon England*, Basil Blackwell, 1981

—, 'Offa's Dyke, Pattern and Purpose', *Antiquaries Journal*, lxxx, 2000, pp. 195–206

—, 'The Origins of Alfred's Urban Policies', in *Alfred the Great: Papers from the Eleventh-Centenary Conferences*, ed. Timothy Reuter, Ashgate, 2003, pp. 219–34

Hill, David, and A. R. Rumble, eds, *The Defence of Wessex:The Burghal Hidage and Anglo-Saxon Fortifications*, Manchester UP, 1996

Hill, David, and Margaret Worthington, *A History and Guide to Offa's Dyke*, Tempus Publishing, 2003

Hill, Paul, *The Age of Æthelstan*, Tempus Publishing, 2004

Hines, John, 'Society, Community, and Identity', in *After Rome*, Short Oxford History of the British Isles, ed. Thomas Charles-Edwards, OUP, 2003, pp. 61–102.

Hodges, R., *The Anglo-Saxon Achievement:Archaeology and the Beginnings of English Society*, Duckworth, 1989

Hodgkin, R. H., *A History of the Anglo-Saxons*, 2 vols, OUP, 1935–9

Hooke, D., *The Landscape of Anglo-Saxon England*, Leicester UP, 1998

Houwen, L. A. J. R. and A. A. MacDonald, eds, *Alcuin of York: Scholar at the Carolingian Court*, Germania Latina III, Egbert Forsten, 1998

Howe, N., *Migration and Mythmaking in Anglo-Saxon England*, New Haven, CT, 1989

Howlett, David, 'The Anglo-Saxon Chronicle and the Idea of Rome in Alfredian Literature', in *Alfred the Great: Papers from the Eleventh-Centenary Conferences*, ed. Timothy Reuter, Ashgate, 2003

Hunter Blair, Peter, *An Introduction to Anglo-Saxon England*, CUP, 1956, 2/1978, 3/2004 [with introduction by Simon Keynes]

Imhof, Michael, and Gregor K. Stasch, *Bonifatius: vom Angelsächsichen Missionar zum Apostel der Deutschen*, Petersberg, 2004

Irvine, Susan, 'The Anglo-Saxon Chronicle and the idea of Rome in

Alfredian Literature', in *Alfred the Great: Papers from the Eleventh-Centenary Conferences*, ed. Timothy Reuter, Ashgate, 2003, pp. 63–77

Jansen, Annemiek, 'The Development of the St Oswald Legends on the Continent', in *Oswald: Northumbrian King to European Saint*, ed. Clare Stancliffe and Eric Cambridge, Paul Watkins, 1995, pp. 230–40.

John, Eric, *Orbis Britanniae and Other Studies*, Leicester UP, 1966

—, 'The Point of Woden', *Anglo-Saxon Studies in Archaeology and History*, 5, 1992

—, *Reassessing Anglo-Saxon England*, Manchester UP, 1996

Kabir, Ananya Jahanara, *Paradise, Death and Doomsday in Anglo-Saxon Literature*, CUP, 2001

Karkov, C., *Authority and the Book: The Ruler Portraits of Anglo-Saxon England*, Boydell Press, 2004

Keene, Derek, 'Alfred and London', in *Alfred the Great: Papers from the Eleventh-Centenary Conferences*, ed. Timothy Reuter, Ashgate, 2003, pp. 235–50

Keeton, George W., *The Norman Conquest and the Common Law*, Ernest Benn, 1966

Kelly, Susan, 'Literacy in Anglo-Saxon Lay Society', in *The Uses of Literacy in Early Medieval Europe*, ed. Rosamond McKitterick, CUP, 1990

Kendrick, T. D., *Anglo-Saxon Art to AD 900*, Methuen, 1938

Keynes, Simon, *The Diplomas of King Æthelred 'the Unready', 978–1016*, CUP, 1980

—, 'Royal Government and the Written Word', in *The Uses of Literacy in Early Medieval Europe*, ed. Rosamond McKitterick, CUP, 1990

—, *The Councils of Clofesho*, Brixworth Lecture 1993, U. Leicester Vaughan Papers, no. 38, 1994

—, 'Anglo Saxon England, 700–900', in *The New Cambridge Medieval History*, II: *c. 700–c. 900*, ed. Rosamond McKitterick, CUP, 1995

—, 'Mercia and Wessex in the Ninth Century', in *Mercia: An Anglo-Saxon Kingdom in Europe*, ed. Michelle P. Brown and Carol A. Farr, Leicester UP, 2001, pp. 310–28

—, 'The Power of the Written Word: Alfredian England, 891–899', in *Alfred the Great: Papers from the Eleventh-Centenary Conferences*, ed. Timothy Reuter, Ashgate, 2003, pp. 175–98

Keynes, Simon, and Michael Lapidge, eds and trans., *Alfred the Great: Asser's Life of King Alfred and Other Contemporary Sources*, Penguin Classics, 1983

Kirby, D. P., *The Earliest English Kings*, Routledge, 1991, revised 2000

Laistner, M. L. W., *Thoughts and Letters in Western Europe: AD 500 to 900*, Methuen, 1931

Lang, James, 'The Imagery of the Franks Casket: Another Approach', in *Northumbria's Golden Age*, ed. Jane Hawkes and Susan Mills, Tempus Publishing, 1999, pp. 247–55

Lapidge, Michael, '*Beowulf*, Aldhelm, the *Liber Monstrorum* and Wessex', *Studi Medievali*, 3rd series, no. 23, 1982, pp. 151–92; reprinted in *Anglo-Latin Literature, 600–899*, Hambledon & London, 1996

—, 'Asser's Reading', in *Alfred the Great: Papers from the Eleventh-Centenary Conferences*, ed. Timothy Reuter, Ashgate, 2003, pp. 27–48

Lapidge, Michael, John Blair, Simon Keynes and Donald Scragg, eds, *The Blackwell Encyclopaedia of Anglo-Saxon England*, Blackwell, 1999

Lapidge, Michael, and Helmut Gneuss, *Learning and Literature in Anglo-Saxon England: Studies Presented to Peter Clemoes*, CUP, 1985

Lawson, M. K., *Cnut:The Danes in England in the Early Eleventh Century*, Longman, 1993; revised as *Cnut. England's Viking King*, Tempus Publishing, 2004

—, *The Battle of Hastings, 1066*, Tempus Publishing, 2002

Leahy, Kevin, *Anglo-Saxon Crafts*, Tempus Publishing, 2004

Levison, Wilhelm, *England and the Continent in the Eighth Century*, Clarendon Press, 1946

Loyn, H. R., *Anglo-Saxon England and the Norman Conquest*, Longman, 1962

—, *The Vikings in Britain*, Blackwell, 1977, revised 1994

—, *The Governance of Anglo-Saxon England, 500–1087*, Edward Arnold, 1984

—, *The English Church, 940–1154*, Longman, 2000

McClure, J. and R. Collins, eds and trans., *Bede:The Ecclesiastical History of the English People*, OUP, 1994

McKiterrick, Rosamond, *Anglo-Saxon Missionaries in Germany: Personal Connections and Local Influences*, Brixworth Lecture 1990, U. Leicester Vaughan Papers, no. 36, 1991

—, 'England and the Continent', in *The New Cambridge Medieval History*, II: *c. 700–c. 900*, ed. Rosamond McKitterick, CUP, 1995

—, *History and Memory in the Carolingian World*, CUP, 2004

McKiterrick, Rosamond, ed., *The Uses of Literacy in Early Medieval Europe*, CUP, 1990

Marcuse, Sibyl, *Musical Instruments: A Comprehensive Dictionary*, Doubleday, 1964, reprinted Norton, 1975

Marenbon, John, *From the Circle of Alcuin to the School of Auxerre: Logic, Theology and Philosophy in the Early Middle Ages*, CUP, 1981

Mason, Emma, *The House of Godwine*, Hambledon & London, 2004

Michelli, Perette, 'The Lindisfarne Gospels', in *Northumbria's Golden Age*, ed. Jane Hawkes and Susan Mills, Tempus Publishing, 1999

Miles, David, *The Tribes of Britain*, Orion, 2005

Mitchell, Bruce, *An Invitation to Old English and Anglo-Saxon England*, Blackwell, 1995

Musset, Lucien, *The Bayeux Tapestry*, Boydell Press, 2005 (trans. Richard Rex)

Myres, J. N. L., *A Corpus of Anglo-Saxon Pottery of the Pagan Period*, 2 vols, CUP, 1977

Nelson, Janet L., 'The political ideas of Alfred of Wessex' in *Kings and Kingship in Medieval Europe*, ed. Anne J. Duggan, 1993, pp. 125–58

—, *Rulers and Ruling Families in Early Medieval Europe: Alfred, Charles the Bald and Others*, Ashgate, 1999

—, 'Carolingian Contacts', in *Mercia: An Anglo-Saxon Kingdom in Europe*, ed. Michelle P. Brown and Carol A. Farr, Leicester UP, 2001, pp. 126–46

—, 'Alfred's Carolingian Contemporaries', in *Alfred the Great: Papers from the Eleventh-Centenary Conferences*, ed. Timothy Reuter, Ashgate, 2003, pp. 293–310

Neuman de Vegvar, Carol, 'The Travelling Twins: Romulus and Remus in Anglo-Saxon England', in *Northumbria's Golden Age*, ed. Jane Hawkes and Susan Mills, Tempus Publishing, 1999, pp. 256–67

Newton, S., *The Origins of Beowulf and the Pre-Viking Kingdom of East Anglia*, Brewer, 1993

Ó Cróinín, Dáibhí, 'Writing', in *From the Vikings to the Normans*, Short Oxford History of the British Isles, ed. Wendy Davies, OUP, 2003, pp. 169–202

Offer, Clifford, *In Search of Clofesho: The Case for Hitchin*, Tessa Publications, 2002

Orchard, Andy, *A Critical Companion to 'Beowulf'*, Boydell Press, 2002

—, 'Latin and the Vernacular Languages: The Creation of a Bilingual Text Culture', in *After Rome*, Short Oxford History of the British Isles, ed. Thomas Charles-Edwards, OUP, 2003

Owen-Crocker, G. R., *Dress in Anglo-Saxon England*, Manchester UP, 1986, revised Boydell Press, 2004

Peddie, John, *Alfred the Good Soldier: His Life and Campaigns*, Millstream Books, 1989

—, *Alfred: Warrior King*, Sutton Publishing, 1999

Petts, David, *Christianity in Roman Britain*, Tempus Publishing, 2004

Prescott, Andrew, *The Benedictional of St Æthelwold: A Masterpiece of Anglo-Saxon Art – A Facsimile*, British Library, 2002

Pryor, Francis, *Britain AD: A Quest for Arthur, England and the Anglo-Saxons*, HarperCollins, 2004

Ramsay, Nigel, Margaret Sparks and T. W. T. Tatton-Brown, eds, *St Dunstan: His Life, Times and Cult*, Boydell Press, 1992

Reno, Frank D., *Historic Figures of the Arthurian Era*, McFarland, 2000

Reuter, Timothy, *Germany in the Early Middle Ages, c. 800–1056*, Longman, 1991

Reuter, Timothy, ed., *Alfred the Great: Papers from the Eleventh-Centenary Conferences*, Ashgate, 2003

Reynolds, Susan, *Kingdoms and Communities in Western Europe, 900–1300*, OUP, 1984, 2/1997

Richards, Julian, *Blood of the Vikings*, Hodder & Stoughton, 2000

Roberts, Jane, Janet L. Nelson and Malcolm Godden, eds, *Alfred the Wise: Studies in Honour of Janet Bately*, D. S. Brewer, 1997

Robertson, J. G., *A History of German Literature*, 4th edn, revised and enlarged by Edna Purdie, Blackwood, 1962

Rollason, David, *Saints and Relics in Anglo-Saxon England*, Blackwell, 1989

—, 'St Cuthbert and Wessex: The evidence of Cambridge, Corpus Christi College MS 183', in *St Cuthbert, his Cult and his Community to AD 1200*, ed. Gerald Bonner, David Rollason and Clare Stancliffe, Boydell Press, 1989

—, *Northumbria, 500–1100: Creation and Destruction of a Kingdom*, CUP, 2003

Rumble, Alexander R., ed., *The Reign of Cnut: King of England, Denmark and Norway*, Leicester UP, 1994

Sawyer, Peter, ed., *The Oxford Illustrated History of the Vikings*, OUP, 1997

Sawyer, P. H., *The Age of the Vikings*, Edward Arnold, 1962

—, *From Roman Britain to Norman England*, Routledge, 1978, 2/1998

Scragg, Donald, *The Battle of Maldon, AD 991*, Blackwell, 1991

Semple, Sarah, 'Illustrations of Damnation in Late Anglo-Saxon Manuscripts', *Anglo-Saxon England*, 32, 2003, pp. 231–47

Sharpe, Richard, 'The Use of Writs in the Eleventh Century', *Anglo-Saxon England*, 32, 2003, pp. 247–91

Smyth, Alfred P., *King Alfred the Great*, OUP, 1995

Stafford, Pauline, 'The Reign of Æthelred II: A Study in the Limitations on Royal Policy and Action', in *Ethelred the Unready: Papers from the Millenary Conference*, ed. David Hill, British Archaeological Reports, British Series, 59, 1978

—, *Queens, Concubines and Dowagers: The King's Wife in the Early Middle Ages*, Batsford, 1983

——, *Unification and Conquest: A Political and Social History of England in the Tenth and Eleventh Centuries*, Edward Arnold, 1989

——, *Queen Emma and Queen Edith: Queenship and Women's Power in Eleventh-century England*, Blackwell, 1997

——, 'Political Women in Mercia', in *Mercia: An Anglo-Saxon Kingdom in Europe*, ed. Michelle P. Brown and Carol A. Farr, Leicester UP, 2001

——, 'Kings, Kingships, and Kingdoms', in *From the Vikings to the Normans*, Short Oxford History of the British Isles, ed. Wendy Davies, OUP, 2003, pp. 11–40

Stancliffe, Clare, and Eric Cambridge, eds, *Oswald: Northumbrian King to European Saint*, Paul Watkins, 1995

Stenton, F. M., *Anglo-Saxon England*, OUP, 1943, 3/1971

Strickland, Matthew, 'Conquest and Military Technology: The Anomaly of Anglo-Saxon England', *Anglo-Norman Studies*, XIX, 1996, pp. 353–82

Sturdy, David, *Alfred the Great*, Constable, 1995

Swanton, Michael, *Opening the Franks Casket*, Brixworth Lecture 1996, U. Leicester Vaughan Papers, no. 40, 1999

Swanton, Michael, ed. and trans., *Three Lives of the Last Englishmen*, Garland, 1984

——, *Anglo-Saxon Prose*, Everyman's Library, 1985, revised 1993

——, *The Anglo-Saxon Chronicle*, J. M. Dent, 1996, revised Phoenix Press, 2000

Swift, Stanley, *Visitor's Guide to Croyland Abbey*, [1980s] revised 1999

Talbot, C.H., ed. and trans., *The Anglo-Saxon Missionaries in Germany*, Sheed and Ward, 1954, revised 1981

Tangl, Michael, *Die Briefen des heligen Bonifatius und Lullus*, Monumentis Germaniae Historica, Weidmann, 1916

Taylor, H. M., and Joan Taylor, *Anglo-Saxon Architecture*, 3 vols, CUP, 1965–78

Thacker, Alan, 'The Cult of King Harold at Chester', in *The Middle Ages in the North-West*, ed. Tom Scott and Pat Starkey, Leopard's Head Press, 1996

Thacker, A., and R. Sharpe, eds, *Local Saints and Local Churches in the Early Medieval West*, OUP, 2002

Temple, E., *Anglo-Saxon Manuscripts, 900–1066*, Harvey Miller, 1976

Tolkien, J.R.R. *Beowulf: The Monsters and the Critics*, Humphrey Milford, 1936

Ullmann, Walter, *A Short History of the Papacy in the Middle Ages*, Methuen, 1972

Walker, Ian W., *Harold: The Last Anglo-Saxon King*, Sutton Publishing, 1997

—, *Mercia and the Origins of England*, Sutton Publishing, 2000

Wallace-Hadrill, J. M., 'The Franks and the English in the Ninth Century', *History*, 35, 1950, pp. 202–18; reprinted in his *Early Medieval History*, Blackwell, 1975, pp. 201–16

—, *Early Germanic Kingship in England and on the Continent*, Clarendon Press, 1971

Ward-Perkins, Bryan, *The Fall of Rome and the End of Civilization*, OUP, 2005

Warren, W. L., 'The Myth of Norman Administrative Efficiency' *Transactions of the Royal Historical Society*, 1984, pp. 113–32

Watts, Victor, ed., *The Cambridge Dictionary of English Place-Names*, CUP, 2005

Webb, J. F., and D. H. Farmer, *The Age of Bede*, Penguin Classics, 1965, revised 1983

Webster, Leslie, 'Ædificia nova: Treasures of Alfred's Reign', in *Alfred the Great: Papers from the Eleventh-Centenary Conferences*, ed. Timothy Reuter, Ashgate, 2003, pp. 79–107

Welch, M., *The English Heritage Book of Anglo-Saxon England*, Batsford, 1992

Whitelock, Dorothy, ed., *English Historical Documents: I: c. 500–1042*, Eyre & Spottiswoode, 2nd edn, 1979

—, *From Bede to Alfred: Studies in Early Anglo-Saxon Literature and History*, Variorum Reprints, 1980

Williams, Ann, *The English and the Norman Conquest*, Boydell, 1995

—, *Kingship and Government in Pre-Conquest England, c. 500–1066*, Macmillan, 1999

Williams, Gareth, 'Military Institutions and Royal Power', in *Mercia: An Anglo-Saxon Kingdom in Europe*, ed. Michelle P. Brown and Carol A. Farr, Leicester UP, 2001

Wilson, David, *Anglo-Saxon Paganism*, Routledge, 1992

Wilson, David M., *The Anglo-Saxons*, Thames & Hudson, 1960, 3rd edn, Penguin Books, 1981

—, *Anglo-Saxon Art from the Seventh Century to the Norman Conquest*, Thames & Hudson, 1984

—, *The Bayeux Tapestry*, Thames & Hudson, 1985, revised 2004

Wormald, Patrick, 'Bede, the *Bretwaldas* and the Origins of the *Gens Anglorum*', in *Ideal and Reality in Frankish and Anglo-Saxon Society: Studies Presented to J. M. Wallace-Hadrill*, ed. Patrick Wormald and others, Basil Blackwell, 1983, pp. 99–129

—, *The Making of English Law: King Alfred to the Twelfth Century*, I: *Legislation and its Limits*, Basil Blackwell, 1999

Wroe-Brown, Robin, 'Bull Wharf: Queenhithe', *Current Archaeology*, 14/2, 1998, pp. 75–7

Yorke, Barbara, *Kings and Kingdoms of Early Anglo-Saxon England*, Routledge, 1990

—, *Wessex in the Early Middle Ages*, Leicester UP, 1995

—, 'The Origins of Mercia', in *Mercia: An Anglo-Saxon Kingdom in Europe*, ed. Michelle P. Brown and Carol A. Farr, Leicester UP, 2001

Yorke, Barbara, ed., *Bishop Æthelwold: His Career and Influence*, Boydell Press, 1988

INDEX

Abbo of Fleury 188, 282
Acca, bishop of Hexham 127
Aclea, battle of 164, 185, 207
Adela, Countess of Flanders 317
Adelard of Bath 236
Ælbert, archbishop of York 62, 152
Ælfgar of Mercia 329, 334
Ælfgifu (1st wife of Æthelred II) 292
Ælfgifu (2nd wife of Æthelred II) *see*
    Emma
Ælfgifu of Northampton 303, 309,
    314–16
Ælfheah, bishop of Winchester,
    archbishop of Canterbury 280,
    301, 304–5, 310, 313
Ælfhelm the Mercian 301, 303
Ælfhere, ealdorman of Mercia 289
Ælfric 244–7, 249, 283
Ælfthyth 276, 289–90, 292
Ælfwine, bishop of Durham 342
Ælfwine (brother of Ecgfrith) 97
Ælle, king of Deira 23, 62
Aelle, king of Sussex xxxiv, 12, 15–16,
    26–7, 33, 99
Aesc *see* Oisc
Æthelbald, king of Mercia 57, 92–3,
    98–100, 102, 110, 120, 142
Æthelbald, king of Wessex 208–9
Æthelberht I, king of Kent 8, 15, 17,
    32, 33–6, 38–9, 43, 48, 51, 257
Æthelberht II, king of Kent 163–4
Æthelberht, king of Wessex 209
Æthelburga, abbess of Barking 143
Æthelburh, queen 65, 67, 70

Æthelflæd, Lady of the Mercians 118,
    197, 226, 240, 264, 265–8, 271
Æthelfrith, king of Bernicia xxxix, 24,
    37, 61, 62–4, 67
Æthelheard, archbishop of Canterbury
    103, 107
Æthelnoth, ealdorman 192
Æthelred I, king of Wessex 188, 189,
    206, 209, 263
Æthelred II 'Unræd', king of England
    145, 198, 232, 235, 256, 276,
    289, 290, 291–4, 298–307, 308,
    316
Æthelred, ealdorman of Mercia 118,
    215, 218, 226, 265
Æthelred, king of Mercia 82, 96, 97–8
Æthelred, king of Northumbria 85,
    169
Æthelric, bishop of Selsey 347
Æthelstan, king of England 119, 193,
    200, 202, 209, 220, 268–75, 284,
    285–6, 289
Æthelstan (son of Æthelred II) 305–6
Æthelswih of Wessex 206
Æthelthryth, abbess of Ely 143–4
Æthelweard, ealdorman 161, 230,
    233, 247, 270
Æthelwine, ealdorman of East Anglia
    282, 295
Æthelwold, bishop of Winchester 245,
    280, 281–2, 289, 290, 292, 304,
    346
Æthelwold, 'king of the Danes'
    199–200, 263–5

Æthelwold Moll, king of Northumbria
    85
Æthelwulf, ealdorman   189
Æthelwulf, king of Wessex   118,
    164–5, 185, 206, 207–9, 216, 289
æthlings   103, 263
afterlife   84, 246
Agilbert, bishop   49, 79, 80
Aidan   68–9, 71, 79, 278
Alaric (the Visigoth)   3
Alchfrith, sub-king of Deira   73, 74
Alcuin of York   10, 40, 61, 75, 85,
    103, 104, 105, 106, 149, 150–4,
    155, 157, 161, 162–3, 165–74
Aldfrith, king of Northumbria   56, 82,
    83, 86, 254
Aldhelm, bishop of Sherborne   xli,
    55–6, 120, 235–6, 240–1, 253–4,
    275
Alexander II, Pope   335, 339
Alfred the Great, king   41, 58, 96, 100,
    117, 130, 149, 164–5, 174, 177,
    184, 187, 189–95, 197, 199,
    205–33, 263, 284, 286
  character and attributes   214
  and the Church   223
  and creation of Anglo-Saxon
      Kingdom   205, 215, 287
  cultural programme   215–18, 221–3
  defence of realm   226–30
  government and reform   218–23
  justice and law   224–5
  and Rome   207–10
Alfred Jewel   217–18
Alfred (son of Æthelred II)   299, 303,
    309, 316–17, 320, 325, 326
Aluberht, bishop of the 'Old Saxons'
    149
Ambrosianus Aurellianus   7
Angles   20, 23–4
Anglo-Saxon Chronicle   212–14, 232,
    235, 243–4, 247–8, 249, 260–1
    and passim
Anglo-Saxon kingdom   205, 215, 233,
    262–3, 287
  consolidation of   263–9
  under Æthelstan   269–75
Anglo-Saxons
  ancestors   1–2
  origin of term   xxxii–xxxiii
  settlement   11–24

Anna, king of East Anglia   95, 143
Annals of Ulster   204, 243, 273, 375
army, standing   229, 298, 311
Arthur, king   7–8
Ashdown, battle of   189, 194
Assandun, battle of   296, 309
Asser   58, 101, 174, 186, 188, 193,
    194, 206, 207, 209, 210–12, 215,
    223, 226
Augustine, archbishop of Canterbury
    8–9, 32, 33–6, 37, 43, 123, 135,
    138
Augustine of Hippo   xxxviii, 5, 221,
    222, 246

Baldred, king of Kent   114, 118, 206
Baldwin II, Count of Flanders   274
Baldwin V, Count of Flanders   232,
    317, 323, 332
Balthidis, queen   40–1
Bamburgh   20, 71–2, 187, 204
Bath   xxvi, 18, 105, 277, 289, 303,
    304, 305
Bayeux Tapestry   332, 335, 354–60
Becket, Thomas   352
Bede   xxxv–xli, 4–11, 62, 161–2, 238,
    244, 254, 353 and passim
Benedict III, Pope   207
Benedict Biscop   47, 62, 75, 77–8, 79,
    86, 91, 152
Benedict, Rule of St   139, 155, 280–1
Benty Grange   26
Beorhtric, king of Wessex   58, 102,
    158, 181, 185
Beorhtwulf, king of Mercia   118, 185
Beornred, abbot of Echternach and
    archbishop of Sens   151
Beornwulf, king of Mercia   101, 117,
    118
Beowulf   xxxi, xli, 1, 24–6, 101, 151,
    234, 235, 240, 249 and passim
Bernicia   20, 23–4, 32, 60, 62, 67, 72,
    73, 204
Bertha of Paris   32, 33, 35, 48
Bewcastle   87–8
Birinus   44, 70, 253
Biscop Baducing see Benedict Biscop
Boethius   210, 221
Boniface, archbishop of Mainz see
    Wynfrith
Book of Kells   68

Brand, abbot of Peterborough 248,
341, 342
bretwalda xliii, 26, 97, 99, 185, 278
Britain
origin of name 2–3, 9
original inhabitants xxxiii–xxxiv, 3,
9
Brixworth, All Saints 110–11
Brunanburh, battle of 10, 200, 235,
244, 270, 275
building, Anglo-Saxon 110–11, 117,
218, 227–8
Burchard, bishop of Würzburg 136
Burgred, king of Mercia 117, 118,
185, 188, 195, 206, 215
burhs 218, 226–8, 230, 265–6, 298
Byrthnoth, ealdorman 193–4, 293,
296

Cadwallon, king of Gwynedd 67
Caedmon 238, 242
Cædwalla, king of Wessex 40, 49–50,
57
calligraphy, Anglo-Saxon 89–91,
148–9, 173, 176, 177, 221, 250,
313
Canterbury 13, 35, 36, 37, 38, 43–8
Capet, Hugh 272
Carloman 135–6, 153, 154
Carmen de Hastinge Proelio 338, 339
Carolingian dynasty 61, 127, 135,
136–7, 148, 153, 209, 217, 233
carvings, Anglo-Saxon 86–9
Ceawlin 17–18, 34
Cedd, bishop 74, 80, 278
Cenwalh, king of Wessex 49, 95
Ceolfrith, abbot 76, 78, 91
ceorls 42–3, 75, 297
Ceolwulf, king of Northumbria 84
Ceolwulf II, king of Mercia 117, 118,
191, 215, 225
Cerdic 12, 16–17, 53, 57, 205
Cerdic dynasty 205, 212–13, 214,
262–3, 272–3
Chad, bishop of Lichfield 81, 278
Charlemagne *see* Charles the Great
Charles II (the Bald) 164, 166, 168,
184, 186, 208, 217, 227
Charles III of West Francia 272
Charles the Great 61, 85, 92, 103,
105, 107, 108–9, 120, 127, 137,

139, 141, 150, 151, 153–4, 158,
162, 165–9, 171–4, 183, 223
Charles Martel 61, 127, 128, 132, 135
Chelsea, Council of 92
Chester 198, 206, 268, 277, 285, 335,
362, 363
Chester, battle of 63
Chester-le-Street 204, 249, 292
Childeric III 136–7
chirographs 259
Christianity 5, 8–9
Anglo-Saxon missions to Germany
120–49
Canterbury and organization of
43–8
and kingship 28
Vikings and 202
see also under individual kingdoms
Church, Anglo-Saxon 32–7, 43–8,
68–9, 105–8, 223, 278–82,
313–14, 324–5, 345–6
church building 110–11, 279, 325,
345
see also Christianity
Clofesho 47, 106–7
Clovis, king of the Franks 28, 33, 61,
121
Cnut, king 144, 182, 256, 278, 283,
291, 297, 300, 302, 303–4, 305,
306, 307, 308–15, 319, 321
Coenwulf, king of Mercia 107,
113–14
Coifi (pagan high priest) 65–6
coinage, Anglo-Saxon 113–17, 206,
215, 278, 284–7, 297, 312–13, 317
Colman, bishop of Lindisfarne 80
Columba, St 32, 68
Columbanus, St 68, 131
concubines 276–7, 303
Conrad II, Emperor 315
Constans II, Emperor 46–7, 48
Constantine II, king of Scots 267, 269
Countisbury Hill, battle of 191
crowning, tradition of 104–5
culture, Anglo-Saxon
cultural legacy 353
under Alfred the Great 215–18,
221–3
see also building; calligraphy; carving;
learning and scholarship; literature;
music

Cumbria 202–3
Cuthbert, archbishop of Canterbury 106, 142
Cuthbert, St 46, 62, 75–7, 177, 192, 203–4, 271, 279
Cuthburg, abbess of Wimborne 56
Cuthred, king of Wessex 57
Cuthred, sub-king of Kent 114
Cyneburh 72, 96
Cynegils, king of Wessex 44, 49, 69–70
Cyneheard 58
Cynewulf, king of Wessex 57–8, 244
Cynric 16–17

Dagobert II, king of the Franks 121–2
Dál Riata (Dalriada) 10, 32, 63, 70
danegeld 302
Danelaw 118, 181, 187, 195–8, 262
Daniel, bishop of Winchester xxxviii, 129, 137
Deerhurst minster 112
defence and fortifications, Anglo-Saxon 226–32, 298
Degsastan, battle of 63
Deira 20, 21, 22, 23–4, 32, 60, 62, 67, 72, 73, 199, 200
Deusdedit, archbishop of Canterbury 45, 96
dialects xxxiv–xxxv, 242, 249
Domesday Book 342, 348–9
Dream of the Rood, The 88, 242, 250
Dryhthelm, vision of 84
Dublin 182, 199, 200
Dumnonia 32, 42
Dunstan, abbot of Glastonbury, archbishop of Canterbury 275, 276, 280–2, 289
Durham 204

Eadbald, king of Kent 43
Eadberht, king of Northumbria 85, 104
Eadberht Præn 103, 107
Eadburga, abbesss 137–8, 145
Eadburh of Mercia 58, 158, 185
Eadfrith, bishop of Lindisfarne 89–90, 249
Eadgifu 272, 273, 289
Eadgyth (daughter of Edward the Elder) 162, 272

Eadgyth of Wilton 260, 277
Eadhild 272
Eadmer 332
Eadred, king of England 200, 275–6, 281, 289
Eadric Streona 119, 301–2, 306, 307, 308, 309
Eadsige, archbishop of Canterbury 324
Eadwig, King of England 276, 281
ealdormen 54, 95, 96, 219, 229
Ealdred, bishop of Worcester, archbishop of York 112, 325, 330, 335, 340
Ealhmund, king of Kent 102
Eanbald II, archbishop of York 75, 153, 170
Eanflæd of Deira 65, 72, 74, 79, 80
Eardwulf, king of Northumbria 85, 151, 165
earls and earldoms 219, 310, 311, 314
East Anglia 31
   Christianity in 36–7, 49
   under the Vikings 197, 198
Easter, computation of 56, 79, 80–1
Ecclesiastical History of the English People (Bede) xxxv, xxxviii–xli, 238
Ecgberht, archbishop of York 62, 68, 85, 124, 143, 152
Ecgberht, king of Wessex 26, 59, 77, 86, 102–3, 104, 113, 117–18, 185, 205, 216
Ecgfrith, king of Bernicia xli, 37, 61, 75, 78, 82, 97–8, 144
Ecgfrith, king of Mercia 104, 105
Echternach 127, 151
Eddius 78
Edgar Ætheling 248, 334, 341, 343
Edgar the Peaceable, king of England 231, 276–8, 279, 281, 282, 283, 286, 287, 289, 290
Edington, battle of 194, 205
Edith, queen of England 311, 321, 323–4, 327, 330, 340, 343–4
Edith Swanneck 331, 334, 340
Edmund Ironside 291, 296, 302, 306, 307–8, 334
Edmund, king of the East Angles 188, 198
Edmund, king of England 203, 270, 275, 280, 289
Edward I, king of England 352

Edward II, king of England 352
Edward III, king of England 352
Edward, the Black Prince 352–3
Edward the Confessor 232, 239, 261,
    291, 299, 303, 308, 309, 311,
    316–17, 318–20, 321–8, 330, 333,
    334, 343, 346, 351–2
Edward the Elder, king of Wessex 162,
    164, 197, 199, 209, 216, 223, 226,
    230, 262, 263–8, 271, 272, 284,
    285
Edward the Exile 308, 309
Edward 'the Martyr' 276, 289, 290,
    291, 292, 308
Edwin, Earl 336, 340
Edwin (half-brother of Æthelstan) 271
Edwin, king of Deira 25, 37, 43, 44,
    61, 62, 63, 64–7, 79, 80
Egbert of Trier 161, 273
Einhard 173–4, 211, 214, 217
Ellendun, battle of 114, 117, 206
Elmet 64, 73
Emma of Normandy 299–300, 303,
    307, 309, 310, 312, 314, 315–20,
    322
emporia, Anglo-Saxon 55, 111, 113,
    115–16, 178, 201–2
English language 38, 205, 233, 234,
    248–51, 254–61, 345, 353
Eorcenwold, bishop of London 55
Eormanric, king of the Ostrogoths 15,
    237
Eric Bloodaxe 198, 200
Erigena, John Scotus 168
Essex 18–19, 31
    Christianity in 36, 48
Ethelburga see Æthelburh
Eustace of Boulogne 326, 337
Exeter Book 239–41

Felix, bishop 44
FitzNigel, Richard 352
Francia 61, 135–7
    Viking raids 183–4, 195, 208
Franks Casket 76, 84, 86–7
Frisia 121, 122, 124, 125, 126, 127,
    128, 129, 131, 156, 183
Fulco of Reims 215
Fulda 134–5, 154–5, 156, 157, 168,
    174–5
Fuller Brooch 218

gafol see tribute
Gaimar, Geoffrey 260–1, 308, 343
Geats 24, 73
genealogy 103–4, 205
gentry 296–7
Geoffrey, count of Anjou 351
Geoffrey of Monmouth 8
Geraint, king of Dumnonia 53, 56
Germanus, bishop of Auxerre 4–6
gesiths 43, 50, 72, 75
Gewis 16, 17
Gewisse people 53
Gildas xxxv, 7, 8, 14, 256
Gloucester 18, 115, 118, 191, 326,
    331
Godiva of Coventry 248, 310, 316
Godwine, Earl of Wessex 182, 232,
    300, 310–11, 314, 316, 317, 318,
    321–9
Godwine (son of Harold II) 340–1
gold 73, 114, 171, 177
Goscelin of St Bertin 260
Gospatric 333
government and administration, Anglo-
    Saxon xliii–xliv, 37–40, 53–5,
    218–21, 258–9, 287–8, 310–15,
    346–7
    see also law
grave goods 19, 26, 36, 52, 114, 179,
    196
Great Heathen army 86
Gregory, abbot of Utrecht 149
Gregory the Great, Pope 23, 32, 33–6,
    40, 135, 215, 222, 278
Gregory III, Pope 106
Grimbald of St Bertin 215, 217
Gruffudd ap Llywelyn of Gwynedd and
    Powys 329, 331
Gumley, synod of 110
Gunnhild 315
Guthlac of Croyland, St 50, 98–9
Guthred 199, 203
Guthrum 117, 190, 191, 192, 194–5,
    197
Gwynedd 275, 329, 331
Gyrth Godwinesson 311, 329, 337,
    339
Gytha 311, 321, 337, 340–1

Hadrian I, Pope 108
Hæstan 229–30

Halfdan 186, 189, 190, 198–9
Halfdan II, king of York 200
Hamwic 54, 59, 115, 130, 159, 227
Harald Hardrada, king of Norway
xliii, 320, 335, 336
Harold I (Harefoot) 303, 315–17
Harold II, king of England xliii, 248,
310, 311, 320, 326, 327, 329, 330,
331–3, 334–9, 340, 343–4, 361–3
Harthacnut I, king of Denmark 183
Harthacnut (son of Cnut) 309, 310,
315, 316–18, 319–20, 321, 335
Hastings, battle of 331, 334, 337–9,
340, 344
Hatfield Chase, battle of 67
Hatfield, synod of 48
Heavenfield, battle of 67, 70
Hedda, abbot 97
Hengest 12, 13–15, 21
Henry I, king of England 349–51, 353
Henry II, king of England 351–2
Henry III, Emperor 232, 315, 324
Henry III, king of England 352
Henry of Huntingdon 351
Hereward the Wake 342–3
Herman the Lotharingian, bishop of
Sherborne 321
Hertford, Synod of 106
hides and hidage 94, 197, 228
high kings xliii–xliv
Hild (Hilda), abbess of Whitby 61–2,
79–80, 143, 238
Hincmar, archbishop of Reims 208
Hingston Down, battle of 185
Historia Brittonum 20
Holme, battle of 200
Honorius, archbishop of Canterbury
43–5
Horsa 13, 14, 21
horses 70–1, 179
Hoxne, battle of 188, 189
Hrabanus see Rabanus
Hrothgar 19, 24, 25, 236, 274
Hrotswitha of Gandersheim 162, 272
Hugh the Great, Count of Paris 272,
273, 274
Huneberc 159–60
Hwicce 32, 94, 95, 99, 102
Hwita, 'Candidus' 167, 168
Hygeburgor see Huneberc
Hygelec, king of the Geats 24, 73, 94

Ine, king of Wessex 40, 41, 53–7, 99,
129, 190, 219
Iona 64, 68, 69, 74, 79, 80
Ireland, raids on 82, 181–2
Irish missionaries 68–9, 122
Irish raiders 9, 32, 202
Islam 46, 61, 67, 139, 140–1
Ivar the Boneless 186

Jænberht, archbishop of Canterbury
106
James the Deacon 65, 66–7
John, king of England 352
John the Old Saxon 215
John of Worcester 335, 336, 351
Judith of Flanders 161, 323, 330, 333
Judith, queen of Wessex 208–9, 289
'Junius' manuscript 242
Justus, bishop of Rochester, archbishop
of Canterbury 34, 43, 65, 67
Jutes 13–15

Kent 13–15, 20, 31, 32–7, 205–6
Christianity in 32–7, 48
government 37–40
kingship 27–8, 31, 104–5
Kingston upon Thames 216, 263, 268,
291

land charters 251–3, 258, 283–4, 347
Lanfranc, archbishop of Canterbury
346
Laurentius, archbishop of Canterbury
36, 37, 43
law, Anglo-Saxon 38–9, 51, 53–5,
144–5, 190, 212, 224–5, 251,
254–8, 269, 282–4, 304, 310,
311–12
Leafwine see Lebuin
learning and scholarship, Anglo-Saxon
89–91, 157, 170–5, 210–18
leases 259
Lebuin, St 158, 161
Leo III, Pope 167, 172
Leo IX, Pope 324, 325
Leofric, abbot of Peterborough 248,
331, 335, 337
Leofric, bishop of Exeter 239
Leofric, Earl of Mercia 248, 310, 316,
318, 322, 326, 329
Leofsige, abbot of Mettlach 273

Leofwine Godwinesson 311, 330, 339
Lichfield 93, 106, 107, 108
life expectancy 128
Lindisfarne 10, 68–9, 70, 71, 74, 77,
   79, 278
   sack of 86, 169, 176–8
Lindisfarne Gospels 68, 89–90, 235,
   249
Lindsey, kingdom of 29, 31, 69, 97, 99
Lioba, abbess of Tauberbischofsheim
   xxxvii, 128, 143, 145–7
literature, Anglo-Saxon 210–18,
   234–48, 245, 253–4, 260
Liudprand, king 61, 131
Lombards 61, 108, 131, 136, 166–7
London 55, 97, 100, 113–17, 178,
   185, 225–6, 297, 303, 315
Longchamp, William 352
Louis IV (d'Outremer) of West Francia
   272, 273
Louis the Pious 166, 183–4
Ludger, bishop of Münster 160–1
Lull, archbishop of Mainz 120, 157,
   174
Lupus, bishop of Troyes 4–6

Macbeth, king of Scots 328
Magnus I, king of Norway 315, 317,
   318, 320, 322
Magonsætan 32, 93, 118
Mainz 135, 157, 174, 330
Malcolm III, king of Scots 328, 331,
   341
Malcolm, king of Scots 203, 315
Maldon, battle of 194, 235, 293–4,
   295, 297
Malmesbury 56
Martin I, Pope 46–7
Maserfelth, battle of 70, 71, 72
Matilda, abbess of Essen 161
Matilda (wife of Emperor Henry V)
   351
Matilda (wife of Henry I) 351
Medeshamstede 94, 96, 110, 112, 189,
   247–8
Mellitus, bishop of London 18, 36, 43
Mercia 19, 32, 92–119
   building projects 110–11
   Christianity in 96–8
   decline of 117–19
   international affairs 108–9

the Mercian Church 105–8
   minsters 111–12
   origins of kingdom 93–6
   trade 113–16
   under Æthelflæd 265–7
   under Vikings 187, 188, 195–6
Merovingian dynasty 33, 61, 121–2,
   125, 128, 136–7, 154
Middle Angles 94
Middle Anglia 32
minsters, Anglo-Saxon 111–12, 178
mints, Anglo-Saxon 116, 198, 285–7,
   313, 335
monasteries xxxv–xxxvi, 86, 89–91,
   170, 295–6
   monastic revival 280–2
Monkwearmouth-Jarrow xxxvi,
   xxxvii, 76, 78, 91, 176
Morcar, Earl of Mercia 334, 336, 340,
   342
Mount Badon, battle of 7–8
Mull, king of Kent 49, 50, 53

navy, Anglo-Saxon 230–2, 300
Nechtansmer, battle of 82
Nennius 8, 20
nobility 75–6, 83, 219
Norman conquest 334–53
Normans and Normandy 181, 199,
   260–1, 299
Northumbria 19–24, 32, 60–91
   administrative structure 64
   Christianity in 49, 65–7, 68–9, 74
   expansionism 73, 82
   formation of kingdom 62–7
   learning and the arts 86–91
   noble clerics 75–80
   Synod of Whitby 80–1
   under Oswald 69–71
   under Vikings 187–8, 197, 199,
   203–4
   waning of 83–6
Nothelm, bishop of London 93

Oda, archbishop of Canterbury 280,
   281
Odberht 103
Odilo, Duke 138
Offa, king of Mercia 13, 58, 92, 94,
   100–5, 106, 107, 108–9, 185, 237
Offa's Dyke 92, 101

Oisc   14
Olaf the Good (the Stout)   314, 315
Olaf Guthfrithsson   200, 202, 269, 275
Olaf Sihtricson, king of York   193, 200
Olaf Tryggvason   297–8
Ordlaf, ealdorman   284
Osburh   206, 219
Oslac 'the Butler'   219
Osred, king of Northumbria   83
Osred II, king of Northumbria   85
Osric, ealdorman   179
Osric, king of Deira   67, 72
Oswald, bishop of Worcester,
     archbishop of York   280, 281,
     282, 295
Oswald, king of Northumbria   28, 44,
     49, 61, 63–4, 67–72, 98, 118–19,
     127, 153, 161–2, 273, 279
Oswine, king of Deira   72, 73, 76
Oswiu, king of Bernicia   61, 63–4,
     71–4, 75, 77, 78–81, 82, 96
Otford   102, 307
Otto I, Emperor (Otto of Saxony)
     162, 272
Owain of Strathclyde   203, 269

paganism   15, 35–6, 49, 122, 132–3,
     137, 142
Papacy   32–6, 36–7, 80–1, 82, 106,
     108–9, 123, 125, 130, 132, 135–6,
     138–9, 148, 149, 151, 165, 172,
     207, 294–5, 313, 324, 325
Paschal I, Pope   115
Pastoral Care (Gregory the Great)
     215–16, 219, 220
Patrick, St   32
Paul the Deacon   166
Paulinus, bishop of York   65, 66–7, 68,
     69, 79
Peada, king of Mercia   45, 72, 73–4,
     96
Pelagius and Pelagianism   5–6
Penda, king of Mercia   45, 49, 67, 70,
     72–3, 95–6, 253
Peter the Deacon   222
Peterborough   112
     see also Medeshamstede
Picts   xxxiii, 3, 5, 9–10, 13–14, 20–1,
     32, 70, 73, 82, 100, 198
Pippin II of Heristal   124, 125, 126,
     127

Pippin III 'the Short'   61, 127, 136–7,
     148, 157
place names   23, 196, 202
Plegmund, archbishop of Canterbury
     96, 215–16, 217
poetry, Anglo-Saxon   235–42
polygamy   138, 142, 303, 315
Powys   xxii, 3, 32, 101, 329
Prittlewell   18–19, 219
Procopius   2, 17

Rabanus, abbot of Fulda   157, 173–5
Radbod   122, 124, 125, 126, 127, 128,
     131, 145
Rædwald   18, 35, 36–7, 44, 49, 62, 63
Ragnald, 'king' of York   267, 270
Ragnar Lothbrok   187, 191
Ralph of Herefordshire (Mantes)   322,
     326, 329, 330
reeves   54, 55, 220, 229, 284, 287, 298
relics   274, 296, 310
Repton   93, 195–6
Richard I, duke of Normandy   292,
     299
Richard II, duke of Normandy   299
Richard II, king of England   353
Riddles   235, 240–1, 251
River Idle, battle of   37, 63
River Winwead, battle of   73, 76–7, 95
Robert I, duke of Normandy   316
Robert II, duke of Normandy   350–1
Robert of Jumièges   322, 325, 327
Romano-British   xxxiv, xxxv, 3–4, 12,
     21, 56, 73
Romescot   313
Rudolf of Fulda   145–6, 147
Runes   250, 251
Ruthwell Cross   88, 242, 250

Sæberht   18, 35, 36, 48
St Brice's Day massacre   298–9
salt   114
Saxons   3, 5, 10, 11, 20
     origin of name   15, 52, 152
scops   236–7
Scotti   xxxiii, 3, 32, 63
Scyld Scefing   205
Seafarer   240
seals   255, 288
Seaxburgha, queen of Wessex   49
Seaxwulf, bishop-abbot   97

Sergius I, Pope 125, 126
Servatus Lupus 163, 164
Sexburga, St 144
sheriffs 311, 346
ships, Anglo-Saxon 29–30, 179, 230–2, 300
shire courts 53, 297, 311, 346–7
shires 53–4, 118, 197, 219, 278, 287, 346–7
Sigeberht, king of East Saxons 44–5, 57–8, 72, 74, 95
Sigeric, archbishop of Canterbury 294–5
Sigulf, abbot of Ferrières 152, 163
Sihtric 268, 271
silver 114, 117, 285, 297
Siward, Earl of Northumbria 310, 318, 322, 326, 329
slaves 22, 23, 40, 41–2, 116, 182, 307
social ranks, Anglo-Saxon 41–3, 75, 296–7
Southampton 115, 185, 194, 297, 307, 317
Stamford Bridge, battle of xliii, 161, 320, 336
Stephen (monk at Ripon) 62
Stigand, bishop of Winchester, archbishop of Canterbury 318, 322, 326, 330, 335, 346
Strathclyde 32, 187, 198, 203, 275
Sturmi (Sturm), abbot of Fulda 134–5, 155, 157
sub-kings/kingdoms 31, 95, 102
Suidbert, bishop 124, 126
Sussex 15–16, 26–7, 32
Sutton Hoo 14, 19, 26, 29, 36, 114, 178, 219
Swein II, king of Denmark 341, 342
Swein, king of Norway 303, 314–15
Swein Forkbeard 297, 298–9, 303–4, 305, 307, 320
Swein Godwineson 311, 322–3, 327, 328
Symeon of Durham 271, 336

Tacitus 27, 236
Tamworth 93, 105, 107
taxation 296, 302, 309, 312, 313, 346
Tetta, abbess of Wimborne 146
thegns 75, 220, 228, 229, 314

Theodore of Tarsus, archbishop of Canterbury 45–8, 77–8, 81, 82, 98, 106, 123, 253, 278
Theodoric the Ostrogoth 210
Thored, earl of Northumbria 292
Thorkell the Tall 300, 301, 302–3, 305, 308
Thurbrand 'the Hold' 306
Thuringia 133–5
Thuroldus of Fécamp 248
tolls 114–15
Tostig, Earl of Northumbria 161, 311, 322, 327, 329, 330, 331, 333–4, 335, 336
Tours 172–3
trade, Anglo-Saxon 109, 113–16, 178, 201–2, 232–3
travellers 158–60
tribute 294, 297, 298, 300, 301, 302
Turold of Fécamp 342

Uhtred of Northumbria 306
Ulf, bishop of Dorchester 241–2, 325
Utrecht 124, 126, 156

Vercelli Book 241–2, 325
Vikings
    First Viking Age 58–9, 86, 91, 117, 118, 176–204, 208, 226–33, 264–5, 279
    origin of term 180
    Second Viking Age 292–4, 296–320
Vita Alfredi Regis Angul Saxonum (Asser) 210–12
Vitalian, Pope 47
Vitalis, Orderic 323, 331, 332, 336, 337, 339, 347
Vortigern 13–14, 15, 20

Wace 338
Wærferth, bishop of Worcester 215, 226, 266
Walburga, abbess of Heidenheim 160
Wales 329, 331, 335
weapons, Anglo-Saxon 50–2, 218, 311
Welf I of Bavaria 161
wergild 41–2, 98, 197 219, 224
Wessex 16–18, 27, 32
    8th-century 53–9
    first Christian kings 48–50
    government 53–5

under Alfred the Great   205–33
    and the Vikings   182, 185–6,
        189–95
Whitby, Synod of   45, 62, 79, 80–1
Widsith   235, 237, 239, 240
Widukind   155
Wigbert, abbot of Fritzlar   134
Wigheard, archbishop of Canterbury
    47, 295
Wight, Isle of   97, 99, 298, 299, 300
Wiglaf, king of Mercia   114, 118,
    185
Wihtred, king of Kent   40, 99
Wilfrid, bishop of York and Ripon
    xli, 48, 50, 62, 68, 69, 74, 75, 77,
        78–83, 97, 121–2, 124, 127, 128,
        161
Willehad, bishop of Bremen   130,
    150–1, 155
William of Jumièges   316
William of Malmesbury   231, 265,
    268, 287, 337, 339, 351
William of Normandy (the Conqueror)
    xliii, xliv, 112, 248, 320, 323, 325,
        332–3, 334, 335–9, 340–3, 344–9,
        350
William of Poitiers   332, 335, 338–9,
    346
Willibald, bishop of Eichstätt   87–8,
    128, 131, 133, 139, 140–1, 148,
        159–60
Willibrord, bishop of Utrecht   61, 68,
    70, 122, 124–8, 131, 137, 148,
        150, 155–6, 161
wills   259
Wimborne   56

Winchcombe   94
Winchester   179, 186, 213, 233, 292
witan   220
Woden   15, 18, 28, 35
women
    rights of   144–5
    saints   143–7
Worcester   94, 239, 243, 266, 282, 352
writs   288, 346
Wulfhere, archbishop of York   200
Wulfhere, king of Mercia   82, 96, 97
Wulfnoth   300, 311
Wulfred, archbishop of Canterbury
    223
Wulfric, abbot of St Augustine's,
    Canterbury   324
Wulfsige, bishop of Sherborne   207,
    214
Wulfstan, bishop of London, archbishop
    of York   255–7, 304, 307
Wulfstan II, bishop of Worcester
    xxxvii, 182, 260, 325, 334
Wynfrith, archbishop of Mainz   xxxii,
    55, 61, 75–6, 83, 100, 106, 120,
        128–39, 141–3, 145, 148–9,
        154–7, 162, 163, 170, 241
Wynnebald, abbot of Heidenheim
    128, 139, 140, 159, 160

Yeavering   64, 66
York   20, 21, 22, 48, 62, 73, 82, 86,
    152–3, 178, 269, 341
    Viking Kingdom of   187–8, 197,
        198–202, 264, 275

Zacharias, Pope   136–7, 139